God's New Israel

God's New Israel

Religious Interpretations
of American Destiny

Revised and Updated Edition

EDITED BY CONRAD CHERRY

THE UNIVERSITY OF NORTH CAROLINA PRESS
Chapel Hill and London

*҉

© 1998 The University of North Carolina Press
All rights reserved
Designed by Heidi Perov
Set in Bembo
by Tseng Information Systems, Inc.
Manufactured in the United States of America

First published in 1971 by Prentice-Hall.

The paper in this book meets the guidelines for permanence
and durability of the Committee on Production Guidelines for
Book Longevity of the Council on Library Resources.

Library of Congress Cataloging-in-Publication Data

God's new Israel : religious interpretations of American destiny /
[compiled by] Conrad Cherry. — Rev. and updated ed.
p.   cm.
First published in 1971 by Prentice-Hall.
Includes bibliographical references and index.

ISBN 0-8078-2449-6 (alk. paper).
ISBN 0-8078-4754-2 (pbk. : alk. paper)

1. United States—History—Philosophy.
2. Messianism, Political—United States.
I. Cherry, Conrad, 1937–
E175.9.G64   1998
973—dc21   98-14071
CIP

02 01 00 99 98   5 4 3 2 1

Americans have tended to find their religious faith in
various forms of belief about their own existence as a people.
MAX LERNER, *America as a Civilization*

It has been often remarked that the people of the United
States come nearer to a parallel with Ancient Israel, than any other
nation upon the globe. Hence *Our American Israel* is a term frequently
used; and common consent allows it apt and proper.
ABIEL ABBOT, *Thanksgiving Sermon*, 1799

Contents

Preface to the Revised and Updated Edition

The original edition of this anthology was published in 1971 and remained in print for over twenty years. Compiled and written primarily with the college and seminary student in mind, the first version of the book enjoyed widespread use in the classroom, and its selections and commentaries were cited by scholarly interpreters of the American "civil religion." By the 1990s, however, it was quite apparent that the book needed to be updated, and at the urging of several colleagues in American religious history I have revised the book to take into account developments that have occurred over the last quarter century. The revisions have been thorough. I have added selections and editorial glosses in the last part to bring the chronology down to the present, but I have also revised all of the editor's introductions, added and substituted some selected readings in earlier parts, and altered the bibliographic citations in the notes and suggested readings. I believe that the changes result in a book more usable by contemporary Americans concerned about the shape of their religious past and present.

The fundamental purpose of the book remains the same, however. The volume aims to trace the theme of American destiny under God, the theme that has functioned as a motivating American mythology, through major developments in U.S. history. Most of the documents are still from the pens of religious and political leaders, but the influence of all the authors of the documents extended well beyond their specific professions. American religious and political literature alone is so saturated with the theme that a full selection of documents bearing significantly on the subject would fill several volumes. The persons who have been selected for inclusion here reflect the attitudes and aspirations of their day even if, in some cases, they are critics of their Zeitgeist. Above all, they preserve the basic continuity of the theme but also bring to light the variations on it that have arisen as Americans have undertaken to define the call of their destiny in different ways.

The book is neither a history of American religious denominations nor a history of American theology. It is, instead, a history of Americans' religious perspective on themselves as a people. As such, it is a treatment of a central belief in America's civil religion. The majority (but by no means all) of the people whose views are represented here are Protestant because the first well-delineated versions of American destiny were Protestant and because the basic convictions of the national religion were blended with a generalized Protestantism during the nineteenth century. Some of the nation's most distinguished theologians do speak within these pages, but their ideas are cast, like those of the other spokespersons, in a popular vein for wide consumption.

The presupposition underlying the volume is that any vital myth does not hide in the hinterland of a "realm of ideas" but impinges upon the life of a people as a spring of their action. To give serious attention to the myth of American destiny in its various forms is to heed the concrete courses of action that are excited by it and that in turn affect it. The introductions to the seven parts of this book note the shifts in the myth occasioned by changing historical circumstances and indicate the links between the myth and the events it inspires and vindicates. More extensive discussion of the historical settings and, in some cases, of the mythology itself may be found in the references cited in the notes and suggested readings.

Conrad Cherry
Indianapolis, Indiana
Fall 1997

God's New Israel

✢✣

Introduction

The belief that America has been providentially chosen for a special destiny has deep roots in the American past, and it is a belief that still finds expression in our so-called "secular age." It has resided at the heart of the attempt by Americans to understand their nation's responsibility at home and abroad. It is a conviction that has manifested itself most vividly in occasions of public worship when American citizens have met to share common religious sentiments. Below are descriptions of two such religious ceremonies. The first is set within the intimacy of a small rural community; the second is set in a metropolis and reaches millions of persons through television. Despite differences in setting, style, and ideology, both are American sacred ceremonies, which have in common a ritualistic form and a symbolic structure. Both are celebrations of a national religious faith. Both focus on the conviction that America has been called to a special task by God.

Two American Sacred Ceremonies

Boalsburg, a small town in central Pennsylvania, proudly announces from its billboards its claim to historical significance:

Boalsburg
An American Village
Birthplace of Memorial Day

In the spring of the year, when American patriots gather at cemeteries, town halls, shrines, and churches to celebrate Memorial Day the citizens of Boalsburg and vicinity remind themselves that their ancestors brought forth an event that has become a national holiday.[1] Memorial Day is, as W. Lloyd

---

1. Boalsburg did meet a disappointment in 1966 when President Johnson and both houses of Congress officially recognized Waterloo, New York, as the birthplace of the Memorial Day observance. The old-timers, leaders of patriotic organizations, and the press in Boalsburg insist, however, that this was simply a miscarriage of justice: whereas Waterloo's claim rests on the

Warner has observed, "both sacred and secular, it is a holy day as well as a holiday and is accordingly celebrated."[2] Along with Thanksgiving Day and the perhaps less explicitly religious observances of the Fourth of July and the birthdays of Washington and Lincoln, Memorial Day is part of an American ceremonial calendar. It is a day of pleasure and relaxation for most Americans, but it is also—particularly for war veterans in the towns and small cities of the northeastern and midwestern United States—a sacred day when the war dead are mourned, the spirit of redemptive sacrifice is extolled, and pledges to American ideals are renewed.

In Boalsburg and the surrounding communities elaborate preparations precede the day itself. During the week or two prior to May 30th, students in the public elementary schools construct flag displays which are pictured in the local newspapers. Graves of the war dead are decorated by families and patriotic organizations. The Veterans of Foreign Wars and the American Legion of the area hold meetings to plan for the holy day and services to commemorate their dead. As the day nears, merchants and residents put up American flags, and newspaper editorials encourage patriotic observance and sometimes lament languid patriotic zeal in the community. On the Sunday before Memorial Day, churches feature sermons on the virtue of human sacrifice for God and country, and veterans and their families gather at the Twenty-Eighth Division Memorial Shrine in Boalsburg to hear messages on the same theme. The climax of the celebration occurs, however, at the end of Memorial Day when all the patriotic groups and celebrants converge at the cemeteries to bring their ceremonies to a collective conclusion.

At 6 P.M. on May 30th, 1967, a crowd gathered on Church Street in Boalsburg to watch a brief parade made up of a high school band, color guards of the VFW and the Legion, fire trucks, and Girl Scouts and Brownies bearing wreaths of flowers. The crowd followed the march two blocks to the cemetery behind Zion Lutheran Church. As people found their places in front of the speakers' platform, the Girl Scouts placed their flowers on the soldiers' graves and a drill team fired a rifle salute. For over a hundred yards behind the crowd stretched the cemetery containing stones marking those fallen in American wars. Among these was the grave of Amos Meyers, the private who was killed on the last day of the battle of Gettysburg at the age of twenty-three and whose mother decorated his grave on that first Memorial Day in 1864. The minister of Zion Lutheran Church offered an invocation, and the district representative to the state legislature in Harrisburg rose to give the address.

---

original decoration of soldiers' graves there on May 5, 1866, the first grave decorations in Boalsburg occurred almost two years earlier.

2. W. Lloyd Warner, *American Life: Dream and Reality* (Chicago: University of Chicago Press, 1953), p. 1.

It was a typical Memorial Day message that lifted up images the people anticipated on this occasion. The nation's and community's war dead were honored as the speaker symbolically united the ethnic and religious groups. He called upon his hearers to remember on this day the sacrificed dead—the Smiths and Steins killed in Vietnam, the Maloneys and Rossis who fell in the Pacific islands, the Heidlers and Lozoskis who made the "supreme sacrifice" in the battle of Meuse-Argonne. And only if the living of the community pledge themselves to the principles for which these men died—democratic freedom and the defense of freedom against tyranny and oppression around the world—will these blood sacrifices not have been in vain. The sacrifices are the sanctification of America's "divine mission" of preserving and dispensing freedom.

Since the spirit of protest against United States involvement in Vietnam was very much in the air in the spring of 1967, several Memorial Day speakers attempted to draw a distinction between democratic freedom and certain types of dissent. "Those who practice civil disobedience," said a Legionnaire at a town a few miles from Boalsburg, "must expect to suffer the penalties provided for violating our laws. It is not an exercise of free expression to burn a draft card, nor to desecrate the flag of the United States."

The Memorial Day celebration is an American sacred ceremony, a religious ritual, a modern cult of the dead. Although it shares the theme of redemptive sacrifice with Christianity and other religions, and although its devotees would insist that the God called upon is the same as the God of their traditional religions, the Memorial Day rite is a civic service that aims to unite Americans beyond their separate religious differences. Lloyd Warner has described the essential function of the rite:

> Each man's church provides him and those of his faith with a set of beliefs and a way of acting to face these problems [of our own, our friends' and all men's death]; but his church and those of other men do not equip him with a common set of social beliefs and rituals which permit him to unite with all his fellows to confront this common and most feared of all his enemies. The Memorial Day rite and other subsidiary rituals connected with it form a cult which partially satisfies this need for common action on a common problem. It dramatically expresses the sentiments of unity of all the living among themselves, of all the living to all the dead, and of all the living and dead as a group to the gods.[3]

Joined with the unifying and existential problem-solving function of the cult is the conviction repeatedly expressed by the speakers that this nation has the providentially bestowed responsibility of acting as guardian and preserver of freedom. American soldiers have presented themselves as sacrifices on the

---

3. Ibid., p. 24.

altar of history that America's God-given task of rescuing oppressed peoples might not fail, that the nation may continue to be a beacon of freedom to all the world, that the sacred principles contained in the Declaration of Independence and the Constitution might remain untarnished.

There are, of course, large segments of American society that would feel little or no affinity with the Memorial Day ceremony. Many citizens in our larger cities have never witnessed the celebration of Memorial Day as a sacred event, and there are signs that since the 1960s the celebration has waned as a powerful collective-national religious event.[4] Yet Memorial Day remains a holy day for those rural and small-town Americans who have been largely bypassed by the effects of urbanization, it continues to be taken with special seriousness by those who have been to war and those who have sent their sons to war, and its vigorous celebration has a way of resurfacing during episodes of U.S. military engagements abroad. Memorial Day is by no means America's only sacred ceremony, however, and is not the only way Americans as citizens attempt to cope with death. In her funerals for great men, especially her political leaders, America has created another religious ceremony that meets anxiety over death in a corporate way and that transcends sectarian religious differences. The funeral for Senator Robert F. Kennedy was one such ceremony.

After Senator Kennedy's death on June 6, 1968, hundreds of thousands of Americans waited outside St. Patrick's Cathedral in New York City to pay their last respects, and millions of citizens who could not take their places in those long lines were able to assume a kind of presence there through their television sets. By way of television they witnessed the funeral on Saturday, followed the funeral train at its point of passage to Washington, and grieved with the family at the burial. Once again in the 1960s Americans participated in a ceremony honoring a leader who had been stopped by an act of destructive violence. In the funeral Robert Kennedy was vested with a meaning that derived from his "American dream" or his vision of American destiny. The funeral was another sacred ceremony in which the dilemma of death was met corporately, religious differences were transcended, and death was construed in terms of America's destiny under God. The day of the funeral, unlike Memorial Day, was altogether a holy day, devoid of mixture with a holiday spirit. And because of the suddenness and circumstances of Kennedy's death, the intensity of emotion permeating the funeral was undoubtedly much greater than that of the Memorial Day ceremony. Nevertheless, many of the same themes, symbols, and invocations were present.

Senator Kennedy's funeral was obviously a religious affair; it was "religious"

---

4. For an analysis of the receding of the event as a collective expression see Catherine Albanese, "Requiem for Memorial Day: Dissent in the Redeemer Nation," in *Civil Religion, Church and State*, ed. Martin E. Marty (New York: K. G. Saur, 1992), pp. 234–46.

in the sense in which most Americans think of that term since it had the trappings of one of the traditional Western religious communities. It was, after all, a Roman Catholic funeral mass. It was at the same time a civil-religious ceremony that appealed to Americans regardless of their denominational persuasions. The occasion was one in which the Catholic doctrines of hope, resurrection, and heavenly reward for a life well lived were drawn upon as resources of comfort by a mourning Kennedy family and other Christians. It was also an occasion when the Kennedys and numerous other Americans found a degree of comfort in the conviction that Robert Kennedy had met his death in the midst of an endeavor to secure freedom for all Americans and thereby fulfill that portion of America's destiny.

The funeral liturgy affirmed in the face of death, "For those who have been faithful all the way, life is not ended but merely changed. And when this earthly abode dissolves, an eternal dwelling place awaits them in Heaven." Senator Kennedy, quoting from and commenting on a speech by his brother, offered a different kind of affirmation:

> "Our future may lie beyond our vision, but it is not completely beyond our control. It is the shaping impulse of America that neither faith nor nature nor the irresistible tides of history, but the work of our own hands, matched to reason and principle, will determine our destiny. There is pride in that, even arrogance, but there is also experience and truth. In any event, it is the only way we can live."
> This is the way he lived.[5]

Those words invited their hearers to a hope and a sense of social responsibility in a way that the promise of an "eternal dwelling place" alone could not.

In his eulogy Archbishop Terence J. Cooke also sensed the national religious meaning of the occasion and of Robert Kennedy's life and death. To be sure, the message was sensitive to the deep personal loss that the Kennedy family had sustained and appropriately commented on Robert Kennedy as devoted husband, father, and son. The liturgy's reference to eternal life after death was cited at the beginning and at the end of the eulogy, providing the frame for the substance of the address. The greater part of Archbishop Cooke's eulogy, however, was a placing of Robert Kennedy in the context of an American dream and was a challenge to Americans to prevent the waste of Kennedy's life by fulfilling that dream.

Although Robert Kennedy could have chosen a much less arduous manner of life, the archbishop said, it was because he was driven by the ideal of building "a better world for his fellow man" that he accepted the demanding challenge of public service. "We admire the ability to identify so that

5. From a transcript of the eulogy furnished by the office of Senator Edward Kennedy.

Negro people spoke of him as 'one of ours.' We admire his vision in confronting the problems of poverty and civil rights." It was a dream that he had for America that evoked this admiration and enlisted his followers: "the dream of an America purged of prejudice, assuring freedom for all her citizens, a land of truly equal opportunity." The proper response to this man's tragic death, therefore, is to occupy ourselves with his dream of America's destiny. "Our sense of shame and discouragement tears alone will not wash away. Somehow, by the grace of God, and with the strength that still lies deep within the soul of America, we must find the courage to take up again the laborious work to which Senator Kennedy devoted all his energies: the building of a great and honorable nation. Especially in this hour, we must keep faith with America and her destiny and we must not forsake our trust in one another." Participation in America's historic destiny is the socially responsible way to meet Senator Kennedy's death. "We have always believed in our national destiny marked by unity in lofty ideals. We believe that our country came into existence to secure the blessings of freedom, equality, and peace for ourselves and those who will come after us."[6]

In this funeral Americans joined in a sacred ceremony, the scope of which crossed denominational religious boundaries. Many citizens had participated in another such ceremony only a few weeks earlier at the funeral for Dr. Martin Luther King, Jr., and in still another only a few short years earlier at the funeral for President John F. Kennedy. American history is, in fact, replete with leaders who have been canonized in the national consciousness as exemplars of American ideals and as particular bearers of America's destiny under God. When those leaders have met their deaths they have become, in the national memory as well as in the ceremonies and speeches that surround their deaths, martyrs for the American cause, even in some cases redeemers.[7]

There are, of course, differences between the two sacred ceremonies considered here, differences of content as well as emotional climate. The human "freedom" for which the supreme sacrifice has been made and which constitutes the essence of American destiny does not, for example, have the same meaning or call for the same kind of response in the two ceremonies. In the Memorial Day celebration it means the freedom of all peoples of the world to share in American democratic principles, a freedom that Americans are obligated to safeguard. In the Kennedy funeral, "freedom" stands for the civil

---

6. From a transcript of the eulogy provided by the office of Archbishop Cooke.

7. The most obvious example of the process is Lincoln. Since Lincoln's assassination occurred on Good Friday, hundreds of speakers on the following Sunday ("Black Easter") were quick to note that assassination day was also crucifixion day. Said one: "Jesus Christ died for the world: Abraham Lincoln died for his country." Cf. the apotheosizing of Jefferson who died on Independence Day, discussed in Merrill D. Peterson, *The Jefferson Image in the American Mind* (New York: Oxford University Press, 1960), pp. 3ff.

right of all American citizens to enjoy full and equal participation in their society. Despite such important differences, the two ceremonies have in common a symbolic, thematic, and ritualistic structure. Both are cults of the dead in which the living are united with one another, the living are united with the dead, and all are united with God and what are believed to be his purposes in history. Both ceremonies stress the belief that God has in store—has always had in store—for this nation a special destiny for which the supreme sacrifice has been made and to the fulfillment of which all Americans must dedicate themselves. And both rites are able to unite Americans beyond their religious divisions.

In the early part of the twentieth century the French sociologist Emile Durkheim observed that it is ritual that causes religious persons' faith to come alive, that quickens and sustains their religious belief. "In fact," Durkheim wrote, "whoever has really practiced a religion knows very well that it is the cult which gives rise to [the] impressions of joy, of interior peace, of serenity, of enthusiasm which are, for the believer, an experimental proof of his beliefs." Durkheim also noted that society itself (in addition to specifically "religious" groups within society) employs ritual to reaffirm its common sentiments:

> There can be no society which does not feel the need of upholding and reaffirming at regular intervals the collective sentiments and the collective ideas which make its unity and its personality. Now this moral remaking cannot be achieved except by the means of reunions, assemblies and meetings where the individuals, being closely united to one another, reaffirm in common their common sentiments; hence come ceremonies which do not differ from regular religious ceremonies, neither in their object, the results which they produce, or the processes employed to attain these results.[8]

Memorial Day and Robert Kennedy's funeral are only two of the many rituals (all of which are not, of course, rituals for the dead) in which Americans "reaffirm in common their common sentiments." They are ritualistic ceremonies that appeal to their participants as American citizens, elevate American leaders to the status of heroes or martyrs, and celebrate what are held to be American ideals.

The sentiment that is continually reaffirmed by these sacred ceremonies is the conviction that America is a nation called to a special destiny by God. A consideration of the character and shape of the national religion to which this conviction belongs is prerequisite to understanding the development of the theme of this book.

8. Emile Durkheim, *The Elementary Forms of the Religious Life*, trans. J. W. Swain (New York: Free Press, 1965), pp. 464, 474–75.

The American Civil Religion

It has become a commonplace to refer to radical pluralism as the cardinal mark of religion in America. The settlement of this land by peoples of different — often antagonistic — churchly orientations and the influx of numerous religious groups during periods of heavy immigration meant that Americans eventually had to learn to live with other Americans of diverse religious traditions. The disestablishment of religion by federal and state constitutions meant that no one religion was favored by the laws of the land and that religious organizations in this country had to become altogether "voluntaristic." Every American religion must recruit and hold its members through methods of persuasion rather than coercion, relying upon the free consent of the people rather than upon the arm of the state.

The truth of this portrait of the American religious development has often obscured the other truth, however, that many Americans have periodically celebrated a common religion. In the words of the sociologist Robert Bellah, "there actually exists alongside of and rather clearly differentiated from the churches an elaborate and well-institutionalized civil religion in America."[9] Although this civil religion is not established by the laws of the land, it is supported and perpetuated by the mores and folk practices of American society. It finds ritual expression in public occasions like the two sacred ceremonies discussed above.

Bellah takes John F. Kennedy's inaugural address as an example of the verbalization of the civil religion and as a clue to the way in which the civil religion may be differentiated from the religious denominations of this country. Kennedy began and closed his address with references to God and God's relation to American tasks and principles. In the opening statement he said,

> I have sworn before you and Almighty God the same solemn oath our forebears prescribed nearly a century and three quarters ago.
>
> The world is very different now. For man holds in his mortal hands the power to abolish all forms of human poverty and to abolish all forms of human life. And yet the same revolutionary beliefs for which our forebears fought are still at issue around the globe — the belief that the rights of man come not from the generosity of the state but from the hand of God.

Kennedy's closing statement reflects the recurrent conviction in American sacred ceremonies:

> Finally, whether you are citizens of America or of the world, ask of us the same high standards of strength and sacrifice that we shall ask of

9. Robert N. Bellah, "Civil Religion in America," *Daedalus*, Winter 1967, p. 1.

you. With a good conscience our only sure reward, with history the final judge of our deeds, let us go forth to lead the land we love, asking His blessing and His help, but knowing that here on earth God's work must truly be our own.

As Bellah points out, similar God-references are standard rhetoric in presidential inaugural addresses and "are almost invariably to be found in the pronouncements of American presidents on solemn occasions, though usually not in the working messages that the president sends to Congress on various concrete issues." To the cynic who would insist that the invocations of God are merely ritualistic expressions that a president must use to get votes or to gain the support of pious people, Bellah replies, "What people say on solemn occasions need not be taken at face value, but it is often indicative of deep-seated values and commitments that are not made explicit in the course of everyday life."[10] Commenting on the rhetoric of a different public ceremony, Alan Trachtenberg offers a similar judgment: "Speeches might be dismissed as highly conventional and insincere. Sincerity, however, is not a necessary qualification for cultural significance; surely the conventions of language themselves suggest predispositions among Americans to react in certain ways at certain times."[11]

It is significant that Kennedy did not refer to Jesus Christ, to the Roman Catholic church, or to any specifically Catholic doctrine. This does not mean that on this occasion President Kennedy ceased to be a Catholic; it does mean that the particular doctrines of his Catholic faith were inappropriate to the public occasion. It indicates that the religious point of view he was propounding was not to be confused with his Catholicism. His religious language was aimed altogether toward the American as a citizen. He mentioned the fact that his oath of office was made before both the people and Almighty God. "In American political theory," Bellah comments, "sovereignty rests, of course, with the people, but implicitly, and often explicitly, the ultimate sovereignty has been attributed to God." Kennedy reinforced this appeal to an ultimate authority when he said, "the rights of man come not from the generosity of the state but from the hand of God." Again, in Bellah's words, "the rights of man are more basic than any political structure and provide a point of revolutionary leverage from which any state structure may be radically altered." Finally, in his statement that "here on earth God's work must truly be our own," Kennedy gave voice to the continuous theme in American history that it is this nation's destiny—for Kennedy, in conjunction with "the citizens of the world"—to carry out God's will on earth. Kennedy's inaugural address

10. Ibid., p. 2.

11. Alan Trachtenberg, *Brooklyn Bridge: Fact and Symbol* (New York: Oxford University Press, 1965), p. 117.

recalls the God-references in the Declaration of Independence: the mention of the "Laws of Nature and of Nature's God" that entitle any people to independence; the statement that all people "are endowed by their Creator with certain inalienable Rights"; the appeal to "the Supreme Judge of the world for the rectitude of our intentions"; and the urging of "a firm reliance on the protection of divine Providence."[12]

The Declaration of Independence, the inaugural addresses of presidents, the celebration of American sacred ceremonies indicate that the disestablishment of the church has never meant that the American political sphere was denied a religious dimension. In fact, that dimension has so permeated the political, educational, and social life of America that it has constituted a civil religion that cannot be identified with Protestantism, Catholicism, or Judaism as such. Americans may be participants in *both* the religious dimension of their civil life *and* one of the traditional religions. The American church historian Sidney Mead is so convinced of the presence of this civil religion at the very foundations of American life and of its potential catholicity that he has said, "just as the ideal of America has been that 'of molding many peoples into the visible image of the citizen,' so it was implied that the religious ideal was that of melding the many diverse sectarianisms into one cosmopolitan religion."[13]

The sacred ceremonies and Kennedy's inaugural provide some clues to the beliefs that make up the civil religion. This nation's destiny under God, the guarantee of human rights by the hand of God, the need for sacrifice and martyrdom for the fulfillment of the nation's destiny—all these are parts of the belief structure of the civil religion. When dealing with any religion, however—be it Christianity, Buddhism, or the American civil religion—it is a highly questionable practice to detail beliefs in isolation from their historical settings. In some cases a religion's reformulation of a belief—in responding to the problems, or in absorbing the spirit, of a given milieu—involves little more than a shift in phraseology. In other instances, however, changes in expression reflect changes in the very substance of the belief. The readings in this book are concerned with the central, continuous belief around which other convictions in the civil religion cluster. The readings also portray the changes—some of them quite drastic—that have occurred in the formulation of the belief. At this point the contours of the general religious context in which that belief is set should emerge in a sketch of three features of the American civil religion: (1) the sources of its beliefs and symbols, (2) its institutions, (3) the relation between the civil religion and other religions in this country.

12. Bellah, "Civil Religion," pp. 4–6.
13. Sidney E. Mead, "The 'Nation With the Soul of a Church,'" *Church History*, Sept. 1967, p. 263.

The Sources of the Beliefs and Symbols of the Civil Religion

The deepest source lies in the Old and New Testaments, but the more immediate source is the history of America or certain events of that history which have been judged revelatory. In the ceremonies of the civil religion the images of God's deliverance of and demands upon his chosen people and the rebirth that can issue from sacrificial death are definitely biblical images. But they are given immediacy by being translated into events of American history. God's demands upon his chosen people become demands upon America at this particular juncture of her history. Rebirth through sacrificial death becomes the rebirth of the nation through the sacrifices of its war dead and martyrs. Biblical events serve as the archetypes, but *the immediate events of revelation—those paradigmatic events by which the celebrants of the civil religion interpret the meaning of their national life and the purposes of God in history—are events in the American experience.*[14] As will become apparent in many of the selections in this anthology, two chief revelatory events for the civil religion are the American Revolution (joined with the entire constitutional period) and the American Civil War. The first was a moment when God delivered the colonies from Pharaoh Britain and the "evils" of the Old World, revealed the purposes of the nation, and adopted the Young Republic as an example and instrument of freedom and republican government for the rest of the world. The Civil War was the nation's first real "time of testing" when God tried the permanence of the Union or, in some interpretations, brought judgment upon his wayward people. Documents like the Declaration of Independence and the Gettysburg Address function as scriptures that interpret these events and hence preserve the traditions of the civil religion. Washington becomes both Moses and Joshua, both the deliverer of the American people out of bondage and the leader of the chosen people into the Promised Land of independence. Lincoln assumes the role of a Christ figure in the national memory: one who tragically dedicated himself to the destiny of a united nation and whose death summed up the sacrifices that redeemed the nation for that destiny.

Other events, persons, and documents in American history have taken on sacred meaning, but these are sufficient to point to the way in which that history most immediately supplies the civil religion with its symbolic material. It is somewhat misleading, therefore, to refer to the civil or national religion as a "common denominator" faith, as if it were formed by reducing Christianity and Judaism to their bare essentials. The belief structure is primarily constituted by the inflow of a history that *Americans as Americans* hold in common. Although the national religion borrows heavily from the Jewish and Christian religions, it is not the borrowed elements but the American experience itself that creates the commonality of the civil faith. "The Lord hath more light

14. Cf. Bellah, "Civil Religion," p. 18.

yet to break forth out of his Holy Word" was a declaration of John Robinson, pastor of the settlers of Plymouth in 1620 while they were still exiles at Leyden. It is also a statement that catches the spirit of the American civil religion which supposes that the light of God's revelation continually breaks forth in crucial events of American history.

The Institutional Framework of the Civil Religion

Clearly the foremost institution is the nation itself, with the public school serving as a subinstitution. Churches and synagogues have also provided a haven for the myths, symbols, and ceremonies of the civil religion.

John E. Smylie has convincingly argued that the nation gradually assumed the traditional role of the church for most Americans. As these shores were inundated by a host of diverse religious organizations and as our laws made clear that no one religious denomination could operate as a national religion, the word "church" made sense to Americans only in the plural. Every church became for the citizens of this land "a voluntary society, perhaps the most important among others, but hardly the organ through which God made his ultimate historical demands and offered his fullest earthly rewards." Lacking special endorsement by the state, the American churches gave up the functions normally associated with the universal church. But where the churches moved out, the nation moved in. "Gradually in America the nation emerged as the primary agent of God's meaningful activity in history. Hence Americans bestowed on it a catholicity of destiny similar to that which theology attributes to the universal church." Early colonial groups believed that their own church covenants were vehicles of God's action in history, but eventually the Declaration of Independence, the Constitution, and the Bill of Rights became the covenants that bound together the people of the nation and secured to them God's blessing, protection, and call to historic mission.[15]

Historically, the public schools of this country have played an inestimable role both in advancing the traditions of the civil religion and in undergirding the religious function of the nation. It is questionable that today the schools any longer perform that role on a broad national front, given their frequent neglect of key events and leaders in American history. In the past, however, they have provided the place of instruction (often, admittedly, the place of unexamined propaganda) in the "sacred history" of the civil religion. Until recently the public schools were unabashedly Protestant in their prayers, morning devotions, and general religious orientation, but they were also the depositories and purveyors of the events and documents of the civil religion.

---

15. John Edwin Smylie, "National Ethos and the Church," *Theology Today*, Oct. 1963, pp. 313–17.

The Supreme Court rulings forbidding devotional Bible reading and prayer were more an effort to disentangle the practices and beliefs of the diverse American religions (including, according to the Court, the "religion of secularism") from those of the civil religion than an attempt to put an end to the civil religion in the schools.

Although the civil religion has developed its own ceremonies, scriptures, events of revelation, and institutions, it has also found immeasurable support from the American churches. The Americanization of the churches and synagogues has been so well documented that it only needs mentioning here. To a great extent the churches of this land came to abide by the suggestion of the Founding Fathers that the different religious groups should not only exist for the sake of their own beliefs and practices but should also assume responsibility for maintenance of the public order, the dissemination of the essential religious beliefs (for example, the existence of a Deity, the governance of the world by his providence, the reward of virtue and the punishment of crime), and the promotion of the public welfare. The presence of the American flag in the churches, the celebration of national events by religious groups, the frequent mixing of biblical and "sacred" American history in sermons are some of the obvious signs that the national religion has often found a home in the American churches. The obvious signs are often misleading, however, for the history of the relationship between the national religion and the denominations has been complex.

The Relation between the Civil Religion and Other Religions in America

At least three modes of this relationship have turned up in the American experience.

Robert Bellah notes one mode when he uses Kennedy's inaugural address as an indication that the civil religion "exists alongside of" and is "rather clearly differentiated from the churches." In this address as well as in the two sacred ceremonies discussed above, sectarian religious beliefs do not intrude; in fact, religious differences are transcended to the plane of a national faith made up of images and beliefs that Americans hold in common. The religious references do have their deepest source in the biblical tradition of the churches, but they are so woven into the fabric of national history that they lose any potentially sectarian color. In this relationship, therefore, the national religion and the denominations remain quite distinct. An American may be a Methodist, a Conservative Jew, or a Roman Catholic and at the same time participate in the civil religion—without insisting that the civil religion be expressed in specifically Methodist, Jewish, or Catholic terms.

Although this type of relationship has had its defenders in American history from Jefferson and Franklin to Lincoln to Dewey, only recently has it become a vital option in America. Only after Protestantism lost its powerful grip on the public life of the nation did the civil religion begin to dislodge itself from Protestant articulation and custody. During the nineteenth century and well into the twentieth, most leading spokespersons for the civil religion couched its beliefs in terms that were unmistakably Protestant. It took such factors as the impact of non-Protestant immigrants, a Supreme Court determined to de-Protestantize the public schools, and a pluralization of values in many regions of American life through modern means of communication to break through this confusion of Protestantism and the religion of America.

A second kind of relationship between the civil religion and other religions, therefore, has a long historical precedent, though that precedent has been rather decisively broken in most regions of American life. It is marked by a thorough blending of a generalized Protestantism with the national religion. The Protestantism is "generalized" in that it is nondenominational. Its representatives tend to define America as a "Christian civilization," but their Christianity is seldom big enough to include Roman Catholicism.

Lyman Beecher, that colorful and influential Congregational minister of the nineteenth century, was quite a man of his time when he mixed his Protestantism and his civil religion in about equal doses. Beecher's Protestantism was generalized because he was extremely capable of glossing over theological differences but also, as Sidney Mead has remarked, because "Protestantism had become for him a principle of high generality which, he thought, permeated and was being incarnated in the democratic institutions of the Republic."[16] Despite the generality of his Protestantism, however, like so many other nineteenth-century Protestants, Beecher could find no room in his civil faith for Roman Catholics. His popular and oft-delivered address, "A Plea for the West," took up that central theme in the civil religion: "America is, in the providence of God, destined to lead the way in the moral and political emancipation of the world." Beecher anchored the theme to what he considered "equally plain," namely, "that the religious and political destiny of our nation is to be decided in the West." Beecher drew upon a lively vision of the West as he encouraged easterners to pour their resources into educational and religious enterprises on the frontier, but he gave his plea urgency by warning that the West had to be educated and made religious before it was completely inundated by European immigrants who would wreck democratic principles with a "Catholic system" that is "adverse to liberty."

Finally, the civil religion and other religions in America have existed in a relationship of tension. The most obvious instances of the tension appear in those groups, like the Jehovah's Witnesses, that spurn patriotic symbols, reject American sacred ceremonies, and refuse to allow the nation to function

16. Mead, "Soul of a Church," p. 280.

for them as a "church." But clergy and scholars within the so-called religious "mainstream" have also insisted that a tension exists between their own traditions and the American "culture faith."

During the 1950s and early 1960s a flood of criticism flowed from the pens of Protestants, Catholics, and Jews who were convinced that the Americanization of their faiths resulted in a banal, watered-down version of their potent religious traditions. Charges against the "American Shinto," that vague "religion in general" which is the heart of the "American way of life," ranged from claims of its sentimental piety and theological naiveté to indictments of its idolatrous worship of American values and narrow-minded nationalism. Much was made of the way in which God and religion were *used* in our culture by politicians, clergymen, popularizers of religion, and businessmen for their own higher ends: for the support of particular national tasks, for the swelling of church membership rolls, for gaining "peace of mind" in a troubled world, for achieving success in a society of capitalistic competition. Professor Will Herberg summed up the reasons for his condemnation of the civil religion:

> . . . civic religion has always meant the sanctification of the society and culture of which it is the reflection, and that is one of the reasons why Jewish-Christian faith has always regarded such religion as incurably idolatrous. Civic religion is a religion which validates culture and society, without in any sense bringing them under judgment. . . .
>
> The burden of this criticism of American religion from the point of view of Jewish-Christian faith is that contemporary religion is so naively, so innocently *man-centered*. Not God, but man—man in his individual and corporate being—is the beginning and end of the spiritual system of much present-day American religiosity. . . . God is conceived as man's "omnipotent servant," faith as a sure-fire device to get what we want.[17]

There have been some who have replied to the critics of the civil religion. Sidney Mead has written, "The 'American religion,' contrary to Will Herberg's much popularized misunderstanding, is *not* 'the American way of life' as we know and experience it, any more than the Christian faith *is* the way of life that ordinary professing 'Christians' commonly exemplify in their everyday activities."[18] Along the same line Robert Bellah has insisted that the critics "take as criteria the best in their own religious tradition and as typical the worst in the tradition of the civil religion," conveniently overlooking the

---

17. Will Herberg, *Protestant-Catholic-Jew* (Garden City, N.Y.: Doubleday & Company, Anchor Books, 1960), pp. 263, 268. Similar criticisms have been abundant, but see especially Martin E. Marty, *The New Shape of American Religion* (New York: Harper & Row, Publishers, 1959); A. Roy Eckardt, "The New Look in American Piety," *Christian Century*, Nov. 17, 1954; Peter Berger, *The Noise of Solemn Assemblies* (Garden City, N.Y.: Doubleday & Company, 1961).

18. Mead, "Soul of a Church," pp. 274–75.

fact that spokesmen for the civil religion have often drawn upon a vivid belief in a transcendent God who cannot be reduced to human designs, in order to censure American society.[19] Abraham Lincoln, for example, who identified with no particular denomination, was able to perform this "prophetic" role for the civil religion during the sectional crisis. And one is reminded of John Kennedy's use of the idea of "the rights of man from the hand of God" as a revolutionary lever. Mead and Bellah are concerned to draw a distinction between *religious nationalism* and *national religion*. Religious nationalism implies a corporate attitude of unconditional reverence for the nation and for its pretended or real goals. National religion, on the other hand, suggests a national attitude of reverence for a transcendent sovereign authority whose designs cannot be identified one-to-one with the designs of the nation. In the latter case America can function as a "church" or as an inclusive institution whose ideals and goals bind a people together under a sovereign God. When those ideals or goals themselves usurp the transcendent authority, or when the nation's every move receives uncritical religious endorsement, the national religion slips into the idolatry of religious nationalism. Many readings in this book will show that the sense of national destiny has frequently led Americans to make the passage from national religion to religious nationalism. Other readings will demonstrate, however, that Americans have sometimes recoiled from the passage and have understood the deluding temptations of the path.

This much must be said on behalf of the critics of the American civil religion: their indictment of the utilitarian distortions of religion has been very much to the point. However much they may have identified the whole of the civil religion with its worst side, the critics have portrayed the idolatry involved when the civil religion sanctifies, without question, the values or goals of American society. To that extent, when other American religions exist in a relation of tension with the civil religion, the tension can point up the distortions of the latter.

The accumulated tradition of the civil religion by no means guarantees that it will persist as a vital religious orientation in American life, for it faces serious problems and challenges in late-twentieth-century America.

Much of the symbolism of the civil religion, for instance, has lost its clarity and specificity. Words such as freedom, democracy, providence, and God which recur in the celebrations of the national faith seem to lack uniform meaning for contemporary Americans. This problem of language is not so much a case of the death of the symbols themselves as it is a matter of the symbols becoming ambiguous. In fact, the ambiguity seems to increase the symbols' capacity to conjure up, like words of Black Magic, diverse and potent images.

19. Bellah, "Civil Religion," p. 12.

As W. H. Auden has put the matter, "words like Communism, Capitalism, Imperialism, Peace, Freedom, Democracy, have ceased to be words the meaning of which can be inquired into and discussed, and have become right or wrong noises to which the response is as involuntary as a knee reflex."[20]

When the civil religion's central symbol, God, becomes ambiguous but retains its evocative powers, the resultant problem is much more serious than a mere problem of language. If that symbol does not refer clearly to a transcendent reality that brings all nations to judgment, the national religion is more than a little inclined to ignore the narrowness and evil within the nation. Reinhold Niebuhr's understanding of God as one "who laughs at human pretensions without being hostile to human aspirations" can exercise a powerful check on chauvinism without destroying the national spirit. When a transcendent perspective of that kind is lacking, the lost causes and less than virtuous aspirations of a people are hidden under a cloak of self-righteousness. Americans have more than once been blinded to their vices by their pretensions to virtue (as well as by their real virtues). As Sidney Mead has so aptly put it, while Americans have consistently viewed themselves as the bearers of a special destiny under God, "God, like Alice's Cheshire Cat, has sometimes threatened gradually to disappear altogether or, at most, to remain only as a disembodied and sentimental smile."[21] In theological terms the God who smiles innocuously on American undertakings is a sentimental Deity whose wrath has ceased to burn toward national sins. In more secular terms the American people have failed to measure themselves by their own highest national ideals.

The civil religion, like any religion which becomes an established part of a culture, is always in danger of sanctifying the virtues of a society while ignoring its vices. Although the danger is not characteristic of the contemporary scene alone, America's present position as a great world power intensifies the peril. Americans have long lived under the conviction that their nation always comes to the defense of other countries for the sake of "free institutions" and "democratic governments." Can we admit, rhetoric to the contrary notwithstanding, that we have also rushed to the aid of military dictatorships when we believe such action will serve our own national interests? The powerful *and clear* symbolizing of a transcendent reality is a religious assurance that such pretensions and shortcomings of the nation will be brought to light.

The civil religion faces another dilemma. How inclusive can that religion become without losing its identity? For the sake of a healthy openness it is called upon to embrace a plurality of values and standpoints both within the nation and in the world at large. Within the national boundaries, however, it

20. From an excerpt of Auden's speech made upon acceptance of the 1967 Medal for Literature of the National Book Committee, *The Washington Post Book World*, Dec. 24, 1967, p. 8.

21. Sidney E. Mead, *The Lively Experiment* (New York: Harper & Row, Publishers, 1963), p. 152.

has found no way of embracing agnostic or atheistic elements. Perhaps it is absurd to expect a civil *religion* to include these elements within its own fold. But as a *civil* religion, it definitely has a responsibility to these components of the national life. Since the civil religion is so intimate a part of American society, it is capable of obstructing the full participation of Americans in the nation's public life. When it performs that function it fails to support the democratic principle that no person or group of persons shall be disadvantaged by either their religious or their nonreligious beliefs. "We have had a Catholic president; it is conceivable that we could have a Jewish one. But could we have an agnostic president? Could a man with conscientious scruples about using the word *God* the way Kennedy and Johnson have used it be elected chief magistrate of our country?"[22] One may expect that the further pluralization of American society will permit a positive answer to that question; in the meantime Americans must wrestle with the issue of how inclusive American public life really is when it is informed by the historic attitudes of the civil religion.

A more urgent aspect of this same dilemma turns on whether the civil religion will truly encompass the African American, the poor, the American Indian, and all those other citizens who have been excluded from a white, male-dominated, affluent mainstream. The civil religion certainly has the resources for meeting this problem in its doctrine of human rights, and its representatives have not neglected civil rights when articulating the theme of "America's destiny under God." Solutions to this paramount problem will not come easily, however, inasmuch as the social issues which have increasingly divided Americans since the end of World War II portend a loss of corporate identity, a loss of what Durkheim called "collective religious sentiments."

Finally, the question of the possible inclusiveness of the civil religion has international implications. In the midst of a twentieth-century quest for world order and understanding, a *national* civil religion—one that draws its traditions from a national history and institutionalizes itself in a nation—seems terribly provincial. Does not the civil religion tighten the hold of national prejudices on the American mind? Although the civil religion need not play this deleterious role, that has been its overwhelming tendency. Although the ideals and goals of the civil religion need not exclude connection with what John Kennedy called the ideals and goals of the "citizens of the world," Americans, like citizens of other nations, are apt to confine their visions within the limits of national self-interest. Still, two improvements of the American civil religion seem to be at least within the realm of possibility: it could begin to incorporate international or transnational symbols and creeds into its framework, and it could take the position that it is only *one* of a host of more or less acceptable civil religions in the world.

22. Bellah, "Civil Religion," p. 15.

American Destiny under God

Beheld from the angle of governing mythology, the history of the American civil religion is a history of the conviction that the American people are God's New Israel, his newly chosen people. The belief that America has been elected by God for a special destiny in the world has been the focus of American sacred ceremonies, the inaugural addresses of our presidents, the sacred scriptures of the civil religion. It has been so pervasive a motif in the national life that the word "belief" does not really capture the dynamic role that it has played for the American people, for it passed into "the realm of motivational myths."[23] It became a myth in the sense that it provided a religious outlook on history and its purpose, and by finding a place in the feelings and choices as well as in the ideas of the people, it proved to be capable of moving them to action. When interpreters of the civil religion have appealed to this myth, therefore, they not only have struck a responsive chord in their auditors, for if they have dramatized their subject, they have been able to elicit a commitment.

A sense of providential calling is not, of course, an exclusive possession of the American people. Other nations have been sustained by the belief that God or Fate or historical circumstance has elected them to a preeminent role in history. The sentiment is probably as old as nationalism itself; at any rate, it has furnished other nations and groups of people with a sense of purpose as they have developed their corporate ideals and their historical tasks.[24] The fact that the conviction is not uniquely American, however, by no means derogates from its importance in the American experience. It has sustained the American people since the colonial period, and it has taken on a distinctively American appearance as it has both motivated and vindicated American projects. It has been such a powerful myth for the nation that it has decisively shaped our foreign relations as well as our own internal developments.

It would, of course, be highly misleading to assume that this pervasive and continuous theme of American destiny has received uniform interpretation throughout American history. The various challenges that have faced the American people—the settlement of a wilderness frontier, the formation of a republic, the fighting of wars, the preservation of peace—have evoked different interpretations of America's high calling. And occasionally within the same period of history, with respect to the same challenge, Americans have been deeply divided over the meaning of the national mission. The following documents and their introductions are concerned with these variations on the one theme of American destiny under God. It is well to note beforehand,

23. The phrase is Sidney Mead's in his discussion of the motif, *The Lively Experiment*, p. 75.
24. See *Many Are Chosen: Divine Election and Western Nationalism*, ed. William R. Hutchison and Hartmut Lehman (Minneapolis: Fortress Press, 1994).

however, that there have been two basic versions when the theme has been applied to the relation between America and other peoples.

America has been regarded either as a "light to the nations" which by force of example will positively influence other peoples and perhaps draw them to an American haven of freedom, or as a chosen people with an obligation actively to win others to American principles and to safeguard those principles around the world. The first pattern is what Clinton Rossiter called the "true American Mission" and the "finest expression of American nationalism":

> It assumes that God, at the proper stage in the march of history, called forth certain hardy souls from the old and privilege-ridden nations; that He carried these previous few to a new world and presented them and their descendents with an environment ideally suited to the development of a free society; and that in bestowing His grace He also bestowed a peculiar responsibility for the success of popular institutions. Were the Americans to fail in their experiment in self-government, they would fail not only themselves, but all men wanting or deserving to be free.[25]

This view of American destiny had its classic expression during the Revolution and the constitutional period, but it had been nursed by the Puritans of Massachusetts Bay and has appeared repeatedly in the course of American history. According to the second version, Americans have presupposed that their divine election involves more than being an example for the rest of the world. They have believed that this nation is called to spread abroad the fundamental principles stated in the Bill of Rights, to preserve democratic government around the world, and to protect freedom wherever it is threatened. Such assumptions undergirded the foreign-mission enterprises of the American churches during the late nineteenth and early twentieth centuries, and they have stimulated and vindicated American participation in foreign wars.

The second version of American destiny has had its unlovely manifestations: a muscular imperialism that cloaks American self-interest with platitudes about saving the world for democracy, a racist myth that justifies American actions abroad because of "Anglo-Saxon superiority," etc. But the first version contains within it the seeds of an extreme isolationism that would preclude the nation's responsibility for the international welfare. Again Clinton Rossiter's remarks are appropriate when he says that America's mission understood as example

> can serve as a cloak for the revival of the most short-sighted, ethnocentric stamp of isolationism, but only if internationally-minded Americans permit it to be stolen from their keeping. The American Mission,

25. Clinton Rossiter, "The American Mission," *The American Scholar*, 20 (1950–51), 19–20.

a view of national destiny neither vulgar nor imperialistic, can certainly be squared with a healthy attitude of international cooperation.[26]

The key word here is "cooperation," which means that if the avoidance of isolationism is not to result in some form of imperialism, America must free itself from the messianic illusions which have led it to insist that Americans are the saviors of the world. International cooperation requires an openness to alternatives and compromise, something which is altogether foreign to messianic absolutism.

Many of the contemporary problems facing the civil religion come to a head in the myth of American destiny under God. The ambiguity of the religious symbolism and the diversity of American citizens and their demands to be heard tend to render the direction of American destiny indistinct, and an attitude of international cooperation balks at any nation's assumption that it has a higher destiny than any other nation. Above all, the belief in America as God's New Israel has come to support America's arrogant self-righteousness. It has been all too easy for Americans to convince themselves that they have been chosen to be a free and powerful people not because God or the circumstances of history choose in mysterious ways but because they *deserve* election. The blessings of success, wealth, and power are readily taken as signs of their having merited a special place in history. Yet recent sensitivity to how those blessings have been withheld from Americans has challenged such smug self-satisfaction. And crises at home and abroad have cast dark clouds of doubt over an assumed American exceptionalism. The consequences of such occurrences, however, are to anticipate the concluding sections of this book. A grasp of the recent threats to the mythology of American destiny requires, first of all, an understanding of the rich, complex history of that mythology.

26. Ibid., p. 27.

Part One

ﾞﾞﾞ

The Colonial Errand into the Wilderness

The rudiments of the theme of American destiny under God emerged in the English colonization of the New World. The new nation that was to appear would inherit from the thirteen colonies an English language, legal system, and set of social customs, all appropriately adapted to the American environment. It would fall heir also to a religious view of history that had developed in the mother country. By the time they launched their colonial enterprises in the seventeenth century, the English had been taught from childhood that the course of human history is directed by God's overruling providence and that God's redemptive efforts centered on England and English Christianity. These assumptions about history were frequently joined with the millennialist belief that God and his chosen English saints were actively defeating the powers of Satan, the first major victory being the Protestant Reformation.[1] The establishment of colonies, therefore, was hardly considered an ordinary undertaking. Many in England saw it as an opportunity to extend the influence of their civilization through which God was working for the redemption of humankind. For others colonization was a chance to bring England to its senses by achieving on new soil what they had not been able to do at home. The Quaker William Penn was moved to announce that his "holy experiment" in religious toleration was meant to be God's own "example to the nations." The letters of the Jesuit father Andrew White claimed that the settlement of Maryland was continuously presided over by the providence of God and that the "first and most important design" of the colony was "sowing the seeds of religion and piety."

---

1. As Winthrop S. Hudson and John Corrigan have observed, this perspective on history was greatly influenced by the writings of John Foxe, whose *Book of Martyrs* was officially placed in every cathedral church in 1571 and later came to occupy a place second only to the Bible in Protestant homes. Winthrop S. Hudson and John Corrigan, *Religion in America* (New York: Macmillan Publishing Company, 1992), p. 24. On Foxe see William Haller, *The Elect Nation: The Meaning and Relevance of Foxe's Book of Martyrs* (New York: Harper & Row, Publishers, 1963). On millennialism see Ernest Lee Tuveson, *Redeemer Nation: The Idea of America's Millennial Role* (Chicago: University of Chicago Press, 1968), pp. 1–30.

Religion was by no means the only, or even the dominant, motive for the settlement of most of the colonies. A religious view of history, however, did furnish a framework of self-understanding for colonists and stockholders who were impelled by a variety of motives. In the early literature of Virginia, for example, an admitted economic motive was interwoven with a historical perspective in which the providence of God loomed large. John Rolfe, whose method of cultivating a sweet leaf of tobacco was instrumental in establishing Virginia's staple crop, wrote that the migration to Virginia was a venture of "a peculiar people, marked and chosen by the finger of God" to possess the land. Alexander Whitaker, a clergyman of the Church of England who arrived at Jamestown with Sir Thomas Dale in 1611 and helped Dale found the town of Henrico, explicated the religious meaning of the Virginia planting but not without reference to economics. Whitaker's *Good Newes from Virginia* was sent to the Virginia Company, which directed it into publication in 1613. In that sermon he enumerated the religious reasons why the English should maintain a financial interest in Virginia. God's deliverance of Sir Thomas Gates and the survivors of the *Sea Venture* which wrecked on Bermuda and His saving of the colony from famine were signs of providential blessing on the enterprise. As a Christian nation England was obligated to answer God's call to convert the "heathen" Indians to the Christian faith and civilized customs. England was being challenged to defend its reputation among the nations as a charitable and persevering people. Though counseling patience and condemning a usurious spirit, Whitaker frankly appealed to the economic motive, placing it in his religious framework: "fortie years were expired, before Israel could plant in Canaan, and yet God had called them by the word of his mouth, had led them himselfe by a high hand. Yet may you boldly looke for a shorter time of reward."

The most self-conscious pursuit of destiny under God in the New World was enacted by the Puritans of Massachusetts Bay, and the most articulate colonial spokesmen for the theme of American destiny were the Puritans. Ecclesiastical and civic leaders in New England conceived of America as a place where a Protestant Reformation of church and society could be completed—a task that had not been carried out in England and Europe. They envisioned their journey to these shores less as an escape from religious persecution than as a positive mission for the construction of a model Christian society. They were on an "errand into the wilderness"; their purpose was to build a holy commonwealth in which the people were covenanted together by their public profession of religious faith and were covenanted with God by their pledge to erect a Christian society. Their government also shared in this covenant since one of the roles of government was to protect their Congregational form of church polity and safeguard their religion against dissident groups. The original errand, however, was more than a mission for the Puritans themselves. They believed that, like Israel of old, they had been singled out by God to be an example for the nations (especially for England). With their charter and company in America, the Puritans could in effect construct a republic independent of an English crown that had not allowed them the freedom of their experiment at home. Nevertheless, they insisted that they were English settlers on an English errand: their godly commonwealth was to be a New England that would serve as a working model for Old England. If they succeeded in their errand, they would mark a turning point in history, for their commonwealth would be imitated by the nations. If they failed, they would fail not only themselves but their God and the very course of history.

The sense of destiny in the New World pervaded Puritan literature. John Winthrop, first governor of the Bay Colony, gave the theme one of its earliest and most pointed expressions. Winthrop's *Model of Christian Charity*, written aboard the flagship *Arbella* as it led the Puritan expedition toward the Promised Land, briefly spelled out the terms of the Puritan covenant (terms founded on a divinely ordained social order in which "some must be rich, some poore") and captured both the anticipation and the dread that arose in the heart of Puritan New Israel as it struck a covenant with Jehovah.

Beginning around 1650 much Puritan literature was replete with lamentations over the failure of New England to measure up to its divine calling. Sermons before the General Assembly at election time became particularly mournful as the clergy bewailed the decline of godliness among the people. Numerous signs of decay were cited: conflict among church members and between pastors and laity, the appearance of heretics, violations of Sabbath observance, impious children. And since the Puritan was quite capable of discerning the hand of God in most any natural or historical event, the jeremiads warned that New England's crop failures, Indian wars, droughts, and epidemics were the judgment of a thoroughly provoked God upon his wayward people. It seemed that Winthrop's worst fears aboard the *Arbella* had come true: "if our hearts shall turne away soe that wee will not obey, but shall be seduced and worshipp . . . other Gods, our pleasures, and proffitts, and serve them; it is propounded unto us this day, wee shall surely perishe out of the good Land." Behind this sense of apostasy regarding the internal task of New England hovered the even greater frustration over the failure of New England to become a model for the nations. In fact, it was probably this frustration that led the clergy to look for signs of a broken covenant in the first place. The root of the problem was, quite simply, that England refused to look upon the Holy Commonwealth as its model. Even the Puritans back home, living under improved conditions of religious toleration, became critical of the American Puritans' harsh treatment of dissenting religious groups. In Perry Miller's apt metaphor, the American Puritans must have felt something like the actor with the dramatic role of the century who rehearsed his lines, took a deep breath, and strode onto the stage only to find the theater empty and no spotlight working.[2]

Michael Wigglesworth, usually judged one of three major poets in seventeenth-century America, laments the state of the Puritan New Israel in his *God's Controversy with New England*. A graduate of Harvard, Wigglesworth enjoyed considerable influence as both a minister and a physician in Malden, Massachusetts, but his verse rather than his sermons or medical practice exerted the greatest influence on Puritan New England. Within a year after the publication of his poetic account of Judgment Day, *Day of Doom* (1662), all eighteen hundred copies of the work had been sold. The first edition alone, therefore, had a distribution of one copy to every thirty-five people in Massachusetts.[3] *God's Controversy* did not attain the renown of *Day of Doom*, but it was widely read and was quoted and imitated by other Puritan proclaimers of God's wrath. Like most other lamentations of the period, *God's Controversy* contrasts the vision, zeal, and sacrifices of the original settlers with the shortsightedness, sloth, and materialism of a later generation of New Englanders. Although the judgment of God thunders forth in the poem in the form of warnings and punishments, the hope is still held out that New England may renew its covenant with God if it will but repent of its sinful ways.

There is no evidence that New Englanders were as morally bankrupt as the preachers of doom intimated, but as the years passed there seemed to be a waning of the ardor with which the Puritans pursued their errand into the wilderness. It appeared to the later generations of preachers of doom that their people were more interested in their growing economic prosperity than in their spiritual state, that there was a cooling of religious zeal. Furthermore, the establishment of a tightly knit holy commonwealth in the wilderness suffered a series of disappointments. Massachusetts eventually lost its charter (1684), and dissenting groups (Quakers and Baptists) made inroads into the Puritan Zion. Yet the hope that God had something special in store for New England was never completely abandoned. Therefore, when the revivals of the Great Awakening deluged the colonies in the 1740s, there occurred not only an upsurge of religious vitality but also a revivification of the view of the New World as the place where God was breaking forth new light for the world at large. Jonathan Edwards, the foremost theologian of the eighteenth century and a formidable defender of the Great Awakening, stated the conviction that the revivals might very well mark the beginning of God's religious renewal of all humankind. It appeared to Edwards that America's opportunity

---

2. Perry Miller, *Errand into the Wilderness* (Cambridge, Mass.: Harvard University Press, Belknap Press, 1956), pp. 12–13.

3. Richard Crowder, *No Featherbed to Heaven: A Biography of Michael Wigglesworth, 1671–1705* (East Lansing: Michigan State University Press, 1962), p. 121.

to become a "city upon a hill" had returned through the movement of God's Spirit in the Awakening. In his *Thoughts Concerning the Present Revival of Religion* (1742), Edwards engaged in a typological interpretation of Scripture and world history to describe the likelihood that his age would be the time when the Kingdom of God would spread from America—and especially from the shores of New England.[4]

Many eighteenth-century figures, including Edwards, found their enthusiasm for the Awakening checked by some of the results of the revivals: heated theological controversies, the division of denominations into prorevivalist and antirevivalist factions, uncontrolled emotionalism. Despite the Great Awakening's divisive influence upon Protestant denominations and the Protestant religious consciousness, however, it played an important cohesive role in the colonies. It crossed class and geographical boundaries (the revivals were well received by city dwellers as well as by rural folk, by highly educated as well as by uneducated) and generated a common religious interest. Above all, it aroused anew the sense of American destiny under God, thus contributing to an emerging feeling of American unity and preparing the way for a new nation's bid for a crucial historical mission.

SUGGESTED READING

Bercovitch, Sacvan. *The American Jeremiad.* Madison: University of Wisconsin Press, 1978.

Gaustad, Edwin S. *The Great Awakening in New England.* 1957. Reprint, Chicago: Quadrangle, 1968.

Morgan, Edmund S. *The Puritan Dilemma: The Story of John Winthrop.* Boston: Little, Brown and Company, 1958.

Stout, Harry S. *The New England Soul: Preaching and Religious Culture in Colonial New England.* New York: Oxford University Press, 1986.

Wright, Louis B. *Religion and Empire: The Alliance between Piety and Commerce in English Expansion, 1558-1625.* New York: Octagon Books, 1965.

---

4. Gerald McDermott has pointed out that according to Edwards God singled out New England not because of its virtues but for His own mysterious reasons, and in his other writings Edwards gave a definite international emphasis to the "glorious work" of the revivals. Gerald McDermott, *One Holy and Happy Society: The Public Theology of Jonathan Edwards* (University Park: Pennsylvania State University Press, 1992), pp. 82-90.

ALEXANDER WHITAKER

�急

Good Newes from Virginia

[sent to] The Right Worshipful Sir Thomas Smith, Knight,
Treasurer of the English Colonie in Virginia

ECCLESIASTES II.I.
*"Cast thy bread upon the waters: for after many daies
thou shalt finde it."*

. . .

. . . let me turne your eyes, my brethren of England, to behold the waters of
Virginia: where you may behold a fit subject for the exercise of your Liberalitie, persons enough on whom you may cast away your Bread, and yet not
without hope, after many daies to finde it. Yea, I will not feare to affirme unto
you, that those men whom God hath made able any way to be helpefull to
this Plantation, and made knowne unto them the necessities of our wants, are
bound in conscience by vertue of this precept, to lay their helping hands to
it, either with their purse, persons, or prayers, so farre forth as God hath made
them fit for it. For it is evident that our wise God hath bestowed no gift upon
any man, for their private use, but for the good of other men, whom God
shall offer to their Liberalitie.

Wherefore, since God hath opened the doore of *Virginia*, to our countrey
of England, wee are to thinke that God hath, as it were, by word of mouth
called us in, to bestow our severall Charity on them. And that this may the
better appeare, we have many reasons to encourage us to bee Liberall minded
and open-handed toward them.

First, if we consider the almost miraculous beginning, and continuance of
this plantation, we must needs confesse that God hath opened this passage

From Alexander Whitaker, *Good Newes from Virginia* (London, 1613), pp. 21–35, 44. [In this and
other selections from colonial American literature, I have altered the text slightly (e.g., by substi-
tuting *u* for *v*, adding and eliminating some punctuation marks, expanding abbreviations, breaking up long paragraphs), but I have sought to preserve the early American flavor by retaining the
original form when it does not seem to obscure the meaning for the modern reader.—Editor]

unto us, and led us by the hand unto this work. For the Marriners that were sent hither first to discover this Bay of Chaesapeac, found it onely by the meere directions of Gods providence: for I heard one of them confesse, that even then, when they were entred within the mouth of the Bay, they deemed the place they sought for to have beene many degrees further. The finding was not so strange, but the continuance and upholding of it hath bin most wonderful. I may fitly compare it to the growth of an Infant, which hath been afflicted from his birth with some grievous sicknes, that many times no hope of life hath remained, and yet it liveth still. Againe, if there were nothing else to encourage us, yet this one thing may stirre us up to go on chearefully with it: that the Divell is a capitall enemy against it, and continually seeketh which way to hinder the prosperitie and good proceedings of it. Yea, hath heretofore so farre prevailed, by his Instruments, the covetous hearts of many back-sliding Adventurers at home, and also by his servants here: some striving for superioritie, others by murmurings, mutinies, & plaine treasons; & others by fornication, prophanenes, idlenes, and such monstrous sinnes; that he had almost thrust us out of this kingdome, and had indeed quitted this Land of us, if God had not then (as one awaked out of sleepe) stood up and sent us meanes of great helpe, when we needed most, and expected least reliefe. The saving of those two honorable Knights, Sir Thomas Gates and Sir George Somers, with Captaine Newport and the rest of the Adventurers in the Sea Venture, as also their happy deliverance out of those unhabited and unfrequented (because feared) Islands of the Barmudaes, could proceed from none other, but the singular providence of God. If this worthie Governour, Sir Thomas Gates, had bin hindred but one weeke longer, it might be feared that the famine, which had by that time devoured the most of our countrimen heere, would have consumed the rest. And when hee considering that his weake meanes was not able to restore, or sustaine the burthen of such wofull distresses, had shipped the few remaining for England, and had forsaken with hannibals sighes, the first builded James-Towne: upon the sudden newes met him, of the comming in of that Honorable Lord La war, with a fresh supplie. Whereupon he presently returned to the Towne he had so lately forsaken. Since, when this English Colony hath taken better root; and as a spreading herbe, whose top hath bin often cropped off, renewes her growth, and spreads her selfe more gloriously, than before. So this Plantation, which the divell hath so often troden downe, is by the miraculous blessing of God revived, and daily groweth to more happy and more hopefull successe. I have shut up many things in few words, and have alleadged this onely to prove unto us, that the finger of God hath been the onely true worker heere; that God first shewed us the place, God first called us hither, and here God by his speciall providence hath maintained us. Wherefore, by him let us be encouraged to lay our helping hands to this good work (yea God's work) with all the strength of our abilitie.

Secondly, let the miserable condition of these naked slaves of the divell move you to compassion toward them. They acknowledge that there is a great good God, but know him not, having the eyes of their understanding as yet blinded: wherefore they serve the divell for feare, after a most base manner, sacrificing sometimes (as I have heere heard) their owne Children to him. I have sent one Image of their god to the Counsell in England, which is painted upon one side of a toad-stoole, much like unto a deformed monster. Their priests (whom they call *Quiokosoughs*) are no other but such as our English Witches are. They live naked in bodie, as if their shame of their sinne deserved no covering: Their names are as naked as their bodie: they esteeme it a vertue to lie, deceive and steale as their master the divell teacheth them. Much more might be said of their miserable condition, but I refer the particular narration of these things to some other season. If this bee their life, what thinke you shall become of them after death? but to be partakers with the divell and his angels in hell for evermore. Wherefore, my brethren, put on the bowels of compassion, and let the lamentable estate of these miserable people enter in your consideration: One God created us, they have reasonable soules and intellectuall faculties as well as wee; we all have Adam for our common parent: yea, by nature the condition of us both is all one, the servants of sinne and slaves of the divell. Oh remember (I beseech you) what was the state of England before the gospell was preached in our Countrey? How much better were we then, and concerning our soules health, than these now are? Let the word of the Lord sound out that It may be heard in these parts; and let your faith which is toward God spread it selfe abroad, and shew forth the charitable fruits of it in these barren parts of the world. "And let him know that he which hath converted a sinner from going a stray out of his way, shall save a soule from death, and hide a multitude of sinnes."

But if any of us should misdoubt that this barbarous people is uncapable of such heavenly mysteries, let such men know that they are farre mistaken in the nature of these men, for besides the promise of God, which is without respect of persons, made as well to unwise men after the flesh, as to the wise, etc., let us not thinke that these men are so simple as some have supposed them: for they are of bodie lustie, strong, and very nimble: they are a very understanding generation, quicke of apprehension, suddaine in their dispatches, subtile in their dealings, exquisite in their inventions, and industrious in their labour. I suppose the world hath no better marke-men with their bow and arrowes than they be; they will kill birds flying, fishes swimming, and beasts running: they shoote also with mervailous strength, they shot one of our men being unarmed quite through the bodie, and nailed both his armes to his bodie with one arrow: one of their Children also, about the age of 12 or 13 years, killed a bird with his arrow in my sight. The service of their god is answerable to their life, being performed with great feare and attention, and many strange dumb shewes used in the same, stretching forth their limbes and straining their bodie, much like to the counterfeit women in England who faine themselves bewitched, or possessed of some evill spirit.

They stand in great awe of their *Quiokosoughs* or Priests, which are a generation of vipers even of Sathans owne brood. The manner of their life is much like to the popish Hermits of our age; for they live alone in the woods, in houses sequestred from the common course of men, neither may any man bee suffered to come into their house or to speake with them, but when this Priest doth call him. He taketh no care for his victuals, for all such kinde of things both bread and water, etc. are brought unto a place neere unto his cottage and there are left, which hee fetcheth for his proper neede. If they would have raine, or have lost any thing, they have their recourse to him, who conjureth for them, and many times prevaileth. If they be sicke, he is their Physition, if they bee wounded he sucketh them. At his command they make warre and peace, neither doe they any thing of moment without him. I will not bee teadious in these strange Narrations, when I have more perfectly entered into their secrets, you shall know all.

Finally, there is a civill governement amongst them which they strictly observe, and shew thereby that the law of Nature dwelleth in them: for they have a rude kinde of Common-wealth, and rough governement, wherein they both honour and obey their Kings, Parents, and Governours, both greater and lesse, they observe the limits of their owne possessions, and incroach not upon their neighbours dwellings. Murther is a capitall crime scarce heard of among them: adultery is most severely punished, and so are their other offences. These unnurtured grounds of reason in them, may serve to incourage us: to instruct them in the knowledge of the true God, the rewarder of all righteousnesse, not doubting but that he that was powerfull to save us by his word, when we were nothing, will be mercifull also to these sonnes of Adam in his appointed time, in whom there bee remaining so many footsteps of Gods image.

Wherefore you wealthy men of this world, whose bellies God hath filled with his hidden Treasure: trust not in uncertain riches, neither cast your eyes upon them; for riches taketh her to her wings as an Eagle, and flieth into Heaven. But "bee rich in good works ready to distribute or communicate." How shamefully doe the most of you either miserably detaine, or wickedlie mispend Gods goods, whereof hee made you his stewards? The Covetous person seekes to hide his talent from the good of others and himselfe, honouring it as his God, which should be his servant. The Prodigall men of our land make hast to fling away Gods treasures, as a greevious burthen which they desire to be eased of. Some make no scruple at it, to spend yearely an hundred pounds, two, three, five hundred, and much more about dogs, haukes and hounds and such sports; which will not give five hundred pence to the releefe of Gods poore members. Others will not care to lose two or three thousand pound in a night, at Cards and Dice, and yet suffer poore Lazarus to perish in their streets for want of their Charitable Almes. Yea divers will hyer gardents at great rents, and build stately houses for their whoores, which have no compassion on the Fatherlesse and widdowes. How much better were it for these men to remember the afflictions of Joseph, to extend the bowels of their compassion to the poore, the fatherles, afflicted and the like, than to mispend that which they must give a straite account of at the day of judgement? Are not these miserable people heere better than hawks, hounds, whores, and the like? O you that spend so much on them, thinke it no dishonour to your persons, no impoverishing to your state, to bestow somewhat to the raising up of Christs kingdome, and maintenance of so holy and heavenly an action as this is, God of his goodnesse that hath given you abilitie to performe it, make you willing to help it forward with the best of your power.

"For after many daies thou shalt find it." Hitherto have we spoken of the commandement and the severall branches of the same: Now follows the reason of this Commandement which the Holy Ghost useth heere to stir us up unto liberality, which is taken from the reward which wee shall have of our well-doing, "for after many daies thou shalt find it." The some of which reason is, that though God doe not presently reward our well doing, but doe defer the requitall of it for many daies, yet thy good works shall not perish, but God at the appointed time, shall abundantly recompence thy liberality. Out of this reasons wee may gather two notable conclusions touching the reward of liberality. First wee may conclude from hence, that God doth not alwaies give a present reward to the good works; he doth for the most part defer his rewards manie daies, sometimes many yeares, yea sometimes even till death it selfe, when hee will never cease to reward us according to our works with unspeakeable joyes of blessed immortality. And the wisdome of God doth thus defer his rewards for most singular reasons. For if God should presently reward good works, who then would not be a prodigall giver, who then would bee a faithful giver? For when a man is certaine of present gaine he will not spare to give abundantly, because he seeth an exceeding profit ready to be put into his hands for so doing: and this would stirre up the most covetous wretch in the world to be liberall, gaping out of meere covetousnesse, after an overplus of reward. Wherefore God hath made the time and condition of his rewards doubtfull, that we might not bee covetous of the benefit: but that he might exercise our faith, and teach us with patience of hope to expect the appointed time of his reward. The principall point of perfect charity is, that wee give in faith, whose true nature is to depend upon God for the good successe of our almes, "for Faith is the ground of things that are hoped for, & the evidence of things that are not seene": now if we should have the reward of good works in the view of our eies, and ready as it were to be put into our hands, what place would then be left for practise of faith whose object is unseene, whose hopes bee of afterwards? . . .

Let then your liberall minds (you honourable and charitable Adventurers of Virginia) be stirred up to cast your almes on the waters of Virginia, without hope of present profit. The base affections of the Usurer will not looke for the overplus of encrease, untill the covenanted time of his loane be expired. The husbandman casting his seed into the earth, waiteth upon God until Harvest for a fruitful crop: verily he that beleeveth doth not make haste. Be not over hastie with God: God will not yet reward you, that he may make you more famous in the world, that the world may see your zeale, and beare witnesse to the patience of your faith, not to greedie haste of covetous desires. The worke is honourable, and now more than ever, sustained by most honorable men. O let us not then be weary of well-doing: fortie yeares were expired, before *Israel* could plant in Canaan, and yet God had called them by the word of his mouth, had led them himselfe by an high hand. Yet may you boldly looke for a shorter time of reward. The returnes which you have from the East Indies, though they be exceeding rich, yet is the adventure doubtfull, the expence chargeable, and the expectation of return, of three yeares continuance.

Let me advise you to be as liberall in adventure hither, and I dare affirme, that by Gods assistance, your profitable returnes shall be of more certainty, and much shorter expectation. Remember, I beseech you, how many lives were lost, how many yeares were spent, what discouragements, what great losses the Adventurers of Spaine and Portugale suffered and under-went, before they could be setled in the West Indies, or receive any profitable returne from thence: and now behold what rich loads, what profitable returnes are yearely shipped from thence. Shall our Nation, hitherto famous for noble attempts, and the honorable finishing of what they have undertaken, be now taxed for inconstancie, and blamed by the enemies of our protestation, for uncharitable-nesse? Yea, shall we be a scorne among Princes, and a laughing stocke among our neighbour Nations, for basely leaving what we honorably began; yea, for beginning a Discoverie, whose riches other men shall gather, so soone as wee have forsaken it? Awake you true hearted English men, you servants of Jesus Christ, remember that the Plantation is Gods, and the reward your Countries. Wherefore, aime not at your present privat gaine, but let the glory of God, whose Kingdome you now plant, & good of your countrey, whose wealth you seeke, so farre prevaile with you, that you respect not a present returne of gaine for this yeare or two: but that you would more liberally supplie for a little space, this your Christian worke, which you so charitably began. As for those spirits of slander, whom the divell hath stirred up to speak evill of this good Land, and to weaken the hands of our brethren, lest they should go forward, and pull Satan out of his Dominions. Let them take heed, lest the punishment of Shammua and his nine companions, the faithlesse searchers of the Land of Canaan, do befall them: and that they never live to taste of the commodities of this good Land.

But lest I may seeme to exhort you to an unprofitable Liberalitie, or to argue God of forgetfulnes to those that serve him faithfully: heare now what a comfortable promise of reward God hath made unto us in these words: which is, "That after many dayes we shall find." If God should have commanded us to cast away without finding, some discouragement there might have been to our weake nature; but since God hath assuredly promised us, that we shall find in the end, who will not obey the command? who will not be Liberall. God hath been alwayes found true in his word, most faithfull in his promises. If God do promise Abraham that his seed shall inherit the Land of Canaan: Abrahams posterie shall after many daies in the appointed time be planted peaceably in the land of Canaan. If God promise Salomon wisdome and riches: Salomon shall be wiser and richer than any Prince of the earth. If God promiseth that he will give his only Sonne, that whosoever beleeveth in him shall not perish, but have life everlasting: his Sonne Jesus Christ shal be borne into the world at the appointed time, and undergoe the weight of Gods wrath for redemption of beleevers. Shall God then faithfully performe all his promises in so great matters, and be unfaithfull in lesser matters: oh let no such base conceit of the Almightie enter into our minds, as to thinke that he that spared not his owne Sonne, to performe his promises to us, will be so unmindfull of us in so small a thing. . . .

Wherefore you (right wise and noble Adventurers of Virginia) whose hearts God hath stirred up to build him a Temple, to make him an house, to conquer a Kingdome for him here: be not discouraged with those many lamentable assaults that the divell hath made against us: he now rageth most, because he knoweth his kingdome is to have a short end. Goe forward boldly, and remember that you fight under the banner of Jesus Christ, that you plant his Kingdome, who hath already broken the Serpents head: God may deferre his temprall reward for a season, but he assured that in the end you shall find riches and honour in this world, and blessed immortality in the world to come. And you my brethren my fellow labourers, send up your earnest prayers to God for his Church in Virginia, that since his harvest heere is great, but the labourers few, hee would thrust forth labourers into his harvest; and pray also for mee that the ministration of his Gospell may be powerful and effectuall by me to the salvation of many, and advancement of the kingdome of Jesus Christ, to whom with the Father and the holy Spirit, bee all honour and glorie for evermore, Amen.

JOHN WINTHROP

🙥

A Modell of Christian Charity

Written On Boarde the Arrabella, On the Attlantick Ocean. Anno 1630

. . .

Christian Charitie

A Modell Hereof

God Almightie in his most holy and wise providence hath soe disposed of the Condicion of mankinde, as in all times some must be rich, some poore, some highe and eminent in power and dignitie; others meane and in subjeccion.

The Reason Hereof

1. Reason: *First*, to hold conformity with the rest of his workes, being delighted to shewe forthe the glory of his wisdome in the variety and differance of the Creatures and the glory of his power, in ordering all these differences for the preservacion and good of the whole; and the glory of his greatnes that as it is the glory of princes to have many officers, soe this great King will have many Stewards, counting himselfe more honoured in dispenceing his guifts to man by man, than if hee did it by his owne immediate hand.

2. Reason: *Secondly*, That he might have the more occasion to manifest the worke of his Spirit: first, upon the wicked in moderateing and restraineing them: soe that the riche and mighty should not eate upp the poore, nor the poore and dispised rise upp against their superiours and shake off thiere yoake; secondly in the regenerate in exerciseing his graces in them, as in the greate ones, their love, mercy, gentlenes, temperance, etc., in the poore and inferiour sorte, theire faithe, patience, obedience, etc.

3. Reason: *Thirdly*, That every man might have need of other, and from hence they might be all knitt more nearly together in the Bond of brotherly affeccion: from hence it appeares plainely that noe man is made more hon-

ourable than another or more wealthy etc., out of any perticuler and singuler respect to himselfe but for the glory of his Creator and the Common good of the Creature, Man; Therefore God still reserves the propperty of these guifts to himselfe as Ezek: 16.17. he there calls wealthe his gold and his silver, etc. Prov: 3.9 he claimes theire service as his due, honour the Lord with thy riches, etc. All men being thus (by divine providence) rancked into two sortes, riche and poore; under the first, are comprehended all such as are able to live comfortably by theire owne meanes duely improved; and all others are poore according to the former distribution. There are two rules whereby wee are to walke one towards another: JUSTICE and MERCY. These are allwayes distinguished in theire Act and in theire object, yet may they both concurre in the same Subject in eache respect; as sometimes there may be an occasion of shewing mercy to a rich man, in some sudden danger of distresse, and allsoe doeing of meere Justice to a poor man in regard of some perticuler contract, etc. There is likewise a double Lawe by which wee are regulated in our conversacion one towardes another: in both the former respects, the lawe of nature and the lawe of grace, or the morrall lawe or the lawe of the gospell, to omitt the rule of Justice as not propperly belonging to this purpose otherwise than it may fall into consideraction in some perticuler Cases: By the first of these lawes man as he was enabled soe withall [is] commaunded to love his neighbour as himselfe. Upon this ground stands all the precepts of the morrall lawe, which concernes our dealings with men. To apply this to the works of mercy this lawe requires two things: first, that every man afford his help to another in every want or distress. Secondly, That hee performe this out of the same affeccion which makes him carefull of his owne good according to that of our Saviour, Math: [7.12] Whatsoever ye would that men should doe to you. This was practised by Abraham and Lott in entertaineing the Angells and the old man of Gibea.

The Lawe of Grace or the Gospell hath some differance from the former as in these respects: first, the lawe of nature was given to man in the estate of innocency; this of the gospell in the estate of regeneracy. Secondly, the former propounds one man to another, as the same fleshe and Image of god; this as a brother in Christ allsoe, and in the Communion of the same spirit and soe teacheth us to put a difference betweene Christians and otherrs. Doe good to all, especially to the household of faith; upon this ground the Israelites were to putt a difference betweene the brethren of such as were strangers though not of the Canaanites. Thirdly, the Lawe of nature could give noe rules for dealeing with enemies, for all are to be considered as friends in the estate of innocency, but the Gospell commands love to an enemy. Proofe: If thine Enemie hunger feede him: Love your Enemies, doe good to them that hate you, Math: 5.44.

This Lawe of the Gospell propoundes likewise a difference of seasons and occasions. There is a time when a Christian must sell all and give to the poore, as they did in the Apostles times. There is a tyme allsoe when a Christian (though they give not all yet) must give beyond theire abillity, as they of Macedonia. Cor: 2.6. Likewise community of perills calls for extraordinary liberallity and soe doth Community in some speciall service for the Churche. Lastly, when there is noe other meanes whereby our Christian brother may be relieved in this distresse, wee must help him beyond our ability, rather than tempt God, in putting him upon help by miraculous or extraordinary meanes.

. . .

It rests now to make some applicacion of this discourse by the present designe which gave the occasion of writeing of it. Herein are four things to be propounded: first, the persons; secondly, the worke; thirdly, the end; fourthly, the meanes.

1. For the persons, wee are a Company professing our selves fellow members of Christ, in which respect onely though wee were absent from eache other many miles, and had our imploymentes as farre distant, yet wee ought to account our selves knitt together by this bond of love, and live in the exercise of it, if wee would have comforte of our being in Christ. This was notorious in the practise of the Christians in former times, as is testified of the Waldenses from the mouth of one of the adversaries Aeneas Sylvius, mutuo [solent amare] penè antequam norint. They use to love any of theire own religion even before they were acquainted with them.

2. For the worke wee have in hand, it is by a mutuall consent through a speciall overruleing providence, and a more than an ordinary approbation of the Churches of Christ to seeke out a place of Cohabitation and Consorteshipp under a due forme of Government both civill and ecclesiasticall. In such cases as this the care of the publique must oversway all private respects, by which not onely conscience, but meare Civill policy doth binde us; for it is a true rule that perticuler estates cannott subsist in the ruine of the publique.

3. The end is to improve our lives, to doe more service to the Lord, the comforte and encrease of the body of Christe whereof wee are members, that our selves and posterity may be the better preserved from the Common corrupcions of this evill world, to serve the Lord and worke out our Salvacion under the power and purity of his holy Ordinances.

4. For the meanes whereby this must bee effected, they are twofold, a Conformity with the worke and end wee aime at; these wee see are extraordinary, therefore wee must not content our selves with usuall ordinary meanes. Whatsoever wee did or ought to have done when wee lived in England, the same must wee doe and more allsoe where wee goe: That which the most in theire Churches mainteine as a truthe in profession onely, wee must bring into familiar and constant practice, as in this duty of love wee must love brotherly without dissimulation, we must love one another with a pure hearte fervently, wee must beare one anothers burthens, wee must not looke onely on our

owne things but allsoe on the things of our brethren, neither must wee think that the lord will beare with such faileings at our hands as hee dothe from those among whome wee have lived.

. . .

   Thus stands the cause betweene God and us. Wee are entered into Covenant with him for this worke, wee have taken out a Commission, the Lord hath given us leave to draw our owne Articles, wee have professed to enterprise thee Accions upon these and these ends, wee have hereupon besought him of favour and blessing: Now if the Lord shall please to heare us, and bring us in peace to the place wee desire, then hath hee ratified this Covenant and sealed our Commission [and] will expect a strickt performance of the Articles contained in it, but if wee shall neglect the observacion of these Articles which are the ends wee have propounded, and dissembling with our God, shall fall to embrace this present world and prosecute our carnall intencions seekeing great things for our selves and our posterity, the Lord will surely breake out in wrathe against us, be revenged of such a perjured people and make us knowe the price of the breache of such a Covenant.

   Now the onely way to avoyde this shipwracke and to provide for our posterity is to followe the counsell of Micah, to doe Justly, to love mercy, to walke humbly with our God. For this end, wee must be knitt together in this worke as one man, wee must entertaine each other in brotherly Affeccion, wee must be willing to abridge our selves of our superfluities, for the supply of others necessities, wee must uphold a familiar Commerce together in all meeknes, gentlenes, patience and liberallity, wee must delight in each other, make others Condicions our owne, rejoyce together, mourne together, labour and suffer together, allwayes haveing before our eyes our Commission and Community in the worke, our Community as members of the same body, soe shall wee keepe the unitie of the spirit in the bond of peace, the Lord will be our God and delight to dwell among us as his owne people and will commaund a blessing upon us in all our wayes, soe that wee shall see much more of his wisdome, power, goodnes and truthe than formerly wee have beene acquainted with. Wee shall finde that the God of Israell is among us, when tenn of us shall be able to resist a thousand of our enemies, when hee shall make us a prayse and glory, that men shall say of succeeding plantacions: the lord make it like that of New England: for wee must Consider that wee shall be as a Citty upon a Hill, the eies of all people are uppon us; soe that if wee shall deale falsely with our god in this worke wee have undertaken and soe cause him to withdrawe his present help from us, wee shall shame the faces of many of gods worthy servants, and cause theire prayers to be turned into Cursses upon us till wee be consumed out of the good land whither wee are goeing: And to shutt upp this discourse with that exhortacion of Moses, that faithfull servant of the Lord in his last farewell to Israell, Deut. 30. Beloved there is now sett before us life, and good, deathe and evill in that wee are Commaunded this day to love the Lord our God, and to love one another, to walke in his wayes and to keepe his Commaundements and his Ordinance, and his lawes, and the Articles of our Covenant with him that wee may live and be multiplied, and that the Lord our God may blesse us in the land whither we goe to possesse it: But if our heartes shall turne away soe that wee will not obey, but shall be seduced and worship . . . other Gods, our pleasures, and proffitts, and serve them; it is propounded unto us this day, wee shall surely perishe out of the good Land whither wee passe over this vast Sea to possesse it;

> Therefore lett us choose life,
> that wee, and our Seede,
> may live; by obeyeing his
> voyce, and cleaveing to him,
> for hee is our life, and
> our prosperity.

MICHAEL WIGGLESWORTH

৯৬

God's Controversy with New England

Written in the time of the great drought Anno 1662

. . .

Beyond the great Atlantick flood
   There is a region vast,
A country where no English foot
   In former ages past:
A waste and howling wilderness,   5
   Where none inhabited
But hellish fiends, and brutish men
   That Devils worshiped.

This region was in darkness plac't
   Far off from heavens light,   10
Amidst the shaddows of grim death
   And of eternal night.
For there the Sun of righteousness
   Had never made to shine
The light of his sweet countenance,   15
   And grace which is divine:

Until the time drew nigh wherein
   The glorious Lord of hostes
Was pleasd to lead his armies forth
   Into those forrein coastes.   20
At whose approach the darkness sad
   Soon vanished away,
And all the shaddows of the night
   Were turned to lightsome day.

From *Proceedings of the Massachusetts Historical Society*, vol. XII (1871–1873), pp. 83–93.

The dark and dismal western woods   25
    (The Devils den whilere)
Beheld such glorious gospel-shine,
    As none beheld more cleare.
Where sathan had his scepter sway'd
    For many generations,   30
The King of Kings set up his throne
    To rule amongst the nations.

The stubborn he in pieces brake,
    Like vessels made of clay:
And those that sought his peoples hurt   35
    He turned to decay.
Those curst Amalekites, that first
    Lift up their hand on high
To fight against Gods Israel,
    Were ruin'd fearfully.   40

Thy terrours on the Heathen folk,
    O Great Jehovah, fell:
The fame of thy great acts, o Lord,
    Did all the nations quell.
Some hid themselves for fear of thee   45
    In forrests wide & great:
Some to thy people croutching came,
    For favour to entreat.

Some were desirous to be taught
    The knowledge of thy wayes,   50
And being taught, did soon accord
    Therein to spend their dayes.
Thus were the fierce & barbarous
    Brought to civility,
And those that liv'd like beasts (or worse)   55
    To live religiously.

O happiest of dayes wherein
    The blind received sight,
And those that had no eyes before
    Were made to see the light!   60
The wilderness hereat rejoyc't,
    The woods for joy did sing,
The vallys & the little hills
    Thy praises echoing.

Here was the hiding place, which thou,   65
    Jehovah, didst provide
For thy redeemed ones, and where
    Thou didst thy jewels hide
In per'lous times, and saddest dayes
    Of sack-cloth and of blood,   70
When th' overflowing scourge did pass
    Through Europe, like a flood.

While almost all the world beside
    Lay weltring in their gore;
We, only we, enjoyd such peace   75
    As none enjoyd before.
No forrein foeman did us fray,
    Nor threat'ned us with warrs:
We had no enemyes at home,
    Nor no domestick jarrs.   80

The Lord had made (such was his grace)
    For us a Covenant
Both with the men, and with the beasts,
    That in this desart haunt:
So that through places wilde and waste   85
    A single man, disarm'd,
Might journey many hundred miles,
    And not at all be harm'd.

Amidst the solitary woods
    Poor travellers might sleep   90
As free from danger as at home,
    Though no man watch did keep.
Thus were we priviledg'd with peace,
    Beyond what others were.
Truth, Mercy, Peace, with Righteousness,   95
    Took up their dwelling here.

Our Governor was of our selves,
    And all his Bretheren,
For wisdom & true piety,
    Select, & chosen men.   100
Who, Ruling in ye fear of God,
    The righteous cause maintained,
And all injurious violence,
    And wickedness, restrained.

Our temp'rall blessings did abound: 105
  But spirituall good things
Much more abounded, to the praise
  Of that great King of Kings.
Gods throne was here set up; here was
  His tabernacle pight: 110
This was the place, and these the folk
  In whom he took delight.

Our morning starrs shone all day long:
  Their beams gave forth such light,
As did the noon-day sun abash, 115
  And 's glory dazle quite.
Our day continued many yeers,
  And had no night at all:
Yea many thought the light would last,
  And be perpetuall. 120

Such, o New-England, was thy first,
  Such as thy best estate:
But, Loe! a strange and suddain change
  My courage did amate.
The brightest of our morning starrs 125
  Did wholly disappeare:
And those that tarried behind
  With sack-cloth covered were.

Moreover, I beheld & saw
  Our welkin overkest, 130
And dismal clouds for sun-shine late
  O'respread from east to west.
The air became tempestuous;
  The wilderness gan quake:
And from above with awfull voice 135
  Th' Almighty thundring spake.

Are these the men that erst at my command
  Forsook their ancient seats and native soile,
To follow me into a desart land,
  Contemning all the travell and the toile, 140
Whose love was such to purest ordinances
  As made them set at nought their fair inheritances?

Are these the men that prized libertee
  To walk with God according to their light,

To be as good as he would have them bee,   145
     To serve and worship him with all their might,
Before the pleasures which a fruitfull field,
     And country flowing-full of all good things, could yield,

Are these the folk whom from the brittish Iles,
     Through the stern billows of the watry main,   150
I safely led so many thousand miles,
     As if their journey had been through a plain?
Whom having from all enemies protected,
     And through so many deaths and dangers well directed,

I brought and planted on the western shore,   155
     Where nought but bruits and salvage wights did swarm
(Untaught, untrain'd, untam'd by vertue's lore)
     That sought their blood, yet could not do them harm?
My fury's flaile them thresht, my fatall broom
     Did sweep them hence, to make my people elbow-room.   160

Are these the men whose gates with peace I crown'd,
     To whom for bulwarks I salvation gave,
Whilst all things else with rattling tumults sound,
     And mortall frayes send thousands to the grave?
Whilest their own brethren bloody hands embrewed   165
     In brothers blood, and fields with carcases bestrewed?

Is this the people blest with bounteous store,
     By land and sea full richly clad and fed,
Whom plenty's self stands waiting still before,
     And powreth out their cups well tempered?   170
For those dear sake an howling wildernes
     I lately turned into a fruitfull paradeis?

Are these the people in whose hemisphere
     Such bright-beam'd, glist'ring, sun-like starrs I placed,
As by their influence did all things cheere,   175
     As by their light blind ignorance defaced,
As errours into lurking holes did fray,
     As turn'd the late dark night into a lightsome day?

Are these the folk to whom I milked out
     And sweetnes stream'd from consolations brest;   180
Whose soules I fed and strengthened throughout
     With finest spirituall food most finely drest?

On whom I rained living bread from Heaven,
　　Withouten Errour's bane, or Superstition's leaven?

With whom I made a Covenant of peace, 185
　　And unto whom I did most firmly plight
My faithfulness, If whilst I live I cease
　　To be their Guide, their God, their full delight;
Since them with cords of love to me I drew,
　　Enwrapping in my grace such as should them ensew. 190

Are these the men, that now mine eyes behold,
　　Concerning whom I thought, and whilome spake,
First Heaven shall pass away together scrold,
　　Ere they my lawes and righteous wayes forsake,
Or that they slack to runn their heavenly race? 195
　　Are these the same? or are some others come in place?

If these be they, how is it that I find
　　In stead of holiness Carnality,
In stead of heavenly frames an Earthly mind,
　　For burning zeal luke-warm Indifferency, 200
For flaming love, key-cold Dead-heartedness,
　　For temperance (in meat, and drinke, and cloaths) excess?

Whence cometh it, that Pride, and Luxurie,
　　Debate, Deceit, Contention, and Strife,
False-dealing, Covetousness, Hypocrisie 205
　　(With such like Crimes) amongst them are so rife,
That one of them doth over-reach another?
　　And that an honest man can hardly trust his Brother?

How is it, that Security, and Sloth,
　　Amongst the best are Common to be found? 210
That grosser sins, in stead of Graces growth,
　　Amongst the many more and more abound?
I hate dissembling shews of Holiness.
　　Or practise as you talk, or never more profess.

Judge not, vain world, that all are hypocrites 215
　　That do profess more holiness then thou:
All foster not dissembling, guilefull sprites,
　　Nor love their lusts, though very many do.
Some sin through want of care and constant watch,
　　Some with the sick converse, till they the sickness catch. 220

Some, that maintain a reall root of grace,
   Are overgrown with many noysome weeds,
Whose heart, that those no longer may take place,
   The benefit of due correction needs.
And such as these however gone astray   225
   I shall by stripes reduce into a better way.

Moreover some there be that still retain
   Their ancient vigour and sincerity;
Whom both their own, and others sins, constrain
   To sigh, and mourn, and weep, and wail, & cry;   230
And for their sakes I have forborn to powre
   My wrath upon Revolters to this present houre.

To praying Saints I always have respect,
   And tender love, and pittifull regard:
Nor will I now in any wise neglect   235
   Their love and faithfull service to reward;
Although I deal with others for their folly,
   And turn their mirth to tears that have been too jolly.

For thinke not, O Backsliders, in your heart,
   That I shall still your evill manners beare: 240
Your sinns me press as sheaves do load a cart,
   And therefore I will plague you for this geare
Except you seriously, and soon, repent,
   Ile not delay your pain and heavy punishment.

And who be those themselves that yonder shew?   245
   The seed of such as name my dreadfull Name!
On whom whilere compassions skirt I threw
   Whilest in their blood they were, to hide their shame!
Whom my preventing love did neer me take!
   Whom for mine own I mark't, lest they should me forsake!   250

I look't that such as these to vertue's Lore
   (Though none but they) would have Enclin'd their ear:
That they at least mine image should have bore,
   And sanctify'd my name with awfull fear.
Let pagan's Brats pursue their lusts, whose meed   255
   Is Death: For christians children are an holy seed.

But hear O Heavens! Let Earth amazed stand;
   Ye Mountaines melt, and Hills come flowing down:
Let horror seize upon both Sea and Land;

Let Natures self be cast into a stown. 260
I children nourisht, nurtur'd and upheld:
   But they against a tender father have rebell'd.

What could have been by me performed more?
   Or wherein fell I short of your desire?
Had you but askt, I would have op't my store, 265
   And given what lawfull wishes could require.
For all this bounteous cost I lookt to see
   Heaven-reaching-hearts, & thoughts, Meekness, Humility.

But lo, a sensuall Heart all void of grace,
   An Iron neck, a proud presumptuous Hand; 270
A self-conceited, stiff, stout, stubborn Race,
   That fears no threats, submitts to no command:
Self-will'd, perverse, such as can beare no yoke;
   A Generation even ripe for vengeance stroke.

Such were that Carnall Brood of Israelites 275
   That Josua and the Elders did ensue,
Who growing like the cursed Cananites
   Upon themselves my heavy judgements drew.
Such also was that fleshly Generation,
   Whom I o'rewhelm'd by waters deadly inundation. 280

They darker light, and lesser meanes misused;
   They had not such Examples them to warn:
You clearer rules, and Precepts, have abused,
   And dreadfull monuments of others harm.
My gospels glorious light you do not prize: 285
   My Gospels endless, boundless grace you clean despize.

My painfull messengers you disrespect,
   Who toile and sweat and sweale themselves away,
Yet nought at all with you can take effect,
   Who hurrie headlong to your own decay. 290
In vain the Founder melts, and taketh pains:
   Bellows and Lead's consum'd, but still your dross remains.

What should I do with such a stiff-neckt race?
   How shall I ease me of such Foes as they?
What shall befall despizers of my Grace? 295
   I'le surely beare their candle-stick away,
And Lamps put out. Their glorious noon-day light
   I'le quickly turn into a dark Egyptian night.

Oft have I charg'd you by my ministers
   To gird your selves with sack cloth, and repent.   300
Oft have I warned you by my messengers;
   That so you might my wrathfull ire prevent:
But who among you hath this warning taken?
   Who hath his crooked wayes, & wicked works forsaken?

Yea many grow to more and more excess;   305
   More light and loose, more Carnall and prophane.
The sins of Sodom, Pride, and Wantonness,
   Among the multitude spring up amain.
Are these the fruits of Pious Education,
   To run with greater speed and Courage to Damnation?   310

If here and there some two, or three, shall steere
   A wiser course, then their Companions do,
You make a mock of such; and scoff, and jeere
   Becaus they will not be so bad as you.
Such is the Generation that succeeds   315
   The men, whose eyes have seen my great & awful deeds.

Now therefore hearken and encline your ear,
   In judgement I will henceforth with you plead;
And if by that you will not learn to fear,
   But still go on a sensuall life to lead: 320
I'le strike at once an All-Consuming stroke;
   Nor cries nor tears shall then my fierce intent revoke.

Thus ceast his Dreadful-threatning voice
   The High & lofty-One.
The Heavens stood still Appal'd thereat;   325
   The Earth beneath did groane:
Soon after I beheld and saw
   A mortall dart come flying:
I lookt again, & quickly saw
   Some fainting, others dying.   330

The Heavens more began to lowre,
   The welkin Blacker grew:
And all things seemed to forbode
   Sad changes to ensew.
From that day forward hath the Lord   335
   Apparently contended

With us in Anger, and in Wrath:
   But we have not amended.

Our healthfull dayes are at an end,
   And sicknesses come on   340
From yeer to yeer, becaus our hearts
   Away from God are gone.
New-England, where for many yeers
   You scarcely heard a cough,
And where Physicians had no work,   345
   Now finds them work enough.

Now colds and coughs, Rhewms, and sore-throats,
   Do more & more abound:
Now Agues sore & Feavers strong
   In every place are found.   350
How many houses have we seen
   Last Autumn, and this spring
Wherein the healthful were too few
   To help the languishing.

One wave another followeth,   355
   And one disease begins
Before another cease, becaus
   We turn not from our sins.
We stopp our ear against reproof,
   And hearken not to God: 360
God stops his ear against our prayer,
   And takes not off his rod.

Our fruitful seasons have been turnd
   Of late to barrenness,
Sometimes through great & parching drought,   365
   Sometimes through rain's excess.
Yea now the pastures & corn fields
   For want of rain do languish:
The cattell mourn, & hearts of men
   Are fill'd with fear & anguish.   370

The clouds are often gathered,
   As if we should have rain:
But for our great unworthiness
   Are scattered again.

We pray & fast, & make fair shewes,   375
     As if we meant to turn:
But whilst we turn not, God goes on
     Our field, & fruits to burn.

And burnt are all things in such sort,
     That nothing now appears,   380
But what may wound our hearts with grief,
     And draw foorth floods of teares.
All things a famine do presage
     In that extremity,
As if both men, and also beasts,   385
     Should soon be done to dy.

This O New-England hast thou got
     By riot, & excess:
This hast thou brought upon thy self
     By pride & wantonness.   390
Thus must thy worldlyness be whipt.
     They, that too much do crave,
Provoke the Lord to take away
     Such blessings as they have.

We have been also threatened   395
     With worser things then these:
And God can bring them on us still,
     To morrow if he please.
For if his mercy be abus'd,
     Which holpe us at our need   400
And mov'd his heart to pitty us,
     We shall be plagu'd indeed.

Beware, O sinful Land, beware;
     And do not think it strange
That sorer judgements are at hand,   405
     Unless thou quickly change.
Or God, or thou, must quickly change;
     Or else thou art undon:
Wrath cannot cease, if sin remain,
     Where judgement is begun.   410

Ah dear New England! dearest land to me;
     Which unto God hast hitherto been dear,

And mayst be still more dear than formerlie,
    If to his voice thou wilt incline thine ear.

Consider wel & wisely what the rod,   415
    Wherewith thou art from yeer to yeer chastized,
Instructeth thee. Repent, & turn to God,
    Who wil not have his nurture be despized.

Thou still hast in thee many praying saints,
    Of great account, and precious with the Lord,   420
Who dayly powre out unto him their plaints,
    And strive to please him both in deed & word.

Cheer on, sweet souls, my heart is with you all,
    And shall be with you, maugre Sathan's might:
And whereso'ere this body be a Thrall,   425
    Still in New-England shall be my delight.

JONATHAN EDWARDS

The Latter-Day Glory Is
Probably to Begin in America

It is not unlikely that this work of God's Spirit [i.e. the religious revival],
so extraordinary and wonderful, is the dawning, or at least a prelude of that
glorious work of God, so often foretold in scripture, which, in the progress
and issue of it, shall renew the world of mankind. If we consider how long
since the things foretold as what should precede this great event, have been
accomplished; and how long this event has been expected by the church of
God, and thought to be nigh by the most eminent men of God, in the church;
and withal consider what the state of things now is, and has for a considerable
time been, in the church of God, and the world of mankind; we cannot reasonably think otherwise, than that the beginning of this great work of God
must be near. And there are many things that make it probable that this work
will begin in America. —It is signified that it shall begin in some very re-
mote part of the world, with which other parts have no communication but
by navigation, in Isa. lx. 9. "Surely the isles shall wait for me, and the ships
of Tarshish first, to bring my sons from far." It is exceeding manifest that this
chapter is a prophecy of the prosperity of the church, in its most glorious state
on earth, in the latter days; and I cannot think that any thing else can be here
intended but America by the isles that are far off, from whence the first-born
sons of that glorious day shall be brought. Indeed, by *the isles*, in prophecies of
gospel-times, is very often meant Europe. It is so in prophecies of that great
spreading of the gospel that should be soon after Christ's time, because it was
far separated from that part of the world where the church of God had till
then been, by the sea. But this prophecy cannot have respect to the conversion
of Europe, in the time of that great work of God, in the primitive ages of the
Christian church; for it was not fulfilled then. The isles and ships of Tarshish,
thus understood, did not wait for God first; that glorious work did not begin
in Europe, but in Jerusalem, and had for a considerable time been very won-

From Jonathan Edwards, "Some Thoughts Concerning the Present Revival of Religion in New
England," *The Works of President Edwards*, IV (New York: S. Converse, 1830), 128–33.

derfully carried on in Asia, before it reached Europe. And as it is not *that* work of God which is chiefly intended in this chapter, but some more glorious work that should be in the latter ages of the Christian church; therefore, some other part of the world is here intended by the isles, that should be, as Europe then was, far separated from that part of the world where the church had before been, and with which it can have no communication but by the ships of Tarshish. And what is chiefly intended is not the British isles, nor any isles near the other continent; they are spoken of as at a great distance from that part of the world where the church had till then been. This prophecy therefore seems plainly to point out America, as the first-fruits of that glorious day.

God has made as it were two worlds here below, two great habitable continents, far separated one from the other: The latter is as it were now but newly created; it has been, till of late, wholly the possession of Satan, the church of God having never been in it, as it has been in the other continent, from the beginning of the world. This new world is probably now discovered, that the new and most glorious state of God's church on earth might commence there; that God might in it begin a new world in a spiritual respect, when he creates the *new heavens* and *new earth*.

God has already put that honour upon the other continent, that Christ was born there literally, and there made the "purchase of redemption." So, as Providence observes a kind of equal distribution of things, it is not unlikely that the great spiritual birth of Christ, and the most glorious "application of redemption," is to begin in this. The elder sister brought forth Judah, of whom Christ came, and so she was the mother of Christ; but the younger sister, after long barrenness, brought forth Joseph and Benjamin, the beloved children, Joseph who had the most glorious apparel, the coat of many colours; who was separated from his brethren, and was exalted to great glory out of a dark dungeon—who fed and saved the world when ready to perish with famine, and was as a fruitful bough by a well, whose branches ran over the wall, and was blessed with all manner of blessings and precious things of heaven and earth, through the good-will of him that dwelt in the bush—was, as by the horns of an unicorn, to push the people together to the ends of the earth, i.e. conquer the world. See Gen. xlix. 2, etc. and Deut. xxxiii. 13, etc. And Benjamin, whose mess was five times so great as that of any of his brethren, and to whom Joseph, that type of Christ, gave wealth and raiment far beyond all the rest, Gen. xlv. 22.

The other continent hath slain Christ, and has from age to age shed the blood of the saints and martyrs of Jesus, and has often been as it were, deluged with the church's blood. —God has, therefore, probably reserved the honour of building the glorious temple to the daughter that has not shed so much blood, when those times of the peace, prosperity and glory of the church, typified by the reign of Solomon, shall commence.

The Gentiles first received the true religion from the Jews: God's church of ancient times had been among them, and Christ was of them. But, that there may be a kind of equality in the disposition of Providence, God has so ordered it, that when the Jews come to be admitted to the benefits of the evangelical dispensation, and to receive their highest privileges of all, they should receive the gospel from the Gentiles. Though Christ was of them, yet they have been guilty of crucifying him; it is therefore the will of God, that the Jews should not have the honour of communicating the blessings of the kingdom of God in its most glorious state to the Gentiles; but on the contrary, they shall receive the gospel in the beginning of that glorious day from the Gentiles. In some analogy to this, I apprehend, God's dealings will be with the two continents. America has received the true religion of the old continent; the church of ancient time has been there, and Christ is from thence. But that there may be an equality, and inasmuch as that Continent has crucified Christ, they shall not have the honour of communicating religion in its most glorious state to us, but we to them.

The old continent has been the source and original of mankind in several respects. The first parents of mankind dwelt there; and there dwelt Noah and his sons; there the second Adam was born, and crucified, and raised again: and it is probably that, in some measure to balance these things, the most glorious renovation of the world shall originate from the new continent, and the church of God in that respect be from hence. And so it is probable that will come to pass in spirituals, which has taken place in temporals, with respect to America: that whereas, till of late, the world was supplied with its silver, and gold, and earthly treasures from the old continent, now it is supplied chiefly from the new; so the course of things in spiritual respects will be in like manner turned. —And it is worthy to be noted, that America was discovered about the time of the reformation, or but little before: Which reformation was the first thing that God did towards the glorious renovation of the world after it had sunk into the depths of darkness and ruin, under the great anti-christian apostacy. So that, as soon as this new world stands forth in view, God presently goes about doing some great thing in order to make way for the introduction of the church's latter-day glory—which is to have its first seat in, and is to take its rise from that new world.

It is agreeable to God's manner, when he accomplishes any glorious work in the world, in order to introduce a new and more excellent state of his church, to begin where no foundation had been already laid, that the power of God might be the more conspicuous; that the work might appear to be entirely God's, and be more manifestly a creation out of nothing: agreeable to Hos. i. 10. "And it shall come to pass, that in the place where it was said unto them, Ye are not my people, there it shall be said unto them, Ye are the sons of the living God." When God is about to turn the earth into a paradise, he does not begin his work where there is some good growth already, but in the wilderness, where nothing grows, and nothing is to be seen but dry sand and barren rocks; that the light may shine out of darkness, the world be replenished from emptiness, and the earth watered by springs from a droughty desert: agreeable to many prophecies of scripture, as Isa. xxxii. 15. "Until the spirit be poured from on high, and the wilderness become a fruitful field." And chap. xli. 18, 19. "I will open rivers in high places, and fountains in the midst of the valleys: I will make the wilderness a pool of water, and the dry land springs of water. I will plant in the wilderness the cedar, the shittah-tree, and the myrtle, and the oil-tree: I will set in the desert, the fir-tree, and the pine, and the box-tree together." And chap. xliii. 20. "I will give waters in the wilderness, and rivers in the desert, to give drink to my people, my chosen." And many other parallel scriptures might be mentioned. Now as when God is about to do some great work for his church, his manner is to begin at the lower end; so, when he is about to renew the whole habitable earth, it is probable that he will begin in this utmost, meanest, youngest and weakest part of it, where the church of God has been planted last of all; and so the first shall be last, and the last first; and that will be fulfilled in an eminent manner in Isa. xxiv. 19. "From the uttermost part of the earth have we heard songs, even glory to the righteous."

There are several things that seem to me to argue, that the sun of righteousness, the sun of the new heavens and new earth, when he rises—and "comes forth as the bridegroom" of his church, "rejoicing as a strong man to run his race, having his going forth from the end of heaven, and his circuit to the end of it, that nothing may be hid from the light and heat of it," shall rise in the west, contrary to the course of things in the old heavens and earth. The movements of Providence shall in that day be so wonderfully altered in many respects that God will as it were change the course of nature, in answer to the prayers of his church; as he caused the sun to go from the west to the east, when he promises to do such great things for his church; a deliverance out of the hand of the king of Assyria, is often used by the prophet Isaiah, as a type of the glorious deliverance of the church from her enemies in the latter-days. The resurrection as it were of Hezekiah, the king and captain of the church (as he is called, 2 Kings xx. 5) is given as an earnest of the church's resurrection and salvation, Isa. xxxviii. 6, and is a type of the resurrection of Christ. At the same time there is a resurrection of the sun, or coming back and rising again from the west, whither it had gone down; which is also a type of the sun of righteousness. The sun was brought back ten degrees; which probably brought it to the meridian. The sun of righteousness has long been going down from east to west; and probably when the time comes of the church's deliverance from her enemies, so often typified by the Assyrians, the light will rise in the west, till it shines through the world like the sun in its meridian brightness.

The same seems also to be represented by the course of the waters of the sanctuary, Ezek. xlvii, which was from west to east; which waters undoubtedly represented the Holy Spirit, in the progress of his saving influences, in the latter ages of the world; for it is manifest, that the whole of those last chapters of Ezekiel treat concerning the glorious state of the church at that time. And if we may suppose that this glorious work of God shall begin in any part of America, I think, if we consider the circumstances of the settlement of New England, it must needs appear the most likely, of all American colonies, to be the place whence this work shall principally take its rise. And, if these things be so, it gives us more abundant reason to hope that what is now seen in America, and especially in New England, may prove the dawn of that glorious day; and the very uncommon and wonderful circumstances and events of this work, seem to me strongly to argue that God intends it as the beginning or forerunner of something vastly great.

Part Two

Revolution, Constitution, and a New Nation's Destiny

Although the Great Awakening brought about a renewal of the idea that the New World was the Promised Land, the birth of the republic lent special credence to the idea. The birth pangs of the Revolutionary War both announced the coming of independence and awakened the colonists to a new errand into the wilderness. Victory was interpreted as both a hard-earned opportunity for American self-determination and a proof of God's blessing on American tasks. The achievement of constitutional government was seen as the first step in a bold experiment that would assure basic human freedoms; it was also understood as a serious effort to erect an American model for the Old World. God's New Israel was transformed into a republic; a colonial destiny became a national destiny.

Protestant clergy were instrumental in rallying support for the revolutionary cause, and their success was due in great part to their ability to arouse in the people a sense of American destiny under God. There were clergy and laypeople in practically every denomination who either remained neutral or favored the British side, but as a whole the churches supported the Revolution. The strongest advocacy came from Congregationalists, Presbyterians, and Baptists. Aggressive missionary activity on the part of the Anglican Society for the Propagation of the Gospel angered many a non-Anglican colonist, and the attempt of the S.P.G. to convince the British government to establish an episcopate in America raised colonial fears to a pitch. For those of Puritan background, an Anglican bishop symbolized both political and religious tyranny. The more positive religious base for revolution resided in a Puritan political ideology that stressed a citizen's *primary* loyalty to God rather than king and described government as the result of a compact which, when broken, required adjustment even to the point of rebellion.

More colonists were prepared for armed resistance by the clergy's Sunday and election sermons and weekly lectures than by the books and pamphlets of a Locke or a Paine. Rural communities seldom exposed to the latest newspapers and books received from their clergymen instruction in the meaning of covenantal government and the "inalienable rights" of man. Of more immediate import was the "preaching up" of the Revolution itself on Sundays, fast days, and times of military recruitment. Curiously, such sermons were often cast in the form of the lamentation or jeremiad which had become a major part of the Puritan homiletical arsenal. Now, however, the jeremiad was bent to a most practical purpose. The sins of God's New Israel were examined so that it might repent and gird itself with holiness for the defeat of the enemy. The minister's lamentation was paralleled by successive recommendations of the Continental Congress that days of "publick humiliation, fasting, and prayer" be observed by the thirteen colonies in order to "confess and deplore our many sins" and implore God to "turn from his wrath." Both sermon and congressional recommendation constituted a call to action. "What carried the ranks of militia and citizens," Perry Miller has written, "was the universal persuasion that they, by administering to themselves a spiritual purge, acquired the energies God had always, in the manner of the Old Testament, been ready to impart to His repentant children. Their first responsibility was not to shoot redcoats but to cleanse themselves; only thereafter to take aim."[1]

Nicholas Street, graduate of Yale and pastor of East Haven (Congregational) Church, supported the Revolution by preaching on political topics and actively raising men, money, and goods for the Continental army.[2] Street's jeremiad, *The American States Acting Over the Part of the Children of Israel in the Wilderness*, was typical of the time. It insisted that the agonies of war had befallen the colonies because of their sins and warned against letting the injustices and cruelties of Pharaoh Britain obscure the wickedness of American Israel. Only after God's chosen people had been "humbled and reformed" would they be delivered from British bondage, make their way through the Red Sea of armed conflict and the wilderness of indecision, and reach the Promised Land of independence.

The end of the Revolutionary War offered American orators an occasion to rejoice in victory, praise God for the triumph, and look ahead with confidence to the destiny beckoning an independent people. Although public exultations usually avoided undisguised self-righteousness (the claim was often made that God had granted the colonies victory despite their unworthiness), there was little doubt in any patriot's mind that victory had come because the revolutionary *cause* (freedom) was just. Exhilaration quickly gave way to apprehension as Americans faced postwar poverty and the confusion resulting

1. Perry Miller, "From the Covenant to the Revival," *The Shaping of American Religion*, ed. James W. Smith and A. Leland Jamison (Princeton, N.J.: Princeton University Press, 1961), p. 333.

2. See Harry K. Eversull, *The Evolution of an Old New England Church* (East Haven, Conn.: Tuttle, Morehouse & Taylor, 1924), pp. 57–86.

from government by confederation. Nevertheless, the conviction that God had given in the victory a sure sign of his approval of the new nation was firmly planted in the American mind.

When Governor Trumbull asked his friend Ezra Stiles, president of Yale, to preach the Connecticut election sermon in 1783, Stiles was offered a chance to give full vent to current American optimism and let his imagination wander over the opportunities awaiting "God's American Israel." The sermon, *The United States Elevated to Glory and Honour,* was lengthy, running over one hundred pages in its printed form. As Stiles addressed the body of state representatives, his words actually stretched toward a much wider audience. "He was talking over their heads," Edmund Morgan has judged, "to the world that lay three thousand miles over the water. America, he was saying, had not merely conquered George III; America had conquered monarchy. America was the future of Europe. In the coming years, as American ships carried the flag around the globe, the power of freedom would everywhere become apparent."[3] America's destiny was disclosed: the nation was to be the pinnacle of liberty, "both civil and religious," and Stiles found ample evidence that America had already begun to realize that glorious historical role. Particularly striking was Stiles's paean to George Washington: Washington was portrayed as God's anointed and a paragon of virtue. Following the Revolution, praises of Washington reached such heights (he was compared most often with Moses, Gideon, and Joshua, but occasionally also with Jesus Christ) that a number of clergy warned against apotheosizing the general.[4] Clearly, Washington became the first "saint" in the American civil religion.

The formulation of a constitution encouraged further definition of American destiny. The Constitutional Convention was preacherless, though eight of the state ratifying conventions had clerical representatives; it was also prayerless, despite Benjamin Franklin's suggestion that the sessions be opened with prayer to overcome "partial interests." The Convention's product, however, by no means lacked religious support and grounding. Reformed or Calvinist theories of government, for example, had long preferred a "mixed state" containing a system of checks and balances to guard against the human tendency to pursue one's own self-interests. A view of human nature and government deeply rooted in New England religion was expressed by John Witherspoon—Presbyterian clergyman, delegate to the Continental Congress, signer of the

---

3. Edmund S. Morgan, *The Gentle Puritan: A Life of Ezra Stiles, 1727–1795* (New Haven, Conn.: Yale University Press, 1962), pp. 454–55.

4. James H. Smylie, "American Clergymen and the Constitution of the United States of America, 1781–1796" (Th.D. dissertation, Princeton Theological Seminary, 1958), pp. 342–52. Regarding the impact of Washington on American oratory see William A. Bryan, *George Washington in American Literature, 1775–1865* (New York: Columbia University Press, 1952), pp. 51–85.

Declaration of Independence, president of the College of New Jersey, member of the New Jersey ratifying convention:

> Pure democracy cannot subsist long, nor be carried far into the departments of state—it is very subject to caprice and the madness of popular rage. . . . Hence it appears, that every good form of government must be complex, so that the one principle may check the other. It is of consequence to have as much virtue among the particular members of a community as possible; but it is folly to expect that a state should be upheld by integrity in all who have a share in managing it. They must be so balanced, that when every one draws to his own interest or inclination, there may be an overpoise upon the whole.[5]

When the Constitution went to the states for debate and ratification, defenders of the document were quick to depict its significance in terms of American destiny. New Hampshire, which had the honor of being the ninth state to ratify the Constitution and hence put it into effect on June 21, 1788, included as a member of its ratifying convention Samuel Langdon, a New England Congregational minister and the president of Harvard from 1774 until 1780. In an election sermon before the General Court of New Hampshire on June 5, 1788, Langdon urged ratification and drew parallels between the laws of Israel and the federal Constitution. The sermon, *The Republic of the Israelites an Example to the American States*, detailed evidences of God's providence in the events of American history and prescribed ways to "make a wise improvement" of what God had granted the New Israel. The states were to secure the human liberties fought for in the Revolution with the establishment of and adherence to a sound federal Constitution. Thereby the states could claim their destiny under God and "RISE! RISE to fame among all nations." Like many other New England ministers at this time, Langdon did not feel that the Constitution excluded the need for state government to preserve and support the Christian religion. And although Langdon insisted in his election sermon that the Christian religion "is confined to no particular nation, sect, or denomination," there is little doubt that he believed his own brand of Protestantism to be that religion's purest form. During the constitutional period, citizens were divided over the question whether the states should support a "religious establishment"; and although the tendency clearly was toward complete disestablishment, it was not until 1833 (in Massachusetts) that the last vestige of religious establishment was abolished in the states.

The American Founding Fathers were as vigorous in their pronouncements on America's providential destiny as any clergyman. Benjamin Franklin,

---

5. John Witherspoon, "Lectures on Moral Philosophy," *Works*, III (Philadelphia: William W. Woodward, 1802), 435.

Thomas Jefferson, and John Adams—all of whose "rationalist" ideas on religion were later to be severely criticized by those of more traditional religious leanings—were never so rationalistic or Deistic that they envisioned God as a watchmaker who simply wound up the universe and then let events take their course. Their God was intimately involved in the events of American history. Divine providence was the force that moved the United States to liberty; eventually providence would, through the example of the United States, direct the world to the same end. In a diary entry for February 1765, Adams wrote, "I always consider the settlement of America with reverence and wonder, as the opening of a grand scene and design in Providence for the illumination of the ignorant, and the emancipation of the slavish part of mankind all over the earth."[6] Franklin and Jefferson preferred the image of Israel's exodus from Egypt and eventual arrival in Canaan as the best representation of the American struggle for freedom. On July 4, 1776, Congress directed Franklin, Jefferson, and Adams to design a seal for the United States. Franklin proposed a portrayal of "Moses lifting his hand and the Red Sea dividing, with Pharaoh in his chariot being overwhelmed by the waters, and with a motto in great popular favor at the time, 'Rebellion to tyrants is obedience to God.'" Jefferson suggested "a representation of the children of Israel in the wilderness, led by a cloud by day and pillar of fire by night."[7]

No one spoke more deliberately of the American Israel's destiny than Thomas Jefferson. He was later to conclude his second inaugural address with an image similar to the one he suggested for the seal: "I shall need . . . the favor of that Being in whose hands we are, who led our fathers, as Israel of old, from their native land and planted them in a country flowing with all the necessaries and comforts of life." According to Jefferson, America was to act as a model democratic republic, thereby serving as "the world's best hope." "A just and solid republican government maintained here," he wrote to John Dickinson in 1801, "will be a standing monument and example for the aim and imitation of the people of other countries."[8] Geographically separated from the tyrannies and corruptions of Europe, America could perform its experiment in self-government unmolested by outside forces and outmoded traditions. In that way the republic would become the hope and example for all freedom-loving peoples. The major themes in Jefferson's version of American destiny were presented in his first inaugural address.

"Jeffersonian isolationism expressed an essentially cosmopolitan spirit,"

---

6. Quoted in Ernest Lee Tuveson, *Redeemer Nation: The Idea of America's Millennial Role* (Chicago: University of Chicago Press, 1968), p. 25.

7. Irving L. Thompson, "Great Seal of the United States," *Encyclopedia Americana*, XIII (1967), 362.

8. A. E. Bergh, ed., *The Writings of Thomas Jefferson*, X (Washington, D.C.: The Thomas Jefferson Memorial Association, 1907), 217.

Daniel Boorstin has said.[9] It was for the sake of all people that America was to isolate itself and perform an experiment in republican democracy. Yet the Jeffersonian view of American destiny also contained the seeds of American self-righteousness. Believing that it had escaped the wickedness of the Old World and the guilt of the past, God's New Israel would find it all too easy to ignore its own shortcomings and all too difficult to admit a loss of innocence.

SUGGESTED READING

Bailyn, Bernard. *The Ideological Origins of the American Revolution.* Cambridge, Mass.: Belknap Press of Harvard University Press, 1967.

Bridenbaugh, Carl. *Mitre and Sceptre: Transatlantic Faiths, Ideas, Personalities, and Politics, 1689–1775.* New York: Oxford University Press, 1962.

Gaustad, Edwin S. *Sworn on the Altar of God: A Religious Biography of Thomas Jefferson.* Grand Rapids, Mich.: W. B. Eerdmans, 1996.

Hatch, Nathan O. *The Sacred Cause of Liberty: Republican Thought and the Millennium in Revolutionary New England.* New Haven, Conn.: Yale University Press, 1977.

Mead, Sidney E. "American Protestantism During the Revolutionary Epoch" and "Thomas Jefferson's 'Fair Experiment'—Religious Freedom," Chaps. 3 and 4, *The Lively Experiment.* New York: Harper & Row, Publishers, 1963.

Noll, Mark A. *Christians in the American Revolution.* Grand Rapids, Mich.: Christian University Press, 1977.

9. Daniel J. Boorstin, *The Lost World of Thomas Jefferson* (Boston: Beacon Press, 1948), p. 229.

NICHOLAS STREET

❧

The American States Acting
Over the Part of the Children of Israel
in the Wilderness and Thereby Impeding
Their Entrance into Canaan's Rest

DEUTERONOMY VIII. 2.
"And thou shalt remember all the way which the Lord
thy God led these forty years in the wilderness, to humble thee, and
to prove thee, to know what was in thine heart, whether thou
wouldest keep his commandments or no."

The history of the children of Israel in Egypt, their sufferings and oppression under the tyrant Pharaoh, their remarkable deliverance by the hand of Moses out of that state of bondage and oppression, and their trials and murmurings in the wilderness, is well known by those who have been conversant with their bibles, and have attended to those important lessons contained in the five Books of Moses. But why God thus dealt with that people, perhaps has not been duly attended to by those that have made conscience of reading the sacred story. But the text tells us, that it was to humble them, and to prove them, that they might know what was in their hearts, and whether they would keep his commandments, or no. All the events which befel them in the way; the miraculous protections, deliverances, provisions and instructions which God gave them, and withal, the frequent and severe punishments which were inflicted for their disobedience, was to discover to themselves and others, all that infidelity, inconstancy, hypocrisy, apostacy, rebellion and perverseness which lay hid in their hearts; the discovery of which was of singular use both to them, and to the church of God in all succeeding ages. For as Watts has it,

A sermon preached at East Haven, Connecticut, April 1777 (New Haven, Conn.: Thomas and Samuel Green, 1777), pp. 3–25, 27–34.

> There, as in a glass our hearts may see,
> How fickle and how false they be.

God, by them, designed to let after generations know what was in their
hearts. But it is not generally known and believed till it comes to the trial;
and then it is found that we are prone to act over the same stupid vile part
that the children of Israel did in the wilderness, under the most instructive
and speaking providences that ever obtained in the world. . . .

I. I am to show that the hearts of the children of men are naturally the same
from generation to generation. This is so plain a point that I need not stand
long for the proof of it, tho' it may be profitable to illustrate it by some examples. "For of one blood God made all nations of men that dwell upon the
face of the earth," Acts 17.26. And this blood is under one common attainder
by guilt; "for by one man's disobedience many were made sinners," says the
apostle, Rom. 5.19. And the apostle speaking of the natural state of the heart
says, that "it is enmity against God, not subject to his law, neither indeed can
be," Rom. 8.7. And our Savior testifieth that "out of the heart of man proceed
evil thoughts, murders, adulteries, fornication, thefts, covetousness, wickedness, deceit, lasciviousness, an evil eye, blasphemy, pride, foolishness. All these
things come from within and defile the man." Mark 7.21, 22, 23. And we find
this radical evil of the heart early breaking forth and exemplifying itself in
the lives of all the generations of men that have been upon the earth, from
Adam our primogenitor to the present race of men that inhabit the earth. . . .

Tho' we have all the wickedness of the world to teach us what there is in
our hearts, and our daily experience to instruct us, yet we do not learn the
depths of wickedness that lodge in that cavern, till a suitable temptation draws
it forth into exercise. The children of Israel were not aware ('tis like) of the
hundredth part of the wickedness that lay lurking in their hearts, while they
were in Egypt in their cruel state of bondage to Pharaoh. They were doubtless ready then to think, that if they could once get free from that state of
vassalage, that they would serve the Lord with chearfulness, and that none
of his commandments should be grievous. But when they came to the trial,
they found unbelief, distrust of God and of his tender care of them, springing
up in the midst of the most extraordinary manifestations of God's power and
goodness on their behalf that ever were made to a people. And tho' they had
been lately delivered from the severest bondage and oppression, yet they were
as impatient under trials, and as ready to murmur at any difficulties in their
way, as tho' they had newly come out of the most prosperous state. Now if any
one had told them while in their cruel state of bondage, that such were their
hearts, they would not have believed them, 'tis like. Therefore God led them
those forty years in the wilderness to humble and prove them, that they might
know what was in their hearts, as 'tis said in the text. And tho' when we read

their history, we are ready to be moved with indignation towards them; yet we are acting over at this day the same stupid part with them in the wilderness.

We in this land are, as it were, led out of Egypt by the hand of Moses. And now we are in the wilderness, i.e. in a state of trouble and difficulty, Egyptians pursuing us, to overtake us and reduce us. There is the Red Sea before us, I speak metaphorically, a sea of blood in your prospect before you, perhaps. And when you apprehend this in your imaginations, are you not ready to murmur against Moses and Aaron that led you out of Egypt, and to say with the people of Israel, "It had been better for us to serve the Egyptians, than that we should die in the wilderness." Exod. 14.12. And tho' God has been pleased to work marvellously for us at times as he did for them; yet if any new difficulty arises, and if things don't go on so prosperously as at other times, how soon does our faith fail us, and we begin to murmur against Moses and Aaron, and wish ourselves back again in Egypt, where we had some comforts of life, which we are now deprived of? not considering that we chose our leaders, and that in obtaining any deliverance there are great troubles and difficulties generally attending it; neither considering that our ill successes are owing to the sins of the people, as was the case of the people of Israel in the wilderness. We find them ten times as ready to find fault with their leaders, and to ascribe their misfortunes to them, as to recoil in upon themselves, and to say, What have we done? tho' it was owing entirely to them that they were not delivered. And thus we in this land are murmuring and complaining of our difficulties and ill successes at times, thinking our leaders to blame, and the like, not considering at the same time that we are practising those vices that have a natural tendency to destroy us, besides the just judgments of Heaven which they tend to draw down upon us as a people. . . . And when we are favoured with a little success, we are apt to be elated in our minds like the children of Israel after the overthrow of the Egyptians in the red sea, and then with them to rejoice, and to encourage ourselves in the cause in which we are engaged; then we can trust, as we imagine, in God, and hope for his salvation and deliverance. But let the scale turn a little against us, our confidence begins to fail, and we grow distrustful of God and his providence, and begin to murmur and repine.

> Thus the faithless Jews forgot
> The dreadful wonders God had wrought,
> Then they provoke him to his face,
> Nor fear his power, nor trust his grace.
> —Watts

Thus we are acting over the like sins with the children of Israel in the wilderness, under the conduct of Moses and Aaron, who was leading them out of a state of bondage into a land of liberty and plenty in Canaan. Again, we are ready to marvel at the unreasonable vileness and cruelty of the British tyrant and his ministry, in endeavouring to oppress, enslave and destroy these American States, who have been some of his most peaceable and profitable subjects. And yet we find the same wicked temper and disposition operating in Pharaoh king of Egypt above 3000 years ago. . . . When Israel began to increase in Egypt, the king said, "Come on, let us deal wisely with them lest they multiply; and it comes to pass when there falleth out any war, they join unto our enemies and fight against us, and so get them out of the land." Therefore they did set over them task-masters to afflict them with their burdens; they made them to serve with rigour, and they made their lives bitter with hard bondage, etc. And afterwards they laid the burthen heavier, allowing them no straw, and yet requiring the full tale of brick. Exod. 5.6–11. And when they endeavoured to make their escape from this cruel and oppressive tyrant, Pharaoh pursued after Israel with a great army unto the Red Sea. Exod. 14.7–10. So that the British tyrant is only acting over the same wicked and cruel part, that Pharaoh king of Egypt acted towards the children of Israel above 3000 years ago.

But some may be ready to wonder, that since we are gone off from Great-Britain, and have declared ourselves independent States, and insist upon standing by ourselves, that they don't let us alone, especially as they have pretended that we are but of little consequence to Great-Britain. But we find the same disposition in the adversaries of Judah and Benjamin, who troubled them in building, and hired counsellors against them to frustrate their purposes. Afterwards Rehum the chancellor wrote to the king, The Jews are building the rebellious and bad city. If this city be builded, and the walls set up again, say they, then they will not pay toll, tribute, etc. and so thou shalt endamage the revenue of the kings. Now because we have maintenance from the king's palace, and it was not meet for us to see the king's dishonour, etc. this city is a rebellious city, and hurtful to kings; and that they have moved sedition within the same of old. If this city be built, by this means thou shalt have no portion on this side the river, and so they hasted to Jerusalem to stay the work by force. Ezra 4, from the beginning to the 24th verse. Now this was a right Tory letter and conduct; and Sanballat's behaviour towards those that encouraged the work of building the city was just like that of the tories towards those that would build up these American States. See Neh. 2.19. "But when Sanballat the Horonite and Tobiah the servant, the Ammonite, heart it, they laughed us to scorn, and despised us, and said, 'What is this thing that ye do? Will ye rebel against the king?'" Thus there were some men then as well as in these days, that seemed to look upon it as a greater crime to oppose the king in his most arbitrary measures, than to violate the law of the realm and of their God. "And when Sanballat and others heard that the walls of Jerusalem were made up, they were very wroth, and conspired all of them together to come and fight against Jerusalem, and to hinder it." Neh. 4.7, 8.

And Great-Britain is now acting over just the same part towards us in these

American States, endeavouring to prevent our building ourselves up into Free, Independent States. So that the temper and disposition of the world has been much the same throughout all generations. Great men are generally proud, ambitious and aspiring, disdainful of inferiors, and apt to resent the least indignities. We see this in Haman, an aspiring courtier, who when he saw that Mordecai bowed not nor did him reverence, was full of wrath; wherefore Haman sought to destroy all the Jews that were throughout the whole kingdom of Ahassuerus. And Haman said unto the king, " 'There is a certain people scattered abroad, and dispersed among the people in all the provinces of thy kingdom, and their laws are diverse from all people, neither keep they the king's laws; therefore it is not for the king's profit to suffer them. Let it please the king that it may be written that they may be destroyed; and I will pay ten thousand talents of silver to the hands of those that have the charge of the business, to bring it into the king's treasuries.' " And the king grants his desire. Esth. 3.5–11. And the British ministry have been acting over the same wicked, mischievous plot against the American States, as Haman did against the Jews, and we have reason to hope that they will meet with the like fate. But what I mention these instances for, is to let you see that the wickedness of man has been much the same throughout all ages . . . we see that our complaints and trials at this day are nothing new. People have been oppressed under the colour of law, as we are by the British ministry; and have been most cruelly oppressed and insulted by those that have been in power; and have been derided and laughed at by their enemies in their most afflicted state.

II. God frequently brings his own people into a state of peculiar trials, to discover to them and others what there is in their hearts. Thus God tempted Abraham, when he put him upon offering up his son Isaac, Gen. 22.2, 3 (i.e.) tried him with that peculiar trial, that he might discover to himself and others, what there was in his heart; whether he would keep God's commandments or no, however trying or self-denying they might be. And the issue discovered to himself and to others the firmness and fixedness of his principles to the glory of God and his own comfort and satisfaction. For the trial proved his sincerity in the cause of God, and that he would keep his commandments under the most trying circumstances of obedience, that nothing should deter him from the service of his God, tho' his best beloved son, as a sacrifice, should be the test of his obedience. Thus nobly did the faith and obedience of this Father of the faithful display itself under the exercise of peculiar trials . . . and as God is thus pleased to bring his own people into a state of peculiar trials for the discovery of their virtues, so likewise for the discovery of their vices, that they and others may see what corruption there still remains in their hearts unmortified and unsubdued. Thus good Hezekiah was tried with a prosperous scene to discover what was in his heart. God gave him a remarkable victory over the Assyrians and granted him miraculous restoration from a dangerous sickness, and not only so, but God gave him peculiar honour by an embassy from the great and potent king of Babylon; all which probably raised in him too high an opinion of himself, as if these things were done, if not by his power, yet at least for his piety and virtues. So that instead of walking humbly with God, and giving the glory of all entirely to him, he took the honour to himself, and vain-gloriously shewed his riches and precious treasures to the Babylon-ish ambassadors. 2 Kings 20.13. . . .

And so a suitable temptation will frequently draw forth such corruptions into exercise, as persons before were not aware of being in their hearts. This we see in a striking light in Hazael, whom the prophet informed how wicked and cruel he would be when he came to be king, viz. that he would burn their strong holds, and slay their young men with the sword, dash their chil-dren, and rip up their women with child, etc. Hazael when he came to hear the description was shocked at it, and resented the thought, as you see from his reply. 2 Kings 8.13. "And Hazael said, 'But what is thy servant a dog, that he should do this great thing?'" And yet we find, as a worthy author observes upon this passage, that the dog did it. He could not conceive that there was such cruelty and barbarity in his heart as to practise such inhumanity as the prophet pointed out. But when he came to the trial, and was made king, and felt the pleasing power of having the world under him, as it were, then pride, insolence, and a tyrannical disposition sprung up in his heart, like noxious and baleful weeds in an overfattened soil, to the destruction of the design of regal dignity, whereby he became a curse and destroyer of his people, rather than a minister of God for good unto them. But he was not aware, it seems, when the prophet told him that he should be king of Syria, that he should ever be left to practise such inhumanity and barbarity as afterwards he was guilty of.

Neither is it profitable that George the third, when he first came to the throne of Great-Britain, and swore to govern according to the good and wholesome laws of the realm, and issued that proclamation for the suppression of immoralities, would in a few years by a royal edict butcher a great num-ber of his best subjects for not submitting to his arbitrary mandates. Doubtless when he first came to the throne, if it had been suggested to him, that he would have practised all that tyranny, cruelty, and oppression which he has not long since gone into with regard to the American States, he would have been greatly ready to have replied in indignation with Hazael, "Is thy servant a dog that he should do this great thing?" But we find he has done it to our grievous wounding, and to his dishonour and bloody guilt! He that should have been our father and protector has become the bloody murderer of thou-sands of his best subjects! And tho' this seems harsh to assert with regard to one whom we have heretofore addressed with the kind and honorary epithet of a gracious sovereign, yet I now boldly assert him to be a cruel tyrant, who seeks to govern us without law, without reason, or the sacred dictates of revelation; impiously declaring that he has a right to give us laws binding in all cases whatsoever. If such a prince is not a tyrant, then I know not who deserves the name! But he is only with that dog Hazael, acting out the cruelty of his heart and that of his bloody court. The seven abominations that have lain hid there, have now come forth like the locusts from the bottomless pit upon this land to distress and annoy it; burning and laying waste populous towns that were erected without any of his expence or patronage; carrying fire and sword among those who have been his most peaceable and faithful subjects; ravishing the women where the armies have marched; exercising the greatest inhumanity and barbarity towards their prisoners; freezing and starving them to death. And all this done by British troops, who used to be famed for their humanity and generosity to prisoners! Who would have thought that such savage cruelty had been in their hearts? But the trial has brought it out to the disgrace of the British tyrant and his bloody troops. Some are disposed, 'tis true, to talk much of the mercy and mildness of British government, to encourage people to submit to their lawless claims; but I am never disposed to look to that power for mercy, that is devoid of justice, but forever reject the cruel wretch, who for the sake of a lawless domination would sacrifice almost one quarter of the globe to his resentment. I think the trial has discovered what is in the heart of British administration, and I never desire to be gain connected with that government, which instead of speaking peace to us, and to our seed, threatens death and destruction to us and our posterity.

But as the trial has discovered what is in the heart of British administration, so likewise the peculiar situation that the American States have been in has tried what is in our hearts. As *The American Crisis* observes, "These are the times that try men's souls;" and many things are discovered in the trial, which otherwise might have lain concealed in the heart. Tho' as our Savior observes, "Out of the abundance of the heart the mouth speaketh"; yet some will conceal what is within, till a proper temptation draw it forth. The contest has been whether we should submit to the arbitrary, oppressive claims of British administration, or maintain our own rights and repel force by force. Vastly the greatest majority has been for the latter; and the general will is always said to be of the nature of a law. A small part of the States have opposed the general will, and have openly taken part with British administration. Others have been more reserved, and have waited to see which is the safest side, in order to determine their conduct. These are men of no principle, only to save themselves, which is the most sordid of all; for they will be on this side or the other, just as the scale is like to turn for or against the country. Now these are trying times to sift men out, that they and others may know what is in their hearts; whether they will sell their country and their God for a little worldly pelf; or whether they will make a noble sacrifice of all their worldly goods, and even bleed and die for their dear country and dear bought privileges. Many have done it already, and many more seem ready to do it, whose names ought to be honoured and held dear in the annals of the American States, so long as there are any to remember their deeds. But this will not be the fame of all that had their birth and education in this noble land! No, it will be said to the eternal disgrace of some, that instead of standing for the precious land of their nativity and its dear bought privileges, that they vilely betrayed it; and with Esau they sold their birth-right for a mess of pottage; that they turned their sword, which should have been drawn in the defence of their country, against the father that begat them, and against the tender bowels of the mother that bare them, and the loving brothers and sisters that solaced them, and all the dear friends and neighbours that used to aid and assist them.

Oh, this is an image too horrid and shocking to look to! I turn from it as a picture too monstrous to behold! and turn to one of a more diminutive size, tho' not much less despicable than the former. And that is such as aim not to use the sword upon either side, but aim to take a part upon that side that will best secure their darling interest. Their souls are so immersed in silver and gold that they would fall into that scale which would weigh down with the most penny weight! These are they that make gold their hope, and the fine gold their confidence, and deny the God that is above, as Job elegantly expresses it. Job 31.24. . . . Such persons trust that their money and interest will secure them from distresses and troubles, and therefore greedily procure it, and then are ready to join with that party which they think are like to conquer; not considering that the events of war are altogether uncertain, and that that side which appears the most promising at present may be in a few days the most gloomy and threatening. 'Tis not worth while under the most promising prospects to say with David, "My mountain stands so strong that I shall not be moved." For God may hide his face as he did from him, and then with him we shall soon be troubled. But then we should always act upon principle, and be uniform in our conduct, committing our cause to God, who sits in the throne judging righteously, and can save and deliver with few or with many. But some people have no notion about trusting in God; they rise and fall just like a ship at anchor with the ebbing and flowing tide. And these trying times are designed to shew us what is in our hearts; whether we will trust in him at all times, and adhere to the cause which we profess to believe to be right in dark and gloomy days, as well as in those that are more fair and prosperous.

It is no great matter for men to trust in God when every thing looks fair and prosperous; they then deceive themselves, thinking they trust in God, whereas they trust in the fair prospect that is before them. But this is the trial of our sincerity, when every thing looks dark and gloomy, according to human prospects, then to commit our cause to God and trust in him for a favourable issue. This is truly trusting in God. And these shifting scenes of adverse and prosperous appearances are designed to humble us and prove us, that we may know what is in our hearts. There is a variety of temptations arising from our particular state and circumstances, to draw out what there is in our hearts. There are many things to try us whether we are of a public spirit; whether we regard our country, our liberties and privileges more than our own private pelf. And some we shall find shrinking back from the public cause, avoiding all occasions in which the public calls for assistance, while others less able must bear the weight of the public weal or let it sink. Others are tried as to their humanity and benevolence, whether they will assist others with the necessary supports of life, when they can do it, at a reasonable lay. And here, alas! we find the trial betraying what is in the hearts of many, given a wicked, oppressive disposition, refusing to part with their provision at that high price allowed and stated by the legislature of the state; waiting, it seems, to take the advantage of people's necessities, to get a more exorbitant price. This is a wickedness prevailing in the country which we should not have imagined to have been in their hearts had not the trial brought it forth. And God is trying us and proving us by all the variety of his dispensations, that we may know what is in our hearts, and whether we will keep his commandments or no; whether the sabbath-profaner will become a sabbath sanctifier; whether the profane swearer will bridle his tongue, and leave off his profaneness; whether the wanton and intemperate will become chaste and sober; and whether people will reform their ways, mortify their corruptions, and become new creatures. The land have sadly corrupted their way; religion has been losing ground for many years; and all manner of vice and profaneness has become rampant in the land. And God is visiting us for these things with general judgments; and 'tis likely God will keep us in this wilderness of trouble to humble us and prove us, that we may see our errors, and know that God has a righteous controversy with us at this day.

We are apt to think that our cause is so righteous with regard to Great-Britain, that I fear we are ready to forget our unrighteousness towards God. And while we are endeavouring to get rid of the unreasonable commands of an earthly sovereign, I fear we forget to obey the most reasonable commands of the rightful Sovereign of the Universe. Let us look upon the ground on which we stand; consider our guilt and danger, and be humble for our sins, and under all the tokens of God's displeasure against us on the account of our sins, repent and reform whatever is amiss in the midst of us, that we may be prepared for a deliverance out of our troubles; that being delivered out of the hands of our enemies, we may serve God without fear in righteousness and true holiness all the days of our lives.

III. People when they are proved and tried, generally shew what they are. A suitable trial generally shews what people are, whether virtuous or vicious; if they are of a virtuous disposition, a suitable trial will generally bring out their virtues to public view; and if vicious, their vices.

We have been ready to look upon ourselves as a virtuous people in this

land, to be sure in comparison with Great-Britain, and so to encourage ourselves that we should not be vanquished on account of our virtues. But the
trial discovers that there is not so much virtue in the land as well were ready
to imagine. There is a vast deal of wickedness brought out to public view in
this day of trial. Many we find will betray their dear bought country for a
little worldly pelf, preferring their present interest, ease and advantage, to all
the liberties and privileges of their future posterity. And many who aim not
to betray their country are so mercenary that they would imbark on that side
that they think would best serve their interest, without regard to the righteousness of the cause. And others who profess to be zealous in the cause of
their country are so fond of making a fortune, as we say, or of advancing their
interest, that they become blind to the bleeding wounds of their country, and
deaf to the cries of the poor and needy; and will not reach forth the helping
hand to their distresses, unless with the iron hand of oppression to extort an
exorbitant sum for their relief. Indeed the trial shews that there is but little
of a public spirit prevailing amongst people in general at this day. The bigger
part seem exceedingly selfish, striving for the highest price for every article
that they have to part with; and if they think there is a prospect of its arriving to a more extravagant price thro' the exigencies of the country, they will
withhold it from the needy, tho' "the stone should cry out of the wall, and
the beam out of the timber should answer it." Hab. 2.11. . . . If this disposition had not appeared upon the trial, we should have been self-righteous and
trusted in ourselves; and have been ready to have thought if we had any successes, this was owing to our being more righteous than Great-Britain, and so
arrogated the glory to ourselves. . . .

But then oppression is not the only sin that our trials have brought forth to
view, but the sins of treachery, falsehood and deceit have crept out in one place
and another thro' the land, in divers persons who would betray its sacred cause
into the hands of tyranny and oppression. And others under the notion of
being high sons of liberty will act without law and above law, and so encourage
and promote universal tyranny under the notion of a plenitude of liberty. For
to govern without law is tyranny: for law is the guardian of liberty, securing a
people in their rights and liberties; and whosoever endeavours to set law aside
or to supersede it, so far endeavours to destroy the liberties of his country, and
so far to promote a tyrannical government. And yet the trying situation of the
country has discovered some to be of this complexion; and however high they
may think themselves for liberty, they are throwing down the very bulwark
that secures it. But the trial discovers another sort of people, who tho' they
are not for going against law, yet they are not for putting the law in execution, which enervates government and renders the law of no force. And such,
however well meaning they may have been, have inadvertently fallen into an
opinion that has proved very hurtful to the country. For the relaxation of the

laws has encouraged some to act out themselves to the disadvantage of the country. The civil sword has not been a terror to evil doers as heretofore, and a praise and protection to such as do well. And the debtor has shewn the dishonesty of his heart in refusing to pay his honest dues, because courts of judicature have not been kept up in times back, to oblige him to do this justice; and men have hereby been defrauded of their honest dues. And this is not the greatest evil; for this has laid the foundation for the most of that oppression that there is in the midst of us. For the country finding themselves not obliged to part with their monies, feel not the necessity of parting with their provision, and so withhold it from the consumer till an extortionate price draws it out of their hands . . . so that it appears that we have much less public virtue in the country than we were aware of, many being disposed to take the advantage of the distresses of their country, not caring who sinks if they can but swim. . . .

Thus the god of this world blinds the eyes of men. If they were not deluded by the devil and the deceitfulness of their own wicked hearts, they could no more think themselves conscientious and friends to their country, than the thief and the high-way man; for oppression is as much spoken against in Scripture as the forementioned vices, and has as direct a tendency to ruin the country. For these things the wrath of God cometh upon the children of disobedience. And when there is the oppression of the poor, and the sighing of the needy in the midst of us, we can't expect any other, but God will arise to judgment and make his plagues dreadful upon this land. We have been ready to wonder that British troops should be so oppressive and cruel to our people; but it has been observed by some worthy divines, that God is wont to punish people frequently with such a kind of punishment as bespeaks the nature of their crimes. And our Saviour tells us that such measure as you mete, shall be measured to you again. Mat. 7.2. And we have reason to believe that God thus permits us to be oppressed by the British troops, as a righteous correction for the oppressive disposition that prevails in this land. . . .

But besides, the trial has brought out many other vices, which we should have hoped were not so predominant in the land, if the trial had not discovered them. To instance a few: the little regard that is shewn to the sabbath by the soldiery and others, who look upon themselves a little at liberty from the restraints of human laws; and that profaneness that there is in our armies, raised from the midst of us for the defence of our dear land, as well as against people at home, at a time in which the land is involved in the greatest distresses that ever it knew and when there has been the most express prohibitions against profane swearing, issued from the highest authority in America . . . a strange spirit of falsehood has gone forth into the land, so that it is very difficult to ascertain facts of the most interesting nature as to our military operations, bespeaking the want of a spirit of integrity and uprightness in the land. All which forbode ill concerning us as a people. For if public virtue fails and people grow vicious and profane, selfish and oppressive under the sorest judgments and calamities, we have reason to fear the worst; that God will multiply our distresses and increase his judgments, till we are brought to a repentance and reformation. We see that God kept the children of Israel in the wilderness for many years after he had delivered them from the hand of Pharaoh, on the account of their wickedness. He led them so long in the wilderness to humble and prove them that they might know what there was in their hearts; and one trial after another brought it out. And so our trials in this wilderness state are bringing out our corruptions one after another, that we and others may know what there is in our hearts; what pride, what selfishness, what covetousness, what ingratitude, rebellion, impatience and distrust of God and his providence, all these come flowing forth from the midst of us under our trials, in as conspicuous a manner as they did from the children of Israel in the wilderness. Which if it had not been for our trials, that have discovered them, we should not have imagined to have been in such a privileged, gospelized land as this.

IV. The discovering to a people their errors and wickedness is designed to humble and reform them. This is spoken of as being the express end and design of bringing the children of Israel into the wilderness, and leading them there forty years. It was to humble them and prove them, that they might know what there was in their hearts, and whether they would keep his commandments or no. God did it not merely to bring out such a deformed character to view, as they exhibit under their trials; but that being brought forth, they might see their own wickedness and deformity, and be humbled and repent of this their great wickedness and reform their lives, by keeping his commandments for the future. And this is the end and design of God in bringing us into this wilderness of trouble and confusion, that we may know what there is in our hearts, that being brought out to public view, we and others may see what a wicked people we are, and that we may be deeply humbled and abased before God on the same account, repent and reform. 'Tis not because God delights in bringing such a deformed character to view. No, for it is more odious and irksome to him, for he hateth all the workers of iniquity, and he is "of purer eyes than to behold evil, and cannot look on iniquity." Hab. 1.13. A vicious character is like a noisom stench in his nostrils; and therefore when God brings such a character into view, it is that we may be humbled under it, repent and reform. Therefore let us be sollicitous to get a clear view of our manifold guilt, and to be deeply humbled on the account of our own sins, and the manifold high handed abominations that are daily committed in this distinguished land of light and liberty: That there is so much of a disposition in the midst of us to oppress one another, while the land is wading in blood to oppose and resist this wickedness in British administration. Oh, let us see the deformity of this vice thro' the bloody spectacles of those parliamentary acts, that declare that they have a right to tax the American States, and to give laws to us in all cases whatsoever; and in consequence of such a claim have sent their bloody troops to butcher us, till we are reduced to such a cruel yoke of tyranny and oppression. Methinks this shocking scene of oppression is enough to give you to see the deformity of this vice, and to make you flee from it as a monster that devours without pity! And if you do not see it in this horrid picture, look into hell—and there see Dives roaring in the fire of hell for a drop of water to cool his tormented tongue, for denying the crumbs that he had to spare from his own table to a poor, perishing Lazarus! . . . Every sin is of a destructive, deadly nature; and if sin was thus seen and viewed, it would not be so difficult to dissuade people from it. But they view it thro' the devil's spectacles, which makes it to appear more delighting and contenting than ever it is found to be; and he blinds their minds as to the deformity and destructive nature of it, so that he may lead them blindfold down to eternal perdition. Therefore we had need take much pains to bring sinners to a just view of their sins; for till then they will not be humbled for them, nor repent and reform.

And hence it is that God brings people into some trying situation to bring their wickedness out to view, that they may know what there is in their hearts and be humbled for it; and the trials that we have been under in this land have brought out a vast deal of wickedness which we should not have been aware of, if the trial had not betrayed it. And what is the end of this discovery? Why to humble us, to bring us to repentance and a general reformation. Let us then be sensible of the ends of Divine Providence in permitting such wickedness to break out in the midst of us. It is to humble us and to give us to see that we have no cause to trust in ourselves—in our own righteousness, which we are very prone to, that disclaiming all confidence in ourselves, we may trust in him who raiseth the dead—and who will have mercy on whom he will have mercy.

Several useful inferences might be made from this subject, but I shall confine myself to one, with which I shall conclude the discourse.

Seeing it as we have heard, that the wickedness of man has been much the same thro' all generations, hence we may infer that every generation may rationally expect the like punishments and calamities that have been inflicted upon generations back. The history of the world is nothing scarcely but a history of the wickedness and miseries of it. Take the sacred history from the fall of man till Christ's appearance on earth, till his crucifixion, resurrection and ascension to glory, and even from the mission of the Holy Ghost till the completion of the sacred canon, and what do we find but the wickedness of man acted forth in a variety of shapes, together with the just judgments of God pursuing it with a variety of calamities thro' life, till death swallows them up in one undistinguished ruin! This is the general melancholy account of the human race as fallen! Then have we reason to look upon it as strange that we see and feel the like distresses and calamities with the world that has gone before us? Surely no. When we read in sacred or profane history of the unnatural wars that have arisen among those of the same nation, people and language, we are ready to be shock'd at the horrid scene, and to marvel at the outrage, cruelty and devastation that they will make of one another in such a contest! But if God did not restrain the wrath and wickedness of mankind, they would always be acting over the horrid scene, biting and devouring one another!

And the wickedness of the British nation, I mean of the governing part of them, has arrived to that pitch, that they are disposed to act over all that wickedness, cruelty and oppression that Pharaoh and the other cruel tyrants of the earth have been disposed to practise towards those in their power. Witness the cruel and unnatural war that they have levied against us; burning and laying waste many noble towns with a savage barbarity and wantonness of rage; abusing the prisoners that have fallen into their hands, with worse than savage barbarity! freezing and starving them to death with a relentless cruelty! so that the cries of those poor oppressed prisoners have entered, I trust, into the ears of the Lord of Sabbaoth, and that he has arisen to avenge their blood upon those inhumane butchers, who have come above 3000 miles to destroy their neighbours that are more righteous than they! This is the nation that heretofore has been famed for their humanity and generosity to their enemies, especially when prisoners, that have now sunk into such a degree of cruelty and barbarism that they can abuse them after they have surrendered, cane them, strip them of their clothing, and then drive them like a flock of sheep into prison, and there freeze and starve them to death! Oh how is the nation fallen and debased by the most sordid wickedness and inhumanity! and from once being famed for christianity, their conduct would disgrace the most barbarous nation on earth! Thus the wickedness of the human heart, without the restraints of divine grace, will act out a part not much inferior in vileness to that of infernals!

But then tho' I thus inveigh against the cruelty and wickedness of British administration and their sordid troops, yet I would by no means intimate that we are innocent and free from wickedness. No, God has a righteous controversy with us in this land; and our iniquities have arrived to that aggravated height, that they have called for these sore calamities that we feel! And the British nation are the rod of God's anger to scourge and chastise us for our sins, as the Assyrian monarch was to God's people of old. See Isa. 10.5, 6, 7. "Oh Assyrian, the rod of mine anger, and the staff in their hand is mine indignation! I will send him against an hypocritical nation, and against the people of my wrath will I give him a charge to take the spoil, and to take the prey and to tread them down as the mire of the streets; howbeit, he meaneth not so, neither doth his heart think so, but it is in his heart to destroy and cut off nations not a few," etc. Tho' this haughty tyrant had no design of executing God's will and the glory of his justice in punishing an hypocritical people, but only to enlarge his own empire and satisfy his own lusts by sacrificing multitudes of people to his own ambition and covetousness; yet God meant to use him as a rod and the instrument of his anger to chastise and correct his sinful, degenerate, backsliding people. And we have reason to think (let the designs of the British tyrant be what they will) that God designs him as the rod of his anger to correct us for the foul sins and abominations of this highly privileged land! Therefore let us be humble, kiss the rod and accept the punishment of our sins—repent and turn to God by an universal reformation—that God may be intreated for the land, spare his heritage, and not give it up to a reproach but restore to us our liberties as at the first, and our privileges as at the beginning.

EZRA STILES

❧

The United States Elevated to Glory and Honour

DEUTERONOMY XXVI. 19.
"And to make thee high above all nations which he hath made,
in praise, and in name, and in honour; and that thou mayest be
an holy people unto the Lord thy God."

Taught by the omniscient Deity, Moses foresaw and predicted the capital
events relative to Israel, through the successive changes of depression and
glory, until their final elevation to the first dignity and eminence among the
empires of the world. These events have been so ordered as to become a display of retribution and sovereignty; for while the good and evil, hitherto felt
by this people, have been dispensed in the way of exact sovereignty, with a
"not for your sakes, do I this, saith the Lord, be it known unto you—but for
mine holy name's sake."

However it may be doubted whether political Communities are rewarded
and punished in this world only; and whether the prosperity and decline of
other Empires have corresponded with their moral state, as to virtue and
vice: Yet the history of the Hebrew theocracy shews that the secular welfare
of God's ancient people depended upon their virtue, their religion, their observance of that holy covenant which Israel entered into with God on the
plains at the foot of Nebo on the other side Jordan. Here Moses, the man of
God, assembled three millions of people, the number of the United States, re-
capitulated and gave them a second publication of the sacred jural institute,
delivered thirty-eight years before, with the most awful solemnity at Mount
Sinai. A Law dictated with sovereign authority by the Most High to a people,
a world, a universe, becomes of invincible force and obligation without any

A sermon preached before Governor Jonathan Trumbull and the General Assembly of the State
of Connecticut, convened at Hartford at the Anniversary Election, May 8th, 1783. Second edition (Worcester, Mass.: Isaiah Thomas, 1785), pp. 5–9, 58–75, 88–92, 95–98.

reference to the consent of the governed. It is obligatory for three reasons, *viz.* its original justice and unerring equity, the omnipotent Authority by which it is enforced, and the sanctions of rewards and punishments. But in the case of Israel, he condescended to a mutual covenant; and by the hand of Moses led his people to avouch the Lord Jehovah to be their God, and in the most publick and explicit manner voluntarily to engage and covenant with God to keep and obey his Law. Thereupon this great prophet, whom God has raised up for so solemn a transaction, declared in the name of the Lord that the Most High avouched, acknowledged and took them for a peculiar people to himself; promising to be their God and Protector, and upon their obedience to make them prosperous and happy. Deut. xxix. 10 & 14. Chap. xxx. 9 & 19. He forsaw indeed their rejection of God and predicted the judicial chastisement of apostacy, a chastisement involving the righteous with the wicked. But as well to comfort and support the righteous in every age, and under every calamity, as to make his power known among all nations, God determined that a remnant should be saved. Whence Moses and the Prophets by divine direction interspersed their writings with promises that, when the ends of God's moral government should be answered in a series of national punishments, inflicted for a succession of ages, he would by his irresistible power and sovereign grace subdue the hearts of his people to a free, willing, joyful obedience; turn their captivity—recover and gather them "from all the nations whither the Lord their fathers possessed—and multiply them above their fathers—and rejoice over them for good, as he rejoiced over" their fathers. Deut. xxx 3 [-9]. Then the words of Moses, hitherto accomplished but in part, will be literally fulfilled; when this branch of the posterity of Abraham shall be nationally collected, and become a very distinguished and glorious people under the Great Messiah the Prince of Peace. He will then make them "high above all nations which he hath made in praise, and in name, and in honour," and they shall become "a holy people unto the Lord" their God.

I shall enlarge no further upon the primary sense and literal accomplishments of this and numerous other prophecies respecting both Jews and Gentiles, in the latter day glory of the church. For I have assumed the text only as introductory to a discourse upon the political welfare of God's American Israel, and as allusively prophetick of the future prosperity and splendour of the United States.

. . .

Already does the new constellation of the United States begin to realize this glory. It has already risen to an acknowledged sovereignty among the republicks and kingdoms of the world. And we have reason to hope, and I believe to expect, that God has still greater blessings in store for this vine which his own right hand hath planted, to make us "high among the nations in praise, and in name, and in honour." The reasons are very numerous, weighty, and conclusive.

In our civil constitutions, those impediments are removed which obstruct the progress of society towards perfection: Such, for instance, as respect the tenure of estates, and arbitrary government. The vassalage of dependent tenures, the tokens of ancient conquests by Goths and Tartars, still remain all over Asia and Europe. In this respect, as well as others, the world begins to open its eyes. One grand experiment in particular has lately been made. The present Empress of Russia, by granting lands in freehold in her vast wilderness of Volkouskile, together with religious liberty, has allured and already draughted from Poland and Germany a colonization of six hundred thousand souls in six years only, from 1762 to 1768.

Liberty, civil and religious, has sweet and attractive charms. The enjoyment of this, with property, has filled the English settlers in America with a most amazing spirit, which has operated, and still will operate, with great energy. Never before has the experiment been so effectually tried, of every man's reaping the fruits of his labour and feeling his share in the aggregate system of power. The ancient republicks did not stand on the people at large; and therefore no example or precedent can be taken from them. Even men of arbitrary principles will be obliged, if they would figure in these states, to assume the patriot so long that they will at length become charmed with the sweets of liberty.

Our degree of population is such as to give us reason to expect that this will become a great people. It is probable that within a century from our independence the sun will shine on fifty million of inhabitants in the United States. This will be a great, a very great nation, nearly equal to half Europe. Already has our colonization extended down the Ohio and to Koskaseah on the Mississippi. And if the present ratio of increase should be rather diminished in some of the elder settlements, yet an accelerated multiplication will attend our general propagation and overspread the whole territory westward for ages. So that before the Millennium, the English settlements in America may become more numerous millions than that greatest dominion on earth, the Chinese empire. Should this prove a future fact, how applicable would be the text, when the Lord shall have made his American Israel "high above all nations which he hat made," in numbers, "and in praise, and in name, and in honour!"

I am sensible some will consider these as visionary Utopian ideas. And so they would have judged had they lived in the apostolick age and been told that by the time of Constantine the empire would have become christian. As visionary that the twenty thousand souls which first settled New-England should be multiplied to near a million in a century and a half. As visionary that the Ottoman empire must fall by the Russian. As visionary to the Catholicks is the certain downfall of the Pontificate. As Utopian would it have been to the loyalists, at the battle of Lexington, that in less than eight years the independence and sovereignty of the United States should be acknowledged by four European sovereignties, one of which should be Britain herself. How wonderful the revolutions, the events of Providence! We live in an Age of Wonders. We have lived an age in a few years. We have seen more wonders accomplished in eight years than are usually unfolded in a century.

God be thanked, we have lived to see peace restored to this bleeding land, at least a general cessation of hostilities among the belligerent powers. And, on this occasion, does it not become us to reflect how wonderful, how gracious, how glorious has been the good hand of our God upon us in carrying us through so tremendous a warfare! We have sustained a force brought against us which might have made any empire on earth to tremble — and yet our bow has abode in strength; and having obtained help of God, we continue unto this day. Forced unto the last solemn appeal, America watched for the first blood: this was shed by Britons on the 19th of April, 1775; which instantly sprung an army of 20,000 into spontaneous existence, with the enterprizing and daring resolution of entering Boston and forcibly disburdening it of its bloody legions. Every patriot trembled until we had proved our armour, until it could be seen whether this hasty concourse was susceptible of exercitual arrangement and could face the enemy with firmness. They early gave us the decided proof of this, in the memorable battle of Bunker-Hill. We were satisfied. This instantly convinced us, and for the first time convinced Britons themselves, that Americans both would and could fight with great effect. Whereupon Congress put at the head of this spirited army the only man on whom the eyes of all Israel were placed. Posterity, I apprehend, and the world itself, inconsiderate and incredulous as they may be of the dominion of heaven, will yet do so much justice to the divine moral government as to acknowledge that this American Joshua was raised up by God and divinely formed by a peculiar influence of the Sovereign of the Universe for the great work of leading the armies of this American Joseph (now separated from his brethren) and conducting this people through the severe, the arduous conflict, to Liberty and Independence. Surprizing was it with what instant celerity men ascended and rose into generals and officers of every subordination; formed chiefly by the preparatory discipline of only the preceding year, 1774; when the arduous and spirit of military discipline was by heaven, and without concert, sent through the continent like lighting. Surprizing was it how soon the army was organized, took its formation, and rose into a firm system and impregnable arrangement.

To think of withstanding and encountering Britain by land was bold, and much more bold and daring by sea; yet we immediately began a navy and built ships of war with an unexampled expedition. It is presumed never was a 35 gun ship before built quicker than that well built and noble ship the *Raleigh*, which was finished from the keel and equipt for sea in a few months. Soon had we got, though small, a very gallant initial navy, which fought gallantly; and wanted nothing but numbers of ships for successful operations against that superior naval force before which we fell. We have, however, exhibited proof to posterity and the world that a powerful navy may be originated, built and equipped for service in a much shorter period than was before imagined. The British navy has been many centuries growing; and France, Holland, the Baltick powers, or any of the powers of this age, in twenty years may build navies of equal magnitude, if necessary for dominion, commerce, or ornament.

A variety of success and defeat hath attended our warfare both by sea and land. In our lowest and most dangerous estate in 1776 and 1777, we sustained ourselves against the British army of sixty thousand troops commanded by Howe, Burgoyne, Kniphausen, and Clinton, and other the ablest generals Britain could procure throughout Europe, with a naval force of 22,000 seamen in above eighty British men of war. These generals we sent home one after another, conquered, defeated, and convinced of the impossibility of subduing America. While oppressed by the heavy weight of this combined force, heaven inspired us with resolution to cut the Gordian knot when the die was cast irrevocably in the glorious act of INDEPENDENCE. This was sealed and confirmed by God Almighty in the victory of General Washington at Trenton, and in the surprizing movement and battle of Princeton; by which astonishing effort of generalship, General Howe, and the whole British army, in elated confidence and in open-mouthed march for Philadelphia, was instantly stopt, remanded back, and cooped up for a shivering winter in the little borough of Brunswick. Thus God "turned the battle to the gate"; and this gave a "finishing to the foundation" of the American republick. This with the Burgoynade at Saratoga by General Gates, and the glorious victory over the Earl of Cornwallis in Virgina, together with the memorable victory of Eutaw springs, and the triumphant recovery of the southern states by General Greene, are among the most heroick acts and brilliant atchievements which have decided the fate of America. And who does not see the indubitable interposition and energetick influence of Divine Providence in these great and illustrious events? Who but a Washington, inspired by heaven, could have struck out the great movement and manoeuvre of Princeton? To whom but the Ruler of the winds shall we ascribe it that the British reinforcement, in the summer of 1777, was delayed on the ocean three months by contrary winds, until it was too late for the conflagrating General Clinton to raise the siege of Saratoga? What but a providential miracle detected the conspiracy of Arnold, even in the critical moment of the execution of that infernal plot, in which the body of the American army, then at West-Point, with his Excellency General Washington himself, were to have been rended into the hands of the enemy! Doubtless inspired by the Supreme Illuminator of great minds were the joint councils of a Washington and a Rochambeau, in that grand effort of generalship with which they deceived and astonished a Clinton and eluded his vigilance in their transit by New-York and rapid marches for Virginia. Was it not of God that both the navy and army should enter the Chesapeak at the same time? Who but God could have ordained the critical arrival of the Gallick fleet, so as to prevent and defeat the British and assist and co-operate with the combined armies in the siege and reduction of York-Town? Should we not ever admire and ascribe to a supreme energy the wise and firm generalship displayed by General Greene, when (leaving the active, roving Cornwallis to pursue his helter-skelter ill-fated march into Virginia) he coolly and steadily went onwards and deliberately, judiciously, and heroically recovered the Carolinas and the southern states?

How rare have been the defections and apostacies of our capital characters, though tempted with all the charms of Gold, Titles, and Nobility? Whence is it that so few of our army have deserted to the enemy? Whence that our brave sailors have chosen the horrours of prison ships and death, rather than to fight against their country? Whence that men of every rank have so generally felt and spoken alike, as if the cords of life struck unison through the continent? What but a miracle has preserved the UNION OF THE STATES, the PURITY OF CONGRESS, and the unshaken PATRIOTISM OF EVERY GENERAL ASSEMBLY? It is God who has raised up for us a great and powerful ALLY, an ally which sent us a chosen army and a naval force; who sent us a Rochambeau and a Chatelleux, and other characters of the first military merit and eminence, to fight side by side with a Washington and a Lincoln, and the intrepid Americans, in the siege and battle of York-Town. It is God who so ordered the balancing interests of nations as to produce an irresistible motive in the European maritime powers to take our part. Hence the recognition of our independence by Spain and Holland, as well as France. Britain ought to have forseen that it must have given joy to surrounding nations, tired and wearied out with the insolence and haughtiness of her domineering flag, a flag which spreads terrour through the oceans of the terraqueous globe, to behold the era when their forces should have arrived to such maturity and strength that a junction of national navies would produce an aggregate force, adequate to the humiliation of Britain and her gallant and lofty navy. Nor could they resist the operation of this motive, prompting them to assist in the cutting off a member, with which the growing aggrandisment and power of Britain were connected; as thus she would be disarmed of terrour, and they should be at rest. If Britain doth not learn wisdom by these events and disclaim the sovereignty of the ocean, the junction of national navies will settle the point for her in less than half a century. So wonderfully does Divine Providence order the time and coincidence of the publick national motives, co-operating in effecting great publick events and revolutions.

But the time would fail me to recount the wonder working Providence of God in the events of this war. Let these serve as a specimen and lead us to hope that God will not forsake this people, for whom he has done such marvellous things (whereof we are glad and rejoice this day) having at length brought us to the dawn of Peace. O peace! thou welcome guest! all hail, thou heavenly visitant! calm the tumult of nations, and wave thy balmy wing to perpetuity over this region of liberty. Let there be a tranquil period for the unmolested accomplishment of the *Magnalia Dei*, the great events in God's moral government, designed from eternal ages to be displayed in these ends of the earth.

And here I beg leave to congratulate my country upon the termination of this cruel and unnatural war, the cessation of hostilities, and the prospect of peace. May this great event excite and elevate our first, our highest acknowledgments to the SOVEREIGN MONARCH of Universal Nature, to the Supreme Disposer and Controller of all Events; let our pious, sincere and devout gratitude ascend in one general effusion of heart-felt praise and hallelujah, in one united cloud of incense, even the incense of universal joy and thanksgiving to God, from the collective body of the United States.

And while we render our supreme honours to the Most High, the God of armies, let us recollect with affectionate honour the bold and brave sons of freedom, who willingly offered themselves and bled in the defence of their country. Our fellow-citizens, the Officers and Soldiers of the Patriot Army, who, with the Manlys, the Joneses, and other gallant commanders and brave seamen of the American navy, have heroically fought the war by sea and by land, merit of their once bleeding but now triumphant country, Laurels, Crowns, Rewards, and the highest honours. Never was the possession of arms used with more glory, or in a better cause, since the days of Joshua the son of Nun. O WASHINGTON! how do I love thy name! how have I often adored and blessed thy God for creating and forming thee the great ornament of human kind! upheld and protected by the Omnipotent, by the Lord of Hosts, thou hast been sustained and carried through one of the most arduous and most important wars in all history. The world and posterity will, with admiration, contemplate thy deliberate, cool, and stable judgment, thy virtues, thy valour and heroick atchievements, as far surpassing those of Cyrus, whom the world loved and adored. The sound of thy fame shall go out into all the earth, and extend to distant ages. Thou has convinced the world of the Beauty of Virtue—for in thee this Beauty shines with distinguished lustre. Those who would not recognize any beauty in virtue in the world beside will yet reverence it in thee. There is a glory in thy disinterested benevolence, which the greatest characters would purchase, if possible, at the expence of worlds, and which may excite indeed their emulation, but cannot be felt by the venal great—who think every thing, even virtue, and true glory, may be bought and sold, and trace our every action to motives terminating in self.

"Find virtue local, all relation scorn,
See all in self, and but for self be born."

But thou, O Washington, forgottest thyself, when thou lovedst thy bleeding country. Not all the gold of Phir, nor a world filled with rubies and diamonds could effect or purchase the sublime and noble feelings of thine heart in that single, self-moved act when thou renouncedst the Rewards of Generalship and heroically tookest upon thyself the dangerous as well as arduous office of our Generalissimo—and this at a solemn moment when thou didst deliberately cast the die for the dubious, the very dubious alternative of a gibbet or a Triumphal Arch. But beloved, enshielded and blessed by the great Melchizedeck, the King of Righteousness as well as peace, thou hast triumphed gloriously. Such has been thy military wisdom in the struggles of this arduous conflict, such a noble rectitude, amiableness and mansuetude of thy character, something is there so singularly glorious and venerable thrown by heaven about thee that not only does thy country love thee, but our very enemies stop the madness of their fire in full volley, stop the illiberality of their slander at thy name, as if rebuked from heaven with a "touch not mine anointed, and do my HERO no harm." Thy fame is of sweeter perfume than Arabian spices in the gardens of Persia. A Baron de Steuben shall waft its fragrance to the Monarch of Prussia; a Marquis de la Fayette shall waft it to a far greater Monarch and diffuse thy renown throughout Europe; listening angels shall catch the odour, waft it to heaven, and perfume the universe!

And now that our warfare is ended, do thou, O man of God, greatly beloved of the Most High, permit a humble minister of the blessed Jesus, who, though at a distance, has vigilantly accompanied thee through every stage of thy military progress, has watched thine every movement and danger with an heart-felt anxiety and solicitude; and who, with the most sincere and fervent wishes for thy safety and success, has not ceased day nor night to pray for thee and to commend thee and thy army to God—condescend to permit him to express his most cordial congratulations, and to share in the triumphs of thy bosom on this great and joyous occasion. We thank the Lord of Hosts that has given his servant to see his desire upon his enemies, and peace on Israel. And when thou shalt now at length retire from the fatigues of nine laborious campaigns to the tranquil enjoyment, to the sweetness and serenity of domestick life, may you never meet the fate of that ornament of arms and of humanity, the great Belisarius; but may a crown of universal reverence and honour of thy saved country, rest and flourish upon the head of its Veteran General and glorious Defender; until, by the divine Jesus, whom thou hast loved and adored, and of whose holy religion thou art not ashamed, thou shalt be translated from a world of war to a world of peace, liberty, and eternal triumph.

. . .

This great American revolution, this recent political phenomenon of a new sovereignty arising among the sovereign powers of the earth, will be attended to and contemplated by all nations. Navigation will carry the American flag around the globe itself and display the Thirteen Stripes and New Constellation at Bengal and Canton on the Indus and Ganges, on the Whang-ho and the Yang-tse-kiang; and with commerce will import the wisdom and literature of the east. That prophecy of Daniel is now literally fulfilling—there shall be an universal travelling "too and fro, and knowledge shall be increased." This knowledge will be brought home and treasured up in America: and being here digested and carried to the highest perfection, may reblaze back from America to Europe, Asia and Africa, and illumine the world with TRUTH and LIBERTY.

That great Civilian, Dr. John Adams, the learned and illustrious American Ambassadour, observes thus, "But the great designs of Providence must be accomplished;—great indeed! The progress of society will be accelerated by centuries by this revolution. The Emperour of Germany is adopting, as fast as he can, American Ideas of toleration and religious liberty: And it will become the fashionable system of Europe very soon. Light spreads from the day-spring in the west; and may it shine more and more until the perfect day."—So spreading may be the spirit for the restoration and recovery of long lost national rights, that even the Cortes of Spain may re-exist and resume their ancient splendour, authority, and control of royalty. The same principles of wisdom and enlightened politicks may establish rectitude in publick government throughout the world.

The most ample religious liberty will also probably obtain among all nations. Benevolence and religious lenity is increasing among the nations. The Reformed in France, who were formerly oppressed with heavy persecution, at present enjoy a good degree of religious liberty, though by silent indulgence only. A re-establishment of the edict of Nantz would honour the Grand Monarch by doing publick justice to a large body of his best and most loyal subjects. The Emperour of Germany, last year, published an imperial decree granting liberty for the free and unmolested exercise of the protestant religion within the Austrian territories and denominations. The Inquisition has been, in effect, this year suppressed in Spain, where the King, by an edict of 3d of November, 1782, proclaimed liberty for inhabitants of all religions: And by a happily conceived plan for literary reformation, the Aurora of science will speedily blaze into meridian splendour in that kingdom. An emulation for liberty and science is enkindled among the nations and will doubtless produce something very liberal and glorious in this age of science, this period of the empire of reason.

The United States will embosom all the religious sects or denominations in Christendom. Here they may all enjoy their whole respective systems of worship and church government, complete. . . .

Little would Civilians have thought ages ago that the world should ever look to America for models of government and polity. Little did they think of finding this most perfect polity among the poor outcasts, the contemptible people of New-England, and particularly in the long despised civil polity of Connecticit; a polity conceived by the sagacity and wisdom of a Winthrop, a Wyllys, a Ludlow, Haynes, Hopkins, Hooker, and the other first settlers of Hartford, in 1636. And while Europe and Asia may hereafter learn that the most liberal principles of law and civil polity are to be found on this side of the Atlantick, they may also find the true religion here depurated from the rust and corruption of ages, and learn from us to reform and restore the church to its primitive purity. It will be long before the ecclesiastical pride of the splendid European hierarchies can submit to learn wisdom from those whom they have been inured to look upon with sovereign contempt. But candid and liberal disquisition will sooner or later have a great effect. Removed from the embarrassments of corrupt systems, and the dignities and blinding opulence connected with them, the unfettered mind can think with a noble enlargement, and with an unbounded freedom go wherever the light of truth directs. Here will be no bloody tribunals, no cardinals inquisitors-general, to bend the human mind, forcibly to control the understanding, and put out the light of reason, the candle of the Lord, in man; to force an innocent Galileo to renounce truths demonstrable as the light of day. Religion may here receive its last, most liberal, and impartial examination. Religious liberty is peculiarly friendly to fair and generous disquisition. Here deism will have its full chance; nor need libertines more to complain of being overcome by any weapons but the gentle, the powerful ones of argument and truth. Revelation will be found to stand the test to the ten thousandth examination.

There are three coetaneous events to take place whose fruition is certain from prophecy, the annihilation of the Pontificate, the reassembling of the Jews, and the fulness of the Gentiles. That liberal and candid disquisition of Christianity, which will most assuredly take place in America, will prepare Europe for the first event, with which the other will be connected, when, especially on the return of the twelve tribes to the Holy Land, there will burst forth a degree of evidence hitherto unperceived and of efficacy to convert a world. More than three quarters of mankind yet remain heathen. Heaven put a stop to the propagation of Christianity when the church became corrupted with the adoration of numerous deities and images, because this would have been only exchanging an old friend for a new idolatry. Nor is Christendom now larger than it was nine centuries ago. The promising prospects of the *Propaganda fide* at Rome are coming to nothing: and it may be of the divine destiny that all other attempts for gospeling the nations of the earth shall prove fruitless, until the present Christendom itself be recovered to the primitive purity and simplicity. At which time, instead of the Babel confusion of contradicting missionaries, all will harmoniously concur in speaking one language, one holy faith, one apostolick religion to an unconverted world. At this period, and in effecting this great event, we have reason to think that the United States may be of no small influence and consideration. It was of the Lord to send Joseph into Egypt, to save much people, and to shew forth his praise. It is of the Lord that "a woman clothed with the sun, and the moon under her feet," and upon "her head a crown of twelve stars," (not to say thirteen) should "flee into the wilderness, where she hath a place prepared of God" (Rev. xii. 1 & 6), and where she might be the repository of Wisdom, and "keep the commandments of God, and have the testimony of Jesus." It may have been of the Lord that Christianity is to be found in such great purity in this church exiled into the wilderness of America; and that its purest body should be evidently advancing forward, by an augmented natural increase and spiritual edification, into a singular superiority—with the ultimate subserviency to the glory of God, in converting the world.

. . .

SAMUEL LANGDON

The Republic of the Israelites
an Example to the American States

DEUTERONOMY IV. 5–8.
"Behold, I have taught you statutes and judgments, even as
the Lord my God commanded me, that ye should do so in the land whither
ye go to possess it. Keep therefore and do them; for this is your wisdom and your
understanding in the sight of the nations, who shall hear all these statues, and say,
surely this great nation is a wise and understanding people: for what nation is there so
great, which hath God so nigh unto them as the Lord our God is in all things that
we call upon him for? and what nation is there so great, which hath statutes and
judgments so righteous as all this law which I set before you this day?"

Here Moses recommends to Israel the strict observance of all the laws which
he had delivered to them by God's command, relating both to their civil polity
and religion, as the sure way to raise their reputation high among all nations
as a wise and understanding people; because no other nation was blessed with
such excellent national law, or the advantage of applying to the oracle of the
living God, and praying to him in all difficulties with assurance that all their
requests would be answered.

As to every thing excellent in their constitution of government, except
what was peculiar to them as a nation separated to God from the rest of mankind, the Israelites may be considered as a pattern to the world in all ages; and
from them we may learn what will exalt our character, and what will depress
and bring us to ruin.

Let us therefore look over their constitution and laws, enquire into their
practice, and observe how their prosperity and fame depended on their strict
observance of the divine commands both as to their government and religion.

They had both a civil and military establishment under divine direction,
and a complete body of judicial laws drawn up and delivered to them by

A sermon preached at Concord, New Hampshire, before the General Court at the Annual Election, June 5, 1788. (Exeter, N.H.: Lamson and Ranlet, 1788), pp. 6–15, 17–19, 29–43, 45–48.

Moses in God's name. They had also a form of religious worship by the same authority, minutely prescribed, designed to preserve among them the knowledge of the great Creator of the Universe, and teach them to love and serve him, while idolatry prevailed through the rest of the world. And this religion contained not only a public ritual, but a perfect, though very concise, system of morals, comprehended in ten commands, which require the perfection of godliness, benevolence, and rectitude of conduct.

When first the Israelites came out from the bondage of Egypt, they were a multitude without any other order than what had been kept up, very feebly, under the ancient patriarchal authority. They were suddenly collected into a body under the conduct of Moses, without any proper national or military regulation. Yet in the short space of about three months after they had passed the red sea, they were reduced into such civil and military order, blended together by the advice of Jethro, as was well adapted to their circumstances in the wilderness while destitute of property. Able men were chosen out of all their tribes, and made captains and rulers of thousands, hundreds, fifties and tens: and these commanded them as military officers and acted as judges in matters of common controversy.

But the great thing wanting was a permanent constitution, which might keep the people peaceable and obedient while in the desert and after they had gained possession of the promised land. Therefore, upon the complaint of Moses that the burden of government was too heavy for him, God commanded him to bring seventy men, chosen from among the elders and officers, and present them at the tabernacle; and there he endued them with the same spirit which was in Moses, that they might bear the burden with him. Thus a Senate was evidently constituted, as necessary for the future government of the nation, under a chief commander. And as to the choice of this Senate, doubtless the people were consulted, who appear to have had a voice in all public affairs from time to time, the whole congregation being called together on all important occasions. The government therefore was a proper republic.

And beside this general establishment, every tribe had elders and a prince according to the patriarchal order, with which Moses did not interfere; and these had an acknowledged right to meet and consult together, and with the consent of the congregation do whatever was necessary to preserve good order and promote the common interest of the tribe. So that the government of each tribe was very similar to the general government. There was a President and Senate at the head of each, and the people assembled and gave their voice in all great matters: for in those ages the people in all republics were entirely unacquainted with the way of appointing delegates to act for them, which is a very excellent modern improvement in the management of republics.

Moreover, to complete the establishment of civil government, courts were to be appointed in every walled city, after their settlement in Canaan, and elders most distinguished for wisdom and integrity were to be made judges, ready always to sit and decide the common controversies within their respective jurisdictions. The people had a right likewise to appoint such other officers as they might think necessary for the more effectual execution of justice, according to that order given in Deut. 16.18, 19. . . . But from these courts an appeal was allowed in weighty causes to higher courts appointed over the whole tribe, and in very great and difficult cases to the supreme authority of the general Senate and chief magistrate.

A government, thus settled on republican principles, required laws, without which it must have degenerated immediately into aristocracy or absolute monarchy. But God did not leave a people, wholly unskilled in legislation, to make laws for themselves. He took this important matter wholly into his own hands, and beside the moral laws of the two tables, which directed their conduct as individuals, gave them by Moses a complete code of judicial laws. They were not numerous indeed, but concise and plain and easily applicable to almost every controversy which might arise between man and man, and every criminal case which might require the judgment of the court. Of these some were peculiarly adapted to their national form, as divided into tribes and families always to be kept distinct; others were especially suited to the peculiar nature of the government as a theocracy, God himself being eminently their king and manifesting himself among them in a visible manner, by the cloud of glory in the tabernacle and temple. This was the reason why blasphemy and all obstinate disobedience to his laws were considered as high treason and punished with death, especially idolatry, as being a crime against the fundamental principles of the constitution. But far the greater part of the judicial laws were founded on the plain immutable principles of reason, justice, and social virtue, such as are always necessary for civil society. Life and property were well guarded, and punishments were equitably adapted to the nature of every crime. In particular, murder stands foremost among capital crimes and is defined with such precision, and so clearly distinguished from all cases of accidental and undesigned killing, that the innocent were in no danger of punishment and the guilty could not escape. And if we still pay regard to this divine law, which is evidently founded on reason and justice, the modern distinction of manslaughter must be rejected as a popish invention, contrived and added in times when superstition reigned and claimed a power above all laws. These laws were sufficient for a nation which had but little commerce abroad, especially as the oracle of Jehovah might be consulted in all cases of a very extraordinary nature.

Let us now consider the national worship which God established among his people, on which their obedience to the moral law very much depended. For unless they paid constant reverence and homage to their God, agreeable to his nature and will, they would soon break loose from all other obligations to morality.

Now as to their ritual; however contemptible, and even ridiculous, it may seem to men whose ideas are all modern and who proudly contemn divine revelation, and notwithstanding it is now abrogated by a far more glorious revelation of grace and truth by Jesus Christ, no religious institution could be more perfectly accommodated to those early ages of the world, and the situation of the Israelites in the midst of idolaters, or better prepare the way for the truth and mercy of the gospel. In those ages the minds of men were not sufficiently cultivated to receive that religion which is spiritual and simple, detached from sensible objects, and destitute of worldly grandeur. Other nations worshipped their gods with an endless variety of superstitious rites, a multitude of costly sacrifices, and all kinds of external pomp, which they fancied would be acceptable to deities to whom they attributed the imperfections and even the worst vices of men. Their worship gratified all the senses, was accommodated to every passion and lust, and indulgent to gross immoralities; it not only captivated vulgar minds, but bound the greatest heroes, politicians, and philosophers fast in the chains of superstition. Therefore it was necessary that the worship of the true God should not be destitute of that splendour which, in those ages, struck the minds of men with awe and reverence. Without some magnificence the best religion would have appeared contemptible in the view of the world; and the Israelites themselves, dazzled with the pageantry of idols, would almost inevitably have been captivated; as, notwithstanding every guard which could be placed about them, we find the fashion of the rest of the world had surprising power over them. But the ceremonies of worship which God commanded his people to observe were not, like those of the heathen, inhuman, frantic, obscene, varied a thousand ways according to the different characters of their gods; no, but by infinite wisdom they were calculated to promote the knowledge of the divine perfections and obedience to the laws of righteousness, and give the most encouraging hope in the goodness and mercy of God. The ritual of the Israelites was rational, sober, uniform, plainly intended to exhibit the majesty, purity, and mercy of the eternal king; to humble men before him under a continual sense of guilt; and to assure true penitents of free pardon by virtue of the appointed sacrifices, which were types of that one sacrifice which Christ has offered for the sins of the world. And to render their worship more striking, in their own view and in the eyes of the world, their tabernacle and temple, their priesthood with its ornaments, their solemn assemblies and great festivals, were decent and magnificent beyond every thing seen among the nations around.

How unexampled was this quick progress of the Israelites from abject slavery, ignorance, and almost total want of order to a national establishment perfected in all its parts far beyond all other kingdoms and States! from a mere mob to a well regulated nation, under a government and laws far superior to what any other nation could boast!

. . .

Upon a review of what has been said, must it not appear quite unaccountable that the Israelites should so speedily attain to such an height of good policy and legislation, beyond all other nations? Are we not constrained to acknowledge an immediate interposition and direction of heaven? Had the unexperienced multitude been left to themselves to draw up a system of civil and military government for themselves, it would have been entirely beyond their abilities to comprehend so complicated a subject; they must have committed innumerable mistakes, in attempting to introduce and establish it; they would have been in danger of jarring opinions, tumults, and insurrections; and probably before the design could be effected, discouragement and confusion would have forced them to surrender into the hands of despotism. But their God provided every thing necessary for their happiness, and nothing more was left to their own wisdom than to submit to his authority and adhere strictly to his commands. By this, their reputation among the nations would have been equal to the excellency of their laws.

But now you may say, Why then were they not universally celebrated? Why did not princes and politicians from all parts of the world visit them, to learn maxims of polity from so well regulated a nation? Why did not philosophers come and enquire into that system of religion and morality which carried virtue to such an height of perfection? Surely a nation, of which all the parts were so firmly cemented, must be strong and formidable. A people who enjoyed the most rational liberty and yet were under the most voluntary and absolute subjection to authority, free from all the convulsions and revolutions which frequently arise from the raging folly of the populace, must become famous. A wise and impartial administration of justice, according to the most excellent laws, by which all were kept in perfect security and peace, could not but be admired. And the commerce of a people whose morals were governed by the best precepts, whose word might be trusted, who practised no kind of fraud, and whose behavior was always benevolent, sober, prudent, and sincere must be highly valued by the world. Whereas on the contrary, the Israelites were often weak, distressed, and generally despised and hated by all their neighbours. The plain answer to this objection is—They never adhered in practice either to the principles of their civil polity or religion, but on their practice depended the prosperity and honor of the nation. They received their law from God, but they did not keep it. They neglected their government, corrupted their religion, and grew dissolute in their morals, and in such a situation no nation under heaven can prosper.

. . .

And now, my fellow Citizens, and much honored Fathers of the State, you may be ready to ask—"To what purpose is this long detail of antiquated history on this public occasion?" I answer—Examples are better than precepts; and history is the best instructor both in polity and morals. I have presented you with the portrait of a nation, highly favoured by Heaven with civil and religious institutions, who yet, by not improving their advantages, forfeited their blessings and brought contempt and destruction on themselves. If I am not mistaken, instead of the twelve tribes of Israel, we may substitute the thirteen States of the American union and see this application plainly offering itself, *viz.* That as God in the course of his kind providence hath given you an excellent constitution of government, founded on the most rational, equitable, and liberal principles by which all that liberty is secured which a people can reasonably claim, and you are impowered to make righteous laws for promoting public order and good morals; and as he has moreover given you by his Son Jesus Christ, who is far superior to Moses, a complete revelation of his will and a perfect system of true religion, plainly delivered in the sacred writings; it will be your wisdom in the eyes of the nations, and your true interest and happiness, to conform your practice in the strictest manner to the excellent principles of your government, adhere faithfully to the doctrines and commands of the gospel, and practice every public and private virtue. By this you will increase in numbers, wealth, and power, and obtain reputation and dignity among the nations; whereas, the contrary conduct will make you poor, distressed and contemptible.

The God of heaven hath not indeed visibly displayed the glory of his majesty and power before our eyes, as he came down in the sight of Israel on the burning mount; nor has he written with his own finger the laws of our civil polity. But the signal interpositions of divine providence, in saving us from the vengeance of a powerful irritated nation from which we were unavoidably separated by their inadmissible claim of absolute parliamentary power over us; in giving us a WASHINGTON to be captain-general of our armies; in carrying us through the various distressing scenes of war and desolation, and making us twice triumphant over numerous armies, surrounded and captivated in the midst of their career; and finally giving us peace with a large territory and acknowledged independence; all these laid together fall little short of real miracles and an heavenly charter of liberty for these United States. And when we reflect how wonderfully the order of these states was preserved when government was dissolved, or supported only by feeble props; with how much sobriety, wisdom, and unanimity they formed and received the diversified yet similar constitutions in the different states; with what prudence, fidelity, patience, and success the Congress have managed the general government under the great disadvantages of a very imperfect and impotent confederation; we cannot but acknowledge that God hath graciously patronized our cause and taken us under his special care, as he did his ancient covenant people.

Or we may consider the hand of God in another view. Wisdom is the gift of God, and social happiness depends on his providencial government; therefore, if these states have framed their constitutions with superior wisdom and secured their natural rights and all the advantages of society with greater precaution than other nations, we may with good reason affirm that God hath give us our government; that he hath taught us good statutes and judgments, tending to make us great and respectable in the view of the world. Only one thing more remains to complete his favor toward us, which is the establishment of a general government, as happily formed as our particular constitutions, for the perfect union of these states. Without this, all that we glory in is lost; but if this should be effected, we may say with the greatest joy—"*God hath done great things for us.*" The general form of such a constitution hath already been drawn up, and presented to the people, by a convention of the wisest and most celebrated patriots in the land. Eight of the states have approved and accepted it, with full testimonies of joy. And if it passes the scrutiny of the whole, and recommends itself to be universally adopted, we shall have abundant reason to offer elevated thanksgivings to the supreme Ruler of the universe for a government completed under his direction.[1]

Now our part is to make a wise improvement of what God grants us, and not neglect or despise our distinguishing privileges. For the best constitution, badly managed, will soon fall and be changed into anarchy or tyranny. Without constant care of your families, you will have bad servants and your estates will be wasted. So we must pay constant attention to the great family, if we desire to be a free and happy people.

The power in all our republics is acknowledged to originate in the people: it is delegated by them to every magistrate and officer; and to the people all in authority are accountable, if they deviate from their duty and abuse their power. Even the man who may be advanced to the chief command of these United States, according to the proposed constitution; whose office resembles

1. Soon after this Sermon was delivered, the Convention of the State of New Hampshire, met according to adjournment, and on the twenty first day of June accepted the proposed general Constitution of government. This being the ninth State which has acceded to this form of national Union, it will be carried into effect; and there is no reason to doubt of the speedy accession of all the other States, which are now debating on the important question. May all rejoice in the Lord, who has formed us into a nation, and honour him as our Judge, Lawgiver, and King, who hath saved us, and will save us from all enemies and fears, if we thankfully receive and rightly improve his great mercies.

that of a king in other nations, which has always been thought so sacred that they have had no conception of bringing a king before the bar of justice; even he depends on the choice of the people for his temporary and limited power and will be liable to impeachment, trial, and disgrace for any gross misconduct. On the people, therefore, of these United-States it depends whether wise men, or fools, good or bad men, shall govern them; whether they shall have righteous laws, a faithful administration of government, and permanent good order, peace, and liberty; or, on the contrary, feel insupportable burdens and see all their affairs run to confusion and ruin.

Therefore, I will now lift up my voice and cry aloud to the people, to the people of this State in particular, whom I will consider as present by their representatives and rulers, and the congregation here collected from various towns—RISE! RISE to fame among all nations, as a wise and understanding people! political life and death are set before you; be a free, numerous, well ordered, and happy people! The way has been plainly set before you; if you pursue it, your prosperity is sure; but if not, distress and ruin will overtake you.

Preserve your government with the utmost attention and solicitude, for it is the remarkable gift of heaven. From year to year be careful in the choice of your representatives and all the highest powers of government. Fix your eyes upon men of good understanding and known honesty; men of knowledge, improved by experience; men who fear God and hate covetousness; who love truth and righteousness, and sincerely wish the public welfare. Beware of such as are cunning rather than wise; who prefer their own interest to every thing; whose judgment is partial or fickle; and whom you would not willingly trust with your own private interests. When meetings are called for the choice of your rulers, do not carelessly neglect them or give your votes with indifference, just as any party may persuade or a sordid treat tempt you; but act with serious deliberation and judgment, as in a most important matter, and let the faithful of the land serve you. Let not men openly irreligious and immoral become your legislators; for how can you expect good laws to be made by men who have no fear of God before their eyes, and who boldly trample on the authority of his commands? And will not the example of their impiety and immorality defeat the efficacy of the best laws which can be made in favour of religion and virtue? If the legislative body are corrupt, you will soon have bad men for Counsellors, corrupt Judges, unqualified Justices, and officers in every department who will dishonor their stations; the consequence of which will be murmurs and complaints from every quarter. Let a superior character point out the man who is to be your head, for much depends on his inspection and care of public affairs and the influence of his judgment, advice and conduct, although his power is circumscribed. In this choice therefore be always on your guard against parties and the methods taken to make interest for unworthy men, and let distinguished merit always determine your vote. And when all places in government are filled with the best men you can find, behave your-selves as good subjects: obey the laws, cheerfully submit to such taxation as the necessities of the public call for, give tribute to whom tribute is due, custom to whom custom, fear to whom fear, and honor to whom honor, as the gospel commands you. Never give countenance to turbulent men, who wish to dis-tinguish themselves and rise to power by forming combinations and exciting insurrections against government. For this can never be the right way to re-dress real grievances, since you may not only prefer complaints and petitions to the court but have the very authority, which you think has been misused, in your own power and may very shortly place it in other hands. How happy was it for this state that the insurrection, attempted here two years ago, was so seasonably and with so little difficulty suppressed, when the neighbouring state was brought into such a difficult and critical situation by the distracted populace and has now scarcely recovered from that violent political paroxism.[2]

I call upon you also to support schools in all your towns, that the rising generation may not grow up in ignorance. Grudge not any expense propor-tionate to your abilities. It is a debt you owe to your children and that God to whom they belong, a necessary evidence of your regard for their present and future happiness and of your own concern to transmit the blessings you yourselves enjoy to future generations. The human mind without early and continual cultivation grows wild and savage: knowledge must be instilled as its capacities gradually enlarge, or it cannot expand and extend its sphere of activity. Without instruction men can have no knowledge but what comes from their own observation and experience, and it will be a long time be-fore they can be acquainted even with things most necessary for the support and comfort of the present life. Leave your children untaught to read, write, cypher, etc. teach them no trade, or husbandry; let them grow up wholly without care; and they will be more fit for a savage than civil life, and what-ever inheritance you may think to leave them will be of no advantage. But, on the contrary, train them up in the fear of God, in an acquaintance with his word, and all such useful knowledge as your abilities will allow, and they will soon know how to provide for themselves, perhaps may take care of their aged parents, and fill the various stations in life with honor and advantage. Look round and see the growing youth: they are to succeed in your stead; government and religion must be continued by them; from among these will shortly rise up our legislators, judges, ministers of the gospel, and officers of every rank. Can you think of this and not promote schools, academies, and

2. [The insurrection of the "neighboring state" refers to Shays' Rebellion in Massachusetts, the most explosive of a number of relatively bloodless revolts growing out of postwar financial readjustment and representing the protest of poor farmers against heavy taxes and payment of debts. —Editor]

colleges? Can you leave the youth uninstructed in any thing which may prepare them to act their part well in the world? Will you suffer ignorance to spread its horrid gloom over the land? An ignorant people will easily receive idolatry for their religion and must bow their necks to the tyrant's yoke, because they are incapable of using rational liberty. Will you then consign over your posterity to foolish and abominable superstitions instead of religion, and to be the slaves of despotism, when a small proportion of the produce of your labours will make them wise, free, and happy?

Will you hear me patiently a little farther, while I say one thing more of very great importance which I dare not suppress. I call upon you to preserve the knowledge of God in the land and attend to the revelation written to us from heaven. If you neglect or renounce that religion taught and commanded in the holy scriptures, think no more of freedom, peace, and happiness; the judgments of heaven will pursue you. Religion is not a vain thing for you because it is your life: it has been the glory and defence of New-England from the infancy of the settlements; let it be also our glory and protection. I mean no other religion than what is divinely prescribed, which God himself has delivered to us with equal evidence of his authority, and even superior to that given to Israel, and which he has as strictly commanded us to receive and observe. The holy scriptures are given as the only rule of our faith, worship and obedience, and if we are guided by this perfect rule, we shall keep the way of truth and righteousness and obtain the heavenly glory. We are now no more at liberty to draw up schemes of religion for ourselves according to our own deceitful reasonings and vain imaginations, or to comply with the traditions and commands of men, or fall in with the refinements of human wisdom and the fashionable sentiments of the world, than Israel was to substitute modes of serving God different from what he had expressly required. We must believe what the Son of God, who made the worlds and was sent by the Father with a proclamation of mercy to mankind, has declared to us. He died to redeem men from the servitude of sin and reconcile them to God that they may be raised to life eternal. And he is appointed to be like a second Moses, the captain of our salvation to conduct us to heaven. To him therefore we must hearken in all things. The principal doctrines of his gospel are quite simple, plain and important. He teaches us that the commands of God reach to the inward thoughts, principles, and affections of the heart, as well as the outward conduct, and are as pure and perfect as the divine nature; that according to the laws of his moral government all men are sinners and must repent in order to obtain mercy; that remission of sins is obtained only by believing on his name and through his blood shed for us on the cross; that his disciples must receive his word, and obey whatsoever he hath commanded, endeavoring to be holy in all manner of conversation and avoid all the vices and corruptions of the world; that there will be a resurrection from the dead both of the just and unjust and a day of solemn judgment, when all mankind must give an account of their conduct in this world and receive their sentence from him whom the Father hath constituted to be the judge; and that in consequence of their sentence mankind will depart into very opposite states, the wicked into everlasting punishment and the righteous into life eternal, the present visible system of nature being then dissolved in flames. In the belief of these plain truths, and that worship and obedience connected with them, the religion of christians consists. As to worship, no multiplied forms and punctilious ceremonies are prescribed, which only serve to throw a veil over the mind; no certain modes are made necessary; but we must worship God, who is a spirit, in spirit and in truth, by prayer and praise, with love and fear, hope and joy. For such worship christians are united into societies called churches and are required to assemble every Lord's day, that they may glorify God with one heart and voice and be instructed and edified by his word and the two only ordinances of baptism and the Lord's supper, which are very simple but well adapted to the nature and design of our religion.

The christian religion, therefore, is confined to no particular nation, sect, or denomination but is designed to call all men to repentance and newness of life; to encourage their hope in the mercy of god, thro' the only mediator Jesus Christ; persuade them to the most cheerful, persevering obedience; and comfort them, under all the labours and sorrows of the world and the natural dread of death, with the assurance of a glorious immortality. This religion may be believed and practised, so as to answer the main purposes of it, under the various forms in which christian churches now appear: just as the principal ends of civil government may be obtained under the various constitutions which have taken place in different nations, however one may be much more eligible than another.

. . .

My subject hath led me into this long and earnest address to the people. But it suggests some things which may properly be addressed to this honorable court. Will you hear me patiently, while with the utmost respect I say a few words to excite the wise reflections of your own minds.

You will consider that you assemble from time to time as fathers of the large family, which depends on you to take care of its general welfare, and that no local views ought to govern you, nor partial instructions of your constituents bind you to act contrary to the clear conviction of your own minds. You will be cautious of forming parties for any selfish purposes, and of being too hasty in determining important matters, or too slow in your proceedings when business is urgent. In order to form a wise judgment of every thing that comes before you, you are sensible of the propriety of examining things to the bottom, attending patiently to every argument on both sides, and asking conscience, rather than any friend, what ought to be done. Like frugal householders you will save all unnecessary expences and take good care of the treasury, but not suffer the faithful servants of the State to be so stinted in their reward as to discourage them from their duty. Lay no grievous burdens on the people beyond their abilities, but take the earliest, easiest, and most righteous methods to reduce and pay off the public debt, unhappily involved in all the perplexities occasioned by boundless emissions of depreciating paper notes. Be liberal, yet frugal, in grants of money, according to the exigencies of the public. Let no laws be wanting which good order and the proper administration of government and justice require; but make no law which establisheth iniquity. And may I propose it, as worthy of your consideration, whether some reformation may not be necessary as to processes in our courts of justice; whether appeals from court to court are not allowed beyond reason and equity, in the plainest cases, and of too trivial value: by which some of our courts are made mere vehicles, justice is delayed, and the law made unnecessarily expensive, tedious and vexatious; and whether some method may not be thought of to determine the judgment of causes in lower or higher courts in proportion to their value and importance. I beg leave to say one word as to religion. With respect to articles of faith or modes of worship, civil authority have no right to establish religion. The people ought to choose their own ministers and their own denominations, as our laws now permit them; but as far as religion is connected with the morals of the people and their improvement in knowledge, it becomes of great importance to the state; and legislators may well consider it as part of their concern for the public welfare to make provision that all the towns may be furnished with good teachers, that they may be impowered to make valid contracts, and that the fulfilment of such contracts should be secured against the fickle humours of men who are always ready to shift from sect to sect or make divisions in parishes that they may get free from all legal obligations to their ministers. Perhaps a little addition to the law already in force in this state might sufficiently secure the continuance of religious instruction, enlarge rather than diminish liberty of conscience, and prevent envyings, contentions, and crumbling into parties. Will you permit me now to pray in behalf of the people, that all the departments of government may be constantly filled with the wisest and best men; that his excellency the President may have the assistance of an able and faithful Council; that the administration of justice may be in the hands of judges and justices well qualified for their offices, who will not take bribes or in any manner pervert judgment; in a word, that the constitution established may in every respect be well supported by your care, and that the people may know the blessings of good government by the union of your counsels and the wisdom of your proceedings. May the Almighty King of kings always be in the midst of you, direct and assist you, impress your hearts with his fear, and grant present and future blessings in reward of your fidelity.

And now if I have delivered words of truth, agreeably to my text, and pointed out the sure way to be a prosperous and happy people, may these things sink deep into your hearts and be accompanied with the divine blessing! May the general government of these United States, when established, appear to be the beset which the nations have yet known and be exalted by uncorrupted religion and morals! And may the everlasting gospel diffuse its Heavenly light and spread Righteousness, Liberty, and Peace thro' the whole world.

THOMAS JEFFERSON

First Inaugural Address

March 4, 1801

Friends and Fellow-Citizens:

Called upon to undertake the duties of the first executive office of our
country, I avail myself of the presence of that portion of my fellow-citizens
which is here assembled to express my grateful thanks for the favor with which
they have been pleased to look toward me, to declare a sincere consciousness
that the task is above my talents, and that I approach it with those anxious
and awful presentiments which the greatness of the charge and the weakness
of my powers so justly inspire. A rising nation, spread over a wide and fruitful
land, traversing all the seas with the rich productions of their industry, engaged in commerce with nations who feel power and forget right, advancing
rapidly to destinies beyond the reach of the mortal eye—when I contemplate
these transcendent objects, and see the honor, the happiness, and the hopes
of this beloved country committed to the issue, and the auspices of this day,
I shrink from the contemplation, and humble myself before the magnitude
of the undertaking. Utterly, indeed, should I despair did not the presence of
many whom I here see remind me that in the other high authorities provided
by our Constitution I shall find resources of wisdom, of virtue, and of zeal on
which to rely under all difficulties. To you, then, gentlemen, who are charged
with the sovereign functions of legislation, and to those associated with you,
I look with encouragement for that guidance and support which may enable
us to steer with safety the vessel in which we are all embarked amidst the
conflicting elements of a troubled world.

During the contest of opinion through which we have passed the anima-
tion of discussions and of exertions has sometimes worn an aspect which
might impose on strangers unused to think freely and to speak and to write
what they think; but this being now decided by the voice of the nation, an-

From *Inaugural Addresses of the Presidents of the United States* (Washington, D.C.: Government
Printing Office, 1965), pp. 13–16.

nounced according to the rules of the Constitution, all will, of course, arrange themselves under the will of the law, and unite in common efforts for the common good. All, too, will bear in mind this sacred principle, that though the will of the majority is in all cases to prevail, that will to be rightful must be reasonable; that the minority possesses their equal rights, which equal law must protect, and to violate would be oppression. Let us, then, fellow-citizens, unite with one heart and one mind. Let us restore to social inter-course that harmony and affection without which liberty and even life itself are but dreary things. And let us reflect that, having banished from our land that religious intolerance under which mankind so long bled and suffered, we have yet gained little if we countenance a political intolerance as despotic, as wicked, and capable of as bitter and bloody persecutions. During the throes and convulsions of the ancient world, during the agonizing spasms of infuri-ated man, seeking through blood and slaughter his long-lost liberty, it was not wonderful that the agitation of the billows should reach even this distant and peaceful shore; that this should be more felt and feared by some and less by others, and should divide opinions as to measures of safety. But every dif-ference of opinion is not a difference of principle. We have called by different names brethren of the same principle. We are all Republicans, we are all Fed-eralists. If there be any among us who would wish to dissolve this Union or to change its republican form, let them stand undisturbed as monuments of the safety with which error of opinion may be tolerated where reason is left free to combat it. I know, indeed, that some honest men fear that a republican government can not be strong, that this Government is not strong enough; but would the honest patriot, in the full tide of successful experiment, aban-don a government which has so far kept us free and firm on the theoretic and visionary fear that this Government, the world's best hope, may by possibility want energy to preserve itself? I trust not. I believe this, on the contrary, the strongest Government on earth. I believe it the only one where every man, at the call of the law, would fly to the standard of the law, and would meet in-vasions of the public order as his own personal concern. Sometimes it is said that man can not be trusted with the government of himself. Can he, then, be trusted with the government of others? Or have we found angels in the forms of kings to govern him? Let history answer this question.

Let us, then, with courage and confidence pursue our own Federal and Re-publican principles, our attachment to union and representative government. Kindly separated by nature and a wide ocean from the exterminating havoc of one quarter of the globe; too high-minded to endure the degradations of the others; possessing a chosen country, with room enough for our descen-dants to the thousandth and thousandth generation; entertaining a due sense of our equal right to the use of our own faculties, to the acquisitions of our own industry, to honor and confidence from our fellow-citizens, resulting not from birth, but from our actions and their sense of them; enlightened by a benign religion, professed, indeed, and practiced in various forms, yet all of them inculcating honesty, truth, temperance, gratitude, and the love of man; acknowledging and adoring an overruling Providence, which by all its dispensations proves that it delights in the happiness of man here and his greater happiness hereafter—with all these blessings, what more is necessary to make us a happy and a prosperous people? Still one thing more, fellow-citizens—a wise and frugal Government, which shall restrain men from injuring one another, shall leave them otherwise free to regulate their own pursuits of industry and improvement, and shall not take from the mouth of labor the bread it has earned. This is the sum of good government, and this is necessary to close the circle of our felicities.

About to enter, fellow-citizens, on the exercise of duties which comprehend everything dear and valuable to you, it is proper you should understand what I deem the essential principles of our Government, and consequently those which ought to shape its Administration. I will compress them within the narrowest compass they will bear, stating the general principle, but not all its limitations. Equal and exact justice to all men, of whatever state or persuasion, religious or political; peace, commerce, and honest friendship with all nations, entangling alliances with none; the support of the State Governments in all their rights, as the most competent administrations for our domestic concerns and the surest bulwarks against antirepublican tendencies; the preservation of the General Government in its whole constitutional vigor, as the sheet anchor of our peace at home and safety abroad; a jealous care of the right of election by the people—a mild and safe corrective of abuses which are lopped by the sword of revolution where peaceable remedies are unprovided; absolute acquiescence in the decisions of the majority, the vital principle and immediate parent of despotism; a well-disciplined militia, our best reliance on peace and for the first moments of war, till regulars may relieve them; the supremacy of the civil over the military authority; economy in the public expense, that labor may be lightly burthened; the honest payment of our debts and sacred preservation of the public faith; encouragement of agriculture, and of commerce as its handmaid; the diffusion of information and arraignment of all abuses at the bar of the public reason; freedom of religion; freedom of the press, and freedom of person under the protection of the habeas corpus, and trial by juries impartially selected. These principles form the bright constellation which has gone before us and guided our steps through an age of revolution and reformation. The wisdom of our sages and blood of our heroes have been devoted to their attainment. They should be the creed of our political faith, the text of civic instruction, the touchstone by which to try the services of those we trust; and should we wander from them in moments of error or of alarm, let us hasten to retrace our steps and to regain the road which alone leads to peace, liberty, and safety.

I repair, then, fellow-citizens, to the post you have assigned me. With experience enough in subordinate offices to have seen the difficulties of this the greatest of all, I have learnt to expect that it will rarely fall to the lot of imperfect man to retire from this station with the reputation and the favor which bring him into it. Without pretentions to that high confidence you reposed in our first and greatest revolutionary character, whose prominent services had entitled him to the first place of faithful history, I ask so much confidence only as may give firmness and effect to the legal administration of your affairs. I shall often go wrong through defect of judgment. When right, I shall often be thought wrong by those whose positions will not command a view of the whole ground. I ask your indulgence for my own errors, which will never be intentional, and your support against the errors of others, who may condemn what they would not if seen in all its parts. The approbation implied by your suffrage is a great consolation to me for the past, and my future solicitude will be to retain the good opinion of those who have bestowed it in advance, to conciliate that of others by doing them all the good in my power, and to be instrumental to the happiness and freedom of all.

Relying, then, on the patronage of your good will, I advance with obedience to the work, ready to retire from it whenever you become sensible how much better choice it is in your power to make. And may that Infinite Power which rules the destinies of the universe lead our councils to what is best, and give them a favorable issue for your peace and prosperity.

❧

Part Three

❧

Westward the Course of Destiny

In the nineteenth century the American understanding of destiny under God was decisively shaped by westward expansion. In the preceding century a number of writers and speakers had claimed that the new nation was the rightful heir to North America and had rhapsodized the challenges of the continent's western reaches. Yet extension west did not begin in earnest until Jefferson's purchase of the Louisiana Territory from Napoleon in 1803. That acquisition doubled the territory of the nation, secured navigation of the Mississippi, and invited exploration of the Far West. Other large strides in expansion were taken during the administration of James K. Polk (1845–49). As the century progressed and the westward movement increased, American eyes would strain beyond the Pacific horizon toward distant lands that might also be embraced by an American destiny.

The magnitude and rich natural resources of the western American wilderness strengthened the conviction that Americans were the chosen people. Surely this was a land intended for the new children of Israel. As trekkers west mastered the territories with rifle, axe, plow, school, church, and railroad, many Americans became doubly convinced of their divine election. Other peoples had let their resources go to waste; America's mastery of nature must surely bespeak its special character. The shift involved in this interpretation of election has been pointedly summarized by H. Richard Niebuhr: "The old idea of American Christians as a chosen people who had been called to a special task was turned into the notion of a chosen nation especially favored. . . . As the nineteenth century went on, the note of divine favoritism was increasingly sounded."[1]

Despite this pride in the land, the West evoked widely differing—even contradictory—responses from the American people. On the one hand, guidebooks for settlers, Romantic poetry, and letters from pioneers commented on the fertility of the soil and the beauty of the landscapes; on the other,

1. H. Richard Niebuhr, *The Kingdom of God in America* (New York: Harper & Row, Publishers, 1959), p. 179.

the atmosphere buzzed with reports of the manifold dangers and bitter trials of the pioneer. Many Americans saw westward expansion as an opportunity for extending democratic principles; at the same time serious doubts arose whether these principles could survive in such a vast area, doubts that turned into sheer skepticism as eastern Whigs feared political dominance by the West and as slaveholding and nonslaveholding interests competed for western territories. Nineteenth-century literature treated westward expansion both as the long-awaited "passage to India" (involving the concept of empire as maritime dominion) and as the very different cultivation of the "Garden of the World" (involving an empire of agriculture). The western wilderness was looked upon in its twofold religious sense: as a "howling wilderness"—a place of demons and death, a wasteland—and as a potential Garden of Eden—a place of retreat, renewal, and refuge. A tension also existed between the West viewed as a realm of unspoiled nature, devoid of human corruptions, and the West seen as an area inviting the improvements of civilization.[2]

However much the conflict between Nature and Civilization may have continued as a characteristic of American attitudes, in actual fact Americans consistently resolved the conflict in favor of Civilization. Nineteenth-century Anglo-Saxon Americans actively set about to transform Nature in the name of progress: destiny under God came to mean in large part preparing the West to receive civilized customs. During this era, "civilized customs" included the religion of evangelical Protestant Christianity. The American Home Missionary Society was founded in the hope that Protestant revivalist preaching would save the West from barbarism and would turn the western wilderness into a Garden of the Lord. Most eastern Protestants believed, however, that preaching should be complemented by education. Firmly convinced that American destiny would be decided west of the Alleghenies, Protestant Christians directed enormous educational energies toward the area, erecting there a host of seminaries, schools, and academies. These schools modeled themselves after eastern institutions by combining patriotic instruction with religious indoctrination.

A key spokesman for Christian education in the West was Lyman Beecher, father of Henry Ward Beecher and Harriet Beecher Stowe and famed New England clergyman who in 1832 became the first president of Lane Theological Seminary in Cincinnati. In his speech *A Plea for the West*, which he delivered in several cities in the East during a fund drive for his seminary, Beecher de-

2. For these different perspectives on the West see Henry Nash Smith, *Virgin Land* (New York: Random House, Vintage Books, 1950); George H. Williams, *Wilderness and Paradise in Christian Thought* (New York: Harper & Row, Publishers, 1962); Leo Marx, *The Machine in the Garden* (New York: Oxford University Press, 1967); Perry Miller, "The Romantic Dilemma in American Nationalism and the Concept of Nature," *Harvard Theological Review*, vol. 48 (1955), pp. 239–53.

clared that the United States was "destined to lead the way in the moral and political emancipation of the world" and that many of the resources for that destiny lay in the West. If the West were not given the benefits of Christian education, however, it would not adequately absorb the spirit of democracy, and America would fail to assume its redemptive role in history.

In the later sections of the *Plea* (which are not included in the following selection), Beecher singled out Roman Catholics who were immigrating to the West as particularly dangerous forces that must be overcome by Protestant educational institutions. While professing the right of Catholics to adhere to their own religious beliefs and practices under the protection of the law, Beecher nonetheless warned that Catholics carried with them from Europe commitments to a state church that undermined republican government. Clearly for Beecher and many of his fellow Protestants, Christianizing the West meant infusing American democratic institutions with the Protestant religion. For them the religious destiny of the nation was a Protestant destiny. In time Mormons, as well as Roman Catholics, were identified as special perils to that destiny. In an address of 1847 to the American Home Missionary Society, the influential Connecticut Congregational minister Horace Bushnell insisted that the presence of "Romanism" and "Mormonism" were clear signs that the American West was in danger of lapsing into utter "barbarism" or into a social chaos marked by lawlessness, lack of manners and customs, and superstitious religious beliefs. "Man is a religious being," Bushnell said, "and if he cannot come to God through his intelligence, he will come to what sort of God his superstitions offer him. . . . Who could have thought it possible that a wretched and silly delusion, like that of the Mormons, could gather in its thousands of disciples in this enlightened age, build a populous city, and erect a temple rivalling in grandeur even that of the false prophet at Mecca?"[3] Toward the end of the nineteenth century, Josiah Strong, leader in the Home Missionary Society, could still classify the Mormons, who were allegedly formed by the principle of "ecclesiastical despotism," along with Roman Catholics and European immigrants as such, as the most serious threats to the democratic institutions of the land.[4]

Protestant bias shaped these views of Catholics and Mormons, but there was a particularly bitter irony entailed in the fearful portrayals of the Mormons or the Church of Jesus Christ of Latter-day Saints, for in one sense they were the most American of America's indigenous religions. "Even when most at odds with its fellow Americans," Thomas O'Dea has written, Mormonism "was to

3. Horace Bushnell, "Barbarism the First Danger," *The American National Preacher*, Sept. 1847, p. 214.

4. Josiah Strong, *Our Country*, ed. Jurgen Herbst (1891; reprint, Cambridge, Mass.: Belknap Press of Harvard University Press, 1963), pp. 76–82, 107–8.

be typically American, and it was always to feel and express this curious combination of typicality and peculiarity."[5] The peculiarity was apparent in the Latter-day Saints' secret temple ceremonies, their belief in polygamy, their religious convictions premised on private revelations to their prophet Joseph Smith, and the teachings of the *Book of Mormon*. The typicality was evident in the special place that America held in the Mormon religious vision. According to the *Book of Mormon*, Jesus Christ made a post-resurrection appearance on American soil, and much of the history of the Mormons' struggle for sanctuary consists of their efforts to establish a Zion, a holy dwelling place, in the American wilderness. Eventually the Mormon leadership would deem the entire United States a divinely favored country. In the words of early Mormon theologian Parley Pratt, "The United States of America was the favoured nation raised up, with institutions adapted to the protection and free development of the necessary truths, and their practical results."[6]

Driven by their numerous opponents from place to place, the Mormons found their abode of safety in the Great Salt Lake Valley. There President Brigham Young, successor to founder Joseph Smith, interpreted the relation between the Mormon western outpost and the remainder of the nation. The Holy City in the wilderness was for Young the gathering place for the Saints from which there would radiate influences that would turn the entire American continent, and eventually the world, into God's Zion. And Young understood the Constitution of the United States as a divinely inspired document that allowed the Mormons freely to pursue their own destiny: "No item of inspiration is held more sacred with us than the Constitution."

The term "Manifest Destiny," which became a popular slogan in the nineteenth century, provides a key to an important transformation of the belief in America's sense of purpose. "Manifest Destiny," as Albert Weinberg has put it, "expressed a dogma of supreme self-assurance and ambition—that America's incorporation of all adjacent lands was the virtually inevitable fulfillment of a moral mission delegated to the nation by Providence itself." The principal justification for the dogma was a theory of "geographical predestination," or the claim that "nature or the natural order of things destined natural boundaries for nations in general and the United States, the nation of special destiny, in particular."[7] Manifest Destiny was abroad as a concept in America before it became a slogan, but its popularization as a watchword of expansionism occurred in the 1840s, greatly aided by the writings of the journalist John L. O'Sullivan. In the midst of negotiations between England and America over

5. Thomas O'Dea, *The Mormons* (Chicago: University of Chicago Press, 1957), p. 21.
6. Cited in Ibid.
7. Albert K. Weinberg, *Manifest Destiny* (Gloucester, Mass.: Peter Smith, 1958), pp. 1–2, 43.

how the Oregon Territory was to be divided (a treaty finally granted American sovereignty up to the 49th parallel despite Polk's earlier assertion that the American title up to latitude 54°40′ N was "clear and unquestionable"), O'Sullivan brushed aside all legal questions with the claim that the whole territory belonged to the United States by virtue of its Manifest Destiny. One of O'Sullivan's editorials, "The True Title," contained an argument frequently resorted to by nineteenth-century expansionists: The United States is entitled to new territories because of its successful experiment in "liberty and federative self-government," because of its natural right to growth and expansion, because it would utilize its territories beneficently, and because the "God of nature and of nations has marked" adjacent areas "for our own."[8]

The doctrine of Manifest Destiny did not in fact unify the nation or generate a common nationalistic sentiment; on the contrary, it signaled an emergence of sectionalism, a vigorous defense of states' rights, and a western regionalism.[9] Nevertheless, the rhetoric employed on behalf of the doctrine was nationalistic in cast, and the view of destiny under God expressed by that rhetoric transformed the nation's understanding of itself. American destiny became "manifest"; thereby it departed in a significant way from the biblical (and early American) portrayal of the destiny of a chosen people. The traditional doctrine of election held that the ultimate reason for God's choosing Israel was hidden in the mystery of the divine will. According to the exponents of Manifest Destiny, God's New Israel was elected for clear or *manifest* reasons—because of its superior form of government, its geographical location, and its beneficence. The mystery of divine transcendence dissolved. As Albert Weinberg has observed, in this "anthropocentric theology, in which God himself served chiefly as a Providence watchful for mankind and human values, the American approached perilously close to changing the traditional dogma, that man exists *ad majorem gloriam Dei*, into the heresy that God exists *ad majorem gloriam hominis.*"[10]

No people in the West suffered more from the effects of an aggressively pursued Manifest Destiny than the area's Native Americans. Driven from their hunting and farming grounds, herded onto reservations consisting of undesirable land, subjected to the diseases of their white conquerors, and defrauded by unfavorable—and broken—treaties, Native Americans were tragic victims of the doctrine of "geographical predestination." Although Christian missionaries on occasion performed ameliorating roles in the march of the white settlers, on the whole Christianity was in league with "civilizing" efforts that

8. *New York Morning News*, Dec. 27, 1845.

9. See Frederick Merk, *Manifest Destiny and Mission in American History* (New York: Alfred A. Knopf, 1963), pp. 57–60.

10. Weinberg, *Destiny*, p. 128.

were oblivious to the integrity of Native American cultures and religions. American Indians manifestly were not the beneficiaries of Manifest Destiny, construed religiously or otherwise. That was a major point in Chief Seattle's famous oration delivered in 1854 before Isaac Stephens, governor of Washington Territory. Leader of the Duwamish tribe, convert to Roman Catholicism, and friend to the white settlers in Puget Sound, Seattle eventually signed the Port Elliot Treaty which ceded Indian lands to the whites and established a reservation for the area's tribes. In his speech, however, Chief Seattle pointed to the different origins, world views, gods, and destinies of the White Man and the Red Man. And in the face of the inevitable dominance of the Reds by the Whites, Seattle offered an anguished hope for the ultimate survival of the former's destiny in the living spirits of the dead.

A vision of American destiny in the West caught the imagination of the literati as well as the politicians, of poets as well as journalists. The writer who gave the vision its loftiest poetic expression was Walt Whitman. Although he resided on the Atlantic seaboard and had not even traveled west of the Mississippi when he wrote his principal poetry, Whitman celebrated the westward movement in a number of his poems. One of his best-known works, "Pioneers! O Pioneers," depicted the transfer of historical destiny from the Old World to the western pioneers who were the creators of a "newer, mightier world." But it was Whitman's poem of 1871, "Passage to India," that most fully revealed his impressions of the significance of westward expansion.

Whitman himself said that "Passage to India" conveyed "what, from the first . . . more or less lurks in my writings, underneath every page, every line, every where." The poem was inspired by three technological achievements: the completion of the Suez Canal, the spanning of the American continent by the Pacific Railroad, and the laying of the Atlantic submarine cable. Whitman felt that by virtue of these events the separate parts of the world had been linked, Columbus's voyage had been completed, and the once inscrutable purpose of human history had been made manifest:

> Lo, soul, seest thou not God's purpose from the first?
> The earth to be spann'd, connected by network . . .
> The lands to be welded together.

Addressing his passive companion, the soul, the poet represented "India" as the geographic East, the distant past, and the area of "primal thought" where one could recover an Edenic innocence and live in harmony with Nature. The discovery of America and the extension of the nation by the "mighty railroad" were, therefore, portions of a great destiny under God that were central to the entire human drama:

> thou born America
> For purpose vast, man's long probation fill'd,
> Thou rondure of the world at last accomplish'd.[11]

True, Whitman's "Passage to India" articulated a deep American hope that a link might be found with the exotic East and explicated a widely held belief that American history would fulfill human history as a whole. But nineteenth-century versions of American destiny were seldom as cosmopolitan or romantic as Whitman's. Especially during the closing years of the century, when the doctrine of Manifest Destiny was resurrected to justify American imperialism, jingoistic fever ran high and belief in American destiny under God became a muscular nationalism.

The ideology of American imperialism took root long before its clear surfacing during the Spanish-American War and the Philippine acquisition. The early prophets of empire seldom appealed to economic aggrandizement in urging American actions overseas. The appeal was more often to the missionary obligations accruing to a superior American Civilization. In his best seller of 1885, *Our Country*, Josiah Strong elucidated these obligations. Strong contended that the future of civilization devolved upon Anglo-Saxons, since they had developed the two related ideas of civil liberty and "a pure spiritual Christianity." And because the American branch of the Anglo-Saxon race had perfected these two ideas, on America especially did human destiny depend. "Thus," wrote Strong, "while on this continent God is training the Anglo-Saxon race for its mission, a complemental work has been in progress in the great world beyond. God has two hands. Not only is he preparing in our civilization the die with which to stamp the nations, but, by what Southey called the 'timing of Providence,' he is preparing mankind to receive our impress." Like many Americans of the period, Strong used the word "race" not in any strictly biological sense but as a loose reference to ethnic origins and cultural characteristics. And many could have added with Strong, "I do not imagine that the Anglo-Saxon is any dearer to God than a Mongolian or an African. My plea is not, Save America for America's sake, but, Save America for the world's sake." Nevertheless, this kind of nationalistic "racism" provided a rationalization for American overseas expansion.[12]

The cry for American destiny west of the Pacific shores grew shrill dur-

---

11. My remarks on "Passage to India" rely chiefly on three sources: the critical notes of Gay Wilson Allen and Charles T. Davis, *Walt Whitman's Poems* (New York: New York University Press, 1955), pp. 242–48; Alan Trachtenberg, *Brooklyn Bridge: Fact and Symbol* (New York: Oxford University Press, 1965), pp. 16–17; and Smith, *Virgin Land*, pp. 47–51.

12. Cited in Ernest Lee Tuveson, *Redeemer Nation: The Idea of America's Millennial Role* (Chicago: University of Chicago Press, 1968), pp. 165–68.

ing the Philippine crisis. An eloquent spokesman for American imperialism during the crisis was the junior senator from Indiana, Albert J. Beveridge. Returning from a tour of the Philippines and the Far East, Beveridge delivered a senate speech in January 1900 that described the wealth of the archipelago, the importance of the area for United States trade, the alleged indolence of the natives and their current incapacity for self-government, and the way in which American opposition to the war in the Philippines was "the chief factor in prolonging it." Beveridge concluded with the assertion that God prepared the "English-speaking and Teutonic peoples" to be "the master organizers of the world to establish system where chaos reigns," that "God marked the American people as His chosen nation to finally lead in the regeneration of the world."[13]

Beveridge amplified his view of American destiny in his Republican campaign speech of 1900, "The Star of Empire." That speech took its title and its point of departure from a stanza in Bishop George Berkeley's eighteenth-century "Verses on the Prospect of Planting Arts and Learning in America":

> Westward the Course of Empire takes its Way;
> The four first Acts already past,
> A fifth shall close the Drama with the Day;
> Times noblest Offspring is the last.

Neither Beveridge nor many other nineteenth-century Americans whose fancies were captured by this stanza bothered to notice that Berkeley, out of disgust for England and Europe, was suggesting America as a refuge for the arts and that he did not really expect the Golden Age in the New World to radiate to other parts of the globe. The stanza was simply utilized, out of context, as a poetic endorsement of America's mission to spread its institutions and customs westward. Beveridge's "Star of Empire" speech portrayed America's insular acquisitions as the fulfillment of the mission of a divinely anointed nation to civilize savage, degenerate peoples. And Beveridge felt no compunction at mixing a defense of national interests with the call of a "high and holy destiny" to "civilize the world." .

The spirit of Beveridge's imperialism certainly did not grip the American people as a whole. The Treaty of Paris which ended the war with Spain and acquired the Philippine Islands for America passed the Senate only after a long and bitter debate and with one vote above the necessary two-thirds majority. Anti-imperialist sentiment was shared by such respected Americans as Senator George F. Hoar of Massachusetts, presidential aspirant William Jennings Bryan, academicians William James and William Graham Sumner, clergyman Henry Van Dyke, steel master Andrew Carnegie, and many others.[14] Neverthe-

---

13. *Congressional Record*, XXXIII (Washington, D.C.: Government Printing Office, 1900), 711.

14. See Robert L. Beisner, *Twelve Against Empire: The Anti-Imperialists, 1898–1900* (New York: McGraw-Hill Book Company, 1968).

less many Americans had begun by the turn of the century to celebrate their nation as a great world power, one destined to sow the seeds of its civilization abroad. The twentieth century would furnish many opportunities to construe the American mission as the promotion and preservation of American ideas and institutions abroad, and such an interpretation would not always, with Beveridge's candor, acknowledge the nation's own self-interests in the mission.

SUGGESTED READING

Bowden, Henry Warner. *American Indians and Christian Missions: Studies in Cultural Conflict.* Chicago: University of Chicago Press, 1981.

Caskey, Marie. *Chariot of Fire: Religion and the Beecher Family.* New Haven, Conn.: Yale University Press, 1978.

Handy, Robert T. *A Christian America: Protestant Hopes and Historical Realities.* New York: Oxford University Press, 1971.

Hofstadter, Richard. "Manifest Destiny and the Philippines." In *America in Crisis*, ed. Daniel Aaron. New York: Alfred A. Knopf, 1952.

Shipps, Jan. *Mormonism: The Story of a New Religious Tradition.* Urbana and Chicago: University of Illinois Press, 1985.

Waters, Frank. *Brave Are My People: Indian Heroes Not Forgotten.* Santa Fe, N.Mex.: Clear Light Publishers, 1993.

LYMAN BEECHER

A Plea for the West

ISAIAH LXVI, 8
Who hath heard such a thing?
who hath seen such things?
Shall the earth be made to bring
forth in one day?
or shall a nation be born at once?
for as soon as Zion travailed,
she brought forth her children.

Ever since the era of modern missions, sceptical men have ridiculed the efforts of the church to evangelize the world, and predicted their failure. "What," they say, "do these Jews build,—if a fox do but go up upon the wall, it will fall. The world can never be converted to Christianity by the power of man." And full well do we know it, and most deeply do we feel it, and in all our supplications for aid, most emphatically do we confess our utter impotency; and could no power but the power of man be enlisted, it would be indeed of all experiments the most ridiculous and hopeless. But because man cannot convert the world to Christianity, cannot God do it? Has he not promised to do it, and selected his instruments, and commanded his people to be fellow workers with him? And hath he said, and shall he not do it?

Instead of its being a work of difficulty and dilatory movement, when the time to favor Zion comes, it shall outrun all past analogies of moral causes, as if seed-time and harvest should meet on the same field, or a nation should instantly rush up from barbarism to civilization.

But as all great eras of prosperity to the church have been aided by the civil condition of the world, and accomplished by the regular operation of moral causes, I consider the text as a prediction of the rapid and universal exten-

From Lyman Beecher, *A Plea for the West*, Second edition (Cincinnati: Truman and Smith, 1835), pp. 7–40.

sion of civil and religious liberty, introductory to the triumphs of universal Christianity. It is certain that the glorious things spoken of the church and of the world, as affected by her prosperity, cannot come to pass under the existing civil organization of the nations. Such a state of society as is predicted to pervade the earth, cannot exist under an arbitrary despotism, and the predominance of feudal institutions and usages. Of course, it is predicted that revolutions and distress of nations will precede the introduction of the peaceful reign of Jesus Christ on the earth. The mountains shall be exalted—and he shall "overturn, and overturn, and overturn, till he whose right it is, shall reign King of nations—King of saints."

It was the opinion of Edwards, that the millennium would commence in America. When I first encountered this opinion, I thought it chimerical; but all providential developments since, and all the existing signs of the times, lend corroboration to it. But if it is by the march of revolution and civil liberty, that the way of the Lord is to be prepared, where shall the central energy be found, and from what nation shall the renovating power go forth? What nation is blessed with such experimental knowledge of free institutions, with such facilities and resources of communication, obstructed by so few obstacles, as our own? There is not a nation upon earth which, in fifty years, can by all possible reformation place itself in circumstances so favorable as our own for the free, unembarrassed applications of physical effort and pecuniary and moral power to evangelize the world.

But if this nation is, in the providence of God, destined to lead the way in the moral and political emancipation of the world, it is time she understood her high calling, and were harnessed for the work. For mighty causes, like floods from distant mountains, are rushing with accumulating power, to their consummation of good or evil, and soon our character and destiny will be stereotyped forever.

It is equally plain that the religious and political destiny of our nation is to be decided in the West. There is the territory, and there soon will be the population, the wealth, and the political power. The Atlantic commerce and manufactures may confer always some peculiar advantages on the East. But the West is destined to be the great central power of the nation, and under heaven, must affect powerfully the cause of free institutions and the liberty of the world.

The West is a young empire of mind, and power, and wealth, and free institutions, rushing up to a giant manhood, with a rapidity and a power never before witnessed below the sun. And if she carries with her the elements of her preservation, the experiment will be glorious—the joy of the nation— the joy of the whole earth, as she rises in the majesty of her intelligence and benevolence, and enterprise, for the emancipation of the world.

It is equally clear, that the conflict which is to decide the destiny of the

West, will be a conflict of institutions for the education of her sons, for purposes of superstition, or evangelical light; of despotism, or liberty.

· · ·

The thing required for the civil and religious prosperity of the West, is universal education, and moral culture, by institutions commensurate to that result — the all-pervading influence of schools, and colleges, and seminaries, and pastors, and churches. When the West is well supplied in this respect, though there may be great relative defects, there will be, as we believe, the stamina and the vitality of a perpetual civil and religious prosperity.

By whom shall the work of rearing the literary and religious institutions of the West be done?

Not by the West alone.

The West is able to do this great work for herself, — and would do it, provided the exigencies of her condition allowed to her the requisite time. The subject of education is no where more appreciated; and no people in the same time ever performed so great a work as has already been performed in the West. Such an extent of forest never fell before the arm of man in forty years, and gave place, as by enchantment, to such an empire of cities, and towns, and villages, and agriculture, and merchandise, and manufactures, and roads and rapid navigation, and schools, and colleges, and libraries, and literary enterprise, with such a number of pastors and churches, and such a relative amount of religious influence, as has been produced by the spontaneous effort of the religious denominations of the West. The later peopled states of New-England did by no means come as rapidly to the same state of relative, intellectual and moral culture as many portions of the West have already arrived at, in the short period of forty, thirty, and even twenty years.

But this work of self-supply is not complete, and by no human possibility could have been completed by the West, in her past condition.

No people ever did, in the first generation, fell the forest, and construct the roads, and rear the dwellings and public edifices, and provide the competent supply of schools and literary institutions. New-England did not. Her colleges were endowed extensively by foreign munificence, and her churches of the first generation were supplied chiefly from the mother country; — and yet the colonists of New-England were few in number, compact in territory, homogeneous in origin, language, manners, and doctrines; and were coerced to unity by common perils and necessities; and could be acted upon by immediate legislation; and could wait also for their institutions to grow with their growth and strengthen with their strength. But the population of the great West is not so, but is assembled from all the states of the Union, and from all the nations of Europe, and is rushing in like the waters of the flood, demanding for its moral preservation the immediate and universal action of those institutions which discipline the mind, and arm the conscience and the heart. And so various are the opinions and habits, and so recent and imperfect is the acquaintance, and so sparse are the settlements of the West, that no homogeneous public sentiment can be formed to legislate immediately into being the requisite institutions. And yet they are all needed immediately, in their utmost perfection and power. A nation is being "born in a day," and all the nurture of schools and literary institutions is needed, constantly and universally, to rear it up to a glorious and unperverted manhood.

It is no implication of the West, that in a single generation, she has not completed this work. In the circumstances of her condition she could not do it; and had it been done, we should believe that a miraculous, and not a human power had done it.

Who then, shall co-operate with our brethren of the West, for the consummation of this work so auspiciously begun? Shall the South be invoked? The South have difficulties of their own to encounter, and cannot do it; and the middle states have too much of the same work yet to do, to volunteer their aid abroad.

Whence, then, shall the aid come, but from those portions of the Union where the work of rearing these institutions has been most nearly accomplished, and their blessings most eminently enjoyed? And by whom, but by those who in their infancy were aided; and who, having freely received, are now called upon freely to give, and who, by a hard soil and habits of industry and economy, and by experience are qualified to endure hardness as good soldiers and pioneers in this great work? And be assured that those who go to the West with unostentatious benevolence, to identify themselves with the people and interests of that vast community, will be adopted with a warm heart and an unwavering right hand of fellowship.

But how shall this aid be extended to our brethren of the West in the manner most acceptable and efficacious?

Not by prayers and supplications only, nor by charities alone, nor by colonial emigrations; for these, though they might cultivate their own garden, would for obvious reasons be fenced in, and exert but a feeble general influence beyond their own inclosures. Those who go out to do good at the West should go out to mingle with the people of the West, and be absorbed in their multitude, as rain drops fall on the bosom of the ocean and mingle with that world of waters.

Nor is it by tracts, or Bibles, or itinerating missions, that the requisite intellectual and moral power can be applied. There must be permanent, powerful, literary and moral institutions, which, like the great orbs of attraction and light, shall send forth at once their power and their illumination, and without them all else will be inconstant and ephemeral. Let it not, however, for a moment be supposed, that the schools of the West are to be sustained by the emigration of an army of instructors from the East. For though for the present *necessity*, the aid of qualified instructors is not to be repelled, but invited; yet for any permanent reliance, it is but a drop of the bucket to the ocean.

Nothing is more certain, than that the great body of the teachers of the West must be educated at the West. It is by her own sons chiefly, that the great work is to be consummated which her civil, and literary, and religious prosperity demands.

But how shall the requisite supply of teachers for the sons and daughters of the West be raised up? It can be accomplished by the instrumentality of a learned and pious ministry, educated at the West.

Experience has evinced, that schools and popular education, in their best estate, go not far beyond the suburbs of the city of God. All attempts to legislate prosperous colleges and schools into being without the intervening influence of religious education and moral principle, and habits of intellectual culture which spring up in alliance with evangelical institutions, have failed. Schools wane, invariably, in those towns where the evangelical ministry is neglected, and the Sabbath is profaned, and the tavern supplants the worship of God. Thrift and knowledge in such places go out, while vice and irreligion come in.

But the ministry is a central luminary in each sphere, and soon sends out schools and seminaries as its satellites by the hands of sons and daughters of its own training. A land supplied with able and faithful ministers, will of course be filled with schools, academies, libraries, colleges, and all the apparatus for the perpetuity of republican institutions. It always has been so—it always will be.

But the ministry for the West must be educated at the West. The demands on the East, for herself and for pagan lands, forbid the East ever to supply our wants. Nor is it necessary. For the Spirit of God is with the churches of the West, and pious and talented young men are there in great numbers, willing, desiring, impatient to consecrate themselves to the glorious work. If we possessed the accommodations and the funds, we might easily send out a hundred ministers a year—a thousand ministers in ten years—around each of whom schools would arise, and instructors multiply, and churches spring up, and revivals extend, and all the elements of civil and religious prosperity abound.

But we have said that the ministry for the West must be a learned and talented ministry.

No opinion is more false and fatal than that mediocrity of talent and learning will suffice for the West. That if a minister is a good sort of a man, but somehow does not seem to be popular, and find employment, he had better go to the West. No; let him stay at home; and if among the urgent demands for ministerial labor here, he cannot find employment, let him conclude that he has mistaken his profession.

But let him not go to the West. The men who, *somehow*, do not succeed at the East, are the very men who will succeed still less at the West. If there be in the new settlements at the West a lack of schools and educated mind, there is no lack of shrewd and vigorous mind; and if they are not deep read in Latin and Greek, they are well read in men and things. On their vast rivers, they go every where, and see every body, and know every thing, and judge with the tact of perspicacious common sense. They are disciplined to resolution and mental vigor by toils and perils, and enterprises; and often they are called to attend as umpires to the earnest discussions of their most able and eloquent men, which cannot fail to throw prosing dullness in the ministry to a hopeless distance. No where, if a minister is deficient, will he be more sure to be "weighed in the balance and found wanting." On the contrary, there is not a place on earth where piety, and talent, and learning, and argument, and popular eloquence are more highly appreciated, or rewarded with a more frank and enthusiastic admiration. There are chords in the heart of the West which vibrate to the touch of genius, and to the power of argumentative eloquence, with a sensibility and enthusiasm no where surpassed. A hundred ministers of cultivated mind and popular eloquence might find settlement in an hundred places, and without the aid of missions, and only to increase the demand for an hundred more.

Most unquestionably the West demands the instrumentality of the first order of minds in the ministry, and thoroughly furnished minds, to command attention, enlighten the understanding, form the conscience, and gain the heart, and bring into religious organization and order the uncommitted mind and families of the great world; and many a man who might guide respectfully a well-organized congregation here of homogeneous character, and moving onward under the impetus of long continued habits, might fail utterly to call around him the population of a new country.

Of course, the institutions which are to lead in this great work of rearing the future ministry of the West should be second to none in their endowments and adaptation to this end. For it is such a work in magnitude as human instrumentality was never before concentrated upon. All other nations have gone up slowly from semi-barbarism to a civilized manhood, while our nation was commenced with the best materials of a nation at that time the most favored nation in the world, and yet was delayed in its growth, through two centuries, by policy, and power, and war, and taxation, and want of capital. It is less than fifty years since our resources have begun to be developed in great power, and we have entered upon the career of internal improvement and national greatness; and at the East, until recently, these movements were slow, as capital gradually increased, and agriculture, and commerce, and art led the way. But the West is filling up as by ocean waves; and such is her prospective greatness, that the capital of the East and of Europe hold competition for her acceptance and use, so that in a day, she is rising up to the high eminence that all other nations have approached progressively through the revolution of centuries.

But what will become of the West, if her prosperity rushes up to such a majesty of power, while those great institutions linger which are necessary to form the mind, and the conscience, and the heart of that vast world. It must not be permitted. And yet what is done must be done quickly; for population will not wait, and commerce will not cast anchor, and manufactures will not shut off the steam nor shut down the gate, and agriculture, pushed by millions of freemen on their fertile soil, will not withhold her corrupting abundance.

We must educate! We must educate! or we must perish by our own prosperity. If we do not, short from the cradle to the grave will be our race. If in our haste to be rich and mighty, we outrun our literary and religious institutions, they will never overtake us; or only come up after the battle of liberty is fought and lost, as spoils to grace the victory, and as resources of inexorable despotism for the perpetuity of our bondage. And let no man at the East quiet himself, and dream of liberty, whatever may become of the West. Our alliance of blood, and political institutions, and common interests, is such, that we cannot stand aloof in the hour of her calamity, should it ever come. Her destiny is our destiny; and the day that her gallant ship goes down, our little boat sinks in the vortex!

It was to meet these exigences of our common country in the West, that the Lane Seminary was called into being by the munificence of the sons of the West; first by a donation from the two gentlemen whose name it bears, followed by the gift of sixty acres of land, on which the institution is located, by Mr. Elnathan Kemper, and the sale of fifty more at a reduced price and long credit by the same benefactor; to which have been added fifteen thousand dollars by the citizens of Cincinnati and the West, for the construction of two college buildings and two professors' houses. To this has been added by our friends on this side of the mountains, twenty thousand dollars from one individual, for the endowment of the professorship of Theology; and by others, thirty thousand, for the endowment of the two professorships of Biblical Literature and Ecclesiastical History.

What we now need is a chapel for the accommodation of students and a fast increasing community with a place of worship; the endowment of a professorship of Sacred Rhetoric, and a library. For the first, we have dared to rely on our friends in Boston and its vicinity. The library we hope to receive from our friends in New-York; and for the Professorship of Sacred Rhetoric we look up, hoping and believing that God will put into the heart of one or more individuals to endow it.

The motives which call on us to co-operate immediately in this glorious work of consummating the institutions of the West, essential to the perpetuity of her greatness and glory, are neither few, nor feeble, nor obscure.

The territory is eight thousand miles in circumference, extending from the Alleghany to the Rocky mountains, and from the Gulf of Mexico to the

Lakes of the North; and it is the largest territory, and most beneficent in climate, and soil, and mineral wealth, and commercial facilities, ever prepared for the habitation of man, and qualified to sustain in prosperity and happiness the densest population on the globe. By twenty-four thousand miles of steam navigation, and canals and rail roads, a market is brought near to every man, and the whole is brought into near neighborhood.

When I first entered the West, its vastness overpowered me with the impression of its uncontrollable greatness, in which all human effort must be lost. But when I perceived the active intercourse between the great cities, like the rapid circulation of a giant's blood; and heard merchants speak of just stepping up to Pittsburgh—only six hundred miles—and back in a few days; and others just from New-Orleans, or St. Louis, or the Far West; and others going thither; and when I heard my ministerial brethren negotiating exchanges in the near neighborhood—only one hundred miles up or down the river—and going and returning on Saturday and Monday, and without trespassing on the Sabbath;—then did I perceive how God, who seeth the end from the beginning, had prepared the West to be mighty, and still wieldable, that the moral energy of his word and spirit might take it up as a very little thing.

This vast territory is occupied now by ten states and will soon be by twelve. Forty years since it contained only about one hundred and fifty thousand souls; while it now contains little short of five millions. At the close of this century, if no calamity intervenes, it will contain, probably, one hundred millions—a day which some of our children may live to see; and when fully people, may accommodate three hundred millions. It is half as large as all Europe, four times as large as the Atlantic states, and twenty times as large as New-England. Was there ever such a spectacle—such a field in which to plant the seeds of an immortal harvest!—so vast a ship, so richly laden with the world's treasures and riches, whose helm is offered to the guiding influence of early forming institutions!

The certainty of success calls us to immediate effort. If we knew not what to do, if all was effort and expense in untried experiments, there might be some pretext for the paralysis of amazement and inaction. But we know what to do: the means are obvious, and well tried, and certain. The sun and the rain of heaven are not more sure to call forth a bounteous vegetation, than Bibles, and Sabbaths, and schools, and seminaries, are to diffuse intellectual light and warmth for the bounteous fruits of righteousness and peace. The corn and the acorn of the East are not more sure to vegetate at the West than the institutions which have blessed the East are to bless the West.

But these all-pervading orbs of illumination and centres of attraction must be established. Such is the gravitating tendency of society, that no spontaneous effort at arms-length will hold it up. It is by the constant energy and strong attraction of powerful institutions only that the needed intellectual and moral power can be applied; and the present is the age of founding them. If this work be done, and well done, our country is safe, and the world's hope is secure. The government of force will cease, and that of intelligence and virtue will take its place; and nation after nation cheered by our example, will follow in our footsteps, till the whole earth is free. There is no danger that our agriculture and arts will not prosper: the danger is, that our intelligence and virtue will falter and fall back into a dark minded, vicious populace—a poor, uneducated reckless mass of infuriated animalism, to rush on resistless as the tornado, or to burn as if set on fire of hell.

Until Europe, by universal education, is delivered from such masses of feudal ignorance and servitude, she sits upon a volcano, and despotism and revolution will arbitrate her destiny.

Consider, too, how quickly and how cheaply the guarantee of a perpetual and boundless prosperity can be secured. The West needs but a momentary aid, when almost as soon as received, should it be needed, she will repay and quadruple both principle and interest. Lend a hand to get up her institutions, to give ubiquity to her schools and Sabbaths and sanctuaries, while her forests are falling and her ocean floods of population rolling in, and afterwards we will not come here to ask for aid; for there is a wealth and chivalrous munificence there, which, when it has first performed the necessary work of self-preservation, will pour with you a noble tide of rival benevolence into that river which is "to make glad the city of our God."

·   ·   ·

✢✣

Discourses

The Land of Zion—This is the land of Zion. West of us is a body of water that we call the Pacific, and to the east there is another large body of water which we call the Atlantic, and to the north is where they have tried to discover a northwest passage; these waters surround the land of Zion. 4:301.

And what is Zion? In one sense Zion is the pure in heart. But is there a land that ever will be called Zion? Yes, brethren. What land is it? It is the land that the Lord gave to Jacob, who bequeathed it to his son Joseph, and his posterity, and they inhabit it, and that land is North and South America. That is Zion, as to land, as to territory, and location. The children of Zion have not yet much in their possession, but their territory is North and South America to begin with. As to the spirit of Zion, it is in the hearts of the Saints of those who love and serve the Lord with all their might, mind and strength. 2:253.

This American continent will be Zion; for it is so spoken of by the prophets. Jerusalem will be rebuilt and will be the place of gathering, and the tribe of Judah will gather there; but this continent of America is the land of Zion. 5:4.

This is the land of Zion—this is the continent whereon the Lord has commenced his work for the last time, and whereon Jesus will make his appearance the second time, when he comes to gather and save the House of Israel. 8:81–2.

Zion will extend, eventually, all over this earth. There will be no nook or corner upon the earth but what will be in Zion. It will all be Zion. 9:138.

The *City of Zion*—We look forward to the day when the Lord will prepare for the building of the New Jerusalem, preparatory to the City of Enoch's going to be joined with it when it is built upon this earth. We are anticipating to enjoy that day, whether we sleep in death previous to that, or not. We look forward, with all the anticipation and confidence that children can possess in a parent, that we shall be there when Jesus comes; and if we are not there, we will come with him: in either case we shall be there when he comes. 8:342.

We want all the Latter-day Saints to understand how to build up Zion. The

From *Discourses of Brigham Young*, ed. John A. Widtsoe (Salt Lake City, Utah: Deseret Book Company, 1954), pp. 119–21, 358–60. [Numbers at the end of paragraphs refer to volume and pages in Young's *Journal of Discourses*. —Editor]

City of Zion, in beauty and magnificence, will outstrip anything that is now known upon the earth. The curse will be taken from the earth and sin and corruption will be swept from its face. Who will do this great work? Is the Lord going to convince the people that he will redeem the center Stake of Zion, beautify it and then place them there without an exertion on their part? No. He will not come here to build a Temple, a Tabernacle, a Bowery, or to set out fruit trees, make aprons of fig leaves or coats of skins, or work in brass and iron, for we already know how to do these things. He will not come here to teach us how to raise and manufacture cotton, how to make hand cards, how to card, how to make spinning machines, looms, etc., etc. We have to build up Zion, if we do our duty. 10:172.

I have many times asked the questions, "Where is the man that knows how to lay the first rock for the wall that is to surround the New Jerusalem or the Zion of God on the earth? Where is the man who knows how to construct the first gate of the city? Where is the man who understands how to build up the Kingdom of God in its purity and to prepare for Zion to come down to meet it?" "Well," says one, "I thought the Lord was going to do this." So he is if we will let him. This is what we want: we want the people to be willing for the Lord to do it. But he will do it by means. He will not send his angels to gather up the rock to build up the New Jerusalem. He will not send his angels from the heavens to go to the mountains to cut the timber and make it into lumber to adorn the City of Zion. He has called upon us to do this work; and if we will let him work by, through, and with us, he can accomplish it; otherwise we shall fall short, and shall never have the honor of building up Zion on the earth. 13:313.

Purpose of Gathering—A remnant of the people of Israel are to be saved, and they will yet be gathered together. 16:109.

Ephraim has become mixed with all the nations of the earth, and it is Ephraim that is gathering together. 2:268.

We are gathering the people as fast as we can. We are gathering them to make Saints of them and of ourselves. 9:137–138.

We have been gathered to the valleys of these mountains for the express purpose of purifying ourselves, that we may become polished stones in the temple of God. We are here for the purpose of establishing the Kingdom of God on the earth. To be prepared for this work it has been necessary to gather us out from the nations and countries of the world, for if we had remained in those lands we could not have received the ordinances of the holy Priesthood of the Son of God, which are necessary for the perfection of the Saints preparatory to his coming. 12:161.

The Constitution of the United States, an *Inspired Document*—We mean to sustain the Constitution of the United States and all righteous laws. 9:157.

We will cling to the Constitution of our country, and to the government that reveres that sacred charter of freemen's rights; and, if necessary, pour out our best blood for the defense of every good and righteous principle. 10:41.

It was observed this morning that the Government of the United States was the best or most wholesome one on the earth, and the best adapted to our condition. That is very true. 2:310.

To accuse us of being unfriendly to the Government, is to accuse us of hostility to our religion, for no item of inspiration is held more sacred with us than the Constitution under which she acts. As a religious society, we, in common with all other denominations, claim its protection. 2:175.

The signers of the Declaration of Independence and the framers of the Constitution were inspired from on high to do that work. But was that which was given to them perfect, not admitting of any addition whatever? No; for if men know anything, they must know that the Almighty has never yet found a man in mortality that was capable, at the first intimation, at the first impulse, to receive anything in a state of entire perfection. They laid the foundation, and it was for aftergenerations to rear the superstructure upon it. It is a progressive–a gradual work. 7:14.

The general Constitution of our country is good, and a wholesome government could be framed upon it, for it was dictated by the invisible operations of the Almighty; he moved upon Columbus to launch forth upon the trackless deep to discover the American Continent; he moved upon the signers of the Declaration of Independence; and he moved upon Washington to fight and conquer, in the same way as he moved upon ancient and modern Prophets, each being inspired to accomplish the particular work he was called to perform in the times, seasons, and dispensations of the Almighty. God's purposes, in raising up these men and inspiring them with daring sufficient to surmount every opposing power, was to prepare the way for the formation of a true republican government. They laid its foundation; but when others came to build upon it, they reared a superstructure far short of their privileges, if they had walked uprightly as they should have done. 7:13.

We believe that the Lord has been preparing that when he should bring forth his work, that, when the set time should fully come, there might be a place upon his footstool where sufficient liberty of conscience should exist, that his Saints might dwell in peace under the broad panoply of constitutional law and equal rights. In this view we consider that the men in the Revolution were inspired by the Almighty, to throw off the shackles of the mother government, with her established religion. For this cause were Adams, Jefferson, Franklin, Washington, and a host of others inspired to deeds of resistance to the acts of the King of Great Britain, who might also have been led to those aggressive acts, for aught we know, to bring to pass the purposes of God, in thus establishing a new government upon a principle of greater freedom, a basis of self-government allowing the free exercise of religious worship.

It was the voice of the Lord inspiring all those worthy men who bore influence in those trying times, not only to go forth in battle but to exercise wisdom in council, fortitude, courage, and endurance in the tented field, as well as subsequently to form and adopt those wise and efficient measures which secured to themselves and succeeding generations, the blessings of a free and independent government.

This government, so formed, has been blessed by the Almighty until she spreads her sails in every sea, and her power is felt in every land. 2:170.

This, then, is our position towards the Government of the United States and towards the world, to put down iniquity, and exalt virtue; to declare the word of God which he revealed unto us, and build up his Kingdom upon the earth. And, know all men, Governments, Nations, Kindreds, Tongues, and People, that this is our calling, intention, and design. We aim to live our religion, and have communion with our God. We aim to clear our skirts of the blood of this generation, by our faithfulness in preaching the truth of heaven in all plainness and simplicity; and I have often said, and repeat it now, that all other considerations of whatever name or nature, sink into insignificance in comparison with this. To serve God and keep his commandments, are first and foremost with me. If this is higher law, so be it. As it is with me, so should it be with every department of the Government; for this doctrine is based upon the principles of virtue and integrity; with it, the Government, her Constitution, and free institutions are safe; without it no power can avert their speedy destruction. It is the life-giving power to the Government; it is the vital element on which she exists and prospers; in absence she sinks to rise no more. 2:176.

CHIEF SEATTLE

❧

Oration

Yonder sky that has wept tears of compassion upon my people for centuries untold, and which to us appears changeless and eternal, may change. Today is fair. Tomorrow it may be overcast with clouds. My words are like the stars that never change. Whatever Seattle says the great chief at Washington can rely upon with as much certainty as he can upon the return of the sun or the seasons. The White Chief says that Big Chief at Washington sends us greetings of friendship and goodwill. That is kind of him for we know he has little need of our friendship in return. His people are many. They are like that grass that covers vast prairies. My people are few. They resemble the scattering trees of a storm-swept plain. . . . I will not dwell on, nor mourn over, our untimely decay, nor reproach our paleface brothers with hastening it, as we too may have been somewhat to blame. . . .

Your God is not our God. Your God loves your people and hates mine. He folds his strong and protecting arms lovingly about the paleface and leads him by the hand as a father leads his infant son—but He has forsaken His red children—if they really are His. Our God, the Great Spirit, seems also to have forsaken us. Your God makes your people strong every day. Soon they will fill the land. Our people are ebbing away like a rapidly receding tide that will never return. The white man's God cannot love our people or He would protect them. They seem to be orphans who can look nowhere for help. How then can we be brothers?. . . We are two distinct races with separate origins and separate destinies. There is little in common between us.

To us the ashes of our ancestors are sacred and their resting place is hallowed ground. You wander far from the graves of your ancestors and seemingly without regret. Your religion was written upon tables of stone by the iron finger of your God so that you could not forget. The Red Man could never comprehend nor remember it. Our religion is the traditions of our ancestors—the dreams

Delivered in 1854 to the Governor of the Washington Territory. [This is one of several versions of this famous oration in the public domain.—Editor]

of our old men, given them in solemn hours of night by the Great Spirit; and the visions of our sachems; and it is written in the hearts of our people.

Your dead cease to love you and the land of their nativity as soon as they pass the portals of the tomb and wander way beyond the stars. They are soon forgotten and never return. Our dead never forget the beautiful world that gave them being.

Day and night cannot dwell together. The Red Man has ever fled the approach of the White Man, as the morning mist flees before the morning sun. However, your proposition seems fair and I think that my people will accept it and will retire to the reservation you offer them. Then we will dwell apart in peace. . . . It matters little where we pass the remnant of our days. They will not be many. A few more moons; a few more winters—and not one of the descendants of the mighty hosts that once moved over this broad land or lived in happy homes, protected by the Great Spirit, will remain to mourn over the graves of a people once more powerful and hopeful than yours. But why should I mourn at the untimely fate of my people? Tribe follows tribe, and nation follows nation, like the waves of the sea. It is the order of nature, and regret is useless. Your time of decay may be distant, but it will surely come, for even the White Man whose God walked and talked with him as friend with friend, cannot be exempt from the common destiny. We may be brothers after all. We will see. . . .

Every part of this soil is sacred in the estimation of my people. Every hillside, every valley, every plain and grove, has been hallowed by some sad or happy event in days long vanished. The very dust upon which you now stand responds more lovingly to their footsteps than to yours, because it is rich with the blood of our ancestors and our bare feet are conscious of the sympathetic touch. Even the little children who lived here and rejoiced here for a brief season will love these somber solitudes and at eventide they greet shadowy returning spirits. And when the last Red Man shall have perished, and the memory of my tribe shall have become a myth among the White Men, these shores will swarm with the invisible dead of my tribe, and when your children's children think themselves alone in the field, the store, the shop, upon the highway, or in the silence of the pathless woods, they will not be alone. At night when the street of your cities and villages are silent and you think them deserted, they will throng with the returning hosts that once filled and still love this beautiful land. The White Man will never be alone.

Let him be just and deal kindly with my people, for the dead are not powerless. Dead, did I say? There is no death, only a change of worlds.

WALT WHITMAN

Passage to India

I

Singing my days,
Singing the great achievements of the present,
Singing the strong light works of engineers,
Our modern wonders, (the antique ponderous Seven outvied,)
In the Old World the east the Suez canal,   5
The New by its mighty railroad spann'd,
The seas inlaid with eloquent gentle wires;
Yet first to sound, and ever sound, the cry with thee O soul,
The Past! the Past! the Past!

The Past—the dark unfathom'd retrospect!   10
The teeming gulf—the sleepers and the shadows!
The past—the infinite greatness of the past!
For what is the present after all but a growth out of the past?
(As a projectile form'd, impell'd, passing a certain line, still keeps
    on,
So the present, utterly form'd, impell'd by the past.)   15

2

Passage O soul to India!
Eclaircise the myths Asiatic, the primitive fables.

Not you alone proud truths of the world,
Nor you alone ye facts of modern science,
But myths and fables of eld, Asia's, Africa's fables,   20
The far-darting beams of the spirit, the unloos'd dreams,

From *The Complete Writings of Walt Whitman*, IX (New York: G. P. Putnam's Sons, 1902), 186–97.

The deep diving bibles and legends,
The daring plots of the poets, the elder religions;
O you temples fairer than lilies pour'd over by the rising sun!
O you fables spurning the known, eluding the hold of the known,
    mounting to heaven!   25
You lofty and dazzling towers, pinnacled, red as roses, burnish'd
    with gold!
Towers of fables immortal fashion'd from mortal dreams!
You too I welcome and fully the same as the rest!
You too with joy I sing.

Passage to India!   30
Lo, soul, seest thou not God's purpose from the first?
The earth to be spann'd, connected by network,
The races, neighbors, to marry and be given in marriage,
The oceans to be cross'd, the distant brought near,
The lands to be welded together.   35

A worship new I sing,
You captains, voyagers, explorers, yours,
You engineers, you architects, machinists, yours,
You, not for trade or transportation only,
But in God's name, and for thy sake O soul.   40

3

Passage to India!
Lo soul for thee of tableaus twain,
I see in one the Suez canal initiated, open'd,
I see the procession of steamships, the Empress Eugenie's leading
    the van,
I mark from on deck the strange landscape, the pure sky, the level
    sand in the distance,   45
I pass swiftly the picturesque groups, the workmen gather'd,
The gigantic dredging machines.

In one again, different, (yea thine, all thine, O soul, the same,)
I see over my own continent the Pacific railroad surmounting every
    barrier,
I see continual trains of cars winding along the Platte carrying
    freight and passengers,   50

I hear the locomotives rushing and roaring, and the shrill steam-
  whistle,
I hear the echoes reverberate through the grandest scenery in the
  world,
I cross the Laramie plains, I note the rocks in grotesque shapes,
  the buttes,
I see the plentiful larkspur and wild onions, the barren, colorless
  sage-deserts,
I see in glimpses afar or towering immediately above me the great
  mountains, I see the Wind river and the Wahsatch mountains,   55
I see the Monument mountain and the Eagle's Nest, I pass the
  Promontory, I ascend the Nevadas,
I scan the noble Elk mountain and wind around its base,
I see the Humboldt range, I thread the valley and cross the river,
I see the clear waters of lake Tahoe, I see forests of majestic pines,
Or crossing the great desert, the alkaline plains, I behold
  enchanting mirages of waters and meadows,   60
Marking through these and after all, in duplicate slender lines,
Bridging the three or four thousand miles of land travel,
Tying the Eastern to the Western sea,
The road between Europe and Asia.

(Ah Genoese thy dream! Thy dream!   65
Centuries after thou art laid in thy grave,
The shore thou foundest verifies thy dream.)

                        4

Passage to India!
Struggles of many a captain, tales of many a sailor dead,
Over my mood stealing and spreading they come,   70
Like clouds and cloudlets in the unreach'd sky,

Along all history, down the slopes,
As a rivulet running, sinking now, and now again to the surface
  rising,
A ceaseless thought, a varied train—lo, soul, to thee, thy sight
  they rise,
The plans, the voyages again, the expeditions,   75
Again Vasco de Gama sails forth,
Again the knowledge gain'd, the mariner's compass,
Lands found and nations born, thou born America,

For purpose vast, man's long probation fill'd,
Thou rondure of the world at last accomplish'd.   80

5

O vast Rondure, swimming in space,
Cover'd all over with visible power and beauty,
Alternate light and day and the teeming spiritual darkness,
Unspeakable high processions of sun and moon and countless stars
    above,
Below, the manifold grass and waters, animals, mountains, trees,   85
With inscrutable purpose, some hidden prophetic intention,
Now first it seems my thought begins to span thee.

Down from the gardens of Asia descending radiating,
Adam and Eve appear, then their myriad progeny after them,
Wandering, yearning, curious, with restless explorations,   90
With questionings, baffled, formless, feverish, with never-happy
    hearts,
With that sad incessant refrain, *Wherefore unsatisfied soul?* and
    Whither O mocking life?

Ah who shall soothe these feverish children?
Who justify these restless explorations?
Who speak the secret of impassive earth?   95
Who bind it to us? what is this separate Nature so unnatural?
What is this earth to our affections? (unloving earth, without a
    throb to answer ours,
Cold earth, the place of graves.)

Yet soul be sure the first intent remains, and shall be carried out,
Perhaps even now the time has arrived.   100

After the seas are all cross'd, (as they seem already cross'd,)
After the great captains and engineers have accomplish'd their
    work,
After the noble inventors, after the scientists, the chemist, the
    geologist, ethnologist,
Finally shall come the poet worthy that name,
The true son of God shall come singing his songs.   105

Then not your deeds only O voyagers, O scientists and inventors,
    shall be justified,

All these hearts as of fretted children shall be sooth'd,
All affection shall be fully responded to, the secret shall be told,
All these separations and gaps shall be taken up and hook'd and
 link'd together,
The whole earth, this cold, impassive, voiceless earth, shall be
 completely justified, 110
Trinitas divine shall be gloriously accomplish'd and compacted
 by the true son of God, the poet,
(He shall indeed pass the straits and conquer the mountains,
He shall double the cape of Good Hope to some purpose,)
Nature and Man shall be disjoin'd and diffused no more,
The true son of God shall absolutely fuse them. 115

6

Year at whose wide-flung door I sing!
Year of the purpose accomplish'd!
Year of the marriage of continents, climates and oceans!
(No mere doge of Venice now wedding the Adriatic,)
I see O year in you the vast terraqueous globe given and giving
 all, 120
Europe to Asia, Africa join'd, and they to the New World,
The lands, geographies, dancing before you, holding a festival
 garland,
As brides and bridegrooms hand in hand.

Passage to India!
Cooling airs from Caucasus far, soothing cradle of man, 125
The river Euphrates flowing, the past lit up again,

Lo soul, the retrospect brought forward,
The old, most populous, wealthiest of earth's lands,
The streams of the Indus and the Ganges and their many affluents,
(I my shores of America walking to-day behold, resuming all,) 130
The tale of Alexander on his warlike marches suddenly dying,
On one side China and on the other side Persia and Arabia,
To the south the great seas and the bay of Bengal,
The flowing literatures, tremendous epics, religions, castes,
Old occult Brahma interminably far back, the tender and junior
 Buddha, 135
Central and southern empires and all their belongings, possessors,
The wars of Tamerlane, the reign of Aurungzebe,

The traders, rulers, explorers, Moslems, Venetians, Byzantium, the
    Arabs, Portuguese,
The first travelers famous yet, Marco Polo, Batouta the Moor,
Doubts to be solv'd, the map incognita, blanks to be fill'd,   140
The foot of man unstay'd, the hands never at rest,
Thyself O soul that will not brook a challenge.
The mediaeval navigators rise before me,
The world of 1492, with its awaken'd enterprise,
Something swelling in humanity now like the sap of the earth in
    spring,   145
The sunset splendor of chivalry declining.

And who art thou sad shade?
Gigantic, visionary, thyself a visionary,
With majestic limbs and pious beaming eyes,
Spreading around with every look of thine a golden world,   150
Enhuing it with gorgeous hues.

As the chief historian,
Down to the footlights walks in some great scena,
Dominating the rest I see the Admiral himself,
(History's type of courage, action, faith,)   155
Behold him sail from Palos leading his little fleet,
His voyage behold, his return, his great fame,
His misfortunes, calumniators, behold him a prisoner, chain'd,
Behold his dejection, poverty, death.

(Curious in time I stand, noting the efforts of heroes,   160
Is the deferment long? bitter the slander, poverty, death?
Lies the seed unreck'd for centuries in the ground? lo, to God's
    due occasion,
Uprising in the night, it sprouts, blooms,
And fills the earth with use and beauty.)

7

Passage indeed O soul to primal thought,   165
Not lands and seas alone, thy own clear freshness,
The young maturity of brood and bloom,
To realms of budding bibles,

O soul, repressless, I wish thee and thou with me,
Thy circumnavigation of the world begin,   170

Of man, the voyage of his mind's return,
To reason's early paradise,
Back, back to wisdom's birth, to innocent intuitions,
Again with fair creation.

8

O we can wait no longer,   175
We too take ship O soul,
Joyous we too launch out on trackless seas,
Fearless for unknown shores on waves of ecstasy to sail,
Amid the wafting winds, (thou pressing me to thee, I thee to me,
   O soul,)
Caroling free, singing our song of God,   180
Chanting our chant of pleasant exploration.

With laugh and many a kiss,
(Let others deprecate, let others weep for sin, remorse, humilia-
   tion,)
O soul thou pleasest me, I thee.

Ah more than any priest O soul we too believe in God,   185
But with the mystery of God we dare not dally.

O soul thou pleasest me, I thee,
Sailing these seas or on the hills, or waking in the night,
Thoughts, silent thoughts, of Time and Space and Death, like
   waters flowing,
Bear me indeed as through the regions infinite,   190
Whose air I breathe, whose ripples hear, lave me all over,
Bathe me O God in thee, mounting to thee,
I and my soul to range in range of thee.

O Thou transcendent,
Nameless, the fibre and the breath,   195
Light of the light, shedding forth universes, thou centre of them,
Thou mightier centre of the true, the good, the loving,
Thou moral, spiritual fountain—affection's source—thou reservoir,
(O pensive soul of me—O thirst unsatisfied—waitest not there?
Waitest not haply for us somewhere there the Comrade perfect?) 200
Thou pulse—thou motive of the stars, suns, systems,
That, circling, move in order, safe, harmonious,
Athwart the shapeless vastnesses of space,

How should I think, how breathe a single breath, how speak, if
    out of myself,
I could not launch, to those, superior universes?   205

Swiftly I shrivel at the thought of God,
At Nature and its wonders, Time and Space and Death,
But that I, turning, call to thee O soul, thou actual Me,
And lo, thou gently masterest the orbs,
Thou matest Time, smilest content at Death,   210
And fillest, swellest full the vastnesses of Space.

Greater than stars or suns,
Bounding O soul thou journeyest forth;
What love than thine and ours could wider amplify?
What aspirations, wishes, outvie thine and ours O soul?   215
What dreams of the ideal? what plans of purity, perfection,
    strength,
What cheerful willingness for others' sake to give up all?
For others' sake to suffer all?

Reckoning ahead O soul, when thou, the time achiev'd,
The seas all cross'd, weather'd the capes, the voyage done,   220
Surrounded, copest, frontest God, yieldest, the aim attain'd,
As filled with friendship, love complete, the Elder Brother found,
The Younger melts in fondness in his arms.

9

Passage to more than India!
Are thy wings plumed indeed for such far flights?   225
O soul, voyagest thou indeed on voyages like those?
Disportest thou on waters such as those?
Soundest below the Sanscrit and the Vedas?
Then have thy bent unleash'd.

Passage to you, your shores, ye aged fierce enigmas!   230
Passage to you, to mastership of you, ye strangling problems!
You, strew'd with the wrecks of skeletons, that living, never
    reach'd you.

Passage to more than India!
O secret of the earth and sky!
Of you O waters of the sea! O winding creeks and rivers!   235

Of you O woods and fields! of you strong mountains of my land!
Of you O prairies! of you gray rocks!
O morning red! O clouds! O rains and snows!
O day and night, passage to you!

O sun and moon and all you stars! Sirius and Jupiter!   240
Passage to you!

Passage, immediate passage! the blood burns in my veins!
Away O soul! hoist instantly the anchor!
Cut the hawsers—haul out—shake out every sail!
Have we not stood here like trees in the ground long enough?   245
Have we not grovel'd here long enough, eating and drinking like
    mere brutes?
Have we not darken'd and dazed ourselves with books long
    enough?

Sail forth—steer for the deep waters only,
Reckless O soul, exploring, I with thee, and thou with me,
For we are bound where mariner has not yet dared to go,   250
And we will risk the ship, ourselves and all.

O my brave soul!
O farther farther sail!
O daring joy, but safe! are they not all the seas of God?
O farther, farther, farther sail!   255

ALBERT J. BEVERIDGE

✣

The Star of Empire

Speech opening the Republican Campaign for the West in the
Auditorium, at Chicago, September 25, 1900, in reply to Mr. Bryan's
Indianapolis speech accepting his second Democratic nomination for
President. This speech was used by the Republicans as a
National Campaign document.

"Westward the Star of Empire takes its Way." Not the star of kingly power, for
kingdoms are everywhere dissolving in the increasing rights of men; not the
star of autocratic oppression, for civilization is brightening and the liberties of
the people are broadening under every flag. But the star of empire, as Washington used the word, when he called this Republic an "empire"; as Jefferson
understood it, when he declared our form of government ideal for extending "our empire"; as Marshall understood it, when he closed a noble period of
an immortal constitutional opinion by naming the domain of the American
people "our empire."

This is the "empire" of which the prophetic voice declared "Westward the
Star of Empire takes its Way"—the star of the empire of liberty and law, of
commerce and communication, of social order and the Gospel of our Lord—
the star of the empire of the civilization of the world. Westward *that* star of
empire takes its course. And to-day it illumines our path of duty across the
Pacific into the islands and lands where Providence has called us.

In that path the American government is marching forward, opposed at
every step by those who deny the right of the Republic to plant the institutions
of the Flag where Events have planted that Flag itself. For this is our purpose,
to perform which the Opposition declares that the Republic has no warrant in
the Constitution, in morals or in the rights of man. And I mean to examine
to-night every argument they advance for their policy of reaction and retreat.

It is not true, as the Opposition asserts, that every race without instruction

From Albert J. Beveridge, *The Meaning of the Times and Other Speeches* (Indianapolis: The Bobbs-
Merrill Co., 1908), pp. 118–43.

and guidance is naturally self-governing. If so, the Indians were capable of self-government. America belonged to them whether they were or were not capable of self-government. If they were capable of self-government it was not only wrong, but it was a crime to set up our independent government on their land without their consent. If this is true, the Puritans, instead of being noble, are despicable characters; and the patriots of 1776, to whom the Opposition compares the Filipinos, were only a swarm of land pirates. If the Opposition is right, the Zulus who owned the Transvaal were capable of self-government; and the Boers who expelled them, according to the Opposition, deserve the abhorrence of righteous men.

But while the Boers took the lands they occupy from the natives who peopled them; while we peopled this country in spite of the Indian who owned it; and while this may be justified by the welfare of the world which those events advanced, that is not what is to be done in the Philippines. The American government, as a government, will not appropriate the Filipinos' land or permit Americans as individuals to seize it. It will protect the Filipinos in their possessions. If any American secures real estate in the Philippines, it will be because he buys it from the owner. Under American administration the Filipino who owns his little plot of ground will experience a security in the possession of his property that he has never known before.

The English in Egypt and India have not taken the land from its owners; they have confirmed the occupants in their ownership. In Hawaii we have not taken the land from its owners; we have secured its owners in their peaceable possession. And our administration in the Philippines will also establish there that same security of property and life which is the very beginning of civilization itself.

If it be said that tropical countries can not be peopled by the Caucasian race, I answer that, even if true, it is no reason why they should not be governed by the Caucasian race. India is a tropical country. India is ruled by England to the advantage of India and England alike. Who denies that India's 300,000,000 are better off under English administration than under the bestial tyranny of native rulers, to whom the agony of their subjects was the highest form of amusement?

Dare Mr. Bryan say that he would have India back to its condition before England took it? If he dare not, he is answered. Dare he say that he would withdraw English rule now? If he dare not, he is answered. Dare he say that he would take the English "residents" from the Malay States and turn them back again to the rule of their brutal lords? If he dare not, he is answered. Dare he say that the Boers should restore the Transvaal to its original owners? If he dare not, he is answered. Dare he deny that the greatest progress shown upon the map of earth to-day is the progress of Egypt during the last twenty years under English rule? If he dare not, he is answered. And he dare not. If he proclaims his faith in the Filipino people, who know not the meaning of self-government, I declare my faith in the American people, who have developed the realities of liberty.

Grant, for the purposes of argument, the Opposition's premise that the white man can not people the Philippines. Grant, also, that the Malays of those islands can not, unaided, establish civilization there; build roads, open mines, erect schools, maintain social order, repress piracy and administer safe government throughout the archipelago. And this must be granted; for they are the same race which inhabits the Malay Peninsula. What, then, is the conclusion demanded by the general welfare of the world?

Surely not that this land, rich in all that civilized man requires, and these people needing the very blessings they ignorantly repel, should be remanded to savagery and the wilderness! If you say this, you say that barbarism and undeveloped resources are better than civilization and the earth's resources developed. What is the conclusion, then, which the logic of civilization compels from these admitted premises? It is that the reign of law must be established throughout these islands, their resources developed and their people civilized by those in whose blood resides the genius of administration.

Such are all Teutonic and Celtic peoples. Such are the Dutch; behold their work in Java. Such are the English; behold their work all around the world. Such the German; behold his advance into the fields of world-regeneration and administration. Such were the French before Napoleon diverted their energies; behold their work in Canada, Louisiana, and our great Northwest. And such, more than any people who ever lived, are the Americans, into whose hands God has given the antipodes to develop their resources, to regenerate their people and to establish there the civilization of law-born liberty and liberty-born law.

If the Opposition declares that we ought to set up a separate government over the Philippines because we are setting up a separate government over Cuba, I answer that such an error in Cuba does not justify the same error in the Philippines. I am speaking for myself alone, but speaking thus, I say, that for the good of Cuba more even than for the good of the United States, a separate government over Cuba, uncontrolled by the American Republic, *never should have been promised.*

Cuba is a mere extension of our Atlantic coast-line. It commands the ocean entrances to the Mississippi and the Isthmian Canal. Jefferson's dearest dream was that Cuba should belong to the United States. To possess this extension of American soil has been the wish of every far-seeing statesman from Jefferson to Blaine. Annexation to the greatest nation the world has ever seen is a prouder Cuban destiny than separate nationality. As an American possession, Cuba might possibly have been fitted for statehood in a period not much longer than that in which Louisiana was prepared for statehood.

Even now the work of regeneration—of cleansing cities, building roads, establishing posts, erecting a system of universal education and the action of all the forces that make up our civilization—is speeding forward faster than at any time or place in human history—American administration! But yesterday there were less than ten thousand Cuban children in school; to-day there are nearly one hundred and fifty thousand Cuban children in school—American administration! But yesterday Havana was the source of our yellow-fever plagues; to-day it is nearly as healthy as New Orleans—American administration!

When we stop this work and withdraw our restraint, revolution will succeed revolution in Cuba, as in the Central and South American countries; Havana again fester with the yellow death; systematic education again degenerate into sporadic instances; and Cuba, which under our control should be a source of profit, power and glory to the Republic and herself, will be a source of irritation and of loss, of danger and disease to both. The United States needs Cuba for our protection; *but Cuba needs the United States for Cuba's salvation.*

The resolution for Cuban independence, hastily passed by all parties in Congress, at an excited hour, was an error which years of time, propinquity of location, common commerce, mutual interests and similar dangers surely will correct. The President, jealous of American honor, considers that resolution a promise. And American promise means performance. And so the unnatural experiment is to be tried. What war and nature—aye, what God hath joined together—is to be put asunder.

I speak for myself alone, but speaking thus, I say that it will be an evil day for Cuba when the Stars and Stripes come down from Morro Castle. I speak for myself alone, but I believe that in this my voice is the voice of the American millions, as it is the voice of the ultimate future, when I say that Porto Rico is ours and ours for ever; the Philippines are ours and ours for ever; and Cuba ought to have been ours, and by the free choice of her people some day will be ours, and ours for ever.

We have a foreign nation on our north; another on our southwest; and now to permit another foreign nation within cannon shot of our southeast coast, will indeed create conditions which will require that militarism which the Opposition to the Government pretends to fear. Think of Cuba in alliance with England or Germany or France! Think of Cuba a naval station and ally of one of the great foreign powers, every one of whom is a rival of America! And so my answer to Mr. Bryan's comparison is that, if we have made a mistake in Cuba, we ought not to make the same mistake in the Philippines.

· · ·

Consider, now, the Opposition's proposed method of procedure in the Philippines: It is to establish a stable government there, turn that government over to the Filipinos, and protect them and their government from molestation by any other nation.

Suppose the Opposition's plan in operation. Suppose a satisfactory government is established, turned over to the Filipinos and American troops withdrawn. The new government must experience feuds, factions and revolution. This is the history of every new government. It was so even with the American people. Witness Shays' Rebellion against the National Government, almost shaking its foundations; witness the Whiskey Rebellion in Pennsylvania, which required the first exercise of armed national power to maintain order with a state of the Union. And we were of a self-governing race—at that period we were almost wholly Anglo-Saxon.

How can we expect the Philippine Malays to escape this common fate of all new governments? Remember that as a race they have not that civil cohesion which binds a people into a nation. Remember that every island is envious of every other one; and that in each island every officer is a "general," jealous of his dignity, intriguing for advancement.

How long would this stable government, which the Opposition asks us to "establish," *remain* "stable," if we withdrew our forces? And if resistance broke out in the Visayas, if revolt sprang into flame among the murderous Moros, what would be our duty? It would be to reënter where we had withdraw and restore the stability of the government which the Opposition declares that we shall establish before we withdraw. And so the Opposition program constantly defeats itself and compels us to do over and over again the work which we must perform at the beginning. And all this without benefit to the Philippine people, without improvement to their lands and with immeasurable loss to ourselves recouped not from a single source of profit. But the American flag floating there for ever means not only established liberty, but permanent stability.

Again governments must have money. That is their first necessity; money for salaries, money for the army, money for public buildings, money for improvements. Before the revenues are established, the government must have money. If the revenues are inadequate, nevertheless the government must have money. Therefore, all governments are borrowers. Even the government of the American people—the richest people of history—is a borrower. Even the government of the British people, who for centuries have been accumulating wealth, must borrow; its bonds are in our own bank vaults. Much more, then, must little governments borrow money.

If, then, we "establish a stable government," as the Opposition demands, and turn that government over to the Filipinos, they also must borrow money. But suppose the Philippine government can not pay its debt when it falls due, as has been the case in many instances on our own continent within the last quarter of a century; as is the case to-day with one of the governments of Central America. If that loan is an English loan, England would seize the revenues of the Philippines for the payment of her debt, as she has done before and is doing now. So would France or Germany or whoever was the creditor nation. Should we have a right to interfere? Of course not, unless we were willing to guarantee the Philippine debt. If, then, the first purpose of the Opposition candidate is carried out, we must:

Keep "stable" the government which we first "*establish*," or the very purpose of the establishment of that government is defeated.

If the second proposition of the Opposition is performed we must:

First: Control the finances of the Philippines perpetually; or,

Second: Guarantee the loans the Philippine government makes with other nations; or,

Third: Go to war with those nations to defeat their collection of their just debts.

Is this sound policy? Is it profitable? Is it moral? Is it just to the Filipinos, to the world, to ourselves? Is it humane to the masses of those children who need first of all, and more than all, order, law and peace? Is it prudent, wise, far-seeing statesmanship? *And does the adoption of a similar course in Cuba justify it in the Philippines?*

No. Here is the program of reason and righteousness, and Time and Events will make it the program of the Republic:

First: We have given Porto Rico such a civil government as her situation demands, under the Stars and Stripes.

Second: We will put down the rebellion and then give the Philippines such a civil government as the situation demands, under the Stars and Stripes.

Third: We are regenerating Cuba, and when our preparatory work is done, we should have given Cuba such a civil government as her situation may demand, under the Stars and Stripes.

The sovereignty of the Stars and Stripes can be nothing but a blessing to any people and to any land.

I do not advocate this course for commercial reasons, though these have their weight. All men who understand production and exchange, understand the commercial advantage resulting from our ownership of these rich possessions. But I waive this large consideration as insignificant, compared with the master argument of the progress of civilization, which under God, the American people are henceforth to lead until our day is done. For henceforward in the trooping of the colors of the nations they shall cluster around and follow the Republic's banner.

The mercantile argument is mighty with Americans in merely mercantile times, and it should be so; but the argument of destiny is the master argument in the hour of destiny, and it should be so. The American people never yet entered on a great movement for merely mercantile reasons. Sentiment and duty have started and controlled every noble current of American history. And at this historic hour, destiny is the controlling consideration in the prophetic statesmanship which conditions require of the American people.

It is destiny that the world shall be rescued from its natural wilderness and from savage men. Civilization is no less an evolution than the changing forms of animal and vegetable life. Surely and steadily the reign of law, which is the very spirit of liberty, takes the place of arbitrary caprice. Surely and steadily the methods of social order are bringing the whole earth under their subjection. And to deny that this is right, is to deny that civilization should increase. In this great work the American people must have their part. They are fitted for the work as no people have ever been fitted; and their work lies before them.

If the Opposition say that they grant this, but that the highest considerations of abstract human rights demand that the Philippines shall have such a government as they wish, regardless of the remainder of the world, I answer that the desire of the Filipinos is not the only factor in determining their government, just as the desire of no individual man is the only factor determining his conduct. It is written in the moral law of individuals that "No man liveth to himself alone"; and it is no less written in the moral law of peoples that "No people liveth to itself alone."

The world is interested in the Philippines, and it has a right to be. The world is interested in India, and it has a right to be. Civilization is interested in China and its government, and that is the duty of civilization. You can not take the Philippines out of the operation of those forces which are binding all mankind into one vast and united intelligence. When Circumstance has raised our flag above them, we dare not turn these misguided children over to destruction by themselves or spoliation by others, and then make answer when the God of nations requires them at our hands, "Am I my brother's keeper?"

If you admit that it is the purpose of that Intelligence that rules the universe to civilize and unify mankind, how is this to be accomplished? If you say that it is by leaving each people to themselves to work out their own salvation, I answer that history shows that civilization has been preserved only by the most superior nations extending it. And the method of extending civilization is by colonization where the superior nation can establish itself among the inferior races; or in place of them, if the inferior races can not exist under civilization, as in New Zealand, Australia and the like. The method is by administration where the superior nation can not, because of climatic conditions, establish itself among or supplant the inferior races, as in Java, India, and the like. And finally that method is by creating and developing commerce among all the peoples of the world.

It is thus that America itself was discovered; thus that this Republic was builded; thus that South Africa was reclaimed; thus that Australia was recovered from the Bushman and made the home of civilization; thus that Ceylon was taken from wild men and tangled jungle and brought beneath the rule of religion, law and industry. It is thus that Egypt is being redeemed, her deserts fertilized, her starving millions fed, her fellahs made men and the blessings of just government bestowed upon the land of the Pharaohs. It is thus that the regeneration of India has progressed, her cities been cleansed, the reign of hygiene and health gradually established in the very kingdom of pestilence and disease; and the arbitrary and infamous tyranny of petty princes, holding power of life and death over miserable subjects, reduced to the orderly administration of equal and unpurchased justice under equal and impartial laws.

History establishes these propositions:

First: Every people who have become great, have become colonizers or administrators;

Second: Coincident with this colonization and administration, their material and political greatness develops;

Third: Their decline is coincident with the abandonment of the policy of possession and administration, or departure from the true principles thereof.

And as a corollary to these propositions is this self-evident and contemporaneous truth:

Every progressive nation of Europe to-day is seeking lands to colonize and governments to administer.

And can this common instinct of the most progressive peoples of the world —this common conclusion of the ablest statesmen of other nations—be baseless?

If the Opposition asks why this is the mission of the American people now more than heretofore, I answer that before any people assumes these great tasks it goes through a process of consolidation and unification, just as a man achieves maturity before he assumes the tasks of a man. Great Britain never became a colonizing and administering power until the separate peoples of England, Scotland, Ireland and Wales, welded into a single indivisible people, were ready to go forth as a national unit and do the great work to which the world was calling it.

The German people did not embark upon this natural policy until separate duchies, principalities and kingdoms were finally welded by a common war, common blood, and common interests into a great single and indivisible people ready to go forth as a national unit to the great work to which the world was calling it.

The French became colonizers of lands and administrators of governments only when her great statesmen, from Richelieu to Colbert, had knit the separate and divided French people into a national unit and sent it forth to the work to which the world was calling it; and France declined only when she abandoned that natural law of national power and progress, and Napoleon diverted her energies to the internal strifes of Europe. Then her decline began.

She lost Canada. The Corsican sold Louisiana to us. And to-day French states-men at last realize the fatal operation of this law when once disobeyed, and so again are seeking to become one of the colonizing and administering powers of earth.

The American Republic has been going through the process of fitting it for the execution of this natural law of civilization. Hitherto we have had local divisions. The proposition that we were a single people, a national unit, and not a sum of segregated factions, was denied. And it required war and commerce and time—the shedding of blood, the uniting of communities by railroads and telegraphs, the knitting together of the fabric of Nationality by that wonderful loom of human intelligence called the post; and finally, the common and united effort of a foreign war, to bring us to a consciousness of our power *as a people*. And there is never in nature a power without a corre-sponding purpose. Shall we now stop this process of nature?

We are this at last, a great national unit ready to carry out that univer-sal law of civilization which requires of every people who have reached our high estate to become colonizers of new lands, administrators of orderly gov-ernment over savage and senile peoples. And being thus prepared, the lands and peoples needing our administration are delivered to our keeping, not by our design, but by occurrence beyond our control. In the astronomy of Des-tiny, American Opportunity, American Duty and American Preparedness are in conjunction. Who shall oppose their progress?

These are the laws which history advises are the laws of civilization's growth. These, therefore, are the high ordinances of universal and racial morality which has for its ultimate object "that far-off divine event towards which civilization tends." And it is to this divine order of progress that I appeal in answer to the misapplied individual moralities that would give Australia back to its Bushmen, the United States to its Indians, Ceylon to its natives, and the whole world back to barbarism and night.

If the Opposition says that this program, written not in the statutes of man, but in the nature of things, will smother our institutions with a myriad of soldiers, I answer that the world to-day demonstrates that it will result in the reverse. If they point to Germany, and other nations with vast military estab-lishments, to prove that colonization and administration over lands held as possessions and dependencies result in the supremacy of the soldiery over the common people, I answer that the examples do not sustain, but destroy the proposition.

Consider Germany. Her standing army in times of peace is 562,000 men. Does colonization cause or require them? No; because she maintained that mighty multitude before the present Emperor and his counsellors developed Germany's progressive colonial and administrative policy. No, again; because, of Germany's standing army of 562,000 men, less than 4,000 are in her possessions, the remainder of her mighty host being stationed within the Empire itself. No, again; because Austria, with no colonies at all, has a standing army in times of peace of over 361,000 men, none of whom is employed in the care of possessions. No, again; because France, a republic, has a standing army in times of peace of 616,000 men, of which less than 10,000 are employed in her colonies and possessions except in Algeria and Tunis, which are considered an immediate part of France. No, again; because Italy, with hardly a colonial possession, maintains a standing army in times of peace of nearly 325,000 men. No, again; because Spain, the world's second largest holder of possessions before we won them, maintained a standing army of less than 100,000 men, of whom less than 10,000 were kept in her misruled and oppressed possessions. No, again; because the greatest colonial power that the world has ever seen, the Empire of Great Britain, has a smaller standing army in times of peace than any power of Europe—less than half as many as Germany, almost two-thirds less than the soldiers of France, nearly one-third less than Italy, and one-third less than the soldiers maintained by Austria, an absolutely non-colonizing power.

. . .

If we do our duty in the Philippines, it is admitted that we ought not to govern the Filipinos as fellow-citizens of the Republic. The Platform of the Opposition says that "to make the Filipinos citizens would endanger our civilization." To force upon Malays, who three hundred years ago were savages and who since that time have been schooled only in oppression, that form of self-government exercised the citizens of the United States, would be to clothe an infant in the apparel of a giant and require of it a giant's strength and tasks. If we govern them, we must govern them with common sense. They must first be made familiar with the simplest principles of liberty—equal obedience to equal laws, impartial justice by unpurchasable courts, protection of property and of the right to labor—in short, with the *substance* of liberty which civilized government will establish among them.

The Filipinos must begin at the beginning and grow in the knowledge of free institutions, and, if possible, into the ultimate practice of free government by observing the operation of those institutions among them and by experiencing their benefits. They have experienced unjust, unequal and arbitrary taxation; this is the result of the institutions of tyranny. They must experience equal, just and scientific taxation; this is the result of free institutions. They have experienced arrest without cause, imprisonment without a hearing, and beheld justice bought and sold; these are the results of the institutions of tyranny. They must experience arrest only for cause publicly made known, conviction only after trial publicly conducted and justice impartial, unpurchasable and speedily administered; these are the results of free institutions.

They have experienced the violation of the home and robbery by public officers; these are the results of the institutions of tyranny. They must experience the sanctity of the fireside, the separation of Church and State, the punishment of soldier or public official practising outrage or extortion upon them; these are the results of free institutions. And these are the results which they will experience under the government of the American Institutions, and our *institutions* follow the flag.

The institutions of every nation follow its flag. German institutions follow the flag of the Fatherland. English institutions follow the banner of St. George. French institutions follow the tricolor of France. And just so, American institutions follow the emblem of the Republic. Nay! Our institutions not only follow the flag, *they accompany it.* They troop beneath its fold. Wherever an American citizen goes, he carries the spirit of our institutions. On whatever soil his blood is shed to establish the sovereignty of our flag, there are planted the imperishable seeds of the institutions of our Nation; and there those institutions flourish in proportion as the soil where they are planted is prepared for them.

Free institutions are as definite, certain and concrete as our Constitution itself. Free speech is an institution of liberty. Free schools are an institution of liberty. Freedom of worship is an institution of liberty. Any American school-boy can catalogue free institutions. And as fast as the simplest of these institutions prepares these children Providence has given into our keeping for higher grades, just so fast more complex forms of our institutions will follow as naturally as childhood succeeds infancy, youth succeeds childhood and manhood crowns maturity. Our flag! Our institutions! Our Constitution! This is the immortal order in which American civilization marches.

And so the answer to the politician's battle-cry that "our Constitution follows the flag" is this great truth of popular liberty, OUR INSTITUTIONS FOLLOW THE FLAG.

We are a Nation. We can acquire territory. If we can acquire territory, we can govern it. If we can govern it, we can govern it as its situation may demand. If the Opposition says that power so broad is dangerous to the liberties of the American people, I answer that the American people's liberties can never be endangered at the hands of the American people; and, therefore, that their liberties can not be endangered by the exercise of this power, because this power is power exercised by the American people themselves.

> "*Congress* shall have power to dispose of and make all needful rules and regulations respecting territory belonging to the United States," says the Constitution.

And what is Congress? The agent of the American people. The Constitution created Congress. But who created the Constitution? "We, the people," declares the Constitution itself.

The American people created the Constitution; it is their method. The

American people established Congress; it is their instrument. The American people elect the members of Congress; they are the people's servants. Their laws are the people's laws. Their power is the people's power. And if you fear this power, you fear the people. If you want their power restricted, it is because you want the power of the people restricted; and a restriction of their power is a restriction of their liberty. So that the end of the logic of the Opposition is limitation upon the liberties of the American people, for fear that the liberties of the American people will suffer at the hands of the American people—which is absurd.

If the Opposition asserts that the powers which the Constitution gives to the legislative agents of the American people will not be exercised in righteousness, I answer that that can only be because the American people themselves are not righteous. It is the American people, through their agents, who exercise the power; and if those agents do not act as the people would have them, they will discharge those agents and annul their acts. The heart of the whole argument on the constitutional power of the government is faith in the wisdom and virtue of the people; and in that virtue and wisdom I believe, as every man must, who believes in a republic. In the end, the judgment of the masses is right. If this were not so, progress would be impossible, since only through the people is progress achieved.

The Opposition says that American liberties will be lost if we administer the substance of liberty to those children. Does any man believe that the American institution of free schools will be destroyed or impaired because we plant free schools throughout the Philippines? Does any man believe that equal rights will be impaired here, because we establish equal rights there?

The individual rights of Englishmen have not declined since England became an administrator of external governments; on the contrary, as England has extended her colonies, the individual rights of individual Englishmen have increased. The rights of the Crown have not enlarged as England's empire has extended; on the contrary, they have diminished. The period of England's great activity in external government has been precisely the period of the extension of the suffrage in England itself, of the enactment of laws for the protection of labor and the amelioration of all the conditions of life among the common people of England.

. . .

This is no unprecedented struggle. It is the ever-old and yet the ever-new, because the ever-elemental contest between the forces of a growing nationality and those who resist it; between the forces of extending dominion and those who oppose it; between the forces that are making us the master people of the world and those who think that our activities should be confined to this continent for ever. It is the eternal duel between the forces of progress and reaction, of construction and disintegration, of growth and decay.

Both sides are and always have been sincere. Washington was sincere when he advocated the adoption of the Constitution; Patrick Henry was sincere when he resisted it as the death-blow to our liberties. Jefferson was sincere when he acquired the empire of Louisiana; Josiah Quincy was sincere when he declared in Congress that the Louisiana acquisition meant the dissolution of the Union.

Webster was sincere when he asserted the sovereignty of the Nation, the indestructibility of the Union, and declared that the Constitution could not follow the flag until the American people so decreed; and Calhoun was sincere when he pronounced the doctrine of state sovereignty, the right of nullification, and announced that the Constitution, carrying slavery, followed the flag in spite of the will of the American people. Lincoln was sincere when he proclaimed that the Union was older than the Constitution, that nationality was the indestructible destiny of the American people, and that he would maintain that nationality by arms; and those mistaken ones were sincere who sought to divide the American people and on the field of battle poured out their blood fighting for their faith.

But their sincerity did not make them *right*. Their earnestness, ability, courage could not give them victory. They were struggling against the Fates. They were resisting the onward forces which were making of the American people the master Nation of the world—the forces that established us first as a separate political body, then welded us into a national unit, indivisible; then extended our dominion from ocean to ocean over unexplored wilderness; and now in the ripeness of time fling our authority and unfurl our flag almost around the globe. It is the "divine event" of American principles among the governments of men for which these forces have been working since the Pilgrims landed on the red man's soil. Men—patriotic, brave and wise—have sought to stay that tremendous purpose of destiny, but their opposition was as the feeble finger of a babe against the resistless pour of the Gulf Stream's mighty current.

For God's hand was in it all. His plans were working out their glorious results. And just as futile is resistance to the continuance to-day of the eternal movement of the American people toward the mastery of the world. This is a destiny neither vague nor undesirable. It is definite, splendid and holy.

When nations shall war no more without the consent of the American Republic: what American heart thrills not with pride at that prospect? And yet our interests are weaving themselves so rapidly around the world that that time is almost here.

When governments stay the slaughter of human beings, because the American Republic demands it: what American heart thrills not with pride at that prospect? And yet to-night there sits in Constantinople a sovereign who knows that time is nearly here.

When the commerce of the world on which the world's peace hangs, traveling every ocean highway of earth, shall pass beneath the guns of the great Republic: what American heart thrills not at that prospect? Yet that time will be here before the first quarter of the twentieth century closes.

When any changing of the map of earth requires a conference of the Powers, and when, at any Congress of the Nations, the American Republic will preside as the most powerful of powers and most righteous of judges: what American heart thrills not at that prospect? And yet, that prospect is in sight, even as I speak.

It is the high and holy destiny of the American people, and from that destiny the American bugles will never sound retreat. "Westward the Star of Empire takes its way!" AMERICAN INSTITUTIONS FOLLOW THE AMERICAN FLAG.

Part Four

Civil War and National Destiny

The mortar shell that burst over Fort Sumter in the early morning of April 12, 1861, signaled Confederate batteries ringing Charleston Harbor to open fire on Federal forces occupying the stronghold. That explosion announced the beginning of the bloody Civil War that would claim, through wounds and disease, the lives of 600,000 Americans. It also heralded the onset of history's direst threat to an undivided American destiny. To be sure, the nation was badly divided long before the act of secession and the ensuing war. Antipathy between an industrial North and an agricultural South, abetted by abolitionist and proslavery literature and by contention over western territories, had already spelled the loss of agreement on America's historic role. Yet whatever hopes for an undivided national destiny may have burned deep within American breasts before the war were in danger of being utterly extinguished by the gathering storm.

It comes as no surprise to find both Northern and Southern apologists during the conflict identifying their separate causes with the destiny of the nation. Both felt that they were defending an authentically *American* mission. Both invoked the help of the nation's God. Both viewed their own section as the citadel of the fundamental principles of American government. Both assumed that their military was the advance guard of the New Israel crossing the Red Sea of war.

Henry Ward Beecher stirred up considerable support for the Union side and confidently identified the Northern cause with the nation's destiny. Neither a profound nor an original religious thinker, Beecher was nevertheless one of the most influential and popular ministers of the nineteenth century. He had long used his platform at Plymouth (Congregational) Church of Brooklyn for the discussion of social and political issues. During the war years he directed his oratorical powers to a vigorous defense of the Union and a caustic indictment of the Confederacy.

When news of the firing on Fort Sumter reached New York, Beecher addressed his Plymouth congregation on the religious and national meaning of the impending war. The sermon, "The Battle Set in Array," set forth the themes that Beecher would reiterate during the next four years. Although Beecher professed an abhorrence for war, he insisted that God's chosen were usually called to suffer for their principles, war being the suffering facing God's American Israel. And although he warned against a vengeful spirit, his warning lost much of its force when he portrayed Southerners as "hot, narrow, boastful" and completely devoid of the sentiments of liberty and national patriotism. In a later sermon before the same congregation he would make the polarity between North and South absolute: "I thank them [the Confederacy] that they took another flag to do the Devil's work, and left our flag to do the work of God." Clearly Beecher believed Northern war efforts to be the instruments of God himself as the Union prepared to preserve America as the "chosen refuge of liberty for all the earth" and to stamp out slavery, the last major obstacle to American freedom. (Beecher was a Republican who campaigned for Lincoln in 1860, but he criticized Lincoln for the delay in issuing an emancipation proclamation. From the start Beecher viewed the war as a moral crusade against slavery.)

James Silver has demonstrated how religious leaders and associations were effective in arousing and sustaining the morale of the people in the South during the Civil War. "Because of the limited industrial resources of the South, the success of the Confederacy depended on the degree of intestinal fortitude developed by the man in the street and on the farm. He needed to identify himself as a member of God's chosen people and his country as a fulfillment of the destiny of history." Jewish and Catholic leaders performed significant roles in so boosting Confederate morale, but the strongest support came from Southern Protestantism.[1] Through sermons, tracts, and editorials composed for both civilians and soldiers, Protestant ministers and editors depicted the Southern struggle against Union forces as the attempt of a chosen people to preserve an American destiny abandoned by Yankee infidels.

There was no more active a sustainer of Confederate morale or more energetic a proponent of Southern destiny than Benjamin Morgan Palmer, minister of the First Presbyterian Church in New Orleans. In terms of intellectual capacity, Palmer stood in the shadow of his friend and teacher James Henley Thornwell, professor at Columbia (South Carolina) Theological Seminary and ardent defender of the institution of slavery. Yet Palmer possessed the talent for taking Thornwell's ideas and dramatically relating them to events of the moment. Shortly after Lincoln's election both Thornwell and Palmer preached on slavery as an institution ordained by God, an institution threatened by the victory of the Republican party. Palmer added that the Southern states should bind themselves into a sacred covenant to protect slavery and should "take all

---

1. James W. Silver, *Confederate Morale and Church Propaganda* (New York: W. W. Norton & Company, 1967), pp. 15, 25, 48, 50, 57–59.

necessary steps looking to separate and independent existence." If war should follow on such actions, Palmer said, the South could be certain that "we defend the cause of God and religion" since "the abolition spirit is undeniably atheistic." Palmer's career of oratory on behalf of the Confederacy was launched; he would travel before the war's end throughout the Southern states championing Confederate destiny under God.[2]

On the first of nine Confederate fast days called by President Davis, Palmer delivered a sermon in New Orleans that described the South's divine mission in the war. As a fast day address, "National Responsibility Before God" dwelt on public sins, but they were sins of the nation that preceded the rise of the Confederacy—that is, they were Yankee sins. As Palmer said, "the South has rather been 'sinned against than sinning.'" In the course of reciting national sins, Palmer elaborated the religious and political principles for which the South stood, but the climax was reached toward the end of the sermon where Palmer exulted in the destiny that the Confederacy encountered in the war. The South would fight to preserve the constitutional right of self-government. Palmer believed, therefore, that Southern destiny was in its deepest meaning *the American* destiny under God.

In "National Responsibility" Palmer alluded to certain convictions used in the justification of slavery: the curse of Ham that befell the black race and doomed it to perpetual servitude, the civilizing effects of the institution of slavery on a backward people, etc. In the antebellum South a defense of slavery had been worked out in great detail, often supported in large measure by proof texts from the Bible.[3] During the war Confederate spokesmen like Palmer incorporated slavery into their view of American destiny: the slaves' good fortune depended upon the future of the Confederacy since its institution of slavery shielded a benighted people from a hostile world and provided them with Christianity and other fruits of Western civilization. Whereas an abolitionist like Beecher considered slavery to be the last great obstacle to the achievement of American freedom, a Southerner like Palmer argued that the abolition of the institution would be destructive of the Negro's future. The facile rationalization and oppressive paternalism involved in the proslavery position are detected easily enough, but it is equally evident that pressure for abolition on moral grounds did not receive widespread Northern support and that genuine concern for the welfare of black Americans was hardly characteristic of Northern attitudes either before or after the war. For the most part

2. See Margaret Burr DesChamps, "Benjamin Morgan Palmer, Orator-Preacher of the Confederacy," *Southern Speech Journal*, Sept. 1953, pp. 14–22.

3. See William Sumner Jenkins, *Pro-Slavery Thought in the Old South* (Chapel Hill: University of North Carolina Press, 1935).

the black slave became a pawn on the checkered board of American destiny, shifted about by both Northern and Southern advocates of the war.

Few persons were able to rise above sectional interpretations of national destiny and speak of the Civil War as a judgment of God falling upon the nation as a whole. Abraham Lincoln was one of those few. As the war dragged on and the lists of dead mounted, Lincoln agonized over the ultimate purpose of the tragedy. Late in 1862 he wrote in a personal note, "In the present civil war it is quite possible that God's purpose is something different from the purpose of either party—and yet the human instrumentalities, working just as they do, are of the best adaptation to effect His purpose." The war years deepened Lincoln's sense of the mystery of divine providence and heightened his awareness of the presumption involved in the easy identification of human designs with the will of God. His brooding over the ways of providence, however, by no means led to timidity in his pursuit of victory; on the contrary, it made even more apparent to him the need to bring the war to a close and restore a united nation dedicated to freedom, the "last, best hope of earth." As Lincoln prepared to issue the final Emancipation Proclamation, he included the freedom of the slave in that hope: "In *giving* freedom to the *slave*, we *assure* freedom to the *free*—honorable alike in what we give, and what we preserve. We shall nobly save, or meanly lose, the last, best hope of earth." (Annual Message to Congress, December 1, 1862.) The nation's destiny was for Lincoln that of beaming forth the rays of democratic freedom to the world. He saw that destiny being severely tested by a tragic and ultimately incomprehensible war. Yet, as Lincoln so vividly put it in the Gettysburg Address, the war might well provide the occasion for a renewed pledge to American destiny under God: "It is for us the living . . . to be here dedicated to the great task remaining before us—that from these honored dead we take increased devotion to that cause for which they gave the last full measure of devotion . . . that this nation, under God, shall have a new birth of freedom." [4]

Lincoln's Second Inaugural Address was the finest example of his mature religious interpretation of the Civil War and American destiny. Replete with biblical language and allusions to Old Testament prophecy, the address combined a belief that the war was a divine judgment upon the entire nation with a firm resolve to set the nation back on its course of justice, peace, and freedom.

The Civil War cost the American people a staggering amount of blood and property. But, as Robert Penn Warren has claimed, probably the most enduring cost was psychological. The war handed Southerners "the Great Alibi," the feeling that most any Southern attitudes and actions are excusable because history conspired against the South. "The race problem, according to the Great

---

4. All Lincoln quotes are from William J. Wolf, *The Religion of Abraham Lincoln* (New York: The Seabury Press, 1963), pp. 147, 159, 172.

Alibi, is the doom defined by history—by New England slavers, New England and Middlewestern Abolitionists, cotton, climate, the Civil War, Reconstruction, Wall Street, the Jews. . . . Since the situation is given by history, the Southerner therefore is guiltless; is, in fact, an innocent victim of a cosmic conspiracy." Using the Great Alibi, Southerners as losers of the war are capable of convincing themselves that they are "trapped in history." The psychological heritage of the North is a different kind—what Warren deems a "Treasury of Virtue." If Southerners believe themselves to be trapped in history, "the Northerner, with his Treasury of Virtue, feels redeemed by history, automatically redeemed." Having won the war, preserved the Union, and eliminated slavery, Northerners are inclined to feel that their history has bestowed virtue upon them. They have in their pockets "a plenary indulgence, for all sins past, present, and future, freely given by the hand of history."[5] Both the complacent fatalism of the Great Alibi and the smug self-righteousness of the Treasury of Virtue destroy the heavy sense of *responsibility* that Lincoln believed was bound up with American destiny under God. To feel conspired against by history, or to feel automatically redeemed by it—neither is to assume responsibility for one's historical destiny.

Much of the religious literature appearing immediately after the Civil War fell into one or the other of these psychological traps. Yet there were persons in all regions of the country who sought a maturer, more responsible understanding of the costly war through which they had passed. In the South, for example, Stephen Elliott, a native South Carolinian who became bishop of the Episcopal Church in Georgia, disavowed alibis. Although he had been an advocate of the Confederacy and found the *specific* purposes of God in allowing the Confederacy's defeat to be obscure, he repeatedly insisted that defeat served the *ultimate*, hidden purposes of God and urged his fellow Southerners to dedicate themselves to a sounder, less spurious nationhood in the future.[6] In Connecticut, Horace Bushnell also searched for a profounder meaning to the war than that represented by narrow sectional apologetics.

Bushnell's oration honoring the alumni of Yale who fell in the Civil War developed many of the themes found in Lincoln's Gettysburg Address. The speech, "Our Obligations to the Dead," clearly expressed Bushnell's resolute opposition to states' rights, slavery and secession, but without lapsing into the superficial confusion of Northern victory with absolute righteousness.

5. Robert Penn Warren, *The Legacy of the Civil War* (New York: Random House, Vintage Books, 1964), pp. 53, 55–56, 59.

6. See William A. Clebsch, "Baptism of Blood: A Study of Christian Contributions to the Interpretation of the Civil War in American History" (Th.D. dissertation, Union Theological Seminary, 1957), pp. 139–89. Cf. the selection by the Georgian Methodist Atticus G. Haygood in H. Shelton Smith, Robert T. Handy, Lefferts A. Loetscher, *American Christianity*, II (New York: Charles Scribner's Sons, 1963), 373–77.

Although we may wish it were otherwise, said Bushnell, history is tragic, and both individuals and nations reach maturity by the appropriation of the tragic features of their histories. The tragedy of the Civil War may nurture a common public sentiment, purchase for Americans a genuine historical consciousness, and yield an American government that is an organic covenant rather than simply a collection of states "kenneled under the Constitution." In short, the Civil War is a baptism of blood capable of redeeming America for its destiny under God—the destiny of exhibiting to the world the nature of democratic freedom. Bushnell's paradigm for interpreting the Civil War was a Christian doctrine of atonement. Just as reconciliation between God and human sinners was achieved through the vicarious sacrifice of Christ, so the drawing together of Americans into a common nation under a common destiny is accomplished through the tragic sacrifices of the war dead.

Thoughts like those of Bushnell and Lincoln focus on the Civil War as a possible resource for recognizing the tragic dimensions of a national existence and for critically assessing American goals. Yet, as Robert Penn Warren has seen, certain attitudes resulting from that war have frequently obscured the nation's tragic experiences and weakened Americans' critical powers. During the last three decades of the nineteenth century, American interpretations of national destiny would grow increasingly optimistic; it would seem to many public spokesmen for the destiny that the blood of the Civil War was a small price to pay for progress and wealth.

SUGGESTED READING

Clebsch, William A. *Christian Interpretations of the Civil War.* Philadelphia: Fortress Press, 1969.

Filler, Louis. *The Crusade Against Slavery.* New York: Harper & Row, Publishers, Torchbooks, 1960.

Goen, C. C. *Broken Churches, Broken Nation: Denominational Schisms and the Coming of the American Civil War.* Macon, Ga.: Mercer University Press, 1985.

Korn, Bertram W. *American Jewry and the Civil War.* New York: The World Publishing Company, Meridian Books, 1961.

Moorhead, James H. *American Apocalypse: Yankee Protestants and the Civil War: 1860–1869.* New Haven, Conn.: Yale University Press, 1978.

Wilson, Charles Reagan. *Baptized in Blood: The Religion of the Lost Cause, 1865–1920.* Athens: University of Georgia Press, 1980.

HENRY WARD BEECHER

৵৬

The Battle Set in Array

EXOD. XIV. 15.
"And the Lord said unto Moses, Wherefore criest thou unto me?
speak unto the children of Israel, that they go forward."

Moses was raised up to be the emancipator of three millions of people. At the age of forty, having, through a singular providence, been reared in the midst of luxury, in the proudest, most intelligent, and most civilized court on the globe, with a heart uncorrupt, with a genuine love of his own race and people, he began to act as their emancipator. He boldly slew one of their oppressors. And, seeing dissension among his brethren, he sought to bring them to peace. He was rejected, reproved, and reproached; and finding himself discovered, he fled, and, for the sake of liberty, became a fugitive and martyr. For forty years, uncomplaining, he dwelt apart with his father-in-law, Jethro, in the wilderness, in the peaceful pursuits of a herdsman. At eighty—the time when most men lay down the burden of life, or have long laid it down—he began his life-work. He was called back by the voice of God; and now, accompanied by his brother, he returned, confronted the king, and, moved by Divine inspiration, demanded, repeatedly, the release of his people. The first demand was sanctioned by a terrific plague; a second, by a second terrible judgment; the third, by a third frightful devastation; the fourth, by a fourth dreadful blow; the fifth, by a fifth desolating, sweeping mischief. A sixth, a seventh, an eighth, and a ninth time, he demanded their release. And when was there ever, on the face of the earth, a man that, once having power, would let it go till life itself went with it? Pharaoh, who is the grand type of oppressors, held on in spite of the Divine command and of the Divine punishment. Then God let fly the last terrific judgment, and smote the first-born of Egypt; and there was wailing in every house of the midnight land. And then, in the midst of the first gush of grief and anguish, the tyrant said, "Let them go! Let them go!" And he did

From Henry Ward Beecher, *Patriotic Addresses*, ed. J. R. Howard (New York: Fords, Howard & Hulbert, 1889), pp. 269–88. Preached April 14, 1861, at Plymouth Church of Brooklyn.

let them go; he shoved them out; and they went pell-mell in great confusion on their way, taking up their line of march, and escaped from Egypt.

But as soon as the first anguish had passed away, Pharaoh came back to his old nature,—just as many men whose hearts are softened and whose lives are made better by affliction, come back to the old way of feeling and living, as soon as they have ceased to experience the first effects of the affliction,—and he followed on after the Israelites. As they lay encamped—these three millions of people, men, women, and children—just apart from the land of bondage, near the fork and head of the Red Sea, with great hills on either side of them, and the sea before them, some one brought panic into the camp, saying, "I see the signs of an advancing host! The air far on the horizon is filled with rising clouds!" Presently, through these clouds, began to be seen glancing spears, mounted horsemen, and a great swelling army. Such, to these lately enslaved, but just emancipated people, was the first token of the coming adversary. Surely, they were unable to cope with the disciplined cohorts of this Egyptian king. They, that were unused to war, that had never been allowed to hold weapons in their hands, that were a poor, despoiled people not only, but that had been subjected to the blighting touch of slavery, had lost courage. They did not dare to be free. And there is no wonder, therefore, that they reproached Moses, and said, "Because there were no graves in Egypt, hast thou taken us away to die in the wilderness?"

I have no doubt that, if Pharaoh's courtiers had heard that, they would have said, "Ah! they do not want to be free. They do not believe in freedom."

"Because there were no graves in Egypt, hast thou taken us away to die in the wilderness? Wherefore hast thou dealt thus with us, to carry us forth out of Egypt?"

Were these people miserable specimens of humanity? They were just what slavery makes everybody to be.

"Is not this the word that we did tell thee in Egypt, saying, Let us alone, that we may serve the Egyptians?"

They would rather have had peace with servitude, than liberty with the manly daring required to obtain it.

"For it had been better for us to serve the Egyptians, than that we should die in the wilderness."

That is just the difference between a man and a slave. They would rather have lived slaves, and eaten their pottage, than to suffer for the sake of liberty; a *man* would rather die in his tracks, than live in ease as a slave.

These, then, were the people that Moses undertook to emancipate, and this was the beginning of Moses's life-work.

"And Moses said unto the people, Fear ye not, stand still" —

That was wrong, but he did not know any better.

"Fear ye not, stand still, and see the salvation of the Lord, which he will show you to-day: for the Egyptians, whom ye have seen to-day, ye shall see them again no more forever. The Lord shall fight for you, and ye shall hold your peace."

He was a little too fast. He was right in respect to the result, but wrong in respect to the means.

"And the Lord said unto Moses, Wherefore criest thou unto me? Speak unto the children of Israel, that they go forward."

They were, after all, to do something and dare something for their liberty. No standing still, but going forward!

"Lift up the rod, and stretch out thine hand over the sea, and divide it; and the children of Israel shall go on dry ground through the midst of the sea."

You recollect the rest. They walked through the sea that lay as a protecting wall on either side of them. They reached the other side. They were divided from the camp of the Egyptians by a fiery cloud, and the Egyptians could not touch them. And what was the fat of the Egyptians? They attempted to follow the children of Israel through the sea, when the waters closed together, and their host was destroyed.

God has raised up many men, at different periods of the world, to bring his cause forth from its various exigencies. Wherever a man is called to defend a truth or a principle, a church or a people, a nation or an age, he may be said to be, like Moses, the leader of God's people. And in every period of the world God has shut up his people, at one time or another, to himself. He has brought their enemies behind them, as he brought the Egyptians behind the children of Israel. He has hedged them in on either hand. He has spread out the unfordable sea before them. He has so beset them with difficulties, when they were attempting to live for right, for duty, and for liberty, that they have been like Israel.

When men stand for a moral principle, their troubles are not a presumption that they are in the wrong. Since the world began, men that have stood for the right have had to stand for it, as Christ stood for the world, suffering for victory.

In the history which belongs peculiarly to us, over and over again the same thing has occurred. In that grand beginning struggle in which Luther figured so prominently, he stood in a doubtful conflict. He was in the minority; he was vehemently pressed with enemies on every side; nine times out of ten during his whole life the odds were against him. And yet he died victorious, and we reap the fruit of his victory.

In one of the consequences of that noble struggle, the assertion in the Netherlands of civil liberty and religious toleration, the same thing took place. Almost the entire globe was against this amphibious republic, until England cared for them; and England cared for them very doubtfully and very imperfectly. All the reigning influences, all the noblest of the commanding men of the Continent, were against them. The conflict was a long and dubious one, in which they suffered extremely, and conquered through their suffering.

In the resulting struggle in England, which was borrowed largely from the Continent,—the Puritan uprising, the Puritan struggle,—the same thing occurred. The Puritans were enveloped in darkness. Their enemies were more than their friends. The issue was exceedingly doubtful. Their very victory began in apparent defeat. For when at last, wearied and discouraged, they could no longer abide the restriction of their liberty in England, they fled away to plant colonies upon these shores. On the sea did they venture, but the ocean, black and wild, before they left it was covered with winter.

In every one of these instances darkness and the flood lay before the champions of truth and rectitude. God in his providence said to them, though they were without apparent instrumentalities, "Go forward! Venture everything! Endure everything! Yield the precious truths never! Live forever by them! Die with *them*, if you die at all."

The whole lesson of the past, then, is that safety and honor come by holding fast to one's principles; by pressing them with courage; by going into darkness and defeat cheerfully for them.

And now our turn has come. Right before us lies the Red Sea of war. It is red indeed. There is blood in it. We have come to the very edge of it, and the Word of God to us to-day is, "Speak unto this people that they go forward!" It is not of our procuring. It is not of our wishing. It is not our hand that has struck the first stroke, nor drawn the first blood. We have prayed against it. We have struggled against it. Ten thousand times we have cried, "Let this cup pass from us!" It has been overruled. We have yielded everything but manhood, and principle, and truth, and honor, and we have heard the voice of God saying, "Yield these never!" And these not being yielded, war has been let loose upon this land.

Now, let us look both ways into this matter, that we may decide what it is our duty to do.

1. There is no fact susceptible of proof in history, if it be not true that this Federal Government was created for the purposes of justice and liberty; and not liberty, either, with the construction that traitorous or befooled heads are attempting to give it,—liberty with a devil in it! We know very well what was the breadth and the clarity of the faith of those men who formed the

early constitutions of this nation. If there was any peculiarity in their faith, it was that their notion of liberty was often extravagant. But there was no doubtfulness in their position. And the instruments which accompanied and preceded it, and the opinions of the men that framed it, put this fact beyond all controversy: that the Constitution of the United States was meant to be as we now hold it, as we now defend it, as we have held it, and as we have been defending it. And at length even this is conceded, as I shall have occasion to say further on, by the enemies of liberty in this country. The Vice-President of the so-called Southern Confederacy has stated recently that there was a blunder made in the construction of our Constitution on this very truth of universal liberty, thus admitting the grand fact that that immortal instrument, as held by the North, embodies the views of those who framed it; and that those views are unmistakably in favor of liberty to all.

2. There can be no disputing the fact that, from commercial and political causes, an element of slavery which had a temporary refuge in the beginning in this land swelled to an unforeseen and unexpected power, and for fifty years has held the administrative power of the country in its hands. No man acquainted with our politics hesitates to say, that while the spirit of liberty first suggested our national ideas and fashioned our national institutions, after that work was done the government passed into the hands of the slave-power; and that that power has administered these institutions during the last fifty years for its own purposes, or in a manner that has been antagonistic to the interests of this country.

3. Against this growing usurpation for the last twenty-five years there has been rising up and organizing a proper legal constitutional opposition, wishing not the circumscription or injury of any section in this land, but endeavoring to keep our institutions out of the hands of despotism and on the side of liberty. For twenty-five years there has been a struggle to see to it that those immortal instruments of liberty should not be wrested from their original intent, —that they should be maintained for the objects for which they were created.

4. What are the means that have been employed to maintain our institutions? Free discussion. That, simply. We have gone before the people, in every proper form. For twenty years of defeat, though of growing influence, we have argued the questions of human rights and human liberty, and the doctrines of the Constitution and of our fathers; and we have maintained that the children should stand where the fathers did. At last the continent has consented. We began as a handful, in the midst of mobs and derision and obloquy. We have gone through the experience of Gethsemane and Calvary. The cause of Christ among his poor has suffered as the Master suffered, again and again and again; and at last the public sentiment of the North has been revolutionized. What! revolutionized away from the doctrines of the fathers? No; back to the doctrines of the fathers. Revolutionized against our institutions? No; in

favor of our institutions. We have taken simply the old American principles. That is the history very simply stated. The children have gone back to the old landmarks. We stand for the doctrines and instruments that the fathers gave us.

5. The vast majority of this nation are now on the side of our American institutions, according to their original intent. We ask only this: that our government may be what it was made to be, — an instrument of justice and liberty. We ask no advantages, no new prerogatives, no privileges whatsoever. We merely say, "Let there be no intestine revolution in our institutions, but let them stand as they were made, and for the purposes for which they were created." Is there anything unreasonable, anything wrong in that? Is it wrong to reason? Is it wrong to discuss? Is it wrong to go before a free people with their own business, and, in the field, in the caucus, in the assembly, in all deliberative bodies, to argue fairly, and express the result by the American means, — the omnipotence of the vote? Is that wrong? It is what we have been doing for the last few years. By the prescribed methods of the Constitution, and in the spirit of liberty which it embodied and evoked, we have done our proper work. Before God we cleanse our hands of all imputation of designing injustice or of seeking wrong. We have not sought any one's damage. We have aimed at no invidious restrictions for any. We have simply said, "God, through our fathers, committed to us certain institutions, and we will maintain them to the end of our lives, and to the end of time."

6. Seven States, however, in a manner revolutionary not only of government, but in violation of the rights and customs of their own people, have disowned their country and made war upon it! There has been a spirit of patriotism in the North; but never, within my memory, in the South. I never heard a man from the South speak of himself as an American. Men from the South always speak of themselves as Southerners. When I was abroad, I never spoke of myself as a Northerner, but always as a citizen of the United States. I love our country; and it is a love of the country, and not a love of the North alone, that pervades the people of the North. There has never been witnessed such patience, such self-denial, such magnanimity, such true patriotism, under such circumstances, as that which has been manifested in the North. And in the South the feeling has been sectional, local. The people there have been proud, not that they belong to the nation, but that they were born where the sun burns. They are hot, narrow, and boastful, — for out of China there is not so much conceit as exists among them. They have been devoid of that large spirit which takes in the race, and the nation, and its institutions, and its history, and that which its history prophesies, — the prerogative of carrying the banner of liberty to the Pacific from the Atlantic.

Now, these States, in a spirit entirely in agreement with their past developments, have revolutionized and disowned the United States of America, and set up a so-called government of their own. Shall we, now, go forward under these circumstances?

For the first time in the history of this nation there is a deliberate and extensive preparation for war, and this country has received the deadly thrust of bullet and bayonet from the hands of her own children. If we could have prevented it, this should not have taken place. But it is a fact! It hath happened! The question is no longer a question of choice. The war is brought to us. Shall we retreat, or shall we accept the hard conditions on which we are to maintain the grounds of our fathers? Hearing the voice of God in his providence saying, "Go forward!" shall we go?

I go with those that go furthest in describing the wretchedness and wickedness and monstrosity of war. The only point on which I should probably differ from any is this: that while war is an evil so presented to our senses that we measure and estimate it, there are other evils just as great, and much more terrible, whose deadly mischiefs have no power upon the senses. I hold that it is ten thousand times better to have war then to have slavery. I hold that to be corrupted silently by giving up manhood, by degenerating, by becoming craven, by yielding one right after another, is infinitely worse than war. Why, war is resurrection in comparison with the state to which we should be brought by such a course. And although war is a terrible evil, there are other evils that are more terrible. In our own peculiar case, though I would say nothing to garnish it, nothing to palliate it, nothing to alleviate it, nothing to make you more willing to have it, nothing to remove the just abhorrence which every man and patriot should have for it, yet I would say that, in the particular condition into which we have been brought, it will not be an unmixed evil. Eighty years of unexampled prosperity have gone far toward making us a people that judge of moral questions by their relation to our convenience and ease. We are in great danger of becoming a people that shall measure by earthly rules,—by the lowest standard of a commercial expediency. We have never suffered for our own principles. And now if it please God to do that which daily we pray that he may avert,—if it please God to wrap this nation in war,—one result will follow: we shall be called to suffer for our faith. We shall be called to the heroism of doing and daring, and bearing and suffering, for the things which we believe to be vital to the salvation of this people.

On what conditions, then, may we retreat from this war, and on what conditions may we have peace?

1. We may do it on condition that two-thirds of this nation shall implicitly yield up to the dictation of one-third. You can have peace on that ground. Italy could have had peace at the hands of Francis II. They had nothing to do but to say to that tyrant, "Here is my neck, put your foot on it," to obtain peace. The people of Hungary may have peace, if they will only say to him

of Vienna, "Reign over us as you please; our lives are in your hands." There is never any trouble in having peace, if men will yield themselves to the control of those that have no business to control them. Two-thirds of this nation unquestionably stand on the side of the original articles of our Constitution and in the service of liberty, and one-third deny and reject them. Now if the two-thirds will give up to the one-third, we can have peace—for a little while.

2. We can have peace if we will legalize and establish the right of any discontented community to rebel, and to set up intestine governments within the government of the United States. Yield that principle, demoralize government, and you can have peace—for a little while. You cannot yield that principle and not demoralize government. And if it is right for seven States on the Gulf to secede, it is the right of seven States on the Lakes. If it is the right of seven States on the Lakes, it is the right of five or three States on the Ohio River. If it is the right of a number of States, it is the right of one State. And if it is the right of any State, there is not a State, a half of a State, a county, or a town, that has not the same right. It is the right of disintegration. It is a right that aims at the destruction of the attraction of governmental cohesion. It is a right that invalidates all power in government. And if you will grant this right; if you will consent to have this government broken up; if you are willing that our country should degenerate to the condition of wrangling and rival States,—you can have peace—for a little while.

3. We can have peace if we will agree fundamentally to change our Constitution, and, instead of maintaining a charter of universal freedom, to write it out as a deliberate charter of oppression.

Mr. Stephens, the Vice-President of the so-called Confederate States, declared, in a formal speech, that our Constitution was framed on a fundamental mistake, inasmuch as it took it for granted that men were born for freedom and equality. They have expunged the doctrine of universal liberty, and put in its place the doctrine of liberty for the strong and servitude for the weak. It is said that the African race, by reason of their nationality and savagism, are not fit for liberty, and that the white race, by reason of their nationality and civilization, are fit to govern them. It is merely a plea that weak persons are not fit to take care of themselves, and that strong persons are fit to take care of them; and it is a plea that is just as applicable to any other peoples as to the Anglo-Saxons and the Africans. It is simply a doctrine that might makes right. It may be stated in this form: "You are weak and I am strong, and I am therefore your lawful master." If it is good for the Africans and the Anglo-Saxons, it is good for all other races. And if it is good in reference to races, it is good in reference to individuals. Therefore there is not a workman, there is not a poor man, there is not a man that is low in station, at the North, who is not interested in this matter, who is not touched in his rights, and who is not insulted by the spirit that is latent in the new Constitution of the so-called Confederate States. It holds that there is appointed of God a governing class and a class to be governed,—a class that are born governors because they are strong and smart and well-to-do, and a class that are born servants because they are poor and weak and unable to take care of themselves. Now take that glorious, flaming sentence in the Declaration of Independence, which asserts the right of every man to life, liberty, and the pursuit of happiness, and which pronounces that right to be alike inalienable to all,—take that and strike it out, and put in its place this infernal article of the new Constitution of the Southern States, and you can have peace—for a little while. There is no trouble about having peace. What an unreasonable people we are! If we will only pay enough for peace we can have it.

This diabolical principle is also deliberately held and advocated by the churches of the South. The Southern churches are all sound on the question of the Bible, and infidel on the question of its contents! They believe that this is God's Book; they believe that this Book is the world's charter; and they believe that it teaches the religion of servitude. Every sermon that I have received within the last year from the South has been a various echo of this one atrocious idea, held in common with all the despotic preachers of Europe. Any man that has read Robert South's sermons, has read over and over again all the arguments contained in the raw, jejune productions of Southern clerical advocates for oppression. In all the discussions between Milton and Salmasius, and in all the writings of Roman priests that have sought to bolster up sacerdotal rule, these arguments have been put forth far more ably than our unscholarly Southerners have put them forth. But this is the ground which has been taken by the Christian Church of the South: that in Christ Jesus all men are not created equal,—that white masters are, but that black servants are not!

And that is not all. Not only is this new government framed on this ground, and not only have all the churches of the South taken this ground, so that it may be said of the Southern Confederacy as it was said of one of the old revolted tribes, "They have a priest to their house," but there has just now been raised up in the North a club of the same kind,—a society for the promotion of *national unity*, on the basis of a change of our national instruments of government. This society proposes to restore peace to this country. And how? Exactly as you restore uniformity of color in a room where some things are red, some blue, and some yellow,—by blowing the light out so that in darkness all things will be of the same color! We are very much divided in this land, one part believing in liberty, and the other believing in servitude; and it is proposed to bring these two parts together in unity, by destroying the distinction between them. What is this society's own statement, as contained in the letter which they have put forth with their articles? They make this formal assertion: that that portion of our original Declaration of Independence which makes all men free and equal has been misinterpreted, or is false. They endeavor to say it softly, but it is a thing that cannot be said softly. To breathe it, to whisper it, makes it louder than thunder!

Indeed, it is true that men are not physiologically equal. No man ever believed that they were. They do not weigh alike. They differ in respect to bone and tissue. They are not the same as regards mental caliber. Their dynamic forces are different. They are not capable of exerting the same amount of political influence. In the nations of Europe it was held that the royal head, *jure Divino*, had privileges which the nobles had not; that there belonged to the nobles prerogatives which did not belong to the commonalty; and that the political rights of the great common people were to be graduated according to their status in society. But our fathers said, God gives the same political rights to all alike. The people are king, and the people are nobles. They are equal in this: that they all stand before the same law of justice, and that justice is to be the same to one as to another. The richest and the poorest, the wisest and the most ignorant, the highest and the lowest, are on an equality before the law. The Declaration of Independence taught simply that every man born into life was born with such dignities, with such a nature conferred upon him, that, as a child of God, he has a right to confront government and legislature and laws, and say, "I demand, in common with every other man, equal justice, equal protection, to life, to liberty, and in the pursuit of happiness." And this is what our society in the North for the promotion of national unity undertake, in their first article, to say is a lie!

Now, you can have your American eagle as you want it. If, with the South, you will strike out his eyes, then you shall stand well with Mr. Davis and Mr. Stephens of the Confederate States; if, with the Christians of the South, you will pluck off his wings, you shall stand well with the Southern churches; and if, with the new peace-makers that have risen up in the North, you will pull out his tailfeathers, you shall stand well with the society for the promotion of national unity! But when you have stricken out his eyes so that he can no longer see, when you have plucked off his wings so that he can no longer fly, and when you have pulled out his guiding tail-feathers so that he can no longer steer himself, but rolls in the dirt a mere buzzard, then will he be worth preserving? Such an eagle it is that they mean to depict upon the banner of America!

Now if any man is fierce for peace, and is willing to pay the price demanded for it, he can have it. On those conditions you can have peace as long as the Jews did. For three guilty days they were rid of the Saviour, and then he rose from the grave, with eternal power on his head, and beyond all touch of weakness or death, then ascended on high to the Source of eternal power, there to live, and to live forever!

4. We must accordingly, if we go on to purchase peace on these terms,

become partners in slavery, and consent, for the sake of peace, to ratify this gigantic evil. We cannot wink at it. We are called to bear overt witness either for or against it. Every State in this Union, according to the new Constitution, must be open to slavery. It is the design of not a few men at the North to make this the issue at the next election: whether we shall not reconstruct this government according to the Constitution of the Confederate States, one feature of which is that slavery shall have liberty to go wherever it pleases, — that slavery shall have the right of incursion to any part of this country. If you consent to such a reconstruction as is proposed, you must open every one of your States to the incoming of slavery. Not only that, but every territory on this continent is to be opened to slavery. We are called to take the executive lancet, and the virus of slavery, and lift up the arms of this virgin continent and inoculate it with this terrific poison. If you will do these things, you are to be permitted to escape war.

5. Next in order must of course be silence. When we have gone so far, we shall no longer have any right of discussion, of debate, of criticism, — we shall no longer have any right of *agitation*, as it is called.

On these conditions we may have peace. If we reject these conditions we are to have separation, demoralization of government, and war.

Now are you prepared to take peace on these conditions? You will not get it on any other conditions. If you have peace, you are to stigmatize the whole history of the past; you are to yield your religious convictions; you are to give over the government into the hands of factious revolutionists; you are to suppress every manly sentiment, and every sympathy for the oppressed. Will you take peace on such a ground as that? So far as I myself am concerned, I utterly abhor peace on any such grounds. Give me war redder than blood, and fiercer than fire, if this terrific infliction is necessary that I may maintain my faith of God in human liberty, my faith of the fathers in the instruments of liberty, my faith in this land as the appointed abode and chosen refuge of liberty for all the earth! War is terrible, but that abyss of ignominy is yet more terrible!

What, then, if we will go forward in the providence of God, and maintain our integrity, are the steps that are before us?

1. Instead of yielding our convictions, it is time to cleanse them, to deepen them, to give them more power, to make them more earnest and more religious. There is no reason, now, why we should compromise. There is nothing to be gained by compromising. And it is time that parents should talk on the great doctrine of human rights in the family, and indoctrinate their children with an abhorrence for slavery, and a love for liberty. It is time for schools to have their scholars instructed in these matters. It is time for every church to make its pews flame and glow with enthusiasm for freedom, and with hatred for oppression. While the air of the South is full of pestilent doctrines of slavery, accursed be our communities if we will not be as zealous and enthu-

siastic for liberty as they are against it! If their air is filled with the storm and madness of oppression, let ours be full of the sweet peace and love of liberty!

2. We must draw the lines. A great many men have been on both sides. A great many men have been thrown backward and forward, like a shuttle, from one side to the other. It is now time for every man to choose one side or the other. We want no shufflers; we want no craven cowards; we want *men*; we want every man to stand forth, and say, "I am for liberty, and the Constitution, and the country, as our fathers gave them to us," or else, "I am against them."

Thousands, thank God, of great men have spoken to us; but I think that the war-voice of Sumter has done more to bring men together, and to produce unity of feeling among them on this subject, than the most eloquent-tongued orator.

We must say in this matter, my friends, as Christ said, "He that is not for us is against us." I will have no commerce, I will not cross palms with a man that disowns liberty in such a struggle as is before us! I will not give him shelter or house-room—except as a convicted sinner; then I will take him, as the prodigal was taken, in his rags and nakedness! But so long as he stands up with impudent face against the things that are dearest to God's heart, and dearest to the instincts of this people, I shall treat him as what he is,—a *traitor*! There ought to be but one feeling in the North, and that ought to be a feeling for liberty, which should sweep through the land like a mighty wind.

3. We must not stop to measure costs,—especially the costs of going forward,—on any basis so mean and narrow as that of pecuniary prosperity. We must put our honor and religion into this struggle. God is helping you; for, no matter how much you deplore the state of things, you cannot help yourselves. You may take counsel with your Till and Safe and Bank, you may look at your accounts on both sides, but your talking and looking will make no difference with your affairs. The time is past in which these things could be of any avail. This matter must now be settled. You must have a part in settling it. The question is whether that shall be a manly or an ignoble part!

There are many reasons which make a good and thorough battle necessary. The Southern men are infatuated. They will not have peace. They are in arms. They have fired upon the American flag! That glorious banner has been borne through every climate, all over the globe, and for fifty years not a land or people has been found to scorn it, or dishonor it. At home, among the degenerate people of our own land, among Southern citizens, for the first time, has this glorious national flag been abased, and trampled to the ground! It is for our sons reverently to lift it, and to bear it full high again, to victory and national supremacy! Our arms, in this peculiar exigency, can lay the foundation of future union, in mutual respect. The South firmly believes that *cowardice* is the universal attribute of Northern men! Until they are most thoroughly convinced to the contrary, they will never cease arrogancy and aggression. But if now it please God to crown our arms with victory, we shall have gone far toward impressing Southern men with salutary respect. Good soldiers, brave men, hard fighting, will do more toward quiet than all the compromises and empty, wagging tongues in the world. Our reluctance to break peace, our unwillingness to shed blood, our patience, have all been misinterpreted. The more we have been generous and forbearing, the more thoroughly were they sure that it was because we dared not fight!

With the North is the strength, the population, the courage. There is not elsewhere on this continent that breadth of courage—the courage of a man in distinction from the courage of a brute beast—which there is in the free States of the North. It was General Scott who said that the New Englanders were the hardest to get into a fight, and the most terrible to meet in a conflict, of any men on the globe.

We have no braggart courage; we have no courage that rushes into an affray for the love of fighting. We have that courage which comes from calm intelligence. We have that courage which comes from broad moral sentiment. We have no anger, but we have indignation. We have no irritable passion, but we have fixed will. We regard war and contest as terrible evils; but when, detesting them as we do, we are roused to enter into them, our courage will be of the measure of our detestation. You may be sure that the cause which can stir up the feelings of the North sufficiently to bring them into such a conflict, will develop in them a courage that will be terrific to the men who have to meet it. I could wish no worse punishment to those that decry the courage of the North, than that they shall have to meet her when she is once brought out and fairly in the field.

4. We must aim at a peace built on foundations so solid, of God's immutable truth, that nothing can reach to unsettle it. Let this conflict between liberty and slavery never come up again. Better have it thoroughly settled, though it take a score of years to settle it, than to have an intermittent fever for the next century, breaking out at every five or ten years. It is bad, you say. That has nothing to do with the point. Your house is on fire, and the question is, What will you do? You are in the struggle, and the question, Will you go through it in the spirit of your ancestors, in the spirit of Christians and patriots, in the spirit that belongs to the age of the world in which you live, and settle it so that it shall not be in the power of mischief to unsettle it? Or will you dally? Will you delay? I know which you will do. *This question is now going forward* to a settlement.

5. Let not our feelings be vengeful nor savage. We can go into this conflict with a spirit just as truly Christian as any that ever inspired us in the performance of a Christian duty. Indignation is very different from anger; conscience

from revenge. Let the spirit of fury be far from us; but a spirit of earnestness, of willingness to do, to suffer, and to die, if need be, for our land and our principles—that may be a religious spirit. We may consecrate it with prayer.

All through the struggle of the Revolution, men there were that preached on the Sabbath, and when not preaching went from tent to tent and performed kind offices to those that were sick or wounded, cheered those that were in despondency, encouraged those whose trials were severe, and led or accompanied their brethren to those conflicts which achieved liberty.

I believe that the old spirit will be found yet in the church; and that in that patriotism which dares to do as well as teach, laymen and officers and pastors will be found no whit behind the Revolutionary day.

It is trying to live in suspense, to be in the tormenting whirl of rumor, now to see the banner up, and now to see it trailing in the dust. Early yesterday things seemed inauspicious. Toward evening all appeared calm and fair. To-day disastrous and depressing rumors were current. This evening I came hither sad from the tidings that that stronghold which seemed to guard the precious name and lasting fame of the noble and gallant Anderson had been given up; but since I came into this desk I have received a dispatch from one of our most illustrious citizens, saying that Sumter is reinforced, and that Moultrie is the fort that has been destroyed. But what if the rising sun tomorrow should reverse the message? What if the tidings that greet you in the morning should be but the echo of the old tidings of disaster? You live in hours in which you are to suffer suspense. Now lifted up, you will be prematurely cheering, and now cast down, you will be prematurely desponding. Look forward, then, past the individual steps, the various vicissitudes of experience, to the glorious end that is coming! Look beyond the present to that assured victory which awaits us in the future.

Young men, you will live to see more auspicious days. Later sent, delayed in your voyage into life, you will see the bright consummation, in part at least, of that victory of this land, by which, with mortal throes, it shall cast out from itself all morbific influences, and cleanse itself from slavery. And you that are in middle life shall see the ultimate triumph advancing beyond anything that you have yet known. The scepter shall not depart. The government shall not be shaken from its foundations.

Let no man, then, in this time of peril, fail to associate himself with that cause which is to be so entirely glorious. Let not your children, as they carry you to your burial, be ashamed to write upon your tombstone the truth of your history. Let every man that lives and owns himself an American, take the side of true American principles;—liberty for one, and liberty for all; liberty now, and liberty forever; liberty as the foundation of government, and liberty as the basis of union; liberty as against revolution, liberty, against anarchy, and liberty, against slavery; liberty here, and liberty everywhere, the world through!

When the trumpet of God has sounded, and that grand procession is forming; as Italy has risen, and is wheeling into the ranks; as Hungary, though mute, is beginning to beat time, and make ready for the march; as Poland, having long slept, has dreamt of liberty again, and is waking; as the thirty million serfs are hearing the roll of the drum, and are going forward toward citizenship,—let it not be your miserable fate, nor mine, to live in a nation that shall be seen reeling and staggering and wallowing in the orgies of despotism! We, too, have a right to march in this grand procession of liberty. By the memory of the fathers; by the sufferings of the Puritan ancestry; by the teaching of our national history; by our faith and hope of religion; by every line of the Declaration of Independence, and every article of our Constitution; by what we are and what our progenitors were,—we have a right to walk foremost in this procession of nations toward the bright future.

BENJAMIN M. PALMER

National Responsibility before God

2D. CHRONICLES, 6TH CHAPTER, 34TH, 35TH VERSES:
"If thy people go out to war against their enemies by the
way that thou shalt send them, and they pray unto thee toward this
city which thou hast chosen, and the house which I have built for thy
name; then hear thou from the heavens their prayer and their
supplication, and maintain their cause."

This day is one of surpassing solemnity. In the gravest period of our history, amidst the perils which attend the dismemberment of a great nation and the reconstruction of a new government, we are confronted with another more instant and appalling. Our late Confederates, denying us the right of self-government, have appealed to the sword and threaten to extinguish this right in our blood. Eleven tribes sought to go forth in peace from the house of political bondage: but the heart of our modern Pharaoh is hardened, that he will not let Israel go. In their distress, with the untried sea before and the chariots of Egypt behind, ten millions of people stretch forth their hands before Jehovah's throne, imploring him to "stir up his strength before Ephraim and Benjamin and Manasseh, and come and save them." It was a memorable day when the Hebrew tribes, having crossed the Jordan, stood, the one-half of them upon Mount Ebal and the other half upon Mount Gerizim, and pronounced the solemn Amen to the curses and blessings of the divine law as proclaimed by the Levites. Not less grand and awful is this scene to-day, when an infant nation strikes its covenant with the God of Heaven. This vast assembly is not simply a convention of individuals engaged in acts of personal worship. It is not even the Church holding communion through priestly rites. But, as an integral part of this young nation and in obedience to the call of our civil head, we are met to recognize the God of nations. Confessing the sins of our fathers with our own, and imploring the divine guidance through all our for-

From Benjamin M. Palmer, *National Responsibility before God, A Discourse Delivered on the Day of Fasting, Humiliation and Prayer*, June 13, 1861 (New Orleans: Price-Current Steam Book & Job Printing Office, 1861).

tunes, the people of these Confederate States proclaim this day, "the Lord our God will we serve, and his voice will we obey." It is this sacramental feature of our worship which lends to it such dreadful solemnity. At the moment when we are crystalizing into a nation, at the very opening of our separate career, we bend the knee together before God—appealing to his justice in the adjudication of our cause, and submitting our destiny to his supreme arbitration. The bonds of this covenant, which we seal this day to the Lord, are entered upon the register in which the Recording Angel writes up the deeds of time, before the Eternal throne.

The question then arises at the threshold of our proceedings, what principles underlie and support this act of public and national homage? Our external actions are a mockery, except as they are concrete expressions of some secret and vital truth. As the body is but the organ of the soul, and each gesture but a symbol of the power which reigns within—so in all intelligent action some dominant idea resides, the soul by which it is quickened and informed. The worship now offered in this sanctuary will be found to turn upon the great truth, that the nation is in a clear sense a sort of *person* before God—girded with responsibilities which draw it within his comprehensive government. We must renounce the shallow nominalism which would make such a word as "nation" a dead abstraction, signifying only the aggregation of individuals. It is an incorporated society, and possesses a unity of life resembling the individuality of a single being. It can deliberate and concur in common conclusions which are carried out in a joint action, analogous to the powers of thought and will in a single mind. It stands in definite moral relations, out of which spring such duties and obligations that we can properly speak of the law of nations in which they are expounded, and by which the intercourse with every similar society is regulated. In these respects a nation becomes a *person* capable of executing a trust, and conscious both of rights and obligations. Each has its own precisely defined character, fulfils its appointed mission, is developed through a providential training, and is held to a strict providential reckoning. The importance of this principle is sufficiently apparent. It not only gives significance to these religious solemnities; but it suggests the duty of this new-born nation to consider the part assigned it in the great drama of History, and its dependence upon the blessing of Him who "ruleth in the kingdom of men and giveth it to whomsoever he will." I shall, therefore, be justified in pausing for a moment upon its illustration.

If we ascend the stream of history to its source, we find in Noah's prophetic utterances to his three sons, the fortunes of mankind presented in perfect outline. The benediction upon Shem marked his descendants out for a destiny predominantly religious; and through all time, in ancient days and in modern, both in a true direction and in a false, and as seen in the two representative nations of the Shemitic stock, history attests the fulfilment of this mission.

Through the entire interval between Abraham and Christ, the Hebrews were appointed to testify for the unity of God against the idolatry of mankind; and all Hebrew history turns upon the execution of this trust as its pivot. Since the Christian era, the Arabians, belonging to the same group, moving in a false direction, but yielding a blind obedience to what may be termed their Semitish instinct, gave birth to the Mohammedan imposture, a religion without a mystery and without a sacrifice, which, transforming a religious enthusiasm into martial fanaticism, has tinged the whole current of their history. Still further to mark the destiny of this group, the only members of it, which have left no permanent trace upon the history of mankind, were those upon the banks of the Euphrates, who were seduced by a fertile agriculture and a flourishing commerce from their religious trust, and lapsed into the idolatry and worldliness of the other races.

In like manner, enlargement was promised to Japhet; and through all the past, the hardy and aggressive families of this stock have spread over the larger portion of the earth's surface, fulfiling their mission as the organ of human civilization. In ancient and in modern times—through the Greeks and Romans once, through the English, French and Germans now—the world has been indebted to Japhet for its intellectual culture, for the discoveries of science, for the inventions of art, for the solution of all the great problems of State policy and public law. It would not be difficult to show how this general work of civilizing the world has been providentially subdivided between the families of this great stock—that as of old Greece was supremely devoted to intellectual culture, and Rome to political philosophy, so in later times the same partition of duties has practically been made between the great nations of Europe. Still further to show the controlling power of God over nations, wild and nomadic tribes have been held in reserve, bursting, at appointed times, the bounds of their enclosure and recruiting the wasted energies of a decaying civilization.

Upon Ham was pronounced the doom of perpetual servitude—proclaimed with double emphasis, as it is twice repeated that he shall be the servant of Japhet and the servant of Shem. Accordingly, history records not a single example of any member of this group lifting itself, by any process of self-development, above the savage condition. From first to last, their mental and moral characteristics, together with the guidance of Providence, have marked them for servitude; while their comparative advance in civilization and their participation in the blessings of salvation, have ever been suspended upon this decreed connexion with Japhet and with Shem.

These facts are beyond impeachment; and nothing can be more instructive than to see the outspreading landscape of all history embraced thus within the camera of Noah's brief prophecy. In the largest classification of the human race, we see the hand of God upon nations—not only "appointing the bounds of their habitations," but impressing upon each the type of character that fits it for its mission. If from this wide generalization we turn attention to particular States, we have the same evidence of their separateness and individuality. Thus, from the earliest moment that Egypt was cradled amidst the bulrushes of her own sacred Nile, she exhibits a character throughout and intensely Egyptian; a character as clearly distinct from the Hebrew and the Persian, as these in their turn differ from the Roman and the Greek. And the spaces which all these respectively fill upon the chart of universal history are as exclusively their own, as the places which they occupy upon the surface of the globe. It is noteworthy in this connection that as nations have their assigned missions, so they are preserved in being till their work is done; after which they sink into decrepitude, or are expunged from the roll of the living. Thus Greece was perpetuated until she had carried the arts of sculpture and painting, of poetry, eloquence and song, to a perfection which has never been surpassed; and when she could do no more in philosophy and science, she was trodden in the dust beneath the iron-heeled legions of Rome. When Rome, too, had built up an empire as wide as the world, and could do no more by her systems of jurisprudence and schemes of state-craft, she slid into a military despotism—and the world having no need of experiments in that direction, her mighty fabric gave way under the pressure of barbarian hordes, the present congress of European nations springing ultimately from the political chaos which was thereby induced. So it has been through all the past; so it will continue to be through all the future; and the grand conclusion is but the lesson which is impressed upon us to-day. This lesson is, that nations are in a weighty sense *persons* before God, with individual characters mysteriously impressed upon the parent stock, and fully developed through a providential training; that they work out their historic missions which are unequivocally assigned by a higher power that girt about with grave responsibilities, they are held to account for their fidelity to their trusts; and that their solemn duty is to recognize in every stage of their career that Being by whose guidance and blessing they are conducted to their destinies. In the acknowledgment of this truth we to-day bow the knee before the God of Heaven, whom we have chosen to serve as the God of this nation forever.

Parallel with this truth of the nation's personal responsibility, is another which determines the form of our worship by humiliation and fasting as well as by prayer. I refer to the continuity of a nation's life through a long succession of individuals that die. While the elements which compose the nation are continually passing away, the nation remains entire without disintegration. As the body of a living man is continually wasting and as continually repaired, through the ceaseless flux of its particles; so in the state "one generation goeth and another generation cometh," but the nation preserves its identity through the whole succession. In consequence of this it is that, in God's government over them, the sins of a nation are often punished in generations long posterior to that which is immediately guilty. The measure of criminality being at last filled up by these, the accumulated chastisement descends. This principle our Lord declares to the Jews of his day: that they "filled up the measure of their fathers"; that "upon them would come all the righteous blood shed upon the earth, from the blood of righteous Abel unto the blood of Zacharias, the sons of Barachias, whom they slew between the temple and the altar; verily I say unto you, all these things shall come upon this generation." It is in virtue of this principle that we undertake to confess the sins of our fathers as well as our own; which, upon any other ground, would be a mockery and a sham. As nations in their corporate form cannot be subject to the retributions of the final judgment, the divine government must be enforced alone by temporal sanctions; and the probation which nations enjoy pass along the current of national life through succeeding generations, bringing at last the avenging punishment upon one generation out of many which are equally implicated. If this should seem severe, it should be remembered that it is unavoidable under a state of discipline and probation; and it has the practical comfort, that repenting posterity may often, by humility and faith, turn aside the descending judgment, and secure still the favor and protection of Heaven, forfeited by their fathers.

Under this exposition of principles which underlie our worship, let us, my brethren, like Daniel of old, "confess our sins and the sins of our people, and present our supplication before the Lord our God, in this his holy mountain." There is obviously a distinction between the sins committed really by individuals, but which from their universality we may in a sense bewail as national, and those sins which are referrable to the nation itself in its organized and corporate form. For example, intemperance is painfully prevalent among all classes of our people; yet it is not properly chargeable upon the nation as an organic whole, except so far as the government by its unwise or insufficient legislation may be responsible for the same. So again, "because of swearing the land mourneth," that profane use of God's holy name which dishonors the lips of multitudes; and which of England's classic writers describes as "the superfluity of naughtiness," "a sort of peppercorn rent" which men gratuitously pay to the Devil. Yet in a strict sense it is the sin of individuals who presumptuously say "our lips are our own, who is Lord over us!" In like manner, Sabbath-breaking is affirmed in Scripture to be one of those offences which peculiarly draw down upon a people the righteous resentment of God. Yet the nation is not held answerable for it, except as rulers in their official acts, or the law by its postal and other arrangements, may wantonly tread it in the dust. However proper it might be to comment upon these forms of transgression and to bewail them upon this day of public fasting, as the common sins of our people, I prefer for special reasons to restrict your attention to that class of sins which are properly national, as being committed by the people in their public association and in their corporate existence.

1. **We bewail then, in the first place, the fatal error of our Fathers in not making a clear national recognition of God at the outset of the nation's career.** The record of the divine dealings with America was, from the beginning, singularly a religious record. It was certainly remarkable that this Western Continent should have been locked up between two oceans from the knowledge of mankind, through fifteen centuries of the Christian era; and quite as remarkable that its discovery should be ordered at a time when an asylum was required for the victims of religious persecution in the old world. It is certainly true that religious zeal operated as a constraining motive with those who first took possession of these shores. In all the proclamations and grants of Spain and Portugal, the planting of the cross upon these heathen and savage coasts was urged as the leading motive for conquest and colonization— and the Continent was formally taken possession of by the first discoverers as distinctly in the name of Almighty God, as by the authority of their Christian Majesties, Ferdinand and Isabella. It is familiar even to our children that the hardships of the first settlement in these United States were cheerfully endured through the faith and patience of those who simply sought "amidst the depths of the desert gloom" "freedom to worship God." Yet will it be credited, when this most religious people, after the lapse of a century and a half, undertook to establish an independent government, there was a total ignoring of the divine claims and of all allegiance to the divine supremacy? It is true that in the eloquent paper which recited their grievances before the world, and proclaimed the Colonies independent of the British throne, the signers of the Declaration appealed to the Divine Omniscience "for the rectitude of their intentions," and pledged their faith to each other "with a firm reliance on the protection of divine Providence." It is therefore the more remarkable that, eleven years after, in that great instrument by which the several States were linked together in a common nationality, and which was at once the public charter and the paramount law of the land, not a word is found from which one could possibly infer that such a being as God ever existed. The omission was a fearful one; and it is not surprising that He who proclaims his jealousy of his own glory, should let fall the blow which has shattered *that* nation. Probable reasons may be suggested for its explanation. It certainly was not due to the irreligiousness of the masses, for they were predominantly christian. But the public leaders of the time were largely tinctured with the free-thinking and infidel spirit which swept like a pestilence over Europe in the seventeenth and eighteenth centuries, and which brought forth at last its bitter fruit in the horrors of the French Revolution. It may have been due

likewise to the jealousy entertained of any union between Church and State, at a time when the novel, grand and successful experiment was first tried of an entire separation between the two. But to whatever causes we refer it, the certain fact is that the American nation stood up before the world a helpless orphan, and entered upon its career without a God. Through almost a century of unparalleled prosperity, this error has been but partially retrieved; as the religious spirit of the people has silently compelled the appointment by executive authority, of days of public thanksgiving and prayer—yet to this day, in the great national act of incorporation there is no bond which connects the old American nation with the Providence and Government of Jehovah.

Thanks be unto God, my brethren, for the grace given our own Confederacy, in receding from this perilous atheism! When my eye first rested upon the Constitution adopted by the Confederate Congress, and I read in the first lines of our organic and fundamental law a clear, solemn, official recognition of Almighty God, my heart swelled with unutterable emotions of gratitude and joy. It was the return of the prodigal to the bosom of his father, of the poor exile who has long pined in some distant and bleak Siberia after the associations of his childhood's home. At length, the nation has a God: Alleluia! "the Lord reigneth let the earth rejoice." And now in the beautiful proclamation of our President our whole people through eleven States are called to ratify the covenant, and to set up the memorial stone thereof. It is indeed no ordinary State Paper, filled with cold and starched commonplaces, which by their icy formality so often freeze up the very piety they seem to invoke. But a religious unction pervades every clause and line; and the child of God can recognize the dialect which his ear loves to hear. It summons us to "recognize our dependence upon God," to "humble ourselves under the dispensations of divine providence," to "acknowledge his goodness" and "supplicate his merciful protection." Under the conviction that "none but a righteous cause can gain the divine favor," it "implores the Lord of Hosts to guide and direct our policy in the paths of right, duty, justice and mercy; to unite our hearts and our efforts for the defence of our dearest rights; to strengthen our weakness, crown our arms with success, and enable us to secure a speedy, just and honorable peace," "to inspire us with a proper spirit and temper of heart and mind to bear our evils, to bless us with his favor and protection, and to bestow his gracious benediction upon our government and country." This is truly a Christian patriot's prayer. It breathes no malignant revenge; but it calls the nation to nestle beneath the wings of Almighty power and love. Upon this central truth—that "God is and that He is the rewarder of them that diligently seek him"—all of us can stand. Hebrew or Christian, Protestant or Catholic—all can subscribe this ultimate truth: and here we all meet to-day to say that He is our trust in whom nations as well as men "live and move and have their being." This day is therefore one of infinite solemnity; it is our nation's first Sabbath, when it meets to confess its God. If it shall hold fast to this testimony, it will have an immortal career: and had I a voice loud as seven thunders, I would proclaim from the Potomac to the Rio Grande, that a nation drives against the rocks which denies its responsibility before the God of Heaven. I speak this not as if it were my trade: but as a man, and in full view of all that constitutes true manhood, under the pressure and dictation of the highest philosophy, I affirm that to know and fear God is the perfection of wisdom. He is most a man, who brings up all parts of his nature with an equal culture; and to cleave sacrilegiously between these parts and to throw away those religious longings which can be satisfied only in God, is to forego our highest prerogative and to approximate the level of senseless apes chattering upon the trees of the forest. May God keep this nation under the power of those religious convictions, which to-day move the hearts of our people as they were never moved before!

2. **We have sinned against God in the idolatry of our History, and in the boastful spirit it has naturally begotten**. It is a melancholy proof of human frailty, that our noblest virtues so easily degenerate into the meanest vices. A generous heart cannot but rejoice in an honorable ancestry; and love of country is a filial virtue, which must feel complacency in a public history illustrated by magnanimity and truth. A just self-reliance too is only the off-shoot of true manliness; characteristic of all, whether nations or men, by whom any thing historic is ever achieved. Were these high virtues always sanctified by a religious sense of dependence upon God, they would never be corrupted into the weaknesses either of vanity or arrogance. But woe to the nation that with pride of heart lifts itself against God! The terrible infliction upon Nebuchadnezzar of old, is a lesson for all time. The poor monarch, driven among the beasts of the field and drivelling in his insanity, proclaims through his affecting experience that all "those who walk in pride God is able to abase." Never was such a debt of gratitude for providential blessings contracted by any people, as that due to God from the American nation. He gave them a broad land and full of springs—He emptied out its former inhabitants who melted away as the Canaanites before Israel—and His gracious providence was a wall of fire around their armies through a long and painful war. Yet we have seen how speedily they forgot the God of their salvation, and made an idol of themselves. Looking out from their palaces and towers, they have cried, saying, "is not this great Babylon that we have built for the house of the kingdom, by the might of our power and for the honor of our majesty?" They have lifted up their golden image upon the plain of Dura, and "at the sound of the cornet, flute, harp, sackbut and psaltery, they have fallen down and worshipped it." With insufferable arrogance they have taunted other nations with their adherence to institutions and usages, which are the growth of time, and cannot perish in an hour. Assuming that Constitutional freedom

can only be enjoyed under Republican forms, as propagandists of their own political faith, they have sometimes rudely challenged every other creed as heretical and monstrous. It is too often forgotten that forms of government are not the arbitrary products of legislation, but are an outgrowth from the nation's life—as it were, secreted from within and crystalizing around it as an external shell. Hence the burning resentment created by a crusade against usages which are endeared by habit and consecrated by time. Certainly from this charge of officious intermeddling, a portion of the American people have not been free, springing, even where it is most innocent, from the egotism and self-conceit which says, "we are the people, and wisdom will die with us." But it was reserved to our own day to carry this haughtiness to its climax, in denying the right even of political existence to those who will not pronounce the Shibboleth of Federalism. The empty menaces, too, which have been poured into our ears, and into the ears of all Europe, would be disgusting from their arrogance if they were not contemptible from their impotence. But in the public laughter which they have drawn down from all the world, we cannot fail to see the righteous retribution of God upon this national idolatry of self. Let us—so far as in the past we may have been implicated in this transgression—deeply repent of it. Let us, in the opening of our national career, lay deep the foundations of public virtue in a sense of dependence upon God. Let us, to the end of our history, aim to preserve that modesty of carriage which distinguishes the nobleman from the parvenu, and which always remembers that a nation is great only through the divine favor.

3. **Another form of national sin has been a too great devotion to Party, coupled with the flagrant abuse of the Elective Franchise**. We may indulge no Utopian dreams of exemption from the collisions of party; nor would complete political repose, if long continued, be an advantage. Under a free government where men are permitted to think, they must be expected to differ. Discussion, too, gives light; for truth, like fire, comes out from the contact of flint and steel. Parties which spring from honest and different views of public policy, are seldom sectional. Embracing the whole country, they are perfectly consistent with genuine patriotism; and may even form bonds of union between those who might else be separated by local interests. The simple existence of parties, therefore, is not an evil; or if it be, like the antagonism between the forces of nature, it is conducive to a higher good. This presupposes, however, that the arena of conflict is the hall of legislation, and the weapons of warfare are those of honorable debate. But when it comes to this, that party usurps the place of country—when caucus becomes king, and by boot and thumbscrew all individuality of opinion is crushed out of men—when public platforms become the oracles of inspiration, higher than the constitution and the law—when tricksters and under-whippers, who drill the rank

and file of party, take the place of party, take the place of statesmen who expound and defend great and lofty principles—when, above all, supple cunning carries out, by base and crooked measures, the decrees of secret cabals: then may be seen the handwriting upon the wall, and the glory has departed. Alas! my brethren, am I not reciting the sad and bitter tale of the past? What but this fell spirit of party has riven to its base a government which, a little while ago, we thought as enduring as the everlasting hills? The great statesmen passed away whose hearts could embrace a continent, and we came to men who, whatever their genius, fall under the cutting rebuke of Goldsmith—to men

> "Who, born for the universe, narrowed their mind,
> And to party gave up what was meant for mankind."

We have lived to see fulfilled in the reign of sectionalism the remarkable prophecy of Mr. Jefferson, uttered forty years ago with such startling emphasis: "I had ceased," writes he, "to pay any attention to public affairs, content to be a passenger in our bark to the shore from which I am not distant. But this momentous question (the Missouri controversy) *like a fire bell in the night,* awakened and filled me with terror. *I considered it at once as the knell of the Union.* It is hushed for a moment; but this is a reprieve only, not a final sentence. *A geographical line coinciding with a marked principle, moral and political, once conceived and held up to the angry passions of men, will never be obliterated."* A turbulent and wicked faction, working through a generation and laying its obscene touch upon everything holy in Church and State, at length sprung like the old man of the sea astride of the nation's neck. The work of ruin was accomplished; and now the deep, awful chasm of eternal separation yawns between North and South. May God in his mercy forgive the authors of this mischief, for it never can be repaired!

But what shall be said of the *abuse of the ballot,* the very symbol and instrument of the people's power? What of the timidity, or indifference, or disgust of some who abstain from their privilege, and suffer every true interest of the country to pass by default into the hands of base and designing men? What, of the profaneness of others, like Esau, who for a mess of pottage sell their American birthright? What, of the political brokerage which trades in this dreadful immorality, and sets up the offices of government virtually at public outcry to the highest bidders? What, of the trained ruffianism which hustles with violence from the polls all honest men who can be browbeaten? "Oh! the offence is rank, and smells to Heaven!" Can my poor voice contribute aught this day towards arousing the public conscience to the enormity of measures, by which all national morality is secretly sapped, and the foundations of public liberty are surely undermined? Let us be deeply humbled before God for sins like these; and let us fervently pray they may belong only to the record of the past. For the love of God and Country, let us strive to bring back the purer days of the republic: when honest merit waited, like Cincinnatus at his plow, to be called forth for service, and before noisy candidates cried their wares at the hustings like fishwomen in the market—when a ribald press did not thrust its obtrusive gaze into the sanctities of private life, and the road to office did not lead through the pillory of public abuse and scandal—and when the votes of the people only expressed their virtuous and unbiased will. If not—then in the loss of our national virtue we shall become as incapable of serving God and history, as the poor nation which we have just seen stranded upon these abuses and wrecked forever. May these things be only of the past! May the brand of Cain be on the forehead of him who first attempts, in our new Government, to corrupt the ballot! May he go forth a fugitive from men, until his dishonor shall hide itself in a nameless grave!

4. **As a nation, we have sinned in a grievous want of reverence for the authority and majesty of law**. You remember that fine passage in Hooker which embalms, in words of amber, the whole philosophy of obedience: "of law there can be no less acknowledged than that her seat is in the bosom of God, her voice the harmony of the world; all things in heaven and earth do her homage; the very least as feeling her care, and the greatest as not exempted from her power; both angels and men and creatures of what condition soever, with uniform consent, admiring her as the mother of their peace and joy." Like the attraction of gravitation in physics, law binds together all the spheres of human duty and holds them fast to the throne of God. In all the concentric circles of society, obedience is man's first obligation. Not one is so much a master, but he owes fealty to a power higher than his own. The spirit of insubordination is therefore the highest treason, for it breaks the tie which binds the universe of moral beings together: as though in nature apostate orbs should fly from their centres, and wildly clash in the regions of space.

But if disregard of law be in this general view a crime of such magnitude, it assumes a new malignity when committed by a people living under such a government as ours. Its distinctive folly and wickedness are seen in the fact that it involves the abdication of our supremacy. In a republic, the sovereign is the people; and the laws they obey are the expressions of their own will. To trample upon these is, therefore, to trail their own sovereignty in the mire, to abdicate their own power, to extinguish the national life by shameful felo-de-se. When a monarch like Charles V lays aside the insignia of his royal state and retires to a convent, we can understand the weariness of care and disgust of the world, which induced the step. But no censure mingles with our compassion, because the state survived. His abdication simply transferred the symbol and substance of power to the hands of another, and there was no break in the continuity of the nation's life. But where the people are the ruler no less than the ruled, abdication is a felony; for it can only take place through self-murder. Insubordination to authority is with us therefore the commencement of political destruction—at once the most flagrant and the most senseless of crimes. There is the greater necessity for grinding this truth into the minds of our people, inasmuch as through the simplicity of our republican institutions the ensigns of power are not flaunted before the eye. Under a monarchy, the king and his court become the symbol of authority, the living representative of the law in its majesty. It is an unquestionable advantage of that form of government, that law should be presented in this embodied and concrete form before the masses; who are insensibly taught reverence by the very pomp and ceremony, which many decry without considering this incidental benefit which accrues. But with us, the administration of law is necessarily stripped of this outward splendor: the people should, therefore, be taught the dignity of obedience, as springing from the self-respect which is due to their own sovereignty. Need I pause to show the disasters which, in a popular government, must flow from irreverence of the law? Alas! the present history of our own distracted land furnishes a commentary for the text. It is a sad tale—a tale, sad as that which renewed the grief of Aeneas before the Tyrian queen. It is this arrogant competition of individual opinion finding its climax in the pretensions of "a higher law," which has involved half the nation in the guilt of perjury, and broken the bond of the holiest covenant ever sworn between man and man. It is this same recklessness of obligation, which has lifted up the sword to butcher those who will not bend nor yield to a merciless proscription. It is the same spirit mounting to phrenzy, which has seized upon wise and venerable ministers of the church; who have turned away from the gospel of God, in order to hound on this war of exterminating and bitter revenge. And it is the same demon of misrule which, in three short months, has swept away every guard of private as well as public liberty; and erected, under the shadow of the tomb of Washington, a despotism as irresponsible and cruel as any which has ever crushed the hearts and hopes of mankind.

In this particular manifestation of lawlessness, the South has rather been "sinned against than sinning." But then we have the *lex talionis*; the spirit, whose unrelenting cry is "an eye for an eye—a tooth for a tooth." This right of retaliation finds recognition with us; not softened, as with the ancient Hebrews, by cities of refuge, whither the man-slayer may betake himself. By a too general consent individuals assume the prerogative of the magistrate, in redressing their own wrongs. It may be true, that certain outrages cannot be restrained by the inadequate defences of public law; and when the safety of society may require instant retribution at the hands of the sufferer, who is substantively transformed into the magistrate. But these cases are exceptional and extreme; and if not provided for by special enactment, they are at least sustained by a virtuous sentiment based upon the instinct of self-preservation, characterizing the State as well as the person. Yet, in a civilized and Christian land, when the broad shield of law is supposed to cover all the interests and rights of men, it is flagrant wickedness to live as though society was resolved into its primordial elements: amid all the paths of business or pleasure, to have the treacherous hand trembling upon the concealed weapon, which is aready, in the sudden brawl, to leap forth upon its unsuspecting victim. This spirit must be exorcised from the land, else it will work the destruction of government. Let us choose wise legislators, who shall frame a code sufficient for the public protection. Let us clothe our Judges with the purest ermine, that they may make the temple of justice awful and holy as the sanctuary of God. Let us create a robust and healthy public sentiment, which shall everywhere support the law by an influence as diffused and silent as the pressure of the atmosphere. Let us train our youth to habits of obedience, teaching boys to remain boys, else they will be beaten with rods. Thus may reverence for law pervade all classes; and the daily conduct of our citizens come up as the swelling chorus of that song, which Hooker beautifully describes as "the harmony of the world." We have sinned in this against our race and against God: let our repentance to-day be the deep bass, which shall give the keynote of that song.

5. **As a people, we have been distinguished by a grovelling devotion to merely material interests**. A nation loses its tone when it becomes intensely utilitarian. When noble deeds are weighed in the scales of merchandise; and expedience stands behind its counter to measure off virtue by the ell, and weigh honor by the pound avoirdupois. The American devotion to material interests is by no means inexplicable. A great and practical race like our own, thrown upon a new Continent, and turning its Saxon energy upon the development of hidden treasures, elsewhere unparalleled, finds its covetousness reacted upon by its own prosperity. The age too is an age of physical science, which, exploring the secrets of nature, and subordinating her powers to the uses of man, renders it utilitarian by system. Besides all this, the stimulus of our Republican institutions develops the activity of our people into almost superhuman energy, and sharpens their wit to the highest shrewdness. With the total obliteration of caste, we start together from the same level of democratic equality. Yet, with the avenues to power and distinction open to all aspirants, is it strange that a general competition should exist amongst our people in the accumulation of wealth, which is at once the most obvious and the most easily attained instrument of power? Thus, the greed of gain has rusted into the hearts of our people—the most sordid of all passions, and the most fruitful source of individual and national corruption. The prevalence of this spirit has exposed us to the bitter sarcasm that, as a nation, we have set up the Golden Calf in the midst of the camp as the God of our idolatry. Every interest of the land has suffered from the corroding influence of this sordid utilitarianism. It has infected our schools of learning, cutting down the standard of intellectual

discipline until sound scholarship is fast becoming a thing obsolete as the my-thology of Greece. It has contaminated our Courts of Justice, until jury trial has, in a measure, become a shield for crime, and immunity from punishment is regulated by a graduated tariff. It has seated itself in halls of legislation, and discounts at the tables of the money-changers the rights and claims which a just legislation should protect. The spirit of speculation sweeps over the land with its expansion of credit and its inflated prosperity, until, as periodically as the equinox, we look for financial disaster, which dashes to the ground colos-sal fortunes as easily as the hurricane lays prostrate the giants of the forest.

It is all wrong, my hearers: offensive to God, and ruinous to ourselves. And I do not wonder that, to save us from total demoralization, God has let loose upon us this political storm, in order to bring up from the depth of the nation's heart its dormant virtue. We are learning by the sacrifices of the times, in the same school with our heroic forefathers, that liberty is better than gold, and honor more precious than fortune. The accumulated treasures of past industry and thrift are now cheerfully laid upon the altar of your coun-try's safety. Fathers are consecrating their sons to that Country's service, with an oath more solemn than that which bound Hannibal to eternal enmity with Rome: and tender mothers buckle the shield around them, as did the Spartan mothers of old, saying with equal heroism, "come back with it a conqueror, or be borne back upon it a martyr." I thank God for the storm. It has come in time to redeem us from ruin. Though the heavens be overcast, and lurid light-nings gleam from the bosom of each dark cloud, the moral atmosphere will be purged—and from our heroism shall spring sons and daughters capable of im-mortal destinies. Let me sound it out as with the trumpet of the Resurrection day: the men in all ages who have made history, have been men of faith—men who could hide a great principle deep in their heart, work it out as a poten-tial and substantive fact, and abide the verdict of posterity. All the Poets, all the Statesmen, all the Warriors of the past, were men of faith. Believing in the grand and the true, they could put their heel upon the present; and lifting up the curtain which hides the far off future from other men, they drew up that future by a magnetic attraction to themselves, and lived abreast of it. Any man can do the things that can be done; but they who do the things that can't be done—they are the immortals. It is a heroic day in which to live! Let the pulse of a high and generous patriotism beat in our breasts: that the history we work out may be the school-book from which our children's children shall learn to be true, and brave, and pure, as it becomes the children of the great to be.

I had designed, in connexion with our national responsibilities, to speak of *the obligations we owe to our slave population.* But the subject is excluded by its own largeness from discussion now. It will bear postponement. When this unnatural war shall be concluded, and we shall be free from the imperti-nent interference with our domestic affairs by which we have been so long annoyed, there will be opportunity to say all that the moralist and christian should utter, and what it will be fitting the legislator and the master should hear. We can afford to bide the time.

In conclusion, permit me to say that the present is by far the most important and glorious struggle through which the nation has ever passed. The parallel which has been drawn between it and the contest of the Revolution has not been seen in its full significance by many even of those who have suggested it; certainly not by those who have derided it in terms of measureless contempt. The principles involved in this conflict are broader and deeper than those which underlay that of the Revolution, rendering it of far greater significance to us and to our posterity and to mankind at large. Our fathers fought for no abstract rights as men, but for chartered rights as Englishmen. They claimed that the fundamental principle of English liberty was invaded, when the Colonies were taxed without representation. They were abundantly able to pay the duty which was stamped upon the Royal paper, and the tax levied upon the tea which they threw into the harbor of Boston: but they were not able to submit to any infraction of their Constitutional rights. For this they resisted unto blood: and had the British Ministry been wise, the day had been long postponed before the Crown had lost its brightest jewel, and England found a rival in those very Colonies which once owed her fealty and love. But *our* Revolution rests upon the broader principle laid as the corner stone of the American Constitution: "that governments derive their just powers from the consent of the governed; and that whenever any form of government becomes destructive of the ends for which it was formed, it is the right of the People to alter, or to abolish it, and to institute a new government, organizing its powers in such form as to them shall seem most likely to effect their safety and happiness." The true issue of to-day is not precisely what it was in November last, nor in January last, nor yet in March, when was exhibited the spectacle of the inauguration at Washington. The issue which now unites our whole population as the heart of one man, is *whether ten millions of people have not the inherent right to institute such a government, "as to them shall seem most likely to secure their safety and happiness."* This right is denied to us; and its denial lays the foundation of a despotism under which we cannot consent to live, for it was distinctly repudiated in the Declaration of 1776. We should be unworthy of our Fathers, if we flinched from maintaining to the last extremity the one, great, cardinal principle of American constitutional freedom. I could perhaps manage to live, if Providence had so ordained, under the despotism of the Czar, for it is not wholly irresponsible: the order of the Nobles would be interposed between me and the absolute will of the Autocrat. I could perhaps submit even to the Turk; for he is held in check by far of his own Janizaries. But I will not—so help me God!—I never will submit to the despotism of the mob. It is not the occupant of the White House who is the tyrant of to-day; but the starving millions behind the throne. Hence the wild outburst of revenge and hate, which now astonishes the world. It is the wail of concentrated agony and despair of the unpaid labor which asks for bread, and capital gives it a stone; and which hopes through our extermination and the deportation or massacre of our slaves, to find room for itself upon the broad Savannas of the South. May a merciful God help them of the North! They have sowed the wind, they must reap the whirlwind. They cannot retrieve the past, they must drive on and meet the future: perhaps to experience the fate of Acteon, and be eaten up by their own hounds.

The last hope of self-government upon this Continent lies in these eleven Confederated States. We have retained the one, primary truth, upon which the whole fabric of public liberty was reared by our fathers, and from which the North has openly apostatized. We have too in the institution of Slavery a great central fact, living and embodied, lifting itself up from the bed of history as the mountain cliff from the bed of the deep, blue sea; and in defending it against the assaults of a "rose-water philanthropy," we may place ourselves against all the past and feel the support of God's immovable Providence. Dare we then—dare any of us, man, woman or child—falter upon the path of such a destiny? Dare we quench in eternal night the hope which for a hundred years has been shedding its light upon the world, that man may be self-governed and free? I do not doubt the bravery of our people—I do not distrust their willingness to make all possible sacrifices to maintain their right. But I do fear the absence of sufficient trust in the power and grace of Almighty God. Whatever may be the strength of our self-reliance, let it be built up through a sacred confidence in God as our shield and buckler. Whatever hopes we may cherish from the diplomatic influences which are destined to bear upon this quarrel, let us remember the jealousy of Him who forbade Israel to "go down into Egypt for horses." Let us trust in God, and with an humble self-reliance take care of ourselves; prepared to recognize that gracious Providence which will work our deliverance.

The division of the American people into two distinct nations has not taken me by surprise. It was clearly enough foreshadowed by the parliamentary conflicts through which we have passed; and it has its root deep down in the different nationalities, of which our eclectic population is composed. The analogies of history should have led us to anticipate it. Through all time, nations have been formed first by agglutination, and then by separation. In their original weakness, the most heterogeneous elements are combined and held together by the pressure of necessity: but in their maturity, those concealed differences spring up, which have their root often in the type of character impressed upon the parent stock; and which no lapse of time can obliterate, and no political chemistry can make permanently to coalesce. We have vainly read the history of our fathers, if we failed to see that from the beginning two nations were in the American womb; and through the whole period of gestation the supplanter has had his hand upon his brother's heel. The separation of North and South was as surely decreed of God, and has as certainly been accomplished by the outworking of great moral causes, as was the separation of the Colonies from their English mother; as the genesis of the modern nations of Europe, out of the destruction of ancient Rome. In effecting this separation, the most glorious opportunity has been missed of demonstrating the power of our Republican principles, the progress of American civilization, and the effective control of the Gospel over human passions. In past ages, the sword has been the universal arbiter, and every issue has been submitted to the ordeal of battle. How fondly many of us hoped and pleaded for the rejection of this brutal argument; and for such an adjustment of our difficulties, as both the civilization and the religion of the age demanded! But our overtures of peace were first fraudulently entertained, and then insultingly rejected. I accept that rejection. I will go to my God, and will tell him how we have desired peace, I will tell him how we have sought to realize the scripture idea of "beating the sword into the plowshare": and then I will remit those who have rejected our treaties of amity and commerce, to his retributive judgment. But in this act, let us bow in low humility before His throne; confessing our sins with prayer and fasting, and trusting in His promise to reward them that diligently seek him. Oh! my country! "there is none like unto the God of Jeshurun, who rideth upon the heaven in thy help, and in his excellency on the sky. The eternal God is thy refuge, and underneath are the everlasting arms: and He shall thrust out the enemy from before thee, and shall say, destroy them. Israel then shall dwell in safety alone: the fountain of Jacob shall be upon a land of corn and wine; also his heavens shall drop dew. Happy art thou, O Israel: who is like unto thee, O People saved by the Lord, the shield of thy help, and who is the sword of thy excellency? and thine enemies shall be found liars unto thee, and thou shalt tread upon their high places."

ABRAHAM LINCOLN

ᕲᕦ

Second Inaugural Address

March 4, 1865

Fellow-Countrymen:

At this second appearing to take the oath of the Presidential office there is less occasion for an extended address than there was at the first. Then a statement somewhat in detail of a course to be pursued seemed fitting and proper. Now, at the expiration of four years, during which public declarations have been constantly called forth on every point and phase of the great contest which still absorbs the attention and engrosses the energies of the nation, little that is new could be presented. The progress of our arms, upon which all else chiefly depends, is as well known to the public as to myself, and it is, I trust, reasonably satisfactory and encouraging to all. With high hope for the future, no prediction in regard to it is ventured.

On the occasion corresponding to this four years ago all thoughts were anxiously directed to an impending civil war. All dreaded it, all sought to avert it. While the inaugural address was being delivered from this place, devoted altogether to *saving* the Union without war, insurgent agents were in the city seeking to *destroy* it without war—seeking to dissolve the Union and divide effects by negotiation. Both parties deprecated war, but one of them would *make* war rather than let the nation survive, and the other would *accept* war rather than let it perish, and the war came.

One-eighth of the whole population were colored slaves, not distributed generally over the Union, but localized in the southern part of it. These slaves constituted a peculiar and powerful interest. All knew that this interest was somehow the cause of the war. To strengthen, perpetuate, and extend this interest was the object for which the insurgents would rend the Union even by war, while the Government claimed no right to do more than to restrict the territorial enlargement of it. Neither party expected for the war the mag-

From *Inaugural Addresses of the Presidents of the United States* (Washington, D.C.: Government Printing Office, 1965), pp. 127–28.

nitude or the duration which it has already attained. Neither anticipated that the *cause* of the conflict might cease with or even before the conflict itself should cease. Each looked for an easier triumph, and a result less fundamental and astounding. Both read the same Bible and pray to the same God, and each invokes His aid against the other. It may seem strange that any men should dare to ask a just God's assistance in wringing their bread from the sweat of other men's faces, but let us judge not, that we be not judged. The prayers of both could not be answered. That of neither has been answered fully. The Almighty has His own purposes. "Woe unto the world because of offenses; for it must needs be that offenses come, but woe to that man by whom the offense cometh." If we shall suppose that American slavery is one of those offenses which, in the providence of God, must needs come, but which, having continued through His appointed time, He now wills to remove, and that He gives to both North and South this terrible war as the woe due to those by whom the offense came, shall we discern therein any departure from those divine attributes which the believers in a living God always ascribe to Him? Fondly do we hope, fervently do we pray, that this mighty scourge of war may speedily pass away. Yet, if God wills that it continue until all the wealth piled by the bondsman's two hundred and fifty years of unrequited toil shall be sunk, and until every drop of blood drawn with the lash shall be paid by another drawn with the sword, as was said three thousand years ago, so still it must be said "the judgments of the Lord are true and righteous altogether."

With malice toward none, with charity for all, with firmness in the right as God gives us to see the right, let us strive on to finish the work we are in, to bind up the nation's wounds, to care for him who shall have borne the battle and for his widow and his orphan, to do all which may achieve and cherish a just and lasting peace among ourselves and with all nations.

HORACE BUSHNELL

Our Obligations to the Dead

Brethren of the Alumni:—

To pay fit honors to our dead is one of the fraternal and customary offices of these anniversaries; never so nearly an office of high public duty as now, when we find the roll of our membership starred with so many names made sacred by the giving up of life for the Republic. We knew them here in terms of cherished intimacy; some of them so lately that we scarcely seem to have been parted from them; others of them we have met here many times, returning to renew, with us, their tender and pleasant recollections of the past; but we meet them here no more: they are gone to make up the hecatomb offered for their and our great nation's life. Hence it has been specially desired on this occasion, that we honor their heroic sacrifice by some fit remembrance. Had the call of your committee been different, I should certainly not have responded.

And yet, over-willing as I have been to assume an office so entirely grateful, it is a matter none the less difficult to settle on the best and most proper way of doing the honors intended. I think you will agree with me, that it cannot be satisfactorily done by preparing a string of obituary notices of our dead; that would be more appropriate to some published document, and no wise appropriate to a public discourse. Besides, to withdraw them from the vaster roll of the dead, in which it was their honor to die, and set them in a circle of mere literary clanship, bounding our testimony of homage by the accident of their matriculation here with us, would be rather to claim our honors in them, than to pay them honors due to themselves. We should seem not even to appreciate the grand public motive to which they gave up their life. They honored us in dying for their country, and we fitly honor them, when we class them with the glorious brotherhood in which they fell. Reserving it there-

An oration given at the Commemorative Celebration held in New Haven, on Wednesday of Commencement Week, July 26, 1865, in honor of the Alumni of Yale College, who fell in the War of the Rebellion. From Horace Bushnell, *Building Eras in Religion* (New York: Charles Scribner's Sons, 1881), pp. 319–55.

fore as my privilege, to make such reference specially to them as befits the occasion, I propose a more general subject in which due honors may be paid to all, viz., *The obligations we owe to the dead*, — all the dead who have fallen in this gigantic and fearfully bloody war.

. . .

First of all then, we are to see that we give them their due share of the victory and the honors of victory. For it is one of our natural infirmities, against which we need to be carefully and even jealously guarded, that we fall so easily into the impression which puts them in the class of defeat and failure. Are they not dead? And who shall count the dead as being in the roll of victory? But the living return to greet us and be with us, and we listen eagerly to the story of the scenes in which they bore their part. We enjoy their exultations and exult with them. Their great leaders also return, to be crowded by our ovations, and deafened by our applauses. These, these, we too readily say, are the victors, considering no more the dead but with a certain feeling close akin to pity. If, sometime, the story of their fall is told us, the spot described, far in front or on the rampart's edge, where they left their bodies with the fatal gashes at which their souls went out, we listen with sympathy and sad respect, but we do not find how to count them in the lists of victory, and scarcely to include them in the general victory of the cause. All our associations run this way, and before we know it we have them down, most likely, on the losing side of the struggle. They belong, we fancy, to the waste of victory, — sad waste indeed! but not in any sense a part of victory itself. No, no, ye living! It is the ammunition spent that gains the battle, not the ammunition brought off from the field. These dead are the spent ammunition of the war, and theirs above all is the victory. Upon what indeed turned the question of the war itself, but on the dead that could be furnished; or what is no wise different, the life that could be contributed for that kind of expenditure? These grim heroes therefore, dead and dumb, that have strewed so many fields with their bodies, — these are the price and purchase-money of our triumph. A great many of us were ready to live, but these offered themselves, in a sense, to die, and by their cost the victory is won.

Nay, it is not quite enough, if we will know exactly who is entitled to a part in these honors, that we only remember these dead of the war. Buried generations back of them were also present in it, almost as truly as they. Thus, if we take the two most honored leaders, Grant and Sherman, who, besides the general victory they have gained for the cause, have won their sublime distinction as the greatest living commanders of the world, it will be impossible to think of them as having made or begotten their own lofty endowments. All great heroic men have seeds and roots, far back it may be, out of which they spring, and apart from which they could not spring at all; a sublime fatherhood and motherhood, in whose blood and life, however undistinguished, victory was long ago distilling for the great day to come of their people and nation.

. . .

Still, it is not my intention to occupy you with the part fulfilled by these remoter generations of the past, but with the more general remembrance of such as have fallen in the war itself. I only refer you to these, to show you how very trivial and weak a thing it is, if we speak of our victories, to imagine that only such as come out of the war alive are entitled to credit and reverence on account of them.

But I pass to a point where the dead obtain a right of honor that is more distinctive, and belongs not to the living at all; or if in certain things partly to the living, yet only to them in some less sacred and prominent way. I speak here of the fact that, according to the true economy of the world, so many of its grandest and most noble benefits have and are to have a tragic origin, and to come as outgrowths only of blood. Whether it be that sin is in the world, and the whole creation groaneth in the necessary throes of its demonized life, we need not stay to inquire; for sin would be in the world and the demonizing spell would be upon it. Such was, and was to be, and is, the economy of it. Common life, the world's great life, is in the large way tragic. As the mild benignity and peaceful reign of Christ begins at the principle: "without shedding of blood, there is no remission," so, without shedding of blood, there is almost nothing great in the world, or to be expected for it. For the life is in the blood,—all life; and it is put flowing within, partly for the serving of a nobler use in flowing out on fit occasion, to quicken and consecrate whatever it touches. God could not plan a Peace-Society world, to live in the sweet amenities, and grow great and happy by simply thriving and feeding. There must be bleeding also. Sentiments must be born that are children of thunder; there must be heroes and heroic nationalities, and martyr testimonies, else there will be only mediocrities, insipidities, common-place men, and common-place writings,—a sordid and mean peace, liberties without a pulse, and epics that are only eclogues.

And here it is that the dead of our war have done for us a work so precious, which is all their own,—they have bled for us; and by this simple sacrifice of blood they have opened for us a new great chapter of life. We were living before in trade and commerce, bragging of our new cities and our census reports, and our liberties that were also consciously mocked by our hypocrisies; having only the possibilities of great inspirations and not the fact, materialized more and more evidently in our habits and sentiments, strong principally in our discords and the impetuosity of our projects for money. But the blood of our dead has touched our souls with thoughts more serious and deeper, and begotten, as I trust, somewhat of that high-bred inspiration which is itself the possibility of genius, and of a true public greatness. Saying nothing then for the present of our victors and victories, let us see what we have gotten by the blood of our slain.

And first of all, in this blood our unity is cemented and forever sanctified. Something was gained for us here, at the beginning, by our sacrifices in the fields of our Revolution,—something, but not all. Had it not been for this common bleeding of the States in their common cause, it is doubtful whether our Constitution could ever have been carried. The discords of the Convention were imminent, as we know, and were only surmounted by compromises that left them still existing. They were simply kenneled under the Constitution and not reconciled, as began to be evident shortly in the doctrines of state sovereignty, and state nullification, here and there asserted. We had not bled enough, as yet, to merge our colonial distinctions and make us a proper nation. Our battles had not been upon a scale to thoroughly mass our feeling, or gulf us in a common cause and life. Against the state-rights doctrines, the logic of our Constitution was decisive, and they were refuted a thousand times over. But such things do not go by argument. No argument transmutes a discord, or composes a unity where there was none. The matter wanted here was blood, not logic, and this we now have on a scale large enough to meet our necessity. True it is blood on one side, and blood on the other,—all the better for that; for bad bleeding kills, and righteous bleeding sanctifies and quickens. The state-rights doctrine is now fairly bled away, and the unity died for, in a way of such prodigious devotion, is forever sealed and glorified.

Nor let any one be concerned for the sectional relations of defeat and victory. For there has all the while been a grand, suppressed sentiment of country in the general field of the rebellion, which is bursting up already into sovereignty out of the soil itself. There is even a chance that this sentiment may blaze into a passion hot enough to utterly burn up whatever fire itself can master. At all events it will put under the ban, from this time forth, all such instigators of treason as could turn their peaceful States into hells of desolation, and force even patriotic citizens to fight against the homage they bore their country. However this may be, the seeds of a true public life are in the soil, waiting to grow apace. It will be as when the flood of Noah receded. For the righteous man perchance began to bethink himself shortly, and to be troubled, that he took no seeds into the ark; but no sooner were the waters down, than the oaks and palms and all great trees sprung into life, under the dead old trunks of the forest, and the green world reappeared even greener than before; only the sections had all received new seeds, by a floating exchange, and put them forthwith into growth together with their own. So the unity now to be developed, after this war-deluge is over, is even like to be more cordial than it ever could have been. It will be no more thought of as a mere human compact, or composition, always to be debated by the letter, but it will be that bond of common life which God had touched with blood; a sacredly heroic, Providentially tragic unity, where God's cherubim stand guard over grudges and hates and remembered jealousies, and the sense of nationality becomes even a kind of religion. . . .

Passing to another point of view, we owe it to our dead in this terrible war, that they have given us the possibility of a great consciousness and great public sentiments. There must needs be something lofty in a people's action, and above all something heroic in their sacrifices for a cause, to sustain a great sentiment in them. They will try, in the smooth days of peace and golden thriftiness and wide-spreading growth, to have it, and perhaps will think they really have it, but they will only have semblances and counterfeits; patriotic professions that are showy and thin, swells and protestations that are only oratorical and have no true fire. All the worse if they have interests and institutions that are all the while mocking their principles; breeding factions that can be quieted only by connivances and compromises and political bargains, that sell out their muniments of right and nationality. Then you shall see all high devotion going down as by a law, till nothing is left but the dastard picture of a spent magistracy that, when every thing is falling into wreck, can only whimper that it sees not any thing it can do! Great sentiments go when they are not dismissed, and will not come when they are sent for. We cannot keep them by much talk, nor have them because we have heard of them and seen them in a classic halo. A lofty public consciousness arises only when things are loftily and nobly done. It is only when we are rallied by a cause, in that cause receive a great inspiration, in that inspiration give our bodies to the death, that at last, out of many such heroes dead, comes the possibility of great thoughts, fired by sacrifice, and a true public magnanimity.

In this view, we are not the same people that we were, and never can be again. Our young scholars, that before could only find the forms of great feeling in their classic studies, now catch the fire of it unsought. Emulous before of saying fine things for their country, they now choke for the impossibility of saying what they truly feel. The pitch of their life is raised. The tragic blood of the war is a kind of new capacity for them. They perceive what it is to have a country and a public devotion. Great aims are close at hand, and in such aims a finer type of manners. And what shall follow, but that, in their more invigorated, nobler life, they are seen hereafter to be manlier in thought and scholarship, and closer to genius in action.

I must also speak of the new great history sanctified by this war, and the blood of its fearfully bloody sacrifices. So much worth and character were never sacrificed in a human war before. And by this mournful offering, we have bought a really stupendous chapter of history. We had a little very beautiful history before, which we were beginning to cherish and fondly cultivate. But we had not enough of it to beget a full historic consciousness. As was

just now intimated in a different way, no people ever become vigorously conscious, till they mightily do, and heroically suffer. The historic sense is close
akin to tragedy. We say it accusingly often,—and foolishly,—that history cannot live on peace, but must feed itself on blood. The reason is that, without
the blood, there is really nothing great enough in motive and action, taking
the world as it is, to create a great people or story. If a gospel can be executed
only in blood, if there is no power of salvation strong enough to carry the
world's feeling which is not gained by dying for it, how shall a selfish race
get far enough above itself, to be kindled by the story of its action in the dull
routine of its common arts of peace? Doubtless it should be otherwise, even as
goodness should be universal; but so it never has been, and upon the present
footing of evil never can be. The great cause must be great as in the clashing
of evil; and heroic inspirations, and the bleeding of heroic worth must be the
zest of the story. Nations can sufficiently live only as they find how to ener-
getically die. In this view, some of us have felt, for a long time, the want of a
more historic life, to make us a truly great people. This want is now supplied;
for now, at last, we may be said to have gotten a history. The story of this four
years' war is the grandest chapter, I think, of heroic fact, and tragic devotion,
and spontaneous public sacrifice, that has ever been made in our world. The
great epic story of Troy is but a song in comparison. There was never a better,
and never so great a cause; order against faction, law against conspiracy, liberty and right against the madness and defiant wrong of slavery, the unity
and salvation of the greatest future nationality and freest government of the
world, a perpetual state of war to be averted, and the preservation for mankind of an example of popular government and free society that is a token of
promise for true manhood, and an omen of death to old abuse and prescrip-
tive wrong the world over; this has been our cause, and it is something to say
that we have borne ourselves worthily in it. Our noblest and best sons have
given their life to it. We have dotted whole regions with battlefields. We have
stained how many rivers, and bays, and how many hundred leagues of railroad, with our blood! We have suffered appalling defeats; twice at Bull Run,
at Wilsons' Creek, in the great campaign of the Peninsula, at Cedar Mountain, at Fredericksburg, at Chancellorsville, at Chickamauga, and upon the
Red River, leaving our acres of dead on all these fields and many others less
conspicuous; yet, abating no jog of courage and returning with resolve unbroken, we have converted these defeats into only more impressive victories.
In this manner too, with a better fortune nobly earned, we have hallowed, as
names of glory and high victory, Pea Ridge, Donelson, Shiloh, Hilton Head,
New Orleans, Vicksburg, Port Hudson, Stone River, Lookout Mountain, Re-
saca, Atlanta, Fort Fisher, Gettysburg, Nashville, Wilmington, Petersburg and
Richmond, Bentonville, Mobile Bay, and, last of all, the forts of Mobile City.
All these and a hundred others are now become, and in all future time are to

be, names grandly historic. And to have them is to be how great a gift for the ages to come! By how many of the future children of the Republic will these spots be visited, and how many will return from their pilgrimages thither, blest in remembrances of the dead, to whom they owe their country!

Among the fallen too we have names that will glow with unfading lustre on whatever page they are written; our own brave Lyon, baptizing the cause in the blood of his early death; our Sedgwick, never found wanting at any point of command, equal in fact to the very highest command, and only too modest to receive it when offered; the grandly gifted young McPherson, who had already fought himself into the first rank of leadership, and was generally counted the peerless hope and prodigy of the armies; Reynolds also, and Kearney, and Reno, and Birney; and how many brilliant stars, or even constellations of stars, in the lower degrees of command, such as Rice, and Lowell, and Vincent, and Shaw, and Stedman, and a hundred others in like honor, for the heroic merit of their leadership and death! And yet, when I drop all particular names, dear as they may be, counting them only the smoke and not the fire, letting the unknown trains of dead heroes pack and mass and ascend, to shine, as by host, in the glorious Milky Way of their multitude, — men that left their business and all the dearest ties of home and family to fight their country's righteous war, and fought on till they fell, — then for the first time do I seem to feel the tide-swing of a great historic consciousness. God forbid that any prudishness of modesty should here detain us. Let us fear no more to say that we have won a history and the right to be a consciously historic people. Henceforth our new world even heads the old, having in this single chapter risen clean above it. The wars of Caesar, and Frederic, and Napoleon, were grand enough in their leadership, but there is no grand people or popular greatness in them, consequently no true dignity. In this war of ours it is the people, moving by their own decisive motion, in the sense of their own great cause. For this cause we have volunteered by the million, and in three thousand millions of money, and by the resolute bleeding of our men and the equally resolute bleeding of our self-taxation, we have bought and sanctified consentingly all these fields, all that is grand in this thoroughly principled history.

Again, it is not a new age of history only that we owe to the bloody sacrifices of this war, but in much the same manner the confidence of a new literary age; a benefit that we are specially called in such a place as this, and on such an occasion, to remember and fitly acknowledge. Great public throes are, mentally speaking, changes of base for some new thought-campaign in a people. Hence the brilliant new literature of the age of Queen Elizabeth; then of another golden era under Anne; and then still again, as in the arrival of another birth-time, after the Napoleonic wars of George the Fourth. The same thing has been noted, I believe, in respect to the wars of Greece and Germany. Only it is in such wars as raise the public sense and majesty of a

people that the result is seen to follow. For it is the high-souled feeling raised
that quickens high-souled thought, and puts the life of genius in the glow of
new-born liberty. This we are now to expect, for the special reason also that
we have here, for the first time, conquered a position. Thus it will be seen that
no great writer becomes himself, in his full power, till he has gotten the sense
of position. Much more true is this of a people. And here has been our weakness until now. We have held the place of cliency, we have taken our models
and laws of criticism, and to a great extent our opinions, from the English
motherhood of our language and mind. Under that kind of pupilage we live
no longer; we are thoroughly weaned from it, and become a people in no secondary right. Henceforth we are not going to write English, but American.
As we have gotten our position, we are now to have our own civilization,
think our own thoughts, rhyme in our own measures, kindle our own fires,
and make our own canons of criticism, even as we settle the proprieties of
punishment for our own traitors. We are not henceforth to live as by cotton
and corn and trade, keeping the downward slope of thrifty mediocrity. Our
young men are not going out of college, staled, in the name of discipline, by
their carefully conned lessons, to be launched on the voyage of life as ships
without wind, but they are to have great sentiments, and mighty impulsions,
and souls alive all through in fires of high devotion.

· · ·

I might also speak at large, if I had the time, of the immense benefit these
dead have conferred upon our free institutions themselves, by the consecrating blood of their sacrifice. But I can only say that having taken the sword to
be God's ministers, and to vindicate the law as his ordinance, they have done it
even the more effectively in that they have died for it. It has been a wretched
fault of our people that we have so nearly ignored the moral foundations of
our government. Regarding it as a merely human creation, we have held it
only by the tenure of convenience. Hence came the secession. For what we
create by our will, may we not dissolve by the same. Bitter has been the cost
of our pitifully weak philosophy. In these rivers of blood we have now bathed
our institutions and they are henceforth to be hallowed in our sight. Government is now become Providential,—no more a mere creature of our human
will, but a grandly moral affair. The awful stains of sacrifice are upon it, as
upon the fields where our dead battled for it, and it is sacred for their sakes.
The stamp of God's sovereignty is also upon it; for he has beheld their blood
upon its gate-posts and made it the sign of his passover. Henceforth we are
not to be manufacturing government, and defying in turn its sovereignty because we have made it ourselves; but we are to revere its sacred rights, rest in
its sacred immunities, and have it even as the Caesar whom our Christ himself requires us to obey. Have we not also proved, written it down for all the

ages to come, that the most horrible, God-defying crime of this world is unnecessary rebellion?

I might also speak of the immense contribution made for religion, by the sacrifices of these bleeding years. Religion, at the first, gave impulse, and, by a sublime recompense of reaction, it will also receive impulse. What then shall we look for but for a new era now to break forth, a day of new gifts and powers and holy endowments from on high, wherein great communities and friendly nations shall be girded in sacrifice, for the cause of Christ their Master?

But these illustrations must not be continued farther. Such are some of the benefits we are put in obligations for by the dead in this great war. And now it remains to ask, by what fitting tribute these obligations are to be paid? And it signifies little, first of all, to say: Let the widows of these dead be widows, and their children, children of the Republic. Let them also be the private care of us all. Let the childless families adopt these fatherless. Give the sons and daughters growing up the necessary education: open to them ways of industry; set them in opportunities of advancement. Let our whole people resolve themselves into a grand Sanitary Commission, for these after-blows of suffering and loss occasioned by the war.

Again, it is another of the sacred obligations we owe to the dead, that we sanctify their good name. Nothing can be more annoying to the sense of honor, than the mischievous facility of some, in letting down the merit and repute of the fallen by the flippant recollection of their faults, or, it may be, of their former vices. Who have earned immunity from this petty kind of criticism, if not they who have died for their country? . . .

A great work also is due from us to the dead, and quite as much for our own sakes as theirs, in the due memorizing of their names and acts. Let the nation's grand war monument be raised in massive granite, piercing the sky. Let every State, honored by such names as Sedgwick, and Lyon, and Mansfield, claim the right to their honors for the future ages, by raising, on some highest mountain top, or in some park of ornament, the conspicuous shaft or pillar, that will fitly represent the majesty of the men. The towns and villages will but honor themselves, when they set up their humbler monuments inscribed with the names of the fallen. Let the churches also, and the college halls and chapels, show their mural tablets, where both worship and learning may be quickened by the remembrance of heroic deeds and deaths. In this way, or some other, every name of our fallen Alumni should be conspicuously recorded in the College; that our sons coming hither may learn, first of all, that our mother gives her best to die for their country.

. . .

But there is one other and yet higher duty that we owe to these dead; viz., that we take their places and stand in their cause. It is even a great law of natural duty that the living shall come into the places and works of the dead. The same also is accepted and honored by Christianity, when it shows the Christian son, and brother, and friend, stepping into the places made vacant by the dead, to assume their blessed and great work unaccomplished, and die, if need be, in the testimony of a common martyrdom. They challenged, in this manner, if the commentators will suffer it, the vows of baptism, and "were baptized for the dead,"—consecrated upon the dead, for the work of the dead. God lays it upon us in the same way now, to own the bond of fealty that connects us with the fallen, in the conscious community and righteous kinship of their cause. And then, as brothers baptized for the dead,—Alumni, so to speak, of the Republic,—we are to execute their purpose and fulfill the idea that inspired them. Neither is it enough at this point to go off in a general heroic, promising, in high rhetoric, to give our life for the country in like manner. There is no present likelihood that we shall be called to do any such thing. No, but we have duties upon us that are closer at hand; viz., to wind up and settle this great tragedy in a way to exactly justify every drop of blood that has been shed in it. Like the blood of righteous Abel it cries both to us and to God, from every field, and river, and wood, and road, dotted by our pickets and swept by the march of our armies.

First of all we are sworn to see that no vestige of state sovereignty is left, and the perpetual, supreme sovereignty of the nation established. For what but this have our heroes died? Not one of them would have died for a government of mere optional continuance; not one for a government fit to be rebelled against. But they volunteered for a government in perfect right, and one to be perpetual as the stars, and they went to the death as against the crime of hell. Tell me also this,—if a government is good enough to die *for*, is it not good enough to die *by*, when it is violated? Not that every traitor is, of course, to be visited by the punishment of treason. It is not for me to say who, or how many or few, shall suffer that punishment. But I would willingly take the question to the dead victims of Belle Isle, and Salisbury, and Andersonville, and let them be the judges. There is no revenge in them now. The wild storms of their agony are laid, and the thoughts which bear sway in the world where they are gathered are those of the merciful Christ, and Christ is the judge before whose bar they know full well that their redress is sure. And yet I think it will be none the less their judgment that something is due to law and justice here. As, too, it was something for them to die for the law, I can imagine them to ask whether it is not something for the law to prove its vindicated honor in the fit punishment of such barbarities? May it not occur to them also to ask, whether proportion is not an everlasting attribute of justice? And if punctual retribution is to follow the sudden taking off of one, whether the deliberate and slow starvation of so many thousands is to be fitly ignored and raise no sword of judgment? Neither is it any thing to say, that the awful ruin of the rebellious country is itself a punishment upon the grandest scale, and ought to be sufficient; for the misery of it is, that it falls on the innocent and not on the leaders and projectors, who are the chief criminals. Our liberal friends abroad conjure us to follow the lead of their despotism, and cover up gently all these offenses, because they are only political. Ah! there is a difference which they need to learn. Doubtless governments may be bad enough to make political offenses innocent; nay, to make them even righteous. But we have not fought this dreadful war to a close, just to put our government upon a par with their oppressive dynasties! We scorn the parallel they give us; and we owe it even to them to say, that a government which is friendly, and free, and right, protecting all alike, and doing the most for all, is one of God's sacred finalities, which no hand may touch, or conspiracy assail, without committing the most damning crime, such as can be matched by no possible severities of justice. We are driven in thus on every side, upon the conclusion that examples ought to be and must be made. Only they must be few and such as can be taken apart from all sectional conditions; for we have sections to compose, and the ordinary uses of punishment in cases of private treason do not pertain where the crime is nearly geographic, and is scarcely different from public war.

One thing more we are also sworn upon the dead to do; viz., to see that every vestige of slavery is swept clean. We did not begin the war to extirpate slavery; but the war itself took hold of slavery on its way, and as this had been the gangrene of our wound from the first, we shortly put ourselves heartily to the cleansing, and shall not, as good surgeons, leave a part of the virus in it. We are not to extirpate the form and leave the fact. The whole black code must go; the law of passes, and the law of evidence, and the unequal laws of suit and impeachment for crime. We are bound, if possible, to make the emancipation work well; as it never can, till the old habit of domination, and the new grudges of exasperated pride and passion, are qualified by gentleness and consideration. Otherwise there will be no industry but only jangle; society in fact will be turned into a hell of poverty and confusion. And this kind of relationship never can be secured, till the dejected and despised race are put upon the footing of men, and allowed to assert themselves somehow in the laws. Putting aside all theoretic notions of equality, and regarding nothing but the practical want of the emancipation, negro suffrage appears to be indispensable. But the want is one thing, and the right of compelling it another. Our States have always made their own laws of suffrage, and if we want to resuscitate the state-rights doctrine, there is no so ready way as to rouse it by state wrongs. But there is always a way of doing what wants to be done,—pardon me if I name it even here; for our dead are not asking mere rhetoric of us, but duty. They call us to no whimpering over them, no sad weeping, or doling of soft sympathy, but to counsel and true action. I remember too, that we have taken more than a hundred thousand of these freedmen of the war to fight our common battle. I remember the massacre of Fort Pillow. I remember the fatal assault of Fort Wagner and the gallant Shaw sleeping there in the pile of his black followers. I remember the bloody fight and victory on the James, where the ground itself was black with dead. Ah, there is a debt of honor here! And honor is never so sacred as when it is due to the weak. Blasted and accursed be the soul that will forget these dead! If they had no offices or honors, if they fought and died in the plane of their humility,—Thou just God, forbid that we suffer them now to be robbed of the hope that inspired them!

Do then simply this, which we have a perfect constitutional right to do,—pass this very simple amendment, that the basis of representation in Congress shall hereafter be the number, in all the States alike, of the free male voters therein. Then the work is done; a general free suffrage follows by consent, and as soon as it probably ought. For these returning States will not be long content with half the offices they want, and half the power allowed them in the Republic. Negro suffrage is thus carried without even naming the word.

Need I add, that now, by these strange fortunes of the rebellion rushing on its Providential overthrow, immense responsibilities are put upon us, that are new. A new style of industry is to be inaugurated. The soil is to be distributed over again, villages are to be created, schools established, churches erected, preachers and teachers provided, and money for these purposes to be poured out in rivers of benefaction, even as it has been in the war. A whole hundred years of new creation will be needed to repair these wastes and regenerate these habits of wrong; and we are baptized for the dead, to go forth in God's name, ceasing not, and putting it upon our children never to cease, till the work is done.

My task is now finished; only, alas! too feebly. There are many things I might say, addressing you as Alumni, as professors and teachers, and as scholars training here for the new age to come. But you will anticipate my suggestions, and pass on by me, to conceive a better wisdom for yourselves. One thing only I will name, which is fitting, as we part, for us all, viz., that without any particle of vain assumption, we swear by our dead to be Americans. Our position is gained! Our die of history is struck! Thank God we have a country, and that country has the chance of a future! Ours be it henceforth to cherish that country, and assert that future; also, to invigorate both by our own civilization, adorn them by our literature, consolidate them in our religion. Ours be it also, in God's own time, to champion, by land and sea, the right of this whole continent to be an American world, and to have its own American laws, and liberties, and institutions.

Part Five

National Progress and Wealth

During the last three decades of the nineteenth century American life passed through some transformations that substantially affected perspectives on the national destiny. The composition of the population was radically changed by millions of European immigrants settling in the United States. By 1900 approximately one-third of the population was either foreign born or the children of foreign-born parents. Of no less consequence were the alterations brought to American life by the twin phenomena of industrial expansion and the growth of cities. By 1860 the amount of capital invested in industry, railroads, commerce, and urban property had already outstripped the total economic value of American farms; after 1865 the nation's industry, greatly stimulated by manufacturing demands of the Civil War, surged ahead at an unprecedented pace. In those postwar years the urban population more than doubled as foreign immigrants and rural Americans made their way to burgeoning industrial centers.[1]

With these changes came all the social and economic problems associated with the industrial revolution: city blight and urban ghettos, rural depressions, exploited human and natural resources. Yet the prevalent mood among Americans who prospered, and who expected to prosper, from the changes was one of forward-looking optimism. Beneath the surface of this optimistic exterior there seethed an explosive discontent, but Americans in many walks of life assumed that both they as individuals and their nation as a whole were beckoned by a glorious future. Increased immigration produced a resurgence of nativist fears that all those foreigners would wreck the social, economic, and political structure of the nation; such apprehensions were counterbalanced by the widely proclaimed belief that America was rapidly fulfilling her destiny as a refuge of freedom and opportunity for the oppressed and homeless of

1. For a discussion of these changes and their effects on American religion see Edwin Scott Gaustad, *A Religious History of America* (San Francisco: HarperCollins Publishers, 1990), pp. 198–214; and Winthrop S. Hudson and John Corrigan, *Religion in America* (New York: Macmillan Publishing Company, 1992), pp. 282–305.

the world. Expanding national wealth was concentrated more and more into the holdings of a few corporations and families, but an ideology springing from the times held that the hand of providence was rewarding the American virtues of thrift and hard work by guiding both industrious individuals and the nation toward a splendid position of economic strength.

Rabbi Isaac Mayer Wise, an immigrant to this country from Bohemia in 1846, was not uncritical of nineteenth-century American society, but he did believe that the progress of Western civilization was culminating in America. Arriving in New York City with only two dollars in his pocket, Wise was to become the influential rabbi of Temple Bene Yeshurun in Cincinnati, a promoter of the Union of American Hebrew Congregations, a founder of Hebrew Union College, and the leading American spokesman for Reform Judaism. Wise's life in America was not the typical success story since he brought with him from Europe a solid formal education at the universities of Prague and Vienna. Yet, like so many other European Jews, he had been at best "tolerated" by a culture shaped by a state church. "My father," he once said, "was not permitted to call even a handbreadth of land his own, therefore I never had a fatherland." Wise urged Jewish immigrants to become thoroughly Americanized, to discard as quickly as possible their European languages and habits. "The Jew must become an American, in order to gain the proud self-consciousness of the free-born man." Through Americanization and the retention of the essentials of their religion, Jews could both attain full participation in American life and preserve their Jewish identity.[2]

Americanization did not mean for Wise the mindless approval of everything in American society. He fulminated against this country's ignorance of great literature, its worship of money, its ready acceptance of Protestant influence on politics. Yet the note he sounded repeatedly was that America was the nation of the future. Its future was, in fact, the hope of humanity since it possessed liberty as the very soul of its existence. Wise gave classic expression to this idea in his 1869 lecture before the Theological and Religious Library Association of Cincinnati. There he portrayed America as the Promised Land of freedom progressively realizing its role in history through a combination of free choice and the law of providence.

Religious interpretations of American destiny after the Civil War seldom dwelt simply on America as the Promised Land of liberty. They usually extolled that destiny in terms of the nation's expanding wealth, employing the arguments of the then dominant laissez-faire economic theory. If economic self-interest were allowed free play, it was held, every industrious person would serve the common good of society and contribute to the nation's in-

2. See Israel Knox, *Rabbi in America: The Story of Isaac M. Wise* (Boston: Little, Brown and Company, 1957).

creasing wealth. This theory was buttressed by the individualism of the so-called Protestant ethic that identified virtue with frugality and hard work; it was also supported by a providential view of history that saw the nation's progress proceeding according to laws of God incorporated within a system of unhindered economic competition.

Henry Ward Beecher, who had by no means exhausted his persuasive powers during the Civil War, became one of America's most eloquent spokesmen for a national destiny pursued within a laissez-faire system. Enjoying a liberal salary and large royalties from his publications, Beecher reasoned that poverty more often springs from sin, than sin from poverty:

> There may be reasons of poverty which do not involve wrong but looking comprehensively through city and town and village and country, the general truth will stand, that no man in this land suffers from poverty unless it be more than his fault—unless it be his sin.[3]

In 1877, when bloody railroad strikes broke out in American cities in protest of a ten percent wage cut, Beecher upbraided the railroad employees for not nobly bearing their poverty. He was not always so callous in his attitude toward the poor and occasionally even denounced the corporate swindles and frauds of his day. He consistently maintained, however, that wealth itself was a blessing to be actively sought and that the nation's wealth was a providentially bestowed means for achieving a significant place in history.

Beecher's Thanksgiving Day sermon of 1870, "The Tendencies of American Progress," clearly revealed his individualist ethic and his views of national wealth and progress. Running through the entire sermon was the conviction that American destiny under God was inextricably intertwined with American wealth. "May God give us magnanimity and power and riches," Beecher said, "that we may throw the shadow of our example upon the poor, the perishing, and the ready-to-be-destroyed, for their protection." John Winthrop's exemplary "city upon a hill" had become, in the rhetoric of people like Beecher, a tawdry megalopolis.

Laissez-faire individualism attained its height as an ideology in this country at precisely the time when it was becoming inapplicable to social and economic reality. The appearance of large trusts and vast cities between Reconstruction and 1900 thwarted the dynamics of free competition and frustrated radical individualism. Nevertheless, laissez-faire as an idea-system continued to spread and became a veritable American gospel that appealed to many levels of society. "This faith and philosophy became the most persuasive siren in American life," Ralph Henry Gabriel has written.

---

3. Quoted in Henry F. May, *Protestant Churches and Industrial America* (New York: Harper & Row, Publishers, Torchbooks, 1967), p. 69.

It filled the highways with farm boys trekking to the city. It drained the towns and countryside of Europe. It persuaded the educated young man that the greatest rewards of life were to be found in the business world. It taught the ambitious that power lies in wealth rather than in political office. It penetrated the workshop and paralyzed the effort of the labor leader undertaking a crusade for justice to the working man.[4]

Captains of industry and builders of railroads became national heroes, saints in a cult of success. Horatio Alger's dime novels popularized the cult in a series of rags-to-riches stories which indoctrinated American youth in the belief that virtue is rewarded by wealth.

Andrew Carnegie, who rose from the position of bobbin boy to wealthy steel master, was one of the heroes of his age and an articulate defender of its ideology. His famous essay "Wealth," which first appeared in the *North American Review* in 1889, argued that the foundations of society and the progress of civilization rest upon certain "laws": the sacredness of property, free economic competition, and accumulation of wealth. Carnegie admitted that the development of civilization on the basis of these laws "may be sometimes hard for the individual," but he was convinced "it is best for the race, because it insures the survival of the fittest in every department." Carnegie, Beecher, and many other Americans of the time drew upon the social Darwinism of Herbert Spencer to give their laissez-faire individualism theoretical respectability. The rough-and-tumble of economic competition was believed to effect the improvement of humanity by guaranteeing that only the fittest of the race would survive. Carnegie softened the harshness of his Darwinism by insisting that the wealthy are obligated to abide by the law of stewardship, that is, they should distribute their wealth in such a way that it contributes to the common good and helps those who will help themselves. Carnegie was thoroughly persuaded, however, that obedience to the basic laws of economic competition would "some day . . . solve the problem of the Rich and the Poor, and . . . bring 'Peace on earth, among men Good-Will.'"

It fell principally to the influential clergy of the day to give the Gospel of Wealth religious sanction and, as custodians of the public conscience, to assure a nation scrambling for riches that it was in no danger of corrupting its character or abandoning its divine destiny. Russell Conwell, Baptist minister and founder of the Philadelphia Temple (out of which grew Temple University), assured Americans that the pursuit of wealth was an honorable task. In his lecture *Acres of Diamonds* which he delivered more than six thousand times across the eastern and middle western United States, Conwell admonished his

---

4. Ralph Henry Gabriel, *The Course of American Democratic Thought* (New York: The Ronald Press Company, 1956), pp. 163–64.

hearers, "I say that you ought to get rich, and it is your duty to get rich." The reason is simple: "Money is power, and you ought to be reasonably ambitious to have it. You ought because you can do more good with it than you could without it." For those who doubted the good character of men of wealth and power Conwell had further words of comfort: "ninety-eight out of one hundred of the rich men of America are honest. That is why they are rich. That is why they are trusted with money."

The religious and moral justification of the Gospel of Wealth was rounded out in 1901 by William Lawrence, Episcopal bishop of Massachusetts. In his essay "The Relation of Wealth to Morals," Lawrence acknowledges that certain moral hazards attend wealth, but he insists that "in the long run, it is only to the man of morality that wealth comes," that on the whole "godliness is in league with riches." What is true for the individual is equally true for the nation. "Material prosperity is helping to make the national character sweeter, more joyous, more unselfish, more Christlike." "Clothed with her material forces, the great personality of this Nation may fulfill her divine destiny" of developing her education, industry, art—her culture as a whole. For Lawrence the acquisition of wealth through free economic competition "sweetens" the national character and encourages the growth of American culture—for Lawrence that is the sum and substance of American destiny under God.

The Gospel of Wealth exercised a firm, prolonged control on the hopes of Americans; its control, however, was neither absolute nor endless. Among farmers and industrial workers who were the victims of a monopolistic capitalism unchecked by government regulations, discontent smoldered and then burst forth in strikes and in protests from workingmen's associations and farmers' alliances. Critics of the ideology of acquisitiveness emerged among the country's intellectuals. American pragmatist philosopher Charles Peirce attacked his "century of greed," economist Thorstein Veblen condemned the Gospel of Wealth, journalist Finley Peter Dunne bitingly satirized the philanthropic activities of the captains of industry. During the early years of the twentieth century the muckrakers opened national sores created by the industrial revolution. The ground was being prepared for an emerging concept of a welfare state and the reforms of the progressive movement.

Religious resistance to uncontrolled capitalism was spearheaded by the movement known as the "Social Gospel." The Social Gospel was never really a tightly organized movement; for the most part it was a religious outlook constituted by shared beliefs. Most of its representatives believed in the social principles of Jesus as reliable moral guides for the individual and for society, trusted in the basic goodness of human nature, and expected "that, through the efforts of men of good will, the kingdom of God would soon become a reality, bringing with it social harmony and the elimination of the worst of social injustices."[5] Most proponents of the Social Gospel shared their age's wholehearted belief in progress. Critical though they were of the selfishness and atomistic individualism of the Gospel of Wealth, they were confident that honest efforts on the part of both government and individuals of good will would correct social injustices and that the nation could progressively achieve the Kingdom of God and the Brotherhood of Man.

Efforts on behalf of the improved status of American women in the late nineteenth century were also set within a progressive view of the national destiny. Calls for women's suffrage, equal rights in marriage, and educational opportunities were construed by women leaders as necessary steps toward a national experience characterized by freedom, equality, and social harmony. The coupling of women's earnest appeals for reform with their confidence in national progress was apparent at the Chicago World's Fair in 1893. The Fair celebrated the four hundredth anniversary of Columbus's "discovery" of America with numerous exhibits of mechanical power, technical achievements, and scientific advancements—all as testimony to America's material progress. But through countless congresses devoted to the motto "Not Matter, But Mind; Not Things, But Men," participants in the Fair also insisted that things higher and nobler should be saluted "by the enlightened and progressive spirit of the age."[6] The congresses dealt with such topics as social reform, women's progress, art, and religion.

At the Fair's World's Parliament of Religions, the best attended of the meetings, social reformers and laborers for women's rights joined representatives of the world's religions in sessions consisting of both popular lectures and scholarly papers. One of the twenty women who addressed the Parliament[7] was Frances E. Willard, president of both the national and the world organizations of the Women's Christian Temperance Union. Willard's campaign against alcohol and its deleterious effects on the family had long been joined with her arguments for the equal rights of women under the law and in human relations. The breadth of Willard's reformist concerns was evident in her speech to the Parliament, touching as it did on the themes of temperance, labor, suffrage, marriage, law, Christianity, and moral uprightness. Defending a notion popular with many women at the time, that the male and female natures complement each other in the divine plan of things, Willard brooked no inequality between the two natures: woman is the "companion and counselor,

5. Robert T. Handy, *The Social Gospel in America, 1870–1920* (New York: Oxford University Press, 1966), p. 10.

6. Cited in David F. Burg, *Chicago's White City of 1893* (Lexington: University Press of Kentucky, 1976), p. 236.

7. See Ursula King, "Rediscovering Women's Voices at the World's Parliament of Religions," *A Museum of Faiths: Histories and Legacies of the 1893 World's Parliament of Religions*, ed. Eric J. Ziolkowski (Atlanta: Scholars Press, 1993), pp. 325–43.

not the incumbrance and toy, of man." And her pleas for equality of the sexes were incorporated into her yearning for a "far-off perfection" and a future personal mutuality that would establish the full righteousness of the nation.

Events of the twentieth century would produce attitudes among the American people that would severely shake their progressive optimism. Deep disappointment over the fact that the Great War was not a war to end all war, shock and despair over the Depression, anxiety over the threat of nuclear extinction—such feelings would render highly questionable, if not downright ludicrous, the assumption that America was moving steadily toward the Kingdom of God. Yet even the crises of the twentieth century would not totally invalidate Walt Whitman's description of America as the nation that "counts almost entirely upon the future." The American Israel could no longer depend upon an inevitable progress toward a spectacular place in history, but it could and would continue to count on the future to bring opportunities for renewal of its divine destiny.

SUGGESTED READING

Abell, Aaron I. *American Catholicism and Social Action: A Search for Social Justice, 1865–1950.* Garden City, N.Y.: Doubleday & Company, 1960.

Hofstadter, Richard. *Social Darwinism in American Thought.* Boston: Beacon Press, 1955.

Kennedy, Gail, ed. *Democracy and the Gospel of Wealth.* Boston: D. C. Heath & Company, 1949.

Ruether, Rosemary Radford, and Rosemary Skinner Keller, eds. *The Nineteenth Century.* Vol. 1 of *Women and Religion in America.* San Francisco: Harper & Row, Publishers, 1981.

Weimann, Jeanne Madeline. *The Fair Women.* Chicago: Academy Chicago, 1981.

White, Ronald C., Jr., and C. Howard Hopkins. *The Social Gospel: Religion and Reform in Changing America.* Philadelphia: Temple University Press, 1976.

ISAAC M. WISE

Our Country's Place in History

The Committee of the Theological and Religious Library Association of our city having bestowed the privilege upon me to open a course of lectures, in which so many excellent and distinguished gentlemen participate, I must in the first place express my thanks to the Committee; and in the second place, make the humble confession, that looking upon the galaxy of orators to come after me (in time, of course,), and the intelligent audience before me, I do not consider myself equal to the task so kindly conferred upon me.

Weak men, in battle, seek shelter behind strong fortifications. I have been prudent enough to profit by the experience of others. Conscious of my deficiencies I seek shelter behind a strong subject—a subject dear and precious to all of us, our country, our promised land, the home and fortress of freedom, the blessed spot which flows with milk and honey, upon which we invoke God's gracious blessings. "Our Country's Place in History" is the subject of this lecture, to which I claim your kind attention; and I know you will bestow it, on account of this important theme.

History and a Place in It

History is Providence realized. It is the experience of the human family, because it is the compendium of those events which effected the progress of our race. Individuals and nations, by an undefined impulse, are the actors who realize the plans of a higher power, to the detriment of all that is wicked, the development and preservation of all that is good, and tends to the elevation of man.

A cursory glance upon this physical universe proves the existence of such an impulse in the vast domain of creation as a force of nature, a universal law. Primary matter, imagine it as ether, gas, mist or chaos,—primary matter is poten-

A lecture delivered before the Theological and Religious Library Association of Cincinnati, January 7, 1869.

tial, imbued with the desire of individuation (although no such term is known in physics), to form bodies of a separate existence. So this earth, those stars, and those suns were individualized from primary matter, other celestial bodies are, and will perpetually be formed by the same law, the same "Word of God." The great bodies of the universe, in the architecture of heaven, are active and co-operative individuals. The influence of each contributes directly or indirectly to the rotation and life of the whole; while the primary or non-individualized matter is apparently passive, without a role in the grand drama of the universe.

The same law precisely governs the destiny of man. The human family is a chaos of persons, each imbued with the desire, to rise above this chaos to individual immortality. Tribes and nations, composed of persons, are continually stimulated by the same innate desire, to rise above the level of the chaos to individual existence, to an active and co-operative attitude. Many rise above the chaos, and fulfill their destiny, to realize the designs of Providence; many more remain particles of the chaos, or meteors in the celestial plan.

Like the stars in the solar system, the nations who rose to individuality are clustered around the central and invisible omnipotence, and complete their rotation in obedience to immutable laws. Like the stars, every people must be a unit in the sum total of history—a unit without which the whole sum could not exist; an independent unit in its sphere, and an auxiliary one, attracting and being attracted, bearing and being borne, in the moral universe of Providence. So and not otherwise, we can imagine a government administered by the Supreme Wisdom. This theory rests upon the solid basis of analogy from nature's revelations, and explains the phenomenon of history. In this sense nations have their places in history.

No Fatalism

This theory has nothing in common with fatalism, inasmuch as obedience to the dicta of reason is its direct opposite. It is not even inevitable necessity to the individual or the nation. Both are at liberty to choose their own course; although, if persisting in the deviation, it amounts to an entire failure of their existence to themselves, while others take their places in the realization of the Providential designs. Particles must, man wills, the object is God's. Let us explain. Every individual is appointed to fulfill that destiny in society, for which he is gifted with adequate capacities. This destiny must be fulfilled, although this or that particular individual may revolt, and neglect his appointment to the bitter end of self destruction. Others gifted with the same capacities will take that place in society and fulfill that same destiny. This is individual freedom and universal necessity. Nature offers many an analogy in this respect, one of which will suffice. There is the forest with its numerous trees. Every tree has the destiny to be a part of the forest. Trees die, therefore saplings must grow up to take their respective places. Every sapling has the natural destiny to grow and to take its place as a tree. But nature produces ten saplings, only one of which fulfills its destiny as a tree of the forest, the other nine die, to nourish the roots of that tree. The forest must; man wills. Precisely the same is the case with nations. Every nation has that destiny, to which time, geographical location and the capacities of the race enable it. It may not know, not understand, not attempt to fulfill its destiny, or do it but partially. But then other nations who do fulfill this particular destiny, will replace it, and the designs of Providence must be realized, exactly as the forest remains a forest, however many saplings perish before one becomes a tree. The Philistines might have fulfilled the destiny of the Hebrews, the Phoenicians that of the Greeks, the Macedonians that of Rome, and the Mexicans that of the United States. But they did not, and the succession was necessary to realize the design. There is no fatalism.

Explanations

Without entering upon the principles of just and successful government, the logical sequence of our theory; we will only add this explanation: The destiny which a nation realizes in the designs of Providence, is its place in history. Furthermore, however different the destinies of the various nations, they are similar in one chief characteristic, whose name is PROGRESS. Nations which contribute nothing to the progress of humanity, fulfill no destiny. Nations contributing no longer to the progress of humanity, have ceased to fulfill their destiny, and are in a state of dissolution. Nations, which contribute most to the progress of humanity, fulfill the highest national destiny. For history, as we have said already, "is the compendium of those events which effected the progress of the human race." We are ready now, to discuss our country's place in history.

The Close of the Fifteenth Century

Let us open our text book and cast a glance on the state of affairs towards the close of the fifteenth century. In the political arena, personal liberty was submerged in huge centralized empires with a fair beginning of standing armies as the right hand of despotism. From and after the crusades, the small sovereignties vanished, and with them the last trace of personal freedom and patriarchal government, without any beneficent change in the feudal system. The serf, the peasant, and the burgher, with the exception of a few cities, was the beast of burden, the commodity, the chattel of the lawless nobleman whose life and fortune were property of the crown. The law was barbarous, and barbarism was the law, modified in exceptional cases by conscientious or prudent rulers. . . .

The Church was no better than the State. Europe was one huge despotism. John Wikliff [*sic*] was dead (1384). His followers were few and harmless. Huss and Hieronimus of Prague had ended on the Pyre (1415–16). The Taborites and Orphanites were massacred and the Calixtines subjected again to the sovereign church (1433). A century of quarrels in the church was successfully closed, the reforms proposed by the councils of Basel and Kostnitz were set aside and overcome, the head of the church was so well established in his rights and privileges, the lower clergy and the people so well trained into submission and silence, that Alexander VI occupied undisturbed the highest dignity in Christendom. The inquisition extended its paternal arms from the North sea into the Pyrenean peninsula; the Jews were driven out of Spain, and everything was nicely fixed for the perpetuation of despotism in State and Church. There was no escape from the terrible arm of absolutism. It reached to the very ends of the then known earth, and extended its horrible dominion into the very realms of heaven. The nations failing to fulfill their destiny, the old world having arrived at a dead lock, a new nation, a new world had to be born, and born they were.

The Travail

Mark the wonderful travail at the birth of a new world and a new chapter of history. In the chaos of that despotism, two peculiar germs of a new creation were discernible. We can only call them two unconscious passions. The love of knowledge and of discovery, were those two germs. Philosophy pressed in the straight jacket of orthodox scholasticism, in the dogmatic prison could not be entirely expunged after all. The long dispute of Nominalists and Realists, as well as the dissensions among church authorities, and especially the philosophical and scientific labors of the Arabs, carried into Christendom by Spanish Jews and their books—began to undermine the authority of scholasticism and to secularize philosophy. Men, although few and far apart, especially in Italy and Germany, began to thirst passionately after better knowledge. Although they were unconscious of the object of their desire and its influence upon the new state of affairs which was to come; nevertheless they felt the desire after better knowledge, and were compelled by an impulse from a higher power, to seek it. This gradually gave birth to the humanists, a class of doctors whose knowledge was quite limited, and whose freedom of research was still more so, because the despotism of Church and State extended over all departments of the mind, as well as over the youngest daughter of that age, the child of Guttenberg [*sic*] and Faust. Nevertheless they worked, although they knew not to what purpose. Popes, potentates and other mighty men, with the iron rod of oppression in one hand, assisted with the other in rearing a new fortress to humanity, without knowing what they did. The same was the case with that peculiar desire, to discover unknown islands, unknown roads on the high sea. Nobody knew exactly why, wherefore or whereto. It was a passion, an impulse from a higher power, for which none could account, had they even attempted it. The Italians and especially the Portuguese, were almost frantic with this passion. These were the travails of that age. These were the silent and seemingly insignificant causes which inspired Columbus with the irresistible passion to discover, he knew not what.

The Discovery of America

Contrary to the wisdom of all the wise men of his age, contrary to the resolves of the maritime experts and the maritime nations of his days, Columbus, compelled by the irresistible power of that nameless Spirit of the universe, steered out upon the unknown multitudiness of water, with the daring scheme to discover a direct route to India. Again, contrary to the hopes of those who sent him, of those who accompanied him, and contrary to his own expectation—to the most lofty flight of his imagination—he discovered a new world. A new world, in virgin purity, emerged from the deep, burst upon the enlarged horizon of human knowledge. A new world, so much larger than old princess Europe, and seated so much more secure between her wide oceans than Europe was on the back of the disguised, arbitrary and despotic Jupiter. A new world whose plains are wider, whose rivers broader, whose mountains higher and whose destiny so much loftier than those of her older sisters. A new world, the youngest daughter of Rhea, the proud heiress of their fortunes and their charms. A new world was discovered. Mankind had travailed and given birth to a new world.

Who schemes this masterly design of progress? Who understood its importance at the time? Who comprehended the passionate yearning of that age after knowledge and discovery? None on earth. God alone did. There is no fatalism.

Mexico and South America

Mankind is very slow in comprehending the designs of Providence. A century passed over the discovery of America without deriving any durable benefit from that great event. The love of discovery degenerated into an adventurous and avaricious spirit. Monarchs and violent men were allied for the sole purpose of plundering the new country, enslaving and exterminating its aborigines, and subjecting the new world to the despotic scepter of the old. Mexico, Peru, and other regions of South America and the West Indies, were thinly colonized to find gold, to acquire new domains for tyrannical crowns, new territory for defunct inhabitants. They failed in the choice of a destiny and could not succeed.

The Reformation

Meanwhile the love for better knowledge progressed rapidly in central Europe, especially in Italy, Germany, France, Holland and England. Commerce, and with it the free cities and municipal rights gained considerable importance. The Jews driven from Spain, Portugal and Naples, carried their commercial spirit, their rich literature, and Free Masonry with its cosmopolitan spirit into other parts of Christendom, especially to Holland and Italy. The love of learning, the growing power of the press, and the increase of commerce, liberalized and humanized nations, and roused in them that spirit of liberty which, in the first instance, resulted in the Protestant Reformation, which severed the sinews of ecclesiastical despotism, and paralyzed the right arm of worldly tyranny. From the day when Martin Luther nailed his theses to the church door, to the outbreak of the Thirty Years' War was a century of fierce contest between growing freedom and tenacious despotism, rising philosophy and declining dogmatics, which roused a feeling of independence, a spirit of liberty, and conscious sentiment of self-respect in the hearts of tens of thousands, who could no longer find a home in Europe, and they were driven to America.

The Puritan Fathers

During and after the Thirty Years' War in Germany and the concomitant convulsions in other countries, the liberal element lost considerable ground in Europe. The persecuted of all classes and denominations sought refuge in North America. True, not all like the Puritan Fathers, came to these shores with the pure desire to be free, and unmolested in their form of worship: nevertheless the vast majority of immigrants came to avoid persecution. Also most of the mere adventurers, to say nothing of English Catholics, French Huguenots, German, Dutch and Slavonic sects, Jews, Quakers and Deists; also most of the mere adventurers came to these shores with a certain spirit of liberty and independence, which was strengthened here by the influence of society and by the circumstances, that every pioneer in the forests of the Atlantic shores, or on the broad plains of the West, was sovereign on his domain, out of every foreign government's reach, and compelled to be his own governor, cabinet, legislature, general and army of defence. This made of the original settlers not only matter-of-fact men, capable of self-government, but also independent sons of freedom who abhorred the very idea of subjection and persecution. This spirit increased in intensity with the growth of the population in number and intelligence. The martial spirit also was developed by the course of events. The combat against ferocious beasts; the wars of "the Israelites against the Philistines," of "God's chosen people against the Indian Gentiles," and the struggles of France and England on this continent, made the American soldier. To all these growing elements in the early stage of American history one more must be counted, and that is the preservation of one language for all the colonies. This was the cornerstone to national greatness.

The Revolution

It is, therefore, quite natural, that the slightest irritation by the British Government, reaching outside of the commercial centers to the sovereigns of the forests and the broad plains, should arm them to resolute resistance. Being all sovereigns and soldiers themselves, and having learned an excellent lesson of Oliver Cromwell and his ironsiders, the only true cousins of Americans—the tea pennies and stamp shillings which among any other people would have passed unnoticed, sufficed to set the colonies ablaze, and to enact one of the brightest chapters in history. Glory to the memory of the heroes of the revolution, to the generous godfathers of liberty. Glory to the memory of George Washington and his heroic compatriots. They were the chosen instruments in the hands of Providence, to turn the wheel of events in favor of liberty forever; and they proved worthy of their great mission, of their immortal work. The hearts of a grateful people, canonized with honor and glory, are the indestructible materials of the monument of George Washington and his compatriots. The millions of oppressed men and women in all countries, whose chains have been broken and whose prisons have been razed, are the grand chorus, who sing the praise of the American revolution; and we, the lords and ladies of this broad land of freedom, re-echo the Hallelujah from ocean to ocean, from Maine's rocky coast to the silvery mirror of the Pacific and the sunny gulf of Mexico.

The Choice of Destiny

The revolution was the first grasp after the destiny of the nation, to which it was fully prepared by the spirit of the age, geographical location and special capacities, growing out naturally of former events in the regular routine of cause and effect. But now the question rose what to make of the thirteen independent republics. A new kingdom was the natural suggestion. But who besides God was to be the king of kings and the lord of lords? Washington, like Gideon, was too good a man to be a king. Still had he accepted that dignity, he could not have maintained it for any length of time. Those who understood the spirit of the people which came forth victoriously from the revolution could think of a republic only, on the broadest principles of personal freedom and municipal rights, civil and religious liberty in the most extensive sense of these terms. The framers of the Constitution were wise enough to understand the spirit of their people, courageous enough to confront the destiny of the nation, and honest enough to express their full conviction in the paragraphs of the Constitution and its immortal preamble. The people of the United States, on accepting this Constitution, had formally and solemnly chosen its destiny, to be now and forever the palladium of liberty and its divinely appointed banner-bearer, for the progress and redemption of mankind. It is a glorious destiny, a lofty ideal, which the fathers of our country have chosen for her; an ideal which must inspire every citizen with the holy desire, to take his proper place in the ranks of the people which follows this ideal, this guiding star, this glowing sun of human prosperity; an ideal which in the midst of selfishness, passion, avarice and debasing materialism, must be and was powerful enough, to rally the myriads of free men around the banners of our country and, with death-defying bravery, wield the sword in her protection to the undisturbed fulfillment of her destiny.

Illustration

With the adoption of the Constitution, our country assumed her place in history. It was done by the free choice of the people. Although it must be admitted that a chain of natural causes and effects, from the fifteenth century to the end of the eighteenth, together with geographical causes, educated the colonists to this destiny; nevertheless it can not be denied that every important step in the progress of our early history resulted from free choice, from personal freedom, demonstrating clearly the theory of individual freedom and universal necessity in the government of mankind. This theory, in the government of a nation, is reduced to the practical problem of finding the just equilibrium of personal freedom and the necessary power of the government, the solution of which is the great object of constitutional statesmanship. Our Constitution of the United States is the original American attempt in solution of that problem. This being of itself a contribution to the progress of mankind, it entitled our country to a place in history. But she occupies a larger chapter in the records of humanity than a written document confers; a place which might be best illustrated by historical parallels.

Being the heiress of the preceding phases of civilization, numerous parallels suggest themselves. Let us select one.

The United States occupy the same place in modern history as Greece did in antiquity. Greece, surrounded by water and blessed with numerous harbors, was favored with an extensive commerce and continual intercourse with the world. The same precisely is the case with our country. The oceans are broad enough to protect us against foreign interference in our domestic affairs, which no council of European powers will ever arrange. At the same time our harbors are numerous enough to shelter the navies of the whole world, and to keep us in constant intercourse with all nations. Distances were the great obstacles in our way. But the American mind removed them. The application of steam to navigation and the electro-magnetic force to the telegraph brought us in connection with the world, as closely as Greece ever was, to Egypt, Phoenicia or Italy, and reduced our wide-stretched territories, for all practical purposes, to a compass no larger than that of ancient Greece. Greece was the heiress of an ancient civilization, which was poured into her lap by immigrants from Egypt, Phoenicia, Assyria, Syria and Asia Minor, and the constant intercourse with all those and other nations. Our country is the heiress of the European civilization. All her shipwrecked men and shipwrecked ideas continually pour into our lap with a wealth of thoughts, designs, energies, learning, skill and enterprise which steadily fill our mental coffers, and enlarge our horizon of conceptions. Greece remoulded all those foreign elements into one preeminently Grecial form; so do we continually assimilate and Americanize, absorb and recast all the foreign elements which we receive. So powerful is the affinity of freedom among men that it unites and amalgamates them quicker than any other agency. While the German in Poland, after centuries of domicil, is still a German, the first American-born generation of Germans is American. While the Poles in France remain foreigners, among us they are fastly incorporated. While Czechs in the heart of Germany, after centuries of mutual intercourse, are still Bohemian in feeling, language, customs and ideals; it is extremely easy for us to sustain one language for the whole country. This is one of the most wonderful influences which we know liberty to exercise on man.

Greece did not stop short at her heritage from abroad, but enlarged it, by native genius, to Grecian art, philosophy, science, government and religion; so do we. Our form of government is new. The patent-office at Washington, that great museum of mind, speaks volumes in praise of native genius. The practical sphere, to which necessity has confined and schooled us, testifies sufficiently, that whenever our turn shall come in the idealistic sphere, we will not be found missing in the production of an originally American art, science, philosophy and religion. Greece educated tens thousands of emissaries, to carry her wealth into Asia, Africa and Europe; so do we. We educate millions of free men, to carry our national wealth all over the earth. The very example of our successful revolution set France and all Europe ablaze with hopes of liberty. The millions of letters and journals which we send annually across the ocean, are so many rays of light to oppressed nations, and rouse the millions to think, reflect, wish and hope for freedom, and to appreciate its blessings. Every Negro in our midst is an emissary for the future humanization and civilization of Africa. Those very Chinamen who do now the work of washerwomen in the far West, are our boarding scholars, to become the future teachers of Eastern Asia, which is already near our doors. The very result of our late rebellion encouraged and inspired millions of European hearts with hopes of redemption, and proved that the republic is stronger than any monarchy. This is as important to humanity as our declaration of independence was. Greece, by the conflux of the various families of man, was inhabited by a peculiar people; so is our country. We are originally English, Irish, French, Dutch, German, Polish, Spanish, or Scandinavian; but we are neither. We are Americans. Every child born on this soil is Americanized. Our country has a peculiar people to work out a new and peculiar destiny.

The heiress of the civilized world's blood, experience and wisdom, as Greece was in days of yore; the mistress of the vast domain fortified by heaving oceans, really wealthy as none was before her; the favored high priestess of the goddess of liberty, with the diadem of honor and the breast-plate of justice—though young, gay, fast, blundering and wild—occupies already a prominent place in history. Her commerce influences the commerce of the world, as only a few old countries do. But commerce, the source of wealth and the missionary of civilization, is one of the handmaids of progress. Her inventions in the mechanical arts, her strikes and associations of mechanics and laborers, revolutionize the system of labor all over the world, and redeem the laboring man from the oppression of hard labor, the despotism of capital and cunningness. These are powerful contributions to the progress of humanity. Still, industry herself is but another handmaid of progress. Liberty is the cause, progenitor, preserver and protector of all the blessings which we enjoy and impart to others. Liberty is progress itself. The chapter of liberty in the modern record of nations is our country's place in history. All other blessings of the human family grow from the soil of liberty, warmed by the genial rays of this glorious sun, and fructified by the stream of justice. Liberty is our place in history, our national destiny, our ideal, the very soul of our existence. As long as we cling tenaciously to our destiny and long steadily after our ideal, we will maintain our country's place in history. Greece, Rome and all the other empires afford no precedences to our future, for ours is a new world and a new destiny, which is entirely in our hands. Political parties may struggle and strive for the ascendancy. The conservative and the progressive elements of society are its centripetal and centrifugal forces which cause regular rotation, as long as they are governed by the center of gravity, the ideal of liberty. Money may govern the actions of tens of thousands; it is after all the mere foam on the surface which invariably disappears, as often as the ocean exerts its freedom of heaving up its billows. Sects may quarrel over particular dogmas, doctors disagree on the precise nature of the center of the earth. Liberty neutralizes their disputes, and begets new forms of religion and science. Nothing can arrest our progress, nothing drag down our country from her high place in history, except our own wickedness working a wilful desertion of our destiny, the desertion from the ideal of liberty. As long as we cling to this ideal, we will be in honor, glory, wealth and prosperity.

In the family, in school, in the academy, in church, on the public forum, in the press and everywhere else educate champions for the host of freedom; they are our country's guard. Warm, rouse, inspire every heart for liberty; this is our strength, our prosperity, our future, our destiny. Freedom to all nations; freedom to every man, this is our country's place in history; liberty in the name of my God and my country.

ᴥ

The Tendencies of American Progress

It is well for us to pause, in our career, to consider whither our national life is tending. For we are too apt to become so engrossed in our private affairs as to have but a dim and feeble sense of our relations to the life of the whole community. Or, if we cast a glance upon the tendencies of our times, it is apt to be superficial—a judgment which follows rather our disposition than our reason. To the hopeful, things are always bright; and they are always dark to the cautious. Prosperous men think the country is doing well; and the unfortunate see the signs of impending mischief and of quick-coming ruin on every hand. Men are apt to judge of the drift of things by the impressions made upon them by the things which are nearest, or by the welfare of the special cause to which they are giving their time and zeal. If that zone of life and force which is in contact with them is stormy, they feel that it is stormy away to the horizon, though but a step beyond it may be tranquil; and if the affairs in which men have embarked their chief zeal and their affections are withstood, and are declining, they are apt to think that the whole work of God in the world is weary and slow-paced.

While, then, it is proper that we should recognize superficial prosperity, and personal prosperity, and all forms of experience from the personal standpoint, we are far more earnest to inquire whether under the surface the tendency of things is onward and upward, or level, or working downward. But in order to this we must have some determinate rule or measure. We must not judge by the eye, nor by our senses, nor by a transient criterion.

The most obvious, and historically the first, condition of prosperity in any community is physical thrift, material wealth; and surely there can be no national life of any great worth without that. For there must be prosperity in material things if there is to be prosperity in moral things in the last estate. Still, a nation may be prospered in the field, and at the loom, and on the ship, and on the shore, and yet be degraded and declining. For material welfare,

From Henry Ward Beecher, *The Original Plymouth Pulpit*, vol. V. (Boston: Pilgrim Press, 1871), pp. 203–19.

although it be an indispensable element of national prosperity, is the lowest, and is to be subordinated to all others. Above it is the social and civil development of a nation. Far superior in importance to mere physical wealth is the wealth which comes from institutions, from laws, from the conduct of the people, and from the whole course of civilized society. But yet higher than this is moral and spiritual good. For without faith civilization itself soon becomes tame and powerless.

The highest prosperity, then, is associated with spiritual good. Next to that is social; and lowest of all is material. And in this order we are to judge of prosperity. That material good is prosperous which is working toward the social and toward the spiritual. That social and civil condition of society is wholesome which recognizes the higher law of religious development.

Now, in looking upon our national condition it is not enough that we see unbounded prosperity on the farm, at the forge, in the shop: we must ask whether this prosperity lies in the line of intelligence, of real virtue; whether it guides itself by moral principle.

On the other hand, in looking upon the imperfections and positive evils which attend the various elements of national life, men are not to be discouraged because there is much in them that is still evil; nor because in some places things are going backward, like eddies upon mighty rivers. For this is the law of all progress. But are things, *on the whole*, tending toward, or away from, moral elements? That will determine the question of prosperity.

Look, then, at our own condition territorially. What other nation has such a field for extension, such a field for development, such a field for material prosperity? Russia alone, perhaps, of all nations, has a territory as extensive as America. In all except bulk though, how different! Our climate, from the north line to the very gulf, is congenial to industry. There is no league in which climatic influences forbid prosperity; but the Russian climate is too rigorous. Through perhaps one third, or one-half—through vast spaces at any rate, it is unfavorable even to life itself, and life can never be developed into any great degree of society-force. Our soil, except a central tract (and that less barren than men suppose) is cultivatable throughout. Theirs is largely sterile. Our population is English-speaking, and homogeneous in ideas, though heterogeneous in origin. But all this, a prodigious condition of power if other things favor, is useless—and, worse than useless, will be corrupting—if there are not other elements of prosperity than merely that which is given us, of territory.

Then, our people carry with them everywhere self-government, and *a genius for it*. Partly, this is the quality of race. We spring mainly from a stock in which inheres the tendency to government, and self-government. And partly it is a thing learned. Our people have learned it; and government, therefore, and laws, go with every colony just as surely as yokes and harnesses go with their teams and herds. Men never emigrate without carrying their household wealth and the material for employing the soil in husbandry. But tools and implements are no more necessary in their judgment than are the institutions and the customs which make men societies. Wherever you throw a hundred Americans, you may be sure that almost their first thought will be to constitute themselves into a body politic. They do it as naturally as water comes together in crystals when cold congeals it. They come by a kind of elective affinity under laws and under constitutions.

Contrast that great and unfortunate nation, France, with our own in this respect. Their self-governing instinct seems never to have been developed. The tendency is feeble, and cultivation has never been applied to it. How to be governed they but just know; and how to govern themselves, not at all. But with us this is one of the most marked national features, the indispensable necessity of being governed, and the indispensable determination to let nobody do it for us, but to do it ourselves.

Our people, also, carry institutions which are to moral force what machinery is to physical force. Institutions are but the condensations of power. They are artificial persons, as it were, to whom is given an unweariable existence—a life longer than the life of those that made them. They are the devices of civilization for storing up and preserving and fitting out moral things, and are indispensable to the strength and constancy and perpetuity of communal life.

But all these are but conditions. What now are the general tendencies of the material prosperity of America which are being developed, with such a territory, with such a people on it, with such civic advantages? On the whole, are they toward intelligence, and morality, and a higher spiritual growth?

1. The mass of our working population, I think, were never so well clothed, so bountifully fed and so well housed, as they are now; and the tendency is not backward, but forward. Our working population, to the very lowest stage and class, tend to more refinement in their food, more taste in their apparel, and more culture in their dwellings, year by year. In other words, the lowest material conditions are working upward, and not downward. Plainness of apparel, and of circumstances surrounding, are not signs and tokens either of civil growth or of Christianity. The general impression is, that, as nations are better, they will be economical. I think, on the contrary, they will be profuse, and have the means of being so. The impression is that they will be unadorned. I think they will be more glorious than Solomon was, in all his apparel. The impression is that the law of simplicity in the sense of littleness of having and using characterizes virtue and religion. Far from it. As you go toward the savage state, you go away from complexity, from multitudinous power, down toward simplicity, and when you come to the lowest state—to the simplicity of men that wear skins and leather apparel, and live in huts and caves—you come to the fool's ideal of prosperity. But from that low animal condition starts development, and nations go on opening their faculties; and

every faculty becomes a market, and demands supply. And the more culture
a man has, the more parts of his nature there are which ask for material, for
institutions, for raiment, for comforts of every kind, the more there is in the
single man demanding these things, the more must his circumstances open
up, and become rich and potential. And in looking upon the condition of the
community, if you find that they are increasing in the variety of their food, in
the quality of their food, and in the excellence of cooking their food; if you
find that their dwellings are growing better and better from period to period;
if you find that their furniture is more beautiful, answering other ends than
merely the mechanical and physical ends—ministering to taste, ministering, if
you will, to luxury—if you find these things, they are signs of upward development and of growth. These are the signs which we find all the way through
our people, clear down to the bottom. And we are beginning to find them, as
I knew we should, among the Freedmen themselves. For no sooner was their
bondage broken than they began to feel that they were no longer animals, but
men, and began, partly from imitation, and partly from that instinct which
is common to all men, to gather around about themselves these evidences of
growth, development, power.

We do not think that anywhere on the globe men, on the whole, live so
well as in America—or grumble so much! But that is an indispensable thing.
For as men live better, their criterion of life grows with the betterment. Taste
increases in a greater ratio, oftentimes, than possession; and men are dissatis-
fied, not so much by what they have, as by the proportion which what they
have bears to their ideal. It is our ideals that make us grumblers. And so there
is some comfort in that.

The tendency, also, is to augment the conveniences, the beauty and the resources of homes. There is universal social ambition among the laborers of
America. They feel the dignity of citizenship. Power, with its responsibility,
has produced upon them the effect that we knew it would. It has educated,
it has inspired, it has developed them. And the consequence is, that they feel,
not that they are a class of work men, but that they are members of society.
They call themselves *citizens*. They belong to the common people. They are
a part of the one great loaf; and though each one is but a crumb, unbroken,
every crumb is loaf. And this, too, is a sign of growth in the right direction.
Show me a man who is content with things just as they have been, when he
has it in his power to make them better, and I will show you a man whose
tendency is the wrong way. He is by just so much less than a man who is con-
tented with inferior conditions of manhood.

There are other signs of thrift. The great fermentation and combinations,
everywhere pervading working men are full of promise—and vexation! They
vex the present, but they will bless the future. This has nothing to do with the
wisdom or the folly of any of the particular measures which the laboring men

may take. All causes which come up from the bottom of society find their way up by the hardest; and mistakes are the rude nurses of ignorant men — rude, but faithful. No class and no nation ever was raised from the bottom by very much help from the top. Thus far men have scarcely discerned, and certainly have not learned, that superiority is an ordination of God, and makes the superior class the nurses and helpers of the inferior. But aristocracy has grown out of superiority, for the most part. As soon as any class has had the power to rise, it has separated itself from the lower class, and called itself cream, and desired to be skimmed off!

And so it has been that class after class, as we go down in society, have been obliged to fight their own battle, and largely to fight it against those who should have been their helpers; and instead of succor from those who were wiser and stronger than themselves, they have had resistance.

Now, it is not strange that when men are fighting their way up from the bottom of society, they are at first ignorant of the best modes; that they make mistakes in the instruments selected, and in the measures devised. It is not presumption against the validity and excellence of any cause that its advocates are making many mistakes. Nothing could be worse than contentment in degradation. And there is nothing, with all its mistakes, that is more auspicious than aspiration and enterprise among laboring men. Therefore when I behold them counseling, and gathering themselves into innumerable forms of association, and learning among themselves brotherhood, and forming habits of common thought, common purposes, and common government, whatever may be the inconvenience of the present, I regard such things as pre-eminently auspicious. They show that the laboring classes are not dead; that they are not inert; that they are a living mass; and that they mean to live to some purpose, and are finding out the way to do it. My heart goes with these my fellow-citizens under such circumstances, even when my head does not.

Very significant, too, is the assimilative power of American institutions, as shown in the condition and the conduct of foreign labor in our midst. For it is not our native-born citizens alone that are laborious, that are enterprising, that are accumulating property, that are good citizens, and obedient to the law. There have been thrown upon our shores vast masses, now almost uncountable, of men born under other skies, other institutions, and other customs, with other ideas. They are poured upon us by millions. Many have feared that they would change the color of the nation; that they would gradually undermine its laws; that, like the flowing of the stream which will chafe even rocks, so at last, by continual attrition, this vast mass of men pouring in upon our institutions would take the temper out of them. But they have not. Our institutions are stronger to-day, with all their population from abroad in them and under them, than they were fifty years ago, or even twenty-five years ago. And in those periods of critical peril when everything seemed put in jeopardy, there was no part of our whole population from the north to the south, or from the east to the west, that was more patriotic than our foreign population. And when, afterward, still other moral perils ensued, and the credit of the nation was at stake, there were no parts of our population, taking the country through, that were honester and truer to the national integrity than our foreign population.

And why should they desire to destroy those institutions for which they voyaged the deep and left their own land? It is the peculiar advantage of popular laws and institutions, that they are just such laws and institutions as common men want, and therefore are just such as common men do not want to destroy. Except in a few cities, and, to be plain, except from one nationality, we have scarcely heard a word of lawlessness from the great throng of our foreign population. The Irish are an ingenuous people. They are very frank and open, and they usually speak out what they think, and frequently act too openly and impulsively; and I must admit that there has been some trouble springing from them. Yet I say, without hesitation, that in fifty years all the trouble will have been a cheap price to have paid for the good qualities which that stock will infuse into the Anglo-Saxon stock. It is *good* stock, though it is very hard to work up. But with this single exception good-naturedly named, where have we found trouble from our foreign population?

With occasional and sporadic exceptions, where have we found better citizenship than among them? Where have we found men that, on the whole, not only were conducting themselves better, but were contributing more directly to the welfare of the state, or of the regions where they had settled down, than our emigrant population? They mingle among us; and in one generation they are as indistinguishable from us as if they and their parents had been born in our midst. They do not clog our courts; they do not mob our streets; they do not make aggression upon law nor upon civil liberty. Their virtues, their wisdom, and their industry we ought to recognize, both with surprise and with gratitude.

Nor do I believe that it will be in the power of China to do what all Scandinavia cannot do. I am just as little afraid of the East, or the West—no, I do not know which way China is—I am as little afraid of the *Oriental* as I am of the European. Coming with another tongue, not easily to be changed, and coming with a very different race-temperament, and with very different culture, it may take longer to digest them; but I think that even a Chinaman, when he has been thoroughly swallowed by American institutions, will, though he lies long by them, be at last digested, and that he will make good blood withal. So that I am not afraid of the importation of Chinamen. And though they do not understand it, others will, when I say, *All hail!* and *Welcome!*

There may be many who object to the Chinese on account of their compulsory carriage hither. They are ashamed to admit that this country is shut against the poor and the laboring classes of any land under heaven; but they find fault with the carriage of them by enforced emigration. "Let them come freely," say they. Oh yes, let them come freely, say I, only let them *come*! As for letting them come freely, here are both hands for that. But the difficulty is not that it is an enforced emigration, but that it is a competitious labor. And on that ground I say, shame, *shame* be to any class of men who have themselves made their fortunes by bringing in cheap labor against our own native labor, and have established themselves with our full welcome, and then turn to repel others who come just as they came, bearing what they bore—willingness to work, and ability to work cheaper than our own laborers!

For the law of God is that men, as they come up, cannot afford to work cheap. Nothing can work cheap except that which *is* cheap. If you have only a hand to sell, with no thought in it, and no skill in it, you can afford to sell that hand cheap; but if that hand has forty years of experience and thought; if that hand represents the whole machinery of your mind and soul, you cannot afford to sell it cheap—and I do not want to have you. And in every community there must be these classes. The lowest and most ignorant, who have never gone to school, nor had the means of culture of any sort, will of course work cheap; and they will work cheap because they bring so little in their work. But as working is instruction, they come up; and every step they come up they give more, and ask more, and get more because they give more. It is the *quid pro quo* that makes the price all the time. It is the great law of equivalents.

And so, while one class of foreign population, taking advantage of the opportunity offered, have been laying the foundations of a moderate competence, and have been going up, the prices of their labor have been rising. And I do not object to that. I want the prices of their labor to rise, because I believe that they give more in the same number of hours than they did when they were unskilled laborers.

But we want another class below them. And when *they* come up, we shall want another class below *them*. "The workman is worthy of his hire"; but it is one of the misfortunes of ignorance that it does not know how to be wise.

The very thing that we need more now than almost anything of the lower interests of our land, is labor. With our vast intermediary territories—that land which for a hundred years will hardly see seed-corn for lack of the hands to open the furrows and plant it—are we in a condition to turn away any man who will come here honestly to labor and to thrive? I say, God bless the Swede; and God bless the Dane; and God bless the German, a hundred times over; and God bless the Frenchman and the Italian, if they come here to be good citizens; and God bless the canny Scotchman, and the sturdy Englishman, and the mercurial Irishman; and God bless a little more the Chinaman,—because he needs a little more!

On the whole, then, there is occasion for courage and for thanks in regard to labor, and in regard to the laborer. Labor is remunerative. The field for it is almost illimitable. Its product is wonderful. The laborers are no longer brute beasts. A change is going on perpetually. There is fermentation, there is circulation, there is emulation; and little by little our laboring classes are coming up in intelligence; in organizing power; in forecast; in refinement; in the amplitude of their domestic conditions; in all the things that go to make men happy here, and that make virtue easy and aspiration natural.

And it is a theme for thanksgiving to-day that, while other nations are receiving the terrible scourge; while upon almost a whole continent labor is suspended, or works only at the forge and the foundry, for purposes of destruction, throughout the length and breadth of this great land labor whistles, and sings, and is happy.

2. Again, the general aspect of wealth in America is such as to give occasion for thanksgiving to-day. The prodigious facilities for developing wealth are only just beginning to be perceived by the mass. The future fortunes of America will be fabulous. I suppose that there are to be fortunes on this continent, compared with which what were called fortunes once will seem like penury. The power of organizing seems to be almost the only limit. The wealth is here. It is easy to be developed. It is easy to be concentrated. It is growing easier every decade of years to be administered. And to be the owner of a million dollars will not make a man eligible to the class of rich men much longer. I look forward into that "golden" future, literally, which is opening before us, and marvel whether the most poetic dreams of growing wealth may not fall short of the reality. By and by there is to be a genius shown—there are yet to be reputations, and very noble reputations—for organizing and amassing wealth, compared with which we have had almost nothing in the past history of nations.

There are some who think that riches are always and only dangerous. Riches are dangerous simply because they are power; and all power is dangerous. Power is dangerous whether it be legislative or moral power. Even variety of influence is dangerous. And wealth is more dangerous than other forms simply because it is a more various power, and has certain facilities for adaptation and use which belongs to almost no other power. But it is impossible to civilize a community without riches. I boldly affirm that no nation ever yet rose from a barbarous state except though the mediation of wealth earned. I affirm that the preaching of the Gospel to the heathen will be invalid and void if it does not make them active workmen, and teach them how to make money. And although the evidences of the conversion of the individual are not that he knows how to make money; yet in a nation no religion is a good religion that does not teach industry, and the thrift which comes from industry. For the law of communities is not analogous to the law of the individual. It is possible, in a great, rich, civilized community, for an individual man to be powerful, and preëminently so, and yet be poor; but no poor man can be of very great validity in a poor community. The community must be rich if he is to have power. It is the contrast, it is the self-denial, it is the moral efficiency without those other and external instrumentalities, that make him so marked, if he labors with voluntary poverty. But no *community* can develop into permanent civilization unless it has power ministered to it very largely through the civilizing influences of wealth. This alone will give the activity required; this alone will give the leisure in which men soften, and meliorate, and grow beautiful.

Now, the dangers of wealth in America are very great. They are even greater than we fear. Organized wealth is one great danger which lies ahead, looming up gigantically. And yet, wealth must be organized. The community will have to find ways in which to protect itself, however. If wealth be organized to do as it pleases, it becomes very dangerous. Nevertheless, organized wealth is yet to be a benefactor of the community to an extent that we have never suspected. It tends now to despotism; but it is because it is in the nascent stages.

Great corporations are dangerous. They do not need to be. Scores of millionaires organized together in concert to accomplish great ends need not be any more dangerous than the State is. There may be an empyrean of wealth; and it may be mischievous; but it does not need to be. At present it is so, and is to be watched against. Wealth tends to control all other power in society. Especially is it so in democratic societies, where we have no kings, no nobles, no fixed estate of honor, no titles, no positions which are permanent, and where wealth and character make the distinction, very largely, between man and man. Under such circumstances wealth tends to absorb into its own hands all the power in society. But it is not necessarily so. It is not necessary that riches should control courts and legislatures, and the franchise itself. It is not necessary that wealth, which owns the market, should also own the civil power, though it is a danger that is to be met and overcome. It tends to feed the lower nature; it tends to change refinement to luxury, and luxury to corruption; but it does not need to do this.

These are valid, imminent, pressing dangers, that never have been exaggerated; and yet they are not dangers which necessarily attend the accumulation and organization of great wealth in any community. It will require the vigilance of statesmen, and of philanthropists, and of good citizens, to guard against the dangers of wealth. But it is not philosophical to look only on the diseases of a community. It is wise to look at its hygienic qualities as well.

Is harm and danger, then, all that wealth is accomplishing in our midst? No. It is the almoner of employment, as it is the almoner of bread. It is the almoner of the family. It is the almoner of unnumbered households. It is the almoner of independence. And are we to forget that capital—that is, wealth in activity—with all its friction, is far safer than invested wealth, lying dead? It is money that is working that keeps bright, and it is money that is working that keeps men bright. Although working money is by various exigencies brought into circumstances where it must be limited, overruled, and curtailed, yet we are not to forget on this account that at the same time it is that which is vivifying industry to the bottom of society, and that is carrying out on its broad hands and arms innumerable blessings to every part of the community. The very circulation of the community would cease, almost, the moment that wealth should cease to exist. It is the blood that carries nutrition into every part of the whole system.

Riches, therefore, may be said to be the poor man's providence, provided it is riches in use, and not invested. When men have retired from business, and their wealth is laid up, there is less danger from it; but there is less benefit from it at the same time. The dangers which we see threatening us are not less than real; but looking comprehensively at the general tendency of wealth in America, it is working in subordination to intelligence and to domestic virtue. There is a vast deal of ignorant using of wealth. A great many men use their property for ostentation; and a great many employ it for useless pride; and a great many use it for selfishness, and even for vice. But how to use money is an art just as much to be learned as how to make it. There are a great many men that know how to make money, who do not know how to use it; and there are a great many men that know how to spend money, who do not know how to make it. Both sides are to be learned. Neither comes by nature. There is an art in it as much as there is in learning to paint, or to carve, or to fabricate at the blacksmith's forge, or at the joiner's bench. And men must not be expected to learn it in a generation. There are hundreds and thousands of men who began with literally nothing, and have ended with two or three hundred thousand dollars which they have to organize and commute into forms of civilization; and is it strange that a great many men do not know how to do it; that they sometimes build and furnish extravagantly and out of taste? My wonder is that there is so much taste and discretion exercised. For if you go through town after town, and village after village, and city after city, you will find that extravagant building and furnishing are the exception—not the rule. The rule is that wealth which has been earned wisely is being expended discreetly. I think that wealth to-day is being used more for building up American homes than for almost all other purposes. I think that the people live in better houses here than they do in any other country, the world over. I am sure they do. Men of the same rank in life, of the same professions, and of the same conditions of wealth, live in better houses, more amply stored, and with more conveniences, here than anywhere else. There is more ingenuity in the construction of houses here—and it requires more ingenuity to keep them constructed!—than in any other land on the globe.

. . .

It is not strange to find a man who works at the forge all day, grim and grizzly, going home at night to pursue historical reading. I know farmers that I should dislike to meet in an argument (unless I was on the same side with them!). And they are not cases here and there, selected. It is characteristic of our working people, and of men that are well to do, that they are growing up to make the town in which they live beautiful and intelligent. Their houses themselves are often models of taste and convenience, and are setting examples which one by one the neighbors follow. And so, in the train of industry comes wealth, and of wealth, taste, and of taste, beneficence; and refinement flashes throughout the land. And when I hear men speaking bitterly against wealth, I notice that almost invariably they are men who have not got it. When I hear them deride moneyed men, moneyed kings, moneyed princes, it seems to me that they have not well considered the facts. They only think of here and there, it may be, a Croesus. But if you follow the more moderate fortunes; if you look into the whole career of money in this land, not the Nile, when it comes down with its annual freshet and distributes the slime which is the riches of Egypt over the circumjacent territory, is so great a blessing to Egypt, as is the great diffusion of wealth in this country to America. And nowhere else does wealth so directly point towards virtue in morality, and spirituality in religion, as in America.

So then, I am not afraid to rejoice. Get rich, if you can. Pay anything for riches. Anything? Yes, pay yourself; pay weariness; pay head-cracking thought; pay anything but this—do not pay your honor nor your affection, nor your simplicity, nor your faith in man, nor your love to God. But whatever you can take out of the body, pay. And when you shall have amassed wealth, it will be God's power, if you are wise to use it, by which you can make your home happier, the community more refined, and the whole land more civilized.

Wealth in America, also, is public-spirited (I thought I had got through; but I find two or three more heads). The classes that are amassing money furnish a large proportion of all the funds by which the active charities of society are carried on. The buildings which decorate our community are from the hands mostly, of wealthy men. Architecture is the adopted child of wealth. The fine arts could scarcely exist but for the interposition of wealth. The universities, and academies, and colleges, and public libraries, and reading rooms, and halls for lectures, are the fruit of liberal wealth in America. Cornell, Vassar, Cooper, Williston, Lawrence, and a hundred others, are significant American names. And there are more coming forward, who yet will not simply be known by their money among those that love them, but whose names will become symbolic of some great public charity, or some great public spirit.

Wealth is searching out the neglected classes; is distributing from our cities vagabond children; is opening schools for the laboring classes, to teach them all mechanic arts. I may safely say that no public need can be wisely presented to the wealth of America, and not be liberally, and at times munificently, taken care of. In other lands, governments give much for public institutions; but in America the great bulk of the means required to build up the institutions of civilization, and to support them, is contributed by the people, and by the business men of the people.

Wealth, then, like its owners, has its devil and its temptations; it has its mistakes and perversions; it has its great dangers to society; but its blessings are a hundred-fold. And, on the whole, the general tendency of wealth is such as to lead me to-day to thank God for the increasing wealth of America. May it ever be sanctified. May it ever learn nobler uses, and aspire higher and higher, until the symbolism of the heavenly state, where the very streets are paved with gold, shall be reproduced in the realities and actualities of our life here on earth.

3. I meant to speak of the cause of education, and the reasons for thanksgiving in that direction; and also of the progress of civilization, and all forms of refinement. I can, however, not even mention them, in detail. I only, in closing, shall speak of the religious condition of the land, as a grand reason for thanksgiving.

4. There are many signs, which, if taken alone, will distress the mind, and so distress many timid souls. Such is the prevalence of scientific scepticism, such is the subversion of old landmarks, and the setting aside of cherished beliefs, and the letting go of old systems, and the coming in of violent actions and reactions of men that have drunk new wine (for truth is intoxicating to men whose heads are not strong), that there is an impression that religion is losing ground; that it is becoming an old story—a superstition. But this scene is enacted every three or four hundred years; and religion comes up every time stronger and stronger. I think religion is like the grass of the meadow, which, when burnt over, lies black and charred, but the ashes of which are a stimulating manure, which afterwards fosters a growth that is stronger than that to which the violence was done. And my faith in religion is not in the church, and not in doctrines, and not in books, and not in ministers, nor in anything external to man, but in that nature which God created, and which makes religion indispensable to man. Until man himself dies, there will be a faith, and that faith will fashion to itself both beliefs and services of devotion.

On the other hand, there was never, probably, so intelligent a faith as there is to-day, in so many men. Never were there so many men who thought so much on the subject of religion, and read so much, and argued so much, and looked so far into the themes of their belief as to-day. Not among the educated classes alone, but among plain people of the country, I think there is more reading, and more thinking, and more real heart-interest in religion than ever before.

Then there is a drawing together, a more kindred feeling, which is taking the place of the rancor and sectarian bitterness which prevailed not a great while ago, in many directions.

And it is very noticeable that the different sects of religion are softening, and that men are coming together in conference who only a few years ago thought it their duty to hate and club one another. This growing spirit of love and fellowship in differing churches is one of the signs of the growth of religion.

Religious ethics, also, are more widely diffused. Though there may not be in the general mind as much belief in doctrinal religion as there once was, there is more belief in the ethics of religion than there was ever before. The standards of belief that are set up by the word of God are more universally accepted and applied to-day than formerly they were. Governments conform to the Christian spirit more than ever they did before. Jurisprudence seeks to measure itself more than ever according to the equity that was in Christ Jesus. The heart is regulating itself more by those great laws of simplicity and truth and righteousness, or justice, if I may so say, than ever before. And even business is seeking, among all its contortions, to cast the devil of dishonesty out of itself. I think business never before acknowledged so high a standard as it does to-day. And while the belief in creeds and formularies may have changed, the belief in ethical standards of religion was never so universally employed as to-day.

And humanity—which is sympathy for man in his sorrow and in his need— when was there ever so much of it? When, in any age of the world since Christ was lifted up on Calvary, has such a scene been presented as to-day is witnessed, when France is humbled? My heart is sore for her. And though I know that the wheat before it is bread must be ground; and though I believe in the loaf, yet, when the wheat is living men, I cannot bear to see the grinding. To-day, one vast nation is treading another vast nation under foot; and all the outlying world around—England, with all her dependencies, Germany itself, America, Italy, and all the other nations—by bazars, by fairs, by collections in churches, and by contributions of public-spirited men, is pouring out a tide of wealth to relieve the sufferers. And if war must be, humanity stands by to bind up the wounds that war makes. When before was there such a looking-on, such a spectatorship? In regard to the inhuman wars of the world, humanity was never so wide-spread. Never was there such sensibility among the nations of the earth as there is to-day. A benevolent or cordial and cooperative kindness in the upbuilding of society never was wiser than to-day. And faith in God—not perhaps according to your definition nor according to mine, but faith in an overruling power; faith in an unerring wisdom; faith in a goodness which is paternal; faith in One who looks upon the whole human race as his family, and not as a despot looks upon his subjects; faith that leads men to see roseate colors in the heaven, and not crushing bolts; faith in God, as the almighty good, was never stronger, and never was growing so fast, nor so deep.

Here, then, is our survey. Our territorial condition is prosperous. Our material prosperity is eminent, and it is tending upward rather than downward. Our labor and our laborers are prospering; and they are working upward. Wealth, with all its tendencies, on the whole, is on the line of development toward moral and not toward physical things. Education is widely prevalent, and is taking in more perfectly every class. Refinement is becoming the indispensable element of all prosperity. Religion itself, though losing many of its antique forms and services, as a spirit and as a controlling influence, was never so strong. I thank God for all the signs of the times. I thank God for the health and for the prosperity of the nation.

And now, I have but one word to say more: as we have been put in the van among nations to develop principles in their practical forms that were only known as seed-corn in other lands, my heart's ambition is, first, for the welfare of this whole land, for the sake of the burden of the population which it carries. God bless America. Not because I was born in it; not because it is my America, and because I receive the reflection of its glory, and a dividend of its power. I am not insensible to these things; yet not on those accounts that are personal to me do I implore God's blessing upon America; but because this continent carries such a burden of humanity that its weal or woe will be like an eternal weal or woe, infinite, endless. May God, for the sake of neighboring peoples, bless this land. And as God is making us wise, and rich, and strong, and expert, and fearless, may He take the lion and the bear out of our nature, and give us the spirit of the dove, that we may stand frowning on our shores against no foreign people; that we may be no band of robbers to filch and to steal from the feeble and the poor. May God give us magnanimity and power and riches, that we may throw the shadow of our example upon the poor, the perishing, and the ready-to-be-destroyed, for their protection. And cursed—cursed of God, and of men cursed—be that man who counsels the red right hand of war except when it is needful to fight for our own existence! We have no war that we want to wage except the war of righteousness in ourselves. It is not for us to bombard and destroy other nations, and to follow the vices of tyrannies. What is the use of the reign of the common people, where is the glory of democracy, if it can but ape, and with greater cruelty, the mischiefs of despotism? Let kings war; let aristocrats war; but the common people of a great republic should own the brotherhood of man. And, instead of raising aloft the red hand, let them throw the nursing arm of protection around about their neighbors, and call all men their brethren, and dwell together in fealty, in unity, in sympathy, and in happiness.

THE RIGHT REVEREND WILLIAM LAWRENCE

The Relation of Wealth to Morals

There is a certain distrust on the part of our people as to the effect of material prosperity on their morality. We shrink with some foreboding at the great increase of riches, and question whether in the long run material prosperity does not tend toward the disintegration of character.

History seems to support us in our distrust. Visions arise of their fall from splendor of Tyre and Sidon, Babylon, Rome, and Venice, and of great nations too. The question is started whether England is not today, in the pride of her wealth and power, sowing the wind from which in time she will reap the whirlwind.

Experience seems to add its support. Is it not from the ranks of the poor that the leaders of the people have always risen? Recall Abraham Lincoln and patriots of every generation.

The Bible has sustained the same note. Were ever stronger words of warning uttered against the deceitfulness of riches than those spoken by the peasant Jesus, who Himself had no place to lay His head? And the Church has through the centuries upheld poverty as one of the surest paths to Heaven; it has been a mark of the saint.

To be sure, in spite of history, experience, and the Bible, men have gone on their way making money and hailing with joy each age of material prosperity. The answer is: "This only proves the case; men are of the world, riches are deceitful, and the Bible is true; the world is given over to Mammon. In the increase of material wealth and the accumulation of riches the man who seeks the higher life has no part."

In the face of this comes the statement of the chief statistician of our census—from one, therefore, who speaks with authority: "The present census, when completed, will unquestionably show that the visible material wealth in this country now has a value of ninety billion dollars. This is an addition since 1890 of twenty-five billion dollars. This is a saving greater than all the

From *The World's Work*, I (January 1901), 286–92.

people of the Western Continent had been able to make from the discovery
of Columbus to the breaking out of the Civil War."

If our reasoning from history, experience, and the Bible is correct, we, a
Christian people, have rubbed a sponge over the pages of the Bible, and are in
for orgies and a downfall to which the fall of Rome is a very tame incident.

May it not be well, however, to revise our inferences from history, experience, and the Bible? History tells us that, while riches have been an item and
an indirect cause of national decay, innumerable other conditions entered in.
Therefore, while wealth has been a source of danger, it has not necessarily led
to demoralization.

That leaders have sprung from the ranks of the poor is true and always will
be true, so long as force of character exists in every class. But there are other
conditions than a lack of wealth at the source of their uprising.

And as to the Bible—while every word that can be quoted against the rich is
as true as any other word, other words and deeds are as true; and the parables of
our Lord on the stewardship of wealth, His association with the wealthy, strike
another and complementary note. Both notes are essential to the harmony of
His life and teachings. His thought was not of the conditions, rich or poor,
but of a higher life, the character rising out of the conditions—fortunately,
for we are released from that subtle hypocrisy which has beset the Christian
through the ages, bemoaning the deceitfulness of riches, and at the same time,
working with all his might to earn a competence, and a fortune if he can.

Man "Born to Be Rich"

Now we are in a position to affirm that neither history, experience, nor the
Bible necessarily sustains the common distrust of the effect of material wealth
on morality. Our path of study is made more clear. Two positive principles
lead us out on our path.

The first is that man, when he is strong, will conquer Nature, open up her
resources, and harness them to his service. This is his play, his exercise, his
divine mission.

"Man," says Emerson, "is born to be rich. He is thoroughly related, and is
tempted out by his appetites and fancies to the conquest of this and that piece
of Nature, until he finds his well-being in the use of the planet, and of more
planets than his own. Wealth requires, besides the crust of bread and the roof,
the freedom of city, the freedom of the earth." "The strong race is strong on
these terms."

Man draws to himself material wealth as surely, as naturally, and as necessarily as the oak draws the elements into itself from the earth.

The other principle is that, in the long run, it is only to the man of morality that wealth comes. We believe in the harmony of God's Universe. We know that it is only by working alone His laws natural and spiritual that we can work with efficiency. Only by working along the lines of right thinking and right living can the secrets and wealth of Nature be revealed. We, like the Psalmist, occasionally see the wicked prosper, but only occasionally.

Put two men in adjoining fields, one man strong and normal, the other weak and listless. One picks up his spade, turns over the earth, and works till sunset. The other turns over a few clods, gets a drink from the spring, takes a nap, and loafs back to his work. In a few years one will be rich for his needs, and the other a pauper dependent on the first, and growling at his prosperity.

Put ten thousand immoral men to live and work in one fertile valley and ten thousand moral men to live and work in the next valley, and the question is soon answered as to who wins the material wealth. Godliness is in league with riches.

Now we return with an easier mind and clearer conscience to the problem of our twenty-five billion dollars in a decade.

My question is: Is the material prosperity of this Nation favorable or unfavorable to the morality of the people?

The first thought is, Who has prospered? Who has got the money?

I take it that the loudest answer would be, "The millionaires, the capitalists, and the incompetent but luxurious rich"; and, as we think of that twenty-five billion, our thoughts run over the yachts, the palaces, and the luxuries that flaunt themselves before the public.

Who the Rich Are

As I was beginning to write this paper an Irishman with his horse and wagon drew up at my back door. Note that I say *his* horse and wagon. Twenty years ago that Irishman, then hardly twenty years old, landed in Boston, illiterate, uncouth, scarcely able to make himself understood in English. There was no symptom of brains, alertness, or ambition. He got a job to tend a few cows. Soon the American atmosphere began to take hold. He discovered that here every man has his chance. With his first earnings he bought a suit of clothes; he gained self-respect. Then he sent money home; then he got a job to drive a horse; he opened an account at the savings bank; then evening school; more money in the bank. He changed to a better job, married a thrifty wife, and today he owns his house, stable, horse, wagon, and bicycle; has a good sum at the bank, supports five children, and has half a dozen men working under him. He is a capitalist, and his yearly earnings represent the income on $30,000. He had no "pull"; he has made his own way by grit, physical strength, and increasing intelligence. He has had material prosperity. His older brother, who paid his passage over, has had material prosperity, and his younger brother, whose passage my friend paid, has had material prosperity.

Now we are beginning to get an idea as to where the savings are. They are in the hands of hundreds of thousands of just such men, and of scores of thousands of men whose incomes ten years ago were two and five thousand, and are now five and ten thousand; and of thousands of others whose incomes have risen from ten to thirty thousand. So that, when you get to the multi-millionaires, you have only a fraction to distribute among them. And of them the fact is that only a small fraction of their income can be spent upon their own pleasure and luxury; the bulk of what they get has to be reinvested, and becomes the means whereby thousands earn their wages. They are simply trustees of a fraction of the national property.

When, then, the question is asked, "Is the material prosperity of this nation favorable or unfavorable to the morality of the people?" I say with all emphasis, "In the long run, and by all means, favorable!"

In other words, to seek for and earn wealth is a sign of a natural, vigorous, and strong character. Wherever strong men are, there they will turn into the activities of life. In the ages of chivalry you will find them on the crusades or seeking the Golden Fleece; in college life you will find them high in rank, in the boat, or on the athletic field; in an industrial age you will find them eager, straining every nerve in the development of the great industries. The race is to the strong. The search for material wealth is therefore as natural and necessary to the man as is the pushing out of its roots for more moisture and food to the oak. This is man's play, his exercise, the expression of his powers, his personality. You can no more suppress it than you can suppress the tide of the ocean. For one man who seeks money for its own sake there are ten who seek it for the satisfaction of the seeking, the power there is in it, and the use they can make of it. There is the exhilaration of feeling one's self grow in one's surroundings; the man reaches out, lays hold of this, that, and the other interest, scheme, and problem. He is building up a fortune? Yes, but his joy is also that he is building up a stronger, abler, and more powerful man. There are two men that have none of this ambition: the gilded, listless youth and the ragged, listless pauper to whom he tosses a dime; they are in the same class.

We are now ready to take up the subject in a little more detail. How is it favorable? The parable of my Irish friend gives the answer.

In the first place, and as I have already suggested, the effort to make his living and add to his comforts and power gives free play to a man's activities and leads to a development of his faculties. In an age and country where the greater openings are in commercial lines, there the stronger men and the mass of them will move. It is not a question of worldliness or of love of money, but of the natural use and legitimate play of men's faculties. An effort to suppress this action is not a religious duty, but a disastrous error, sure to fail.

Self-Respect and Self-Mastery

Besides this natural play of the faculties comes the development of self-respect and ambition. In the uprise from a lower to a higher civilization, these are the basal elements. Watch the cart-loads of Polish or Italian immigrants as they are hauled away from the dock. Study their lifeless expression, their hang-dog look, and their almost cowering posture. Follow them and study them five years later: note the gradual straightening of the body, the kindling of the eye, and the alertness of the whole person as the men, women, and children begin to realize their opportunities, bring in their wages, and move to better quarters. Petty temptations and deep degradations that might have overwhelmed them on their arrival cannot now touch them.

With this comes also the power of self-mastery. The savage eats what he kills and spends what he has. In the movement towards civilization through material wealth, questions come up for decision every hour. Shall I spend? Shall I save? How shall I spend? How can I earn more? Shall I go into partnership with a capital of ten dollars, or shall I wait until I have fifty dollars?

Wage earners are not today, as they were in earlier days, hungering for the bare physical necessities of life. They are hungering now, and it marks an upward movement in civilization, for higher things, education, social life, relaxation, and the development of the higher faculties.

To be sure, a certain fraction wilt under the strain, take to drink, to lust, to laziness. There is always the thin line of stragglers behind every army, but the great body of the American people are marching upwards in prosperity through the mastery of their lower tastes and passions to the development of the higher. From rags to clothes, from filth to cleanliness, from disease to health; from bare walls to pictures; from ignorance to education; from narrow and petty talk to books and music and art; from superstition to a more rational religion; from crudity to refinement; from self-centralization to the conception of a social unity.

Here in this last phrase we strike the next step in development. In this increase of wealth, this rapid communication which goes with it, this shrinking of the earth's surface and unifying of peoples through commerce, men and women are realizing their relations to society.

That there are those who in the deepest poverty sustain the spirit of unselfishness and exhibit a self-sacrifice for others which puts their richer neighbors to the blush we know by experience. At the same time, the fact is that for the mass and in the long run grinding poverty does grind down the character; in the struggle for bare existence and for the very life of one's children there is developed an intense self-centralization and a hardness which is destructive of the social instinct and of the finer graces. When, however, through the increase of wealth man has extended his interests, his vision, and his opportunities, "he is thoroughly related." His lines run out in every direction; he lays his finger upon all the broader interests of life, the school, the church, and the college. He reaches through commerce to the ends of the earth. He discovers one bond which is essential to the social unity in this commercial age—the bond of faith in other men; for in credit, on belief in others, our whole social and commercial fabric is built. And when a man has reached this point, he has indeed reached one of the high plateaus of character: from this rise the higher mountain peaks of Christian graces, but here he is on the standing-ground of the higher civilization.

As I write I can almost feel the silent protest of some critics. Are not these qualities, self-respect, self-mastery, a sense of social unity, and mutual confidence, the commonplaces of life? Is this the only response of material wealth in its relation to morality?

These are to us now the commonplaces of life: they are at the same time the fundamentals of character and of morality. If material prosperity has been one of the great instruments (and I believe it has) in bringing the great body of our people even to approach this plateau of character, it has more than justified itself.

One might, however, mention other and finer qualities that follow in these days the train of prosperity. I instance only one. We will strike up one mountain peak: it is that of joyful and grateful service.

The Privilege of Grateful Service

In other days we have heard much of "the sweet uses of adversity": the note still lingers in sermons and will linger as long as Christianity stands. There is, however, the other note that sounds strong in these days,—the privilege of grateful service.

I have in mind now a man of wealth (you can conjure up many like him) who lives handsomely and entertains; he has everything that purveys to his health and comfort. All these things are tributary to what? To the man's efficiency in his complete devotion to the social, educational, and charitable interests to which he gives his life. He is Christ's as much as was St. Paul, he is consecrated as was St. Francis of Assisi; and in recognition of the bounty with which God has blessed him he does not sell all that he has, but he uses all that he has, and, as he believes, in the wisest way, for the relief of the poor, the upbuilding of social standards, and the upholding of righteousness among the people. The Christian centuries, with all their asceticism and monasticism, with their great and noble saints, have, I believe, never witnessed a sweeter, more gracious, and more complete consecration than that which exists in the lives of hundreds of men and women in the cities and towns of this country, who, out of a sense of grateful service to God for His bounty, are giving themselves with all joy to the welfare of the people. And if ever Christ's words have been obeyed to the letter, they are obeyed today by those who are living out His precepts of the stewardship of wealth.

As we think of the voluntary and glad service given to society, to the State, the Church, to education, art, and charity, of the army of able men and women who, without thought of pay, are serving upon directories of savings banks and national banks, life insurance companies, railroads, mills, trusts and corporations, public commissions, and offices of all sorts, schools and colleges, churches and charities; as we run our thoughts over the free services of the doctors, of the lawyers, for their poorer clients, we are amazed at the magnitude of unpaid service, which is now taken for granted, and at the cheerful and glad spirit in which it is carried through. Material prosperity is helping to make the national character sweeter, more joyous, more unselfish, more Christlike. That is my answer to the question as to the relation of material prosperity to morality.

Again I feel a silent protest. Is not the writer going rather far? We did not believe that our twenty-five billions would lead to orgies; but is he not getting rather close to the millennium? Are there no shadows and dark spaces in the radiance which he seems to think that wealth is shedding around us?

Yes, my friendly critic, there are, and to a mention of a few of them I give the pages that are left.

The Spirit of Commercialism

First and most pervasive, I name the spirit of commercialism. It crops up in many forms and places, hydra-headed.

Is it any wonder? When one realizes that in the last ten years seventy millions of people have earned their living, paid their bills, and have at the same time increased the property of the Nation by twenty-five billions of dollars, we reach a slight conception of the intensity, the industry, the enterprise, and the ability with which those people have thought, worked, and reaped. One wonders that religion, charity, or culture have survived the strain at all. When the eye and ambition of a strong man are set upon a purpose, he sometimes neglects other considerations; he is not over nice about the rights of others; he occasionally overrides the weak, crushes out the helpless, and forgets to stop and pick up those that have fallen by the way.

We know how that was in England: we remember the report of the Commission by Lord Shaftesbury as to the horrible condition of the miners, men, women, and children. That was simply one phase in the development of the great movement of modern industrialism. It was a neglect and forgetfulness under a new pressure, rather than deliberate cruelty. The facts once known, attention called,—and reforms began; and they have been going on in behalf of the working people ever since. Much, very much, has been done.

As conditions change, much remains to do. The better adjustment of rights, wages, and taxes will call for the highest intelligence and strongest character. Again, the small tradesman has driven away the little counter where a widow earned her living, the larger tradesman has wiped out the small tradesman, and the department store is now finishing off some of the large tradesmen. It is hard, but it is a part of the great economic movement. It endangers some of the fundamentals of morality, and destroys for the time some of the finer graces.

Ephemeral success sometimes follows deceit, and that breeds a body of commercial frauds; but they cannot endure. A fortune is won by an unscrupulous adventurer; and a hundred fortunes are lost and characters spoiled in trying to follow suit. An ignorant man happens upon wealth or by some mysterious commercial ability wins wealth, and he then thinks himself omniscient. He, not God, is his own creator. He goes to church, but he is Godless. When a nation of people have been seeking for clothes, houses, and comforts in the upbuilding of civilization, is it any wonder that they do not realize that a man's life consisteth not in the abundance of things that he possesseth? There are deceit, hardness, materialism, and vulgarity in the commercial world; and to me the vulgarest of all is not the diamond-studded operator, but the horde of mothers crushing each other around the bargain counter in the endeavor to get something, and that so small, for nothing. The worse of commercialism is that it does not stop at the office, but enters the home, taints the marriage vow, and poisons social life at its springs.

Beyond these rudimentary forms of commercialism, there is another, even more dangerous, because it threatens the liberties and rights of the people. The eye of the public is on it now. I refer to the relation of concentrated masses of wealth to the public service.

I have no time to more than suggest a few of the conditions that have led up to this. Industrial enterprise has drawn many of the strongest and ablest men from political to commercial interests; society and legislation now do for the people what in other days the landlord did; they are concerned more and more with industrial, commercial, and financial questions, from the national tariff to the size of a house-drain. Just at this time, and because of our great industrial development and prosperity, a horde of ignorant voters waiting to be moulded by any strong leader have come to this shore. The wide distribution of wealth has driven merchants and mechanics, widows and trustees of orphans, doctors and ministers, to invest their savings in great enterprises, corporations, and trusts, which, to succeed, must be directed by a few men. We have therefore this situation: a few men responsible for the safekeeping and development of enormous properties, dependent upon legislation, and a great mass of voters, many of them ignorant, represented by their own kind in city or state government, strongly organized by a leader who is in it for what he can get out of it, and who is ever alert with his legislative cohorts to "strike" the great corporations. The people believe that the officers of great corporations so manage that they can get what they want, call it by assessment, bribery, ransom, or what you will, and they brand those otherwise respectable men as cowards and traitors to public liberty.

The Rich Man and the Burglar

A burglar breaks into your house, awakes you, and "strikes" you for $500 which is in your safe downstairs. You expostulate: he answers that he will burn your house. But your children, you cry, will they be safe? He does not know: he wants the money. But if you give it to him, he will try the same on other people. It is against all public duty for you to yield. Again, the threat that he will burn your house; and you, miserable, conscience-stricken that you are doing a cowardly thing, and one against the safety of the public, crawl down-stairs, open the safe, and hand over the cash. You have saved your house and children, but how about your duty to the public and your neighbors, as well as to yourself?

This is very much the position of the great trustees of capital, the heads of our great corporations, at the hands of the modern bandit. Shall they jeopardize the income of women and children, merchants and mechanics, and perhaps drive them into poverty? Or shall they accept the situation, yield to the threat, and trust to the authorities to seize the robber, or through an aroused public opinion so to vote, act, and legislate as to change the law and stop this modern brigandage? That some of the promoters and managers of great corporations are unscrupulous is undoubtedly true. The jail is none too good for them, if only the law would touch them. Nor have we a word of apology or justification for any man who yields to or encourages blackmail. The difficulty, however, is not a simple one. It concerns more than the directors and the politicians; it relates to the rights and liberties of the people. I do not have so much fear of the rich man in office, as I do of the poor but weak man in office and the rich man outside. Through the interplay of aroused public opinion, better legislation, and intelligent action, the relief will come. A younger generation, with its eye keen upon that danger-point is coming to the front.

In some cities of China the houses have no windows on the street, only bare walls and the little door. The families are isolated, narrow, and selfish: there is no public spirit. When the Chinese boy returns home from his Christian Mission School, touched with the spirit of Christian civilization, his first work in bringing civilization to his home is to take a crowbar, knock a hole in the front wall, and make a window, that he may see out and the people see in. He unifies society and creates a public opinion. What is needed as our next step in civilization is to break a hole and make a window that the public may see into the great corporations and trusts and, what is just as important, that the managers may see out and recognize the sentiment of the public.

Light and action—heroic action! There are men today waiting and wanting to act, to throw off the shackles of the modern bandit; but they dare not alone; their trusts are too great. What is wanted is a group of men, high in position, great in power, who at great cost, if need be, will stand and say, "Thus far, up to the lines of the nicest honor, shalt thou go, and no farther."

The people have their eye upon the public service. An administration may pay political debts by pushing ignorant and unworthy men into the lower offices, but when it comes to filling positions of great responsibility the President could not, and would not if he could, appoint men less worthy than Wood in Cuba, Allen in Porto Rico, and Taft in the Philippines, men of force, intelligence, and character. Collegiate education does not insure character, but it does sift men and insure intelligence; and, as President Pritchett of the Massachusetts Institute of Technology pointed out in his inaugural address, though less than one per cent of our population are college men, yet from this very small fraction a majority of the legislative, executive, and judicial places of the General Government which have to do in any large way with shaping the policy and determining the character of the government, are chosen.

The Danger from Luxury

One other dark shadow, and I am done. The persistent companion of riches,— luxury and an ability to have what you want. That vice and license are rampant in certain quarters is clear; that vulgar wealth flaunts itself in the face of the people is beyond question; and that the people are rather amused at the spectacle must be confessed. The theatre syndicate will turn on to the boards whatever the people want; and the general tone of the plays speaks not well for the taste and morality of the people. The strain of temptation overwhelms a fraction of our youth. But one has no more right to test the result of prosperity by the small class of the lazy and luxurious than he has to test the result of poverty by the lazy tramp.

With all this said, the great mass of the people are self-restrained and simple. Material prosperity has come apace, and on the whole it uplifts. Responsibility sobers men and nations. We have learned how to win wealth: we are learning how to use and spend it. Every year marks a long step in advance in material prosperity, and character must march in step. Without wealth, character is liable to narrow and harden. Without character, wealth will destroy. Wealth is upon us, increasing wealth. The call of today is, then, for the uplift of character,—the support of industry, education, art, and every means of culture; the encouragement of the higher life; and, above all, the deepening of the religious faith of the people; the rekindling of the spirit, that, clothed with her material forces, the great personality of this Nation may fulfill her divine destiny.

I have been clear, I trust, in my opinion that material prosperity is in the long run favorable to morality. Let me be as clear in the statement of that eternal truth, that neither a man's nor a nation's life consists in the abundance of things that he possesseth.

In the investment of wealth in honest enterprise and business, lies our path of character. In the investment of wealth in all that goes toward the uplift of the people in education, art, and religion is another path of character. Above all, and first of all, stands the personal life. The immoral rich man is a traitor to himself, to his material as well as spiritual interests. Material prosperity is upon us; it is marching with us. Character must keep step, ay, character must lead. We want great riches; we want also great men.

FRANCES WILLARD

ॐ

A White Life for Two

I dare affirm that the reciprocal attraction of two natures, out of a thousand million, for each other, is the strongest though one of the most unnoted proofs of a beneficent Creator. It is the fairest, sweetest rose of time, whose petals and whose perfume expand so far that we are all inclosed and sheltered in their tenderness and beauty. For, folded in its heart, we find the germ of every home; of those beatitudes, fatherhood and motherhood; the brotherly and sisterly affection, the passion of the patriot, the calm and steadfast love of the philanthropist. For the faithfulness of two, each to the other, alone makes possible the true Home, the pure Church, the righteous Nation, the great, kind Brotherhood of Man.

Marriage is not, as some surface-thinkers have endeavored to make out, an episode in man's life and an event in woman's; it is no unequal covenant; it is the sum of earthly weal or woe to *him* or *her* who shares its mystic sacrament.

This gentle age, into which we have happily been born, is attuning the Twain whom God hath made for such great destiny to higher harmonies than any other age has known, by a reform in the denaturalizing methods of a civilization largely based on force, by which the boy and girl have hitherto been sedulously trained apart. They are now being set side by side in school, in church, in government, even as God sets male and female everywhere side by side throughout his realm of law, and has declared them one throughout his realm of grace. We are, then, beginning to train those with each other who were formed for each other, and the English-speaking home, with its Christian method of a two-fold headship, based on laws natural and divine, is steadily rooting out all that remains of the mediaeval, continental and harem philosophies concerning this greatest problem of all time. The true relations of that complex being whom God created by uttering the mystic thought that had in it the potency of Paradise: "In *our* own image let *us* make man, and let *them* have dominion over all the earth," will ere long be ascertained

From *The World's Parliament of Religions*, vol. 2, ed. John Henry Barrows (Chicago: The Parliament Publishing Company, 1893), pp. 1230–34.

by means of the new correlation and attuning, each to other, of a more complete humanity upon the Christ-like basis that "*there shall be no more curse.*"
The temperance reform is this correlation's necessary and true forerunner, for
while the race-brain is bewildered it cannot be thought out. The labor reform is another part, for only under cooperation can material conditions be
adjusted to a non-combatant state of society; and every yoke lifted from the
laboring man lifts one still heavier from the woman at his side. The equal suffrage movement is another part, for a government organized and conducted
by one half the human unit, a government of the minority, by the minority,
for the minority, must always bear unequally upon the whole. The social
purity movement could only come after its heralds, the three other reforms I
have mentioned, were well under way, because alcoholized brains would not
tolerate its expression; women who had not learned to work would lack the
individuality and intrepidity required to organize it, and women perpetually
to be disfranchised could not hope to see its final purposes wrought out in
law. But back of all were the father and mother of all reforms—Christianity
and education—to blaze the way for all these later comers.

The Woman's Christian Temperance Union is doing no work more important than that of reconstructing the ideal of womanhood. In an age of force,
woman's greatest grace was to cling; in this age of peace she doesn't cling
much, but is every bit as tender and as sweet as if she did. She has strength
and individuality, a gentle seriousness; there is more of the sisterly, less of the
syren—more of the duchess and less of the doll. Woman is becoming what
God intended her to be, and Christ's Gospel necessitates her being, the companion and counselor, not the incumbrance and toy, of man.

Happily for us, every other genuine reform helps to push forward the white
car of social purity. The personal habits of men and women must reach the
same high level. To-day a woman knows that she must walk the straight line
of a white life or men will look upon her with disdain. A man needs, for his
own best good, to find that, in the eyes of women, just the same is true of
him—and evermore, be it remembered, this earnest effort to bring in the day
of "sweeter manners, purer laws" is as much in man's interest as our own.

Why are the laws so shamelessly unequal now? Why do they bear so heavily
upon the weaker, making the punishment for stealing away a woman's honor
no greater than that for stealing a silk gown? Why is the age of protection or
consent but ten years in twenty states of America, and in one, only seven years?
Our laws and social customs make it too easy for men to do wrong. They
are not sufficiently protected by the strong hand of penalty from themselves,
from the sins that do most easily beset them, and from the mad temptations
that clutch at them on every side. The World's Woman's Christian Temperance Union has taken up this sacred cause of protection for the home, and we
shall never cease our efforts until women have all the help that law can furnish

them throughout the world. We ask for heavier penalties, and that the age of consent be raised to eighteen years; we ask for the total prohibition of the liquor traffic, which is leagued with every crime that is perpetrated against the physically weaker sex, and we ask for the ballot, that law and law-maker may be directly influenced by our instincts of self-protection and home protection.

But, as I have said, we are not working for ourselves alone in this great cause of social purity. As an impartial friend to the whole human race in both its fractions, man and woman, I, for one, am not more in earnest for this great advance because of the good it brings to the gentler, than because of the blessing it prophesies for the stronger sex. I have long believed that when that greatest of all questions, the question of a life companionship, shall be decided on its merits, pure and simple, then will come the first fair chance ever enjoyed by young manhood for the building up of genuine character and conduct.

Multiplied forces in law and gospel are to-day conspiring for the deliverance of our young men from the snares of their present artificial environment and exaggerated estimate of their own value; but the elevation of their sisters to the plane of perfect financial and legal independence, from which the girls can dictate the equitable terms. "You must be as pure and true as you require me to be, ere I give you my hand," is the brightest hope that gleams in the sky of modern civilization for our brothers; and the greater freedom of women to make of marriage an affair of the heart and not of the purse, is the supreme result of Christianity, up to this hour.

With all its faults, and they are many, I believe the present marriage system to be the greatest triumph of Christianity, and that it has created and conserves more happy homes than the world has ever before known. Any law that renders less binding the mutual, life-long loyalty of one man and woman to each other, which is the central idea of every home, is an unmitigated curse to that home and to humanity. Around this union, which alone renders possible a pure society and a permanent state, the law should build its utmost safeguards, and upon this union the Gospel should pronounce its most sacred benedictions. But while I hold these truths to be self-evident, I believe that a constant evolution is going forward in the home as in every other place, and that we may have but dimly dreamed the good in store for those whom God for holiest love hath made.

My theory of marriage in its relation to society would give this postulate: Husband and wife are one, and that one is—husband and wife. I believe that they will never come to the heights of purity, of power and peace, for which they were designed in heaven, until this better law prevails. One undivided half of the world for wife and husband equally; co-education to mate them on the plane of mind; equal property rights to make her God's own free woman, not coerced into marriage for the sake of support, nor a bond-slave after she is married, who asks her master for the price of a paper of pins, and gives him back the change.

I believe in uniform national marriage laws; in divorce for one cause only; in legal separation on account of drunkenness and other abominations; but I would guard (*for the children's sake*) the marriage tie by every guarantee that could make it, at the top of society, the most coveted estate of the largest-natured and most endowed, rather than at the bottom, the necessary refuge of the smallest-natured and most dependent women. Besides all this, in the interest of men, in order that their incentives to the best life might be raised to the highest power, I would make women so independent of marriage that men who, by bad habits and niggardly estate, whether physical, mental or moral, were least adapted to help build a race of human angels, should find the facility with which they now enter its hallowed precincts reduced to the lowest minimum. Until God's laws are better understood and more reverently obeyed, marriage cannot reach its best. The present abnormal style of dress among women, heavily mortgages the future of their homes and more heavily discounts that of their children. Add to this the utter recklessness of immortal consequences that characterizes the mutual conduct of so many married pairs, and only the everlasting tendency toward good that renders certain the existence and supremacy of a goodness that is infinite, can explain so much health and happiness as our reeling old world persists in holding while it rolls onward toward some far-off perfection, bathed in the sunshine of God's Omnipotent Love.

Part Six

American Destiny and World War

The United States hesitated before entering the two world wars. Each time most U.S. citizens initially preferred that their nation hold itself aloof from what they took to be strictly European conflicts. But after U.S. entrance, American defenders of the Allied cause often envisioned war as an instrument for the achievement of a higher destiny.

Long before this country committed its men and arms to the First World War, a number of Americans were agitating for military preparedness and direct support of the Allied forces. Most wanted to avoid involvement in the struggle, however, and chose to believe that their nation should operate on the European scene through the power of moral example rather than by force of arms. Woodrow Wilson won the 1916 presidential election as the man who "kept us out of war," and many citizens hoped with Wilson that German belligerency could be negotiated away. "There is such a thing as a man being too proud to fight," Wilson said. "There is such a thing as a nation being so right that it does not need to convince others by force that it is right."[1]

Early in 1917 the Germans proved to be unmoved by moral suasion and announced the reopening of unrestricted submarine warfare. The subsequent loss of eight U.S. ships and rumors of a German plot to involve the United States in a war with Mexico and Japan led to President Wilson's appearance before a special session of Congress on April 2 to ask for a declaration of war. Wilson's was one of history's least bellicose war speeches. "It is a fearful thing," he said, "to lead this great peaceful people into war, into the most terrible and disastrous of all wars, civilization itself seeming to be in the balance." Now that the nation has been forced into this course of action, however, the fight must be for those principles of freedom which it has ever been the destiny of America to safeguard: "We shall fight for the things which we have always carried nearest our hearts—for democracy, for the right of those who submit to authority to have a voice in their own Governments, for the rights and lib-

---

1. Quoted in John Morton Blum, *Woodrow Wilson and the Politics of Morality* (Boston: Little, Brown and Company, 1956), p. 101.

erties of small nations, for a universal dominion of right by such a concert of free peoples as shall bring peace and safety to all nations, and make the world itself at last free." American engagement in war could be for no paltry purpose of merely defending American interests. It had to be a war to end war, a war to make the whole world safe for democracy.

American public opinion was mobilized for the war effort by the government's Committee on Public Information. Operating under the direction of journalist George Creel, the C.P.I. employed the talents of hundreds of writers and artists to launch one of the most effective propaganda campaigns in modern history. The chief aim of the propaganda was to convince the American people that their nation was at war to preserve freedom and democracy in the world and that the "Huns" were the very creatures of Satan, completely devoid of human compassion and totally committed to wrecking the free world. As a result, the Great War came to be seen as an Armageddon, a battle waged by the saints against unmitigated evil.

American clergymen became leading advocates of the righteousness of the nation's cause. It is inaccurate to conclude, however, as one study has done,[2] that the clergy were dupes of a well-planned British and American government propaganda movement. The clergy did not have to be duped. They drew upon their own religious traditions of Israelite war, holy crusade, and "just war" theory in order both to ground their prowar arguments and to give shape to their militant rhetoric. It is clear, however, that the clergy's and the government's cause were one. The clergy were ardent and effective defenders of Wilson's claim that this expeditionary war was being waged on behalf of free people everywhere, and they were prime contributors to the opinion that a holy American army was moving against an altogether evil force. It followed that pacifism was deemed a cowardly, unscriptural position. Randolph H. McKim, Episcopal rector at Epiphany Church in Washington, D.C., summed up an argument frequently heard during the war: "If any man demands how we can make war in the name of Christ, the Prince of Peace, let him remember those words of His, 'I came not to send peace but a sword.' Yes, if He bids us love truth and righteousness, He also bids us hate falsehood and wrong and injustice and cruelty. And he calls us to fight against these things, not only by argument but by the sword, when occasion arises."[3] Words of damnation for the Germans—especially for their leaders—also came easily to religious spokesmen. Revivalist Billy Sunday expressed the imprecation in his

---

2. Ray H. Abrams, *Preachers Present Arms* (Philadelphia: Round Table Press, 1933), pp. xvi, 79ff. et passim.

3. Randolph H. McKim, *For God and Country, or the Christian Pulpit in War-Time* (New York: E. P. Dutton & Co., 1918), pp. 117–18.

own inimitable fashion: "If you turn hell upside down, you will find 'Made in Germany' stamped on the bottom."

Numerous sermons sought to represent American action abroad as a serious attempt to realize the national destiny. A sermon on patriotism by the Right Reverend Monsignor C. F. Thomas of St. Patrick's Church in Washington, D.C., was typical of religious interpretations of American destiny during World War I. Delivered on Washington's Birthday at a memorial mass held for the Knights of Columbus, the sermon was one of a host preached by Catholics, Protestants, and Jews on that sacred day in 1918. All over the District of Columbia patriotic and religious groups gathered for ceremonies eulogizing George Washington and celebrating the principles of freedom for which he stood and for which, it was believed, Americans were currently called to fight. In his Washington tabernacle, Billy Sunday closed a prayer with the remark that it did not really matter if Germany had fifty guns to our one since "the Lord on our side is worth more guns than old Krupp can make." At the Eighth Street Temple, Rabbi Abram Simon said, "We are fighting the old fight of freedom and advancement against intolerance and oppression. This is the fight that George Washington made."[4] Mgr. Thomas's sermon paralleled the hardships of the children of Israel in the wilderness with the hardships of the New Israel at war, pleaded for unity and sacrifice in support of America's mission of preserving the liberties of democratic government, and closed with the claim that the American war task was "just and righteous." Thomas's address pulled together under the rubric of American destiny the war claims declared by Wilson and the government information office. Typical of speeches during American sacred ceremonies, it interpreted war deaths as sacrifices made for the fulfillment of American destiny under God.

A majority of Americans either heartily supported or did not seriously object to the Treaty of Versailles and the plan for a League of Nations that Wilson brought back from the Paris Peace Conference in 1919. Nevertheless, in a final vote in March 1920, the Senate rejected the treaty and the league. Reasons for this rejection were numerous and complex, but a fierce Republican opposition to Wilson, plus the president's own blunder in refusing to marshall bipartisan support for the treaty, were crucial factors. Even though the league and the treaty were defeated, Wilson's speeches on their behalf clearly articulated what the American people had come to believe the U.S. mission in the war had been.

In his speech for ratification before the Senate in 1919, Wilson admitted that he had to make undesirable compromises in the treaty, but he lodged the hope for future world peace, and for rectification of the errors of the treaty, in the League of Nations. Wilson painted a highly idealized picture of American

4. *Washington Post*, Feb. 23, 1918, p. 2.

destiny during the war and after. Certainly Clemenceau of France and Lloyd George of Great Britain did not accept the picture Wilson had drawn.

As Wilson continued his defense of the treaty and the league in a speaking tour across the nation, his words revealed less and less concern for the facts. He talked of the "high-minded, statesmanlike cooperation" at the peace conference and described the United States as interested in nothing less than the "liberation and salvation of the world."[5] But all the rhetoric was of no avail, for America was beginning to turn from the kind of international leadership to which Wilson believed God had called the nation. The 1920s were years of isolationism and narrowing nationalism. Although the United States made some token gestures toward international peace efforts, the nation kept its distance from the real work of the league and raised around itself an economic wall of protective tariffs. The ugliest forms of chauvinism appeared in open hostility toward foreigners and in suspicion of foreign ideas. During the years between the two world wars numerous Americans, particularly clergymen, repented of their wholehearted endorsement of war, and religious pacifism became a widely accepted and respectable position. The coming of the Great Depression, the renewal of political and military upheavals in Europe, and a general war-weariness in the country led to a feeling of disillusionment and to a sense of frustration over the failure of the Great War to yield a secure peace and an enduring prosperity. It was unclear whether the nation had any world destiny it could call its own.

When the totalitarian powers revealed their strategies of aggression in the 1930s, most Americans indicated their disapproval—but with a sense of thankfulness that they were isolated from such disturbing affairs. The attacks on Poland, France, and Britain finally convinced the United States that it might eventually stand alone before the Axis forces. Step by step the nation abandoned its neutrality. With the attack on Pearl Harbor and the subsequent declaration of war, the nation was forced once again to interpret its reason-for-being within the greater context of world affairs. Propaganda released through films, radio, public speeches, newspapers, and popular magazines again mobilized public support for the national war effort, but on the whole there was less war hysteria this time and much less talk of a holy crusade aimed at the final destruction of evil. Because of the disappointments of World War I, Americans were more inclined to view their participation in World War II as a tragic necessity rather than as a glorious blow for righteousness. It was surely seen as a fight for freedom and justice against aggressive tyranny, but not as a struggle for the redemption of the world.

The Federal Council of Churches may serve as a barometer of the change

---

5. For Wilson's speeches during his tour see *War and Peace*, II, ed. R. S. Baker and W. E. Dodd (New York: Harper & Row, Publishers, 1927), 1–416.

in attitude that occurred between the two wars. At the conclusion of the First World War the Council had wired Wilson that the proposed League of Nations was the "political expression of the Kingdom of God on earth." In a statement released in 1942, the council spoke much more cautiously, characterizing the current war as a struggle between nations representing the institution of free peoples against those representing tyranny and adding, "We do not hold that a victory of the United Nations would in itself guarantee the achievement of any Christian goals." Allied victory would simply create much more favorable circumstances for the Christian religion. "A victory of the United Nations would at least afford in many lands a degree of freedom in Christian service of which so far as the human eye can see an Axis victory would rob us."[6] There was evidence of yet another change. Although during the Second World War there was a noticeable decline in religious pacifism, most religious groups came to acknowledge the integrity of that position and supported the right of conscientious objection.

Though American leaders were reluctant to depict America's role in the war as a holy crusade for the redemption of the world, they did not hesitate to appeal to the nation's deep-seated sense of election in their description of war aims. Franklin D. Roosevelt, whose official statements and radio addresses were second only to those of Winston Churchill in their capacity to arouse and sustain the spirit of a people, frequently defined America's role in the war in terms of the national destiny. The president's annual message to Congress on January 6, 1942, suggested a far-reaching national mission at stake in the war. America had joined the free world in the noble task of preserving the divine heritage of human dignity against a cynical contempt for the human race. Roosevelt did see the war as a clear conflict between good and evil, but missing from his address was both the narrow jingoism and the naive utopianism so evident during the First War.

Almost as soon as World War II started, interpretation of American destiny began to center on the problem of how to establish a just and durable peace once an Allied victory had been attained. Thoughtful citizens turned their attention to the possibility of a United Nations organization which would provide a workable alternative to the settlement of disputes by war. The interlocking nature of American destiny, Allied war aims, and national responsibility for world peace was delineated by the Christian ethicist Reinhold Niebuhr in 1943. Written at the time of the formation of the British-American Alliance (which was to be a step toward the United Nations), Niebuhr's brief but trenchant essay, "Anglo-Saxon Destiny and Responsibility," differentiated between a self-righteous and a responsible sense of Anglo-American destiny. Niebuhr claimed that a proper religious understanding of a high national call-

6. *Christian Century*, Dec. 23, 1942, p. 1602.

ing could stimulate the pursuit of justice and peace without giving rein to proud messianism and destructive vindictiveness. The essay was one of the clearest expressions of Niebuhr's political realism, and it possessed a religious insight reminiscent of Lincoln's during the Civil War.

The nuclear obliteration of Hiroshima and Nagasaki toward the war's end was a terrifying warning that civilization could not survive another total war. It was also awesome proof that the American isolationism of the twenties and thirties had been a deceptive means of achieving national security. The destiny of America was inextricably bound up with the destiny of the globe. Interpretations of America's mission in the world would continue to vary, however. The cold war with Russia, the "limited wars" in Korea and Vietnam, the various revolutions throughout the world all would raise troubling questions about the nature and extent of America's international responsibility. Serious problems at home also would pose startling questions. Did a New American Israel any longer exist? Could America really claim a unified destiny under God?

SUGGESTED READING

Abrams, Ray H. "The Churches and the Clergy in World War II," *Annals of the American Academy of Political and Social Science*, Mar. 1948, pp. 110–19.

Handy, Robert T. *Undermined Establishment: Church-State Relations in America, 1880–1920*. Princeton, N.J.: Princeton University Press, 1991.

Johnson, F. Ernest. "The Impact of the War on Religion in America," *American Journal of Sociology*, Nov. 1942, pp. 353–60.

May, Henry F. *The End of American Innocence*. New York: Alfred A. Knopf, 1959.

Mulder, John M. *Woodrow Wilson: The Years of Preparation*. Princeton, N.J.: Princeton University Press, 1978.

Piper, John F., Jr. *The American Churches in World War I*. Athens: Ohio University Press, 1985.

THE RIGHT REVEREND MONSIGNOR C. F. THOMAS

Patriotism

I am glad to welcome you here on this occasion and to aid in your celebration of this memorial day. I applaud your sentiments of love and devotion which prompt you to come. Your presence at this solemn Mass renews your consecration to the highest duties of religion and patriotism.

This day is sacred to the memory of Washington, who still remains first in the hearts of his countrymen for his successful work and heroic sacrifices in winning liberty and freedom for this favored land of ours. The day is honored, and through its memories we are kept in mind of the solemn pledges we inherit to perpetuate what he achieved to remotest generations. And your noble and admirable fraternity links itself closely to all the deepest sentiments or loftiest ideals which the honoring of the day calls forth.

The greatness of Washington shines out in his generosity of soul and largeness of nature, as well as in his genuine courage and heroism. And through them was he able to render grateful recognition for the valuable patriotic services of our forefathers in the faith in bringing about the glorious results of the American Revolution.

Far be it from us to glory in fidelity to truth and duty; but we have inviolably kept the trust handed down to us, and every generation of us has striven to uphold, increase, defend and enrich the precious inheritance of our republican institutions in liberty and freedom.

Your organization has from the beginning served to emphasize the loyalty of energy towards the upbuilding of tendencies and movements, and of succor and support in times of emergency, peril and disaster. And recent sacrifices and services have demonstrated the ever living element or instinct of patriotism which pervades and permeates our being. In every corner of this vast land, loud has been the response to our country's call in the hour of need

Delivered at a Memorial Mass on Washington's Birthday at St. Patrick's Church, Washington, D.C. From *War Addresses from Catholic Pulpit and Platform* (New York: Joseph F. Wagner, otn.d.), pp. 171–77.

and danger, and in this response the clearest tones have been sounded by the enthusiastic and brave and unselfish action of the Knights of Columbus.

This action to which I refer, which has been and is an important factor in the means of defense adopted against the impending peril, and which has received just and merited approbation from private sources and Government authorities, has certainly been duplicated by others; but it evidences a spirit which the whole American people must thoroughly learn. The preservation of what our fathers won on many hard fought fields of battle and completely achieved by patient struggle and heroic sacrifices, the fulfillment of the mission attained by this nation, or entrusted to it, by their victory, is to be the result of many trials and much hardship.

It was a glorious day when this young nation was declared and acknowledged to be free and independent; and when it set out—emerging from the bondage of Old World ideas—to confer on the human race new and incalculable truths founded in the aspirations of democracy. Our fathers indulged in the vision of untold splendor, of radiant happiness, of true civilization, when the States would eventually unfold their capacities to the fullest extent and the people would develop the inherent powers of the human soul and reach almost Utopian heights of success and peace. True to the inspiration imparted, and faithful to the traditions handed down, the citizens of these United States have furnished valuable contributions to the best and purest civilization, and have built up a vast nation, sold in its integrity, strong in its assurance of permanence, vast in its power of achievement, rich in its resources and opulent in its advantages. The providence of God seems to have smiled on their efforts and to have exceedingly blessed their endeavors; and the nation has advanced far beyond the most sanguine expectations of its founders and fathers.

But I think that many have been prone to rest satisfied with the progress so far obtained, or to imagine that the greatness of the nation is so strong that one need not fear the peril of defeat or the disaster of subjugation. They fold themselves, as it were, within their self-conceit or self-consciousness and consider it impossible for all this glory and grandeur, all this power and prestige to be swept away and our institutions demolished. They resent the forcing of the present emergency upon us as unwarranted, as if there was no danger to us from the cataclysm which has befallen the Old World systems and life. It has been hard to convince a great number of our fellow citizens that our participation in this was justifiable, or that our rights and liberties were in any way jeopardized. Failure to rouse universal enthusiasm and support, bitter and severe denunciation of governmental action, attempts to thwart measures of defence or means of aggressive prosecution of the war prove, not perhaps any lack of genuine loyalty or appreciation of the need of adequate defence, but the conviction of an overweening confidence in the unassailable character of our institutions or of a want of the conviction of the necessity of intense personal sacrifice and patriotism.

The ancient Hebrews were led out of Egypt to found a theocratic state in the land of Canaan. Under the guidance of Moses they were fitting themselves for a high divine purpose. They were drilling to influence the world by their preservation of the knowledge of the true God and by the principles and ideas flowing therefrom. But they did not realize what the cost of progress towards that end involved and were not disposed to endure without protest the hardships, pain, hunger and fatigue, the disgust and perils of their pilgrimage towards the shining goal of their liberty from oppression. Disappointment and anger oft moved them to bitter sarcasm and deep murmuring of their lot. Rebuke and resentment against their great captain were frequent because of their sorry plights and severe sufferings into which he led them. They were willing enough to rejoice in liberty acquired and in glory attained, but were too selfish to undergo the trials through which alone they could lay hold onto the end of their desires and efforts. They were glad enough to be free from Pharaoh's yoke and Egyptian bondage, but even the sufferings of that time and ignominy of that lot seemed to them in the desert more tolerable than the hardships they were encountering on their journey to the promised land.

There is in this country a spirit—evident and pronounced—which acknowledges the high state of our progress and the glories of our material prosperity, the incomparable advantages here secured and enjoyed, the magnificent opportunity for the realization of the highest results of democracy; but does not appreciate the need or necessity of sustaining the trials and hardships through which all these can and must be enlarged, strengthened and perpetuated. This nation is grand in the prospects of happiness it holds out to the human race, almost divine in the prophecy it enfolds of future perfection of human life. The principles upon which it is erected are truer than it was ever the fortune of man to invent for the benefit of mankind; the elements which tell for progress and development, for enlightenment and happiness, are here more rooted than ever before in the history of the world. But it must not be forgotten that the enjoyment of our possession, and the perpetuation of our inheritance, even the solidification of our work or achievements, require and demand on our part, now more than ever, the greatest amount of personal sacrifice, endurance, devotion and heroism. We cannot expect to retain or to preserve the present results of past endeavors, the fruit of our fathers' labors and struggles, unless we are determined at all costs, and all hazards, to maintain the precious ideas, spirit, principles, as well as the material accomplishments which they bequeathed to us.

Even after the Hebrews had rooted themselves in Canaan, and attained a kingdom and established themselves as a dominant people in all that Eastern country they found themselves attacked on every side — exposed to incursions from hostile tribes, to subjugation by neighboring nations — always in conflict with dangers and perils, with envy and fear from abroad, and always obliged to intense exertion for defence and for the perpetuation of the glorious principality they had set up. No nation, no people, have endured who were not endowed with the deepest instincts of patriotism and the most unselfish spirit of devotion and sacrifice. And the ancient Hebrews had ingrained into them by severe measures and bitter experience the lesson of suffering and hardship.

We have now to learn the same lesson. We have never been compelled to learn it before. We must learn it now in face of the danger that confronts us. We are to continue. The Providence of God destines this nation to last — indefinitely, we confidently trust. The whole world looks to us to carry to the future what will save the future from disorder, confusion, anarchy, perhaps dissolution. But our trust cannot be fulfilled without the loyalty, love, personal aid and patriotic efforts of each and every individual.

If I read aright the meaning of this day, if I understand at all the significance of this celebration, if I have caught in the least degree the spirit of the immortal Washington, I must emphasize the need of the individual devotion of every citizen of this Republic to the fortunes, whatever they be, in store for it. We may be eager to avail ourselves of the advantages and privileges; we must be just as eager to sustain the trials and help to ward off the dangers that may assail it. We are all anxious that our liberties be preserved; we must be just as anxious to stand behind it when these liberties are threatened with extinction. We rejoice to share it the happiness here conferred upon us; we must be just as willing to sorrow with the country in its misfortunes. And when the country sorrows, when its freedom hangs in the balance, when all that for which it stands finds itself a target for outside attack, when its fondest hopes and yearnings are in danger of being frustrated, there is demanded a universal unity among the citizens — unity of thought, unity of effort, unity of aim, unity in personal devotion and self-sacrifice.

There has been a union here among us ever since Washington's day. There never was seen in the whole history of the world such a union as has existed among us. But that union has now to be perfected by privations we endure and the cost we pay in this time of our nation's greatest crisis.

Perhaps the emergency has arisen precisely to teach us this union. We have not yet really become a nation. There have been so many divergent interests among us. There have been conflicting aims. There are so many different nationalities here beginning to establish themselves. We have been a melting pot; and we have not yet solved the problem — never before presented except to the Roman Empire of old — of amalgamating into one nation members of various other nationalities. We thought we had succeeded. Professor Charles

William Elliott, twenty-two years ago, wrote that we had succeeded. But the present crisis proves we had not. And, in my judgment, there was need of some such circumstances as the present to give us the opportunity to appreciate the benefits of the life and the blessings we enjoy, and by appreciation be urged and impelled and driven to give of the best and dearest in us for the defence of the home of our hearts and the land of our abode. Man never values what comes to him easily. A nation never realizes its happiness or its greatness until the hour when its life is threatened. The soul never takes in the grandeur of life eternal until the mortal life is about to end. So here in these United States I believe there would not and will not be a united people unless we now realize that our future as a people, and as individuals, depends on the personal hardships we suffer, and the sacrifices we offer, in order that safety be secured and our institutions be solidified.

I speak for an undivided nation. I speak for unity of action in the crisis we face. I speak for union of endeavor to secure victory for the American arms now engaged in deadly conflict for the perpetuation of American liberties. I speak for universal sacrifice, and for the devotion of each and every individual, in the giving up of even earthly life itself for the cause which is now the cause of America.

In the work of preparation for the task the Government has undertaken, in the gathering together the elements which shall form a powerful army and equip it to the highest point of efficiency much has been accomplished. Criticism has been severe. Lethargy was deep. Objections were numerous. Supineness was inconceivably great. Opposition was intense in some quarters. But the success has been phenomenal. And there is no reason to fear but that our forces will be equal to the burden placed upon them and fit to give a good and glorious account of themselves on the day of battle and in the hour of actual conflict.

Yet much more remains to be done, and the whole nation must be aroused. Every section must be brought to take part. No man, no woman must be found who does not do all possible, suffer all that is required, positively and willingly sustain hardship and trial, privation and pain, in the endeavor to contribute effectively to the success of the cause everyone has or should have at heart. And the spectacle must be offered to the entire world, of all the millions of which we are made up, rising en masse, struggling, rushing, rolling onward with force irresistible, with ardor the greatest and love the deepest, with unselfishness, to crush the foe of American life and liberty and to render safe for all time to come what we and the nation stand for.

A more inspiring example is not possible, a greater incentive could not be found towards unifying the people of this country in the spirit of heroic patriotism, of enthusiastic support and self-sacrificing devotion to the fortunes and needs of the country than has been given by the Knights of Columbus in what they have done and are still doing to help prepare the nation for its gigantic struggle and to aid in securing victory for its arms.

The day is a fitting occasion to renew and spread over the land a feeling of pride in American institutions, American greatness, American prosperity and a sense of assurance that it will all survive; to reawaken in all the liveliest sentiments of patriotism which cannot exist without the determination to suffer what may be necessary to insure safety and victory, and to send out through the entire land the call for union in hardship and trial as indispensable for union in joy and peace.

And this gathering affords opportunity of imparting to the whole country the stimulus, and of communicating to it the spirit which has animated the Knights of Columbus in every part of the Republic and prompted them to undertake, and enabled them to accomplish the great work which is so prolific of magnificent results in the perfecting of the morale and strength of our forces.

The cause is just and righteous. Our sanctuary has been violated. Our rights despised. Our honor assailed in its tenderest spot. Our champions have gone forth to avenge the insult, to regain the confidence of the world in our greatness and power. And it is incumbent upon every man and woman who glories in the name of American, and who lives under the protection of American freedom and enjoys the benefits of American liberty, to strengthen the arms of those champions by the offering of his energies and possessions. Unless they succeed—and they cannot succeed without the undivided action of our millions—this will no longer be the home of the brave and the land of the free.

WOODROW WILSON

Presenting the Treaty for Ratification

Address to the Senate of the United States.
July 19, 1919.

Gentlemen of the Senate:

The treaty of peace with Germany was signed at Versailles on the twenty-eighth of June. I avail myself of the earliest opportunity to lay the treaty before you for ratification and to inform you with regard to the work of the Conference by which that treaty was formulated.

The treaty constitutes nothing less than a world settlement. It would not be possible for me either to summarize or to construe its manifold provisions in an address which must of necessity be something less than a treatise. My services and all the information I possess will be at your disposal and at the disposal of your Committee on Foreign Relations at any time, either informally or in session, as you may prefer; and I hope that you will not hesitate to make use of them. I shall at this time, prior to your own study of the document, attempt only a general characterization of its scope and purpose.

In one sense, no doubt, there is no need that I should report to you what was attempted and done at Paris. You have been daily cognizant of what was going on there,—of the problems with which the Peace Conference had to deal and of the difficulty of laying down straight lines of settlement anywhere on a field on which the old lines of international relationship, and the new alike, followed so intricate a pattern and were for the most part cut so deep by historical circumstances which dominated action even where it would have been best to ignore or reverse them. The cross currents of politics and of interest must have been evident to you. It would be presuming in me to attempt to explain the questions which arose or the many diverse elements that entered into them. I shall attempt something less ambitious than that and more clearly suggested by my duty to report to the Congress the part it seemed necessary

From *War and Peace*, I, *The Public Papers of Woodrow Wilson*, ed. S. T. Baker and W. E. Dodd (New York: Harper & Row, Publishers, 1927), 537–52.

for my colleagues and me to play as the representatives of the Government of the United States.

That part was dictated by the role America had played in the war and by the expectations that had been created in the minds of the peoples with whom we had associated ourselves in that great struggle.

The United States entered the war upon a different footing from every other nation except our associates on this side of the sea. We entered it, not because our material interests were directly threatened or because any special treaty obligations to which we were parties had been violated, but only because we saw the supremacy, and even the validity, of right everywhere put in jeopardy and free government likely to be everywhere imperiled by the intolerable aggression of a power which respected neither right nor obligation and whose every system of government flouted the rights of the citizen as against the autocratic authority of his governors. And in the settlements of the peace we have sought no special reparation for ourselves, but only the restoration of right and the assurance of liberty everywhere that the effects of the settlement were to be felt. We entered the war as the disinterested champions of right and we interested ourselves in the terms of the peace in no other capacity.

The hopes of the nations allied against the Central Powers were at a very low ebb when our soldiers began to pour across the sea. There was everywhere amongst them, except in their stoutest spirits, a somber foreboding of disaster. The war ended in November, eight months ago, but you have only to recall what was feared in midsummer last, four short months before the armistice, to realize what it was that our timely aid accomplished alike for their morale and their physical safety. That first, never-to-be-forgotten action at Chateau-Thierry had already taken place. Our redoubtable soldiers and marines had already closed the gap the enemy had succeeded in opening for their advance upon Paris,—had already turned the tide of battle back towards the frontiers of France and begun the rout that was to save Europe and the world. Thereafter the Germans were to be always forced back, back, were never to thrust successfully forward again. And yet there was no confident hope. Anxious men and women, leading spirits of France, attended the celebration of the Fourth of July last year in Paris out of generous courtesy,—with no heart for festivity, little zest for hope. But they came away with something new at their hearts; they have themselves told us so. The mere sight of our men,—of their vigor, of the confidence that showed itself in every movement of their stalwart figures and every turn of their swinging march, in their steady comprehending eyes and easy discipline, in the indomitable air that added spirit to everything they did,—made everyone who saw them that memorable day realize that something had happened that was much more than a mere incident in the fighting, something very different from the mere arrival of fresh troops. A great moral force had flung itself into the struggle. The fine physical force of those spirited men spoke of something more than bodily vigor. They carried the great ideals of a free people at their hearts and with that vision were unconquerable. Their very presence brought reassurance; their fighting made victory certain.

They were recognized as crusaders, and as their thousands swelled to millions their strength was seen to mean salvation. And they were fit men to carry such a hope and make good the assurance it forecast. Finer men never went into battle; and their officers were worthy of them. This is not the occasion upon which to utter a eulogy of the armies America sent to France, but perhaps, since I am speaking of their mission, I may speak also of the pride I shared with every American who saw or dealt with them there. They were the sort of men America would wish to be represented by, the sort of men every American would wish to claim as fellow countrymen and comrades in a great cause. They were terrible in battle, and gentle and helpful out of it, remembering the mothers and the sisters, the wives and the little children at home. They were free men under arms, not forgetting their ideals of duty in the midst of tasks of violence. I am proud to have had the privilege of being associated with them and of calling myself their leader.

But I speak now of what they meant to the men by whose sides they fought and to the people with whom they mingled with such utter simplicity, as friends who asked only to be of service. They were for all the visible embodiment of America. What they did made America and all that she stood for a living reality in the thoughts not only of the people of France but also of tens of millions of men and women throughout all the toiling nations of a world standing everywhere in peril of its freedom and the loss of everything it held dear, in deadly fear that its bonds were never to be loosed, its hopes forever to be mocked and disappointed.

And the compulsion of what they stood for was upon us who represented America at the peace table. It was our duty to see to it that every decision we took part in contributed, so far as we were able to influence it, to quiet the fears and realize the hopes of the peoples who had been living in that shadow, the nations that had come by our assistance to their freedom. It was our duty to do everything that it was within our power to do to make the triumph of freedom and of right a lasting triumph in the assurance of which men might everywhere live without fear.

Old entanglements of every kind stood in the way,—promises which Governments had made to one another in the days when might and right were confused and the power of the victor was without restraint. Engagements which contemplated any dispositions of territory, any extensions of sovereignty that might seem to be to the interest of those who had the power to insist upon them, had been entered into without thought of what the peoples concerned might wish or profit by; and these could not always be honorably brushed aside. It was not easy to graft the new order of ideas on the old, and some of the fruits of the grafting may, I fear, for a time be bitter. But, with very few exceptions, the men who sat with us at the peace table desired as sincerely as we did to get away from the bad influences, the illegitimate purposes, the demoralizing ambitions, the international counsels and expedients out of which the sinister designs of Germany had sprung as a natural growth.

It had been our privilege to formulate the principles which were accepted as the basis of the peace, but they had been accepted, not because we had come in to hasten and assure the victory and insisted upon them, but because they were readily acceded to as the principles to which honorable and enlightened minds everywhere had been bred. They spoke the conscience of the world as well as the conscience of America, and I am happy to pay my tribute of respect and gratitude to the able, forward-looking men with whom it was my privilege to cooperate for their unfailing spirit of cooperation, their constant effort to accommodate the interests they represented to the principles we were all agreed upon. The difficulties, which were many, lay in the circumstances, not often in the men. Almost without exception the men who led had caught the truce and full vision of the problem of peace as an indivisible whole, a problem, not of mere adjustments of interest, but of justice and right action.

The atmosphere in which the Conference worked seemed created, not by the ambitions of strong governments, but by the hopes and aspirations of small nations and of peoples hitherto under bondage to the power that victory had shattered and destroyed. Two great empires had been forced into political bankruptcy, and we were the receivers. Our task was not only to make peace with the Central Empires and remedy the wrongs their armies had done. The Central Empires had lived in open violation of many of the very rights for which the war had been fought, dominating alien peoples over whom they had no natural right to rule, enforcing, not obedience, but veritable bondage, exploiting those who were weak for the benefit of those who were masters and overlords only by force of arms. There could be no peace until the whole order of Central Europe was set right.

That meant that new nations were to be created,—Poland, Czecho-Slovakia, Hungary itself. No part of ancient Poland had ever in any true sense become a part of Germany, or of Austria, or of Russia. Bohemia was alien in every thought and hope to the monarchy of which she had so long been an artificial part; and the uneasy partnership between Austria and Hungary had been one rather of interest than of kinship or sympathy. The Slavs whom Austria had chosen to force into her empire on the south were kept to their obedience by nothing but fear. Their hearts were with their kinsmen in the Balkans. These were all arrangements of power, not arrangements of natural union or association. It was the imperative task of those who would make peace and make it intelligently to establish a new order which would rest upon the free choice of peoples rather than upon the arbitrary authority of Hapsburgs or Hohenzollerns.

More than that, great populations bound by sympathy and actual kin to Rumania were also linked against their will to the conglomerate Austro-Hungarian monarchy or to other alien sovereignties, and it was part of the task of peace to make a new Rumania as well as a new slavic state clustering about Serbia.

And no natural frontiers could be found to these new fields of adjustment and redemption. It was necessary to look constantly forward to other related tasks. The German colonies were to be disposed of. They had not been governed; they had been exploited merely, without thought of the interest or even the ordinary human rights of their inhabitants.

The Turkish Empire, moreover, had fallen apart, as the Austro-Hungarian had. It had never had any real unity. It had been held together only by pitiless, inhuman force. Its peoples cried aloud for release, for succor from unspeakable distress, for all that the new day of hope seemed at last to bring within its dawn. Peoples hitherto in utter darkness were to be led out into the same light and given at last a helping hand. Undeveloped peoples and peoples ready for recognition but not yet ready to assume the full responsibilities of statehood were to be given adequate guarantees of friendly protection, guidance and assistance.

And out of the execution of these great enterprises of liberty sprang opportunities to attempt what statesmen had never found the way before to do; an opportunity to throw safeguards about the rights of racial, national and religious minorities by solemn international covenant; an opportunity to limit and regulate military establishments where they were most likely to be mischievous; an opportunity to effect a complete and systematic internationalization of waterways and railways which were necessary to the free economic life of more than one nation and to clear many of the normal channels of commerce of unfair obstructions of law or of privilege; and the very welcome opportunity to secure for labor the concerted protection of definite international pledges of principle and practice.

These were not tasks which the Conference looked about it to find and went out of its way to perform. They were inseparable from the settlements of peace. They were thrust upon it by circumstances which could not be overlooked. The war had created them. In all quarters of the world old-established relationships had been disturbed or broken and affairs were at loose ends, needing to be mended or united again, but could not be made what they were before. They had to be set right by applying some uniform principle of justice or enlightened expediency. And they could not be adjusted by merely prescribing in a treaty what should be done. New states were to be set up which could not hope to live through their first period of weakness without assured support by the great nations that had consented to their creation and won for them their independence. Ill-governed colonies could not be put in the hands of governments which were to act as trustees for their people and not as their masters if there was to be no common authority among the nations to which they were to be responsible in the execution of their trust. Future international conventions with regard to the control of waterways, with regard to illicit traffic of many kinds, in arms or in deadly drugs, or with regard to the adjustment of many varying international administrative arrangements could not be assured if the treaty were to provide no permanent common international agency, if its execution in such matters was to be left to the slow and uncertain processes of cooperation by ordinary methods of negotiation. If the Peace Conference itself was to be the end of cooperative authority and common counsel among the governments to which the world was looking to enforce justice and give pledges of an enduring settlement, regions like the Saar basin could not be put under a temporary administrative regime which did not involve a transfer of political sovereignty and which contemplated a final determination of its political connections by popular vote to be taken at a distant date; no free city like Danzig could be created which was, under elaborate international guarantees, to accept exceptional obligations with regard to the use of its port and exceptional relations with a State of which it was not to form a part; properly safe-guarded plebiscites could not be provided for where populations were at some future date to make choice what sovereignty they would live under; no certain and uniform method of arbitration could be secured for the settlement of anticipated difficulties of final decision with regard to many matters dealt with in the treaty itself; the long-continued supervision of the task of reparation which Germany was to undertake to complete within the next generation might entirely break down; the reconsideration and revision of administrative arrangements and restrictions which the treaty prescribed but which it was recognized might not prove of lasting advantage or entirely fair if too long enforced would be impracticable. The promises governments were making to one another about the way in which labor was to be dealt with, by law not only but in fact as well, would remain a mere humane thesis if there was to be no common tribunal of opinion and judgment to which liberal statesmen could resort for the influences which alone might secure their redemption. A league of free nations had become a practical necessity. Examine the treaty of peace and you will find that everywhere throughout its manifold provisions its framers have felt obliged to turn to the League of Nations as an indispensable instrumentality for the maintenance of the new order it has been their purpose to set up in the world, — the world of civilized men.

That there should be a League of Nations to steady the counsels and maintain the peaceful understandings of the world, to make, not treaties alone, but the accepted principles of international law as well, the actual rule of conduct among the governments of the world, had been one of the agreements accepted from the first as the basis of peace with the Central Powers. The statesmen of all the belligerent countries were agreed that such a league must be created to sustain the settlements that were to be effected. But at first I think there was a feeling among some of them that, while it must be attempted, the formation of such a league was perhaps a counsel of perfection which practical men, long experienced in the world of affairs, must agree to very cautiously and with many misgivings. It was only as the difficult work of arranging an all but universal adjustment of the world's affairs advanced from day to day from one stage of conference to another that it became evident to them that what they were seeking would be little more than something written upon paper, to be interpreted and applied by such methods as the chances of politics might make available if they did not provide a means of common counsel which all were obliged to accept, a common authority whose decisions would be recognized as decisions which all must respect.

And so the most practical, the most skeptical among them turned more and more to the League as the authority through which international action was to be secured, the authority without which, as they had come to see it, it would be difficult to give assured effect either to this treaty or to any other international understanding upon which they were to depend for the maintenance of peace. The fact that the covenant of the League was the first substantive part of the treaty to be worked out and agreed upon, while all else was in solution, helped to make the formulation of the rest easier. The Conference was, after all, not to be ephemeral. The concert of nations was to continue, under a definite Covenant which had been agreed upon and which all were convinced was workable. They could go forward with confidence to make arrangements intended to be permanent. The most practical of the conferees were at last the most ready to refer to the League of Nations the superintendence of all interests which did not admit of immediate determination, of all administrative problems which were to require a continuing oversight. What had seemed a counsel of perfection had come to seem a plain counsel of necessity. The League of Nations was the practical statesman's hope of success in many of the most difficult things he was attempting.

And it had validated itself in the thought of every member of the Conference as something much bigger, much greater every way, than a mere instrument for carrying out the provisions of a particular treaty. It was universally recognized that all the peoples of the world demanded of the Conference that it should create such a continuing concert of free nations as would make wars of aggression and spoliation such as this that has just ended forever impossible. A cry had gone out from every home in every stricken land from which sons and brothers and fathers had gone forth to the great sacrifice that such a sacrifice should never again be exacted. It was manifest why it had been exacted. It had been exacted because one nation desired dominion and other nations had known no means of defense except armaments and alliances. War had lain at the heart of every arrangement of the Europe,—of every arrangement of the world,—that preceded the war. Restive peoples had been told that fleets and armies, which they toiled to sustain, meant peace; and they now knew that they had been lied to: that fleets and armies had been maintained to promote national ambitions and meant war. They knew that no old policy meant anything else but force, force,—always force. And every enlightened judgment demanded that, at whatever cost of independent action, every government that took thought for its people or for justice or for ordered freedom should lend itself to a new purpose and utterly destroy the old order of international politics. Statesmen might see difficulties, but the people could see none and could brook no denial. A war in which they had been bled white to bear the terror that lay concealed in every Balance of Power must not end in a mere victory of arms and a new balance. The monster that had resorted to arms must be put in chains that could not be broken. The united power of free nations must put a stop to aggression, and the world must be given peace. If there was not the will or the intelligence to accomplish that now, there must be another and a final war and the world must be swept clean of every power that could renew the terror. The League of Nations was not merely an instrument to adjust and remedy old wrongs under a new treaty of peace; it was the only hope for mankind. Again and again had the demon of war been cast out of the house of the peoples and the house swept clean by a treaty of peace; only to prepare a time when he would enter in again with spirits worse than himself. The house must now be given a tenant who could hold it against all such. Convenient, indeed indispensable, as statesmen found the newly planned League of Nations to be for the execution of present plans of peace and reparation, they saw it in a new aspect before their work was finished. They saw it as the main object of the peace, as the only thing that could complete it or make it worth while. They saw it as the hope of the world, and that hope they did not dare to disappoint. Shall we or any other free people hesitate to accept this great duty? Dare we reject it and break the heart of the world?

And so the result of the Conference of Peace, so far as Germany is concerned, stands complete. The difficulties encountered were very many. Sometimes they seemed insuperable. It was impossible to accommodate the interests of so great a body of nations,—interests which directly or indirectly affected almost every nation in the world,—without many minor compromises. The treaty, as a result, is not exactly what we would have written. It is probably not what any one of the national delegations would have written. But results were worked out which on the whole bear test. I think that it will be found that the compromises which were accepted as inevitable nowhere cut to the heart of any principle. The work of the Conference squares, as a whole, with the principles agreed upon as the basis of the peace as well as with the practical possibilities of the international situations which had to be faced and dealt with as facts.

I shall presently have occasion to lay before you a special treaty with France, whose object is the temporary protection of France from unprovoked aggression by the power with whom this treaty of peace has been negotiated. Its terms link it with this treaty. I take the liberty, however, of reserving it for special explication on another occasion.

The role which America was to play in the Conference seemed determined, as I have said, before my colleagues and I got to Paris,—determined by the universal expectations of the nations whose representatives, drawn from all quarters of the globe, we were to deal with. It was universally recognized that America had entered the war to promote no private or peculiar interest of her own but only as the champion of rights which she was glad to share with free men and lovers of justice everywhere. We had formulated the principles upon which the armistice had been agreed to and the parleys of peace undertaken,—and no one doubted that our desire was to see the treaty of peace formulated along the actual lines of those principles,—and desired nothing else. We were welcomed as disinterested friends. We were resorted to as arbiters in many a difficult matter. It was recognized that our material aid would be indispensable in the days to come, when industry and credit would have to be brought back to their normal operation again and communities beaten to the ground assisted to their feet once more, and it was taken for granted, I am proud to say, that we would play the helpful friend in these things as in all others without prejudice or favor. We were generously accepted as the unaffected champions of what was right. It was a very responsible role to play; but I am happy to report that the fine group of Americans who helped with their expert advice in each part of the varied settlements sought in every transaction to justify the high confidence reposed in them.

And that confidence, it seems to me, is the measure of our opportunity and of our duty in the days to come, in which the new hope of the peoples of the world is to be fulfilled or disappointed. The fact that America is the friend of the nations, whether they be rivals or associates, is no new fact; it is only the discovery of it by the rest of the world that is new.

America may be said to have just reached her majority as a world power. It was almost exactly twenty-one years ago that the results of the war with Spain put us unexpectedly in possession of rich islands on the other side of the world and brought us into association with other governments in the control of the West Indies. It was regarded as a sinister and ominous thing by the statesmen of more than one European chancellery that we should have extended our power beyond the confines of our continental dominions. They were accustomed to think of new neighbors as a new menace, of rivals as watchful

enemies. There were persons amongst us at home who looked with deep disapproval and avowed anxiety on such extensions of our national authority over
distant islands and over peoples whom they feared we might exploit, not serve
and assist. But we have not exploited them. We have been their friends and
have sought to serve them. And our dominion has been a menace to no other
nation. We redeemed our honor to the utmost in our dealings with Cuba. She
is weak but absolutely free; and it is her trust in us that makes her free. Weak
peoples everywhere stand ready to give us any authority among them that will
assure them a like friendly oversight and direction. They now that there is no
ground for fear in receiving us as their mentors and guides. Our isolation was
ended twenty years ago; and now fear of us is ended also, our counsel and association sought after and desired. There can be no question of our ceasing to be a
world power. The only question is whether we can refuse the moral leadership
that is offered us, whether we shall accept or reject the confidence of the world.

The war and the Conference of Peace now sitting in Paris seem to me to
have answered that question. Our participation in the war established our position among the nations and nothing but our own mistaken action can alter it.
It was not an accident or a matter of sudden choice that we are no longer isolated and devoted to a policy which has only our own interest and advantage
for its object. It was our duty to go in, if we were indeed the champions of
liberty and of right. We answered to the call of duty in a way so spirited, so
utterly without thought of what we spent of blood or treasure, so effective, so
worthy of the admiration of true men everywhere, so wrought out of the stuff
of all that was heroic, that the whole world saw at last, in the flesh, in noble
action, a great ideal asserted and vindicated, by a Nation they had deemed material and now found to be compact of the spiritual forces that must free men
of every nation from every unworthy bondage. It is thus that a new role and
a new responsibility have come to this great Nation that we honor and which
we would all wish to lift to yet higher levels of service and achievement.

The stage is set, the destiny disclosed. It has come about by no plan of our
conceiving, but by the hand of God, who led us into this way. We cannot turn
back. We can only go forward, with lifted eyes and freshened spirit, to follow
the vision. It was of this that we dreamed at our birth. America shall in truth
show the way. The light streams upon the path ahead, and nowhere else.

FRANKLIN D. ROOSEVELT

❧

Annual Message to Congress

January 6, 1942

Mr. Vice President, Mr. Speaker,
Members of the Senate and of the
House of Representatives:

In fulfilling my duty to report upon the state of the Union, I am proud to say to you that the spirit of the American people was never higher than it is today—the Union was never more closely knit together—this country was never more deeply determined to face the solemn tasks before it.

The response of the American people has been instantaneous. It will be sustained until our security is assured.

Exactly one year ago today I said to this Congress: "When the dictators are ready to make war upon us, they will not wait for an act of war on our part. . . . They—not we—will choose the time and the place and the method of their attack."

We know now their choice of the time: a peaceful Sunday morning—December 7, 1941.

We know their choice of the place: an American outpost in the Pacific.

We know their choice of the method: the method of Hitler himself.

Japan's scheme of conquest goes back half a century. It was not merely a policy of seeking living room: it was a plan which included the subjugation of all the peoples in the Far East and in the islands of the Pacific, and the domination of that ocean by Japanese military and naval control of the western coasts of North, Central, and South America.

The development of this ambitious conspiracy was marked by the war against China in 1894; the subsequent occupation of Korea; the war against Russia in 1904; the illegal fortification of the mandated Pacific islands following 1920; the seizure of Manchuria in 1931; and the invasion of China in 1937.

From *The War Messages of Franklin D. Roosevelt*, December 8, 1941, to April 13, 1945 (Washington, D.C., 1945), pp. 26–30.

A similar policy of criminal conquest was adopted by Italy. The Fascists first revealed their imperial designs in Libya and Tripoli. In 1935 they seized Abyssinia. Their goal was the domination of all North Africa, Egypt, parts of France, and the entire Mediterranean world.

But the dreams of empire of the Japanese and Fascist leaders were modest in comparison with the gargantuan aspirations of Hitler and his Nazis. Even before they came to power in 1933, their plans for conquest had been drawn. Those plans provided for ultimate domination, not of any one section of the world, but of the whole earth and all the oceans on it.

With Hitler's formation of the Berlin-Rome-Tokyo alliance, all these plans of conquest became a single plan. Under this, in addition to her own schemes of conquest, Japan's role was to cut off our supply of weapons of war to Britain, Russia, and China—weapons which increasingly were speeding the day of Hitler's doom. The act of Japan at Pearl Harbor was intended to stun us—to terrify us to such an extent that we would divert our industrial and military strength to the Pacific area, or even to our own continental defense.

The plan failed in its purpose. We have not been stunned. We have not been terrified or confused. This reassembling of the Seventy-seventh Congress is proof of that; for the mood of quiet, grim resolution which here prevails bodes ill for those who conspired and collaborated to murder world peace.

That mood is stronger than any mere desire for revenge. It expresses the will of the American people to make very certain that the world will never suffer again.

Admittedly, we have been faced with hard choices. It was bitter, for example, not to be able to relieve the heroic and historic defenders of Wake Island. It was bitter for us not to be able to land a million men and a thousand ships in the Philippine Islands.

But this adds only to our determination to see to it that the Stars and Stripes will fly again over Wake and Guam; and that the brave people of the Philippines will be rid of Japanese imperialism; and will live in freedom, security, and independence.

Powerful and offensive actions must and will be taken in proper time. The consolidation of the United Nations total war effort against our common enemies is being achieved.

That is the purpose of conferences which have been held during the past two weeks in Washington, in Moscow, and in Chungking. That is the primary objective of the declaration of solidarity signed in Washington on January 1, 1942, by twenty-six nations united against the Axis powers.

Difficult choices may have to be made in the months to come. We will not shrink from such decisions. We and those united with us will make those decisions with courage and determination.

Plans have been laid here and in the other capitals for coordinated and cooperative action by all the United Nations—military action and economic action. Already we have established unified command of land, sea, and air forces in the Southwestern Pacific theater of war. There will be a continuation of conferences and consultations among military staffs, so that the plans and operations of each will fit into a general strategy designed to crush the enemy. We shall not fight isolated wars—each nation going its own way. These twenty-six nations are united—not in spirit and determination alone, but in the broad conduct of the war in all its phases.

For the first time since the Japanese and the Fascists and the Nazis started along their blood-stained course of conquest they now face the fact that superior forces are assembling against them. Gone forever are the days when the aggressors could attack and destroy their victims one by one without unity of resistance. We of the United Nations will so disperse our forces that we can strike at the common enemy wherever the greatest damage can be done.

The militarists in Berlin and Tokyo started this war. But the massed, angered forces of common humanity will finish it.

Destruction of the material and spiritual centers of civilization—this has been and still is the purpose of Hitler and his Italian and Japanese chessmen. They would wreck the power of the British Commonwealth and Russia and China and the Netherlands—and then combine all their forces to achieve their ultimate goal, the conquest of the United States.

They know that victory for us means victory for freedom.

They know that victory for us means victory for the institution of democracy—the ideal of the family, the simple principles of common decency and humanity.

They know that victory for us means victory for religion.

And they could not tolerate that. The world is too small to provide adequate "living room" for both Hitler and God. In proof of that Nazis have now announced their plan for enforcing their new German, pagan religion throughout the world—the plan by which the Holy Bible and the Cross of Mercy would be displaced by "Mein Kampf" and the swastika and the naked sword.

Our own objectives are clear: the objective of smashing the militarism imposed by war lords upon their enslaved peoples—the objective of liberating the subjugated nations—the objective of establishing and securing freedom of speech, freedom of religion, freedom from want, and freedom from fear everywhere in the world.

We shall not stop short of these objectives—nor shall we be satisfied merely to gain them and then call it a day. I know that I speak for the American people—and I have good reason to believe I speak also for all the other peoples who fight with us—when I say that this time we are determined not only to win the war, but also to maintain the security of the peace which will follow.

But modern methods of warfare make it a task not only of shooting and fighting but an even more urgent one of working and producing.

Victory requires the actual weapons of war and the means of transporting them to a dozen points of combat.

It will not be sufficient for us and the other United Nations to produce a slightly superior supply of munitions to that of Germany, Japan, Italy, and the stolen industries in the countries which they have overrun.

The superiority of the United Nations in munitions and ships must be over-whelming—so overwhelming that the Axis nations can never hope to catch up with it. In order to attain this overwhelming superiority the United States must build planes and tanks and guns and ships to the utmost limit of our national capacity. We have the ability and capacity to produce arms not only for our own forces but also for the armies, navies, and air forces fighting on our side.

And our overwhelming superiority of armament must be adequate to put weapons of war at the proper time into the hands of those men in the con-quered nations who stand ready to seize the first opportunity to revolt against their German and Japanese oppressors and against the traitors in their own ranks, known by the already infamous name of "Quislings." As we get guns to the patriots in those lands, they too will fire shots heard "round the world."

This production of ours in the United States must be raised far above its present levels, even though it will mean the dislocation of the lives and occu-pations of millions of our own people. We must raise our sights all along the production line. Let no man say it cannot be done. It must be done and we have undertaken to do it.

I have just sent a letter of directive to the appropriate departments and agencies of our government, ordering that immediate steps be taken:

1. To increase our production rate of airplanes so rapidly that in this year, 1942, we shall produce 60,000 planes, 10,000 more than the goal set a year and a half ago. This includes 45,000 combat planes—bombers, dive bombers, pursuit planes. The rate of increase will be continued, so that next year, 1943, we shall produce 125,000 airplanes, including 100,000 combat planes.

2. To increase our production rate of tanks so rapidly that in this year, 1942, we shall produce 45,000 tanks; and to continue that increase so that next year, 1943, we shall produce 75,000 tanks.

3. To increase our production rate of antiaircraft guns so rapidly that in this year, 1942, we shall produce 20,000 of them; and to continue that increase so that next year, 1943, we shall produce 35,000 antiaircraft guns.

4. To increase our production rate of merchant ships so rapidly that in this year, 1942, we shall build 8,000,000 dead-weight tons as compared

with a 1941 production of 1,100,000. We shall continue that increase so that next year, 1943, we shall build 10,000,000 tons.

These figures and similar figures for a multitude of other implements of war will give the Japanese and Nazis a little idea of just what they accomplished in the attack on Pearl Harbor.

Our task is hard—our task is unprecedented—and the time is short. We must strain every existing armament-producing facility to the utmost. We must convert every available plant and tool to war production. That goes all the way from the greatest plants to the smallest—from the huge automobile industry to the village machine shop.

Production for war is based on men and women—the human hands and brains which collectively we call Labor. Our workers stand ready to work long hours; to turn out more in a day's work; to keep the wheels turning and the fires burning twenty-four hours a day and seven days a week. They realize well that on the speed and efficiency of their work depend the lives of their sons and their brothers on the fighting fronts.

Production for war is based on metals and raw materials—steel, copper, rubber, aluminum, zinc, tin. Greater and greater quantities of them will have to be diverted to war purposes. Civilian use of them will have to be cut further and still further, and, in many cases, completely eliminated.

War costs money. So far, we have hardly even begun to pay for it. We have devoted only 15 percent of our national income to national defense. As will appear in my Budget Message tomorrow, our war program for the coming fiscal year will cost 56 billion dollars or, in other words, more than one half of the estimated annual national income. This means cutting luxuries and other non-essentials. In a word, it means an "all-out" war by individual effort and family effort in a united country.

Only this all-out scale of production will hasten the ultimate all-out victory. Speed will count. Lost ground can always be regained—lost time never. Speed will save lives; speed will save this nation which is in peril; speed will save our freedom and civilization—and slowness has never been an American characteristic.

As the United States goes into its full stride, we must always be on guard against misconceptions which will arise naturally or which will be planted among us by our enemies.

We must guard against complacency. We must not underrate the enemy. He is powerful and cunning—and cruel and ruthless. He will stop at nothing which gives him a chance to kill and to destroy. . . .

We must, on the other hand, guard against defeatism. . . .

We must guard against divisions among ourselves and among all the other United Nations. We must be particularly vigilant against racial discrimination in any of its ugly forms. Hitler will try again to breed mistrust and suspicion between one individual and another, one group and another, one race and another, one government and another. . . .

We cannot wage this war in a defensive spirit. As our power and our resources are fully mobilized, we shall carry the attack against the enemy—we shall hit him and hit him again wherever and whenever we can reach him.

We must keep him far from our shores, for we intend to bring this battle to him on his own home grounds.

American armed forces must be used at any place in all the world where it seems advisable to engage the forces of the enemy. In some cases these operations will be defensive, in order to protect key positions. In other cases, these operations will be offensive, in order to strike at the common enemy, with a view to his complete encirclement and eventual total defeat.

. . .

If any of our enemies, from Europe or from Asia, attempt long-range raids by "suicide" squadrons of bombing planes, they will do so only in the hope of terrorizing our people and disrupting our morale. Our people are not afraid of that. We know that we may have to pay a heavy price for freedom. We will pay this price with a will. Whatever the price, it is a thousand times worth it. No matter what our enemies in their desperation may attempt to do to us, we will say as the people of London have said, "We can take it." And what's more, we can give it back—and we will give it back—with compound interest.

When our enemies challenged our country to stand up and fight, they challenged each and every one of us. And each and every one of us has accepted the challenge—for himself and for the nation.

There were only some four hundred United States marines who in the heroic and historic defense of Wake Island inflicted such great losses on the enemy. Some of those men were killed in action; and others are now prisoners of war. When the survivors of that great fight are liberated and restored to their homes, they will learn that a hundred and thirty million of their fellow citizens have been inspired to render their own full share of service and sacrifice.

Our men on the fighting fronts have already proved that Americans today are just as rugged and just as tough as any of the heroes whose exploits we celebrate on the Fourth of July.

Many people ask, "When will this war end?" There is only one answer to that. It will end just as soon as we make it end, by our combined efforts, our combined strength, our combined determination to fight through and work through until the end—the end of militarism in Germany and Italy and Japan. Most certainly we shall not settle for less.

That is the spirit in which discussions have been conducted during the visit of the British Prime Minister to Washington. Mr. Churchill and I under-stand each other, our motives and our purposes. Together, during the past two weeks, we have faced squarely the major military and economic problems of this greatest world war.

All in our nation have been cheered by Mr. Churchill's visit. We have been deeply stirred by his great message to us. We wish him a safe return to his home. He is welcome in our midst, now and in days to come.

We are fighting on the same side with the British people, who fought alone for long, terrible months, and withstood the enemy with fortitude and tenacity and skill.

We are fighting on the same side with the Russian people who have seen the Nazi hordes swarm up to the very gates of Moscow, and who with almost superhuman will and courage have forced the invaders back into retreat.

We are fighting on the same side as the brave people of China who for four and a half long years have withstood bombs and starvation and have whipped the invaders time and again in spite of superior Japanese equipment and arms.

We are fighting on the same side as the indomitable Dutch.

We are fighting on the same side as all the other governments in exile, whom Hitler and all his armies and all his Gestapo have not been able to con-quer.

But we of the United Nations are not making all this sacrifice of human effort and human lives to return to the kind of world we had after the last world war.

We are fighting today for security, for progress, and for peace, not only for ourselves, but for all men, not only for one generation, but for all generations. We are fighting to cleanse the world of ancient evils, ancient ills.

Our enemies are guided by brutal cynicism, by unholy contempt for the human race. We are inspired by a faith which goes back through all the years to the first chapter of the Book of Genesis: "God created man in His own image."

We on our side are striving to be true to that divine heritage. We are fight-ing, as our fathers have fought, to uphold the doctrine that all men are equal in the sight of God. Those on the other side are striving to destroy this deep belief and to create a world in their own image—a world of tyranny and cruelty and serfdom.

This is the conflict that day and night now pervades our lives. No com-promise can end that conflict. There never has been—there never can be—successful compromise between good and evil. Only total victory can reward the champions of tolerance and decency, and freedom, and faith.

REINHOLD NIEBUHR

⳾ⅇ

Anglo-Saxon Destiny and Responsibility

It is becoming increasingly apparent that, whether any other conditions of a stable peace will be fulfilled or not, an Anglo-American alliance, which must be the cornerstone of any durable world order, is in the process of formation. Mr. Churchill's unequivocal words at Harvard, Governor Dewey's statement in favor of lasting co-operation with Britain, and the Republican postwar statement in which isolationism is renounced, all point to at least one step forward in our foreign policy.

This partnership between the English-speaking peoples can of course become a new menace to international justice and peace if it stands alone. The world cannot be organized by an Anglo-Saxon hegemony. Such a leadership could be ten times more just than the Nazis were and yet not be just enough to avoid arousing the resentment of Europe and Asia, in fact, of the entire world. Whatever Britain and America do together must be immediately related to a wider co-operation with the other two great powers, Russia and China, and must finally be made a part of a total constitutional or quasi-constitutional system of the world order in which all the nations, large and small, will have their due responsibilities and rights.

Nevertheless the further steps that must be taken to insure a stable peace all depend upon this first step of Anglo-American solidarity; for if Britain and America cannot agree together, all other necessary agreements become improbable.

The position of the Anglo-Saxon peoples at the crucial and strategic point in the building of a world community is a fact of such tremendous significance that it can only be adequately comprehended in religious terms. It is a position of destiny and carries with it tremendous responsibilities. Without a religious sense of the meaning of destiny, such a position as Britain and America now hold is inevitably corrupted by pride and the lust of power. We may in fact be certain that this corruption will not be absent from our political life. But if the churches in Britain and America are able to speak to the several nations

From *Christianity and Crisis*, October 4, 1943. Reprinted by permission of Reinhold Niebuhr.

as the prophets spoke to Israel, it may be possible to mitigate the pride sufficiently to allow these two nations to serve the world community creatively.

The Prophetic Idea of Destiny

The prophet Amos was certain of two things. One was that Israel had been particularly chosen of God; and the other was that this special mission gave the nation not a special security but a special peril. "You only have I chosen," he declared in God's name, "therefore will I visit you with your iniquities." It would serve no good purpose to try to compare the special destiny of the Anglo-Saxon peoples with that of Israel in olden times. Certainly no one would be so rash today as to claim the kind of destiny for our nations that the prophet's word "only" implies. Nevertheless only those who have no sense of the profundities of history would deny that various nations and classes, various social groups and races are at various times placed in such a position that a special measure of the divine mission in history falls upon them. In that sense God has chosen us in this fateful period of world history.

The world requires a wider degree of community. It must escape international anarchy or perish. If the world community is to be genuine, it cannot, of course, be superimposed by Anglo-Saxon or any other power. All peoples and nations must find their rightful place in the fellowship. Nevertheless, neither the world community nor any other form of human society ever moves as logically or abstractly as some of the "planners" and blueprinters imagine. Some nation or group always has a higher degree of power and responsibility in the formation of community than others.

It so happens that the combined power of the British Empire and the United States is at present greater than any other power. It is also true that the political ideals that are woven into the texture of their history are less incompatible with international justice than any other previous power of history.

The Components of Destiny

Yet as soon as one has said this, one is forced to make qualifications. All historical destiny is compounded of virtue and grace. If the position that any nation or group of nations holds is attributed to the virtue of those nations alone, one has the beginning of that pharisaism which destroys virtue, whether in individual or in national life. The fact is that no nation or individual is ever good enough to deserve the position of leadership that some nations and individuals achieve. If the history that leads to a special mission is carefully analyzed, it always becomes apparent that factors other than the virtues of the leader are partly responsible for the position the individual or collective leader holds. Those who do not believe in God's providence in history will call these factors "accidents" or "fortune." The religious man perceives them as gifts of grace. The grace that determines the lives of men and nations is manifest in all special circumstances, favors, and fortunes of geography and climate, of history and fate that lead to eminence despite the weakness and sinfulness of the beneficiary of such eminence.

These elements in history are either purely accidental or they stand under divine providence. If they are purely accidental, then history itself has no meaning; for in that case it would be the fruit of caprice. That is why secularists usually obscure these factors of history; for it is not possible for man to live in a completely capricious world. But if they are obscured, the sense of destiny becomes purely a vehicle of pride. Those who achieve a special position in history claim a right to it either by virtue of their power or by virtue of their goodness. The Nazi sense of destiny is completely amoral because it regards power as the sole source of eminence. This amoral sense of destiny has been developed more explicitly by the Nazis than by any other modern nation; but no powerful nation is completely free of the pretension that its power is the sole source of its right to rule. Ideas of "manifest destiny" in our own history have this same source.

The Rule of the Virtuous

The idea that we have a right to rule because of our superior virtue is of a higher order than the amoral idea that we have a right to rule because of our power. It recognizes the moral element in history. It is nevertheless a dangerous idea because it obscures the immoral elements in all historical success. If Germany has been the particular bearer of the idea of destiny through power, the Anglo-Saxon world has been constantly tempted to express its sense of destiny pharisaically and to claim eminence by the right of its virtue. It is this element in Anglo-Saxon politics that has subjected it to the charge of "cant" from Continental nations. We have not heard the end of this charge from either Germany or France, from either the Continent or Russia, because there is an element of truth in the charge.

There is no cure for the pride of a virtuous nation but pure religion. The pride of a powerful nation may be humbled by the impotence that defeat brings. The pride of a virtuous nation cannot be humbled by moral and political criticisms because in comparative terms it may actually be virtuous. The democratic traditions of the Anglo-Saxon world are actually the potential basis of a just world order. But the historical achievements of this world are full of violations and contradictions of these principles. "In God's sight" they are not just; and they know it if they place themselves under the divine scrutiny, that is, if they regard their own history prayerfully rather than comparatively and measure themselves by what is demanded of them rather than by comparing their success with the failure of others.

Thus a contrite recognition of our own sins destroys the illusion of eminence through virtue and lays the foundation for the apprehension of "grace" in our national life. We know that we have the position that we hold in the world today partly by reason of factors and forces in the complex pattern of history that we did not create and from which we do not deserve to benefit. If we apprehend this religiously, the sense of destiny ceases to be a vehicle of pride and becomes the occasion for a new sense of responsibility.

The Perils of Eminence

If we know that we have been chosen beyond our deserts, we must also begin to realize that we have not been chosen for our particular task in order that our own life may be aggrandized. We ought not derive either special security or special advantages from our high historical mission. The real fact is that we are placed in a precarious moral and historical position by our special mission. It can be justified only if it results in good for the whole community of mankind. Woe unto us if we fail. For our failure will bring judgment upon both us and the world. That is the meaning of the prophetic word, "Therefore will I visit you with your iniquities." This word must be translated by the church today into meanings relevant to our own history. If this is not done, we are bound to fail. For the natural pride of great nations is such that any special historical success quickly aggravates it until it becomes the source of moral and political confusion.

Without a religious sense of humility and responsibility the Anglo-Saxon world will fail to come to terms with the two great non-Christian nations, Russia and China. It will fail to understand to what degree what is good in the new Russian order represents values of equal justice that we should have, but did not, achieve, and to what extent the evils of tyranny in Russia are simply a false answer to our own unsolved problem of social justice. It will fail to understand to what degree the white man's pride is the chief obstacle in building a world community that brings Asia fully into the world community. It is worth remembering in this connection that long before the Nazi elaborated the idea of Nordic superiority the Anglo-Saxon world betrayed an arrogance toward the darker peoples of which the Latin world, for instance, was comparatively free. Our racial pride is incompatible with our responsibilities in the world community. If we do not succeed in chastening it, we shall fail in our task.

If we should imagine that our victory in this great World War were a justification of our virtue and if our moral pride thus becomes accentuated, we shall fail in our task of finally bringing the fallen foes into the world community on terms that will bring health both to them and the total community. If we should give ourselves to the illusion that this war was a simple contest between right and wrong, and that the victory was a simple triumph of right over wrong; if we fail to understand to what degree Nazi tyranny grew on the soil of our general international anarchy; if we lack the spiritual humility to see these factors of history, we shall be bound to corrupt the peace by vindictiveness.

Self-Righteousness Leads to Vindictiveness

There are already many ominous signs of this vindictiveness, and a careful analysis of various manifestations of the spirit of vengeance reveals very clearly how self-righteousness is the presupposition of vengeance. It is also quite easy to foresee the consequences of any peace that is built upon the assumption that the elimination of Nazi evil will eliminate evil from the world. All these perils are the insecurities to which we are exposed in our historical eminence. They represent the always overhanging divine judgment. They are the modern counterparts of what Amos foresaw in his words, "Therefore will I visit you with your iniquities."

We may be fairly sure that the Anglo-Saxon world will not be good enough or sufficiently contrite to fulfill its historical mission with complete success. It nevertheless has a great opportunity to fulfill it with relative success. But if this is to be accomplished, the Christian church must understand its prophetic mission. It must cease to vacillate between ascetic withdrawal from the world "power politics" and a too simple identification of the nation's purposes with the divine Will. It must contend against both irresponsibility and complacency in our national life.

The world community cannot be realized if the Anglo-Saxon world fails in its historic mission. If it is afraid of the perils of that mission and is affrighted by the moral ambiguities of "power politics," it will fail just as seriously as if it accepts its mission without a religious sense of contrition. It may be that the former temptation is still the primary temptation for America, and the second one that to which Britain is particularly prone. But the differences between the two great parts of the Anglo-Saxon world are less than the similarities. In both cases the Christian faith is still in sufficiently close relation to the national life to encourage the hope that it will help to purify the nations for their mission; in both cases, however, the Christian forces are to some degree the salt that has lost its savor. If the nations should fail therefore, the failure would be the consequence of the prior failure of the Christian church.

Part Seven

✣

Challenges since Mid-Century

Since the middle of the twentieth century America has faced some critical challenges that have decisively shaped its sense of national destiny. Race problems at home have set Americans to pondering whether their nation can justly be termed a Promised Land of liberty, and if so in what sense. Events on the international scene have stirred disquieting questions about the limits of power in America's mission of safeguarding "the rights of democratic freedom" around the globe. And issues regarding the moral condition of the nation have agitated Americans of different political and religious persuasions. The remaining readings in this book cluster around three problems which have become the foci of recent interpretations of American destiny. The interpretations vary widely, but all share the belief that the problems with which they deal have placed the nation at a crossroads of its existence.

America's World Role

American attitudes toward the nation's mission in the world were influenced considerably by the general "turn to religion" in the 1950s. Surveys conducted during that decade indicated a marked increase in church attendance and in the construction of new churches; they also reported that the large majority of Americans professed a belief in God, held that the Bible was the inspired word of God, and thought that religion was "of very great importance."[1] The evangelistic crusades of Billy Graham and his imitators reached the peak of their popularity in the 1950s, and Norman Vincent Peale's *The Power of Positive Thinking* and other books of religious self-help made the best seller lists. This surge of piety was by no means confined to ecclesiastical institutions. It was a religious revival on a broad national scale, and its influence spread to the highest councils of the land. President Dwight D. Eisenhower became both

1. See Will Herberg, *Protestant-Catholic-Jew* (Garden City, N.Y.: Doubleday & Company, 1960), pp. 1ff., 72ff.

a leading spokesman and a stellar symbol of the revival. Eisenhower broke precedent by opening his first inaugural address with a prayer. He instituted the practice of regular prayer breakfasts at the White House and appointed a Congregational minister as the "president's pastor." Under his direction the nation added "under God" to the pledge of allegiance and the postmaster general held a ceremony commemorating a new postage stamp bearing the motto "In God We Trust." Americans looked upon Eisenhower the man as a desirable blend of religion, patriotism, and moral principle (moral principle supposedly unsullied by partisan politics). His statement made during his years as president of Columbia University became the watchword of Americanism in the 1950s: "Democracy is the political expression of a deeply felt religion."[2]

The climate was right for the turn to religion during the Eisenhower years. The anxiety produced by the destructive use of nuclear power at the close of World War II and the tensions of the ensuing Cold War drove many Americans to seek security in religious experiences. Just as clearly, much of the religion of the day was in close league with anticommunism. The usual contrast drawn by public rhetoric was one between the "religious principles of democracy" and "godless communism." Even if all the religious fervor did not align itself with the extremism of Senator Joseph McCarthy's communist-hunt (some of it did), much of it was thoroughly bound up with a national urge to launch a "moral crusade" against atheistic communism. Religious interpretations of American destiny, therefore, tended to support a foreign policy which operated on the assumption that the nation's mission abroad was to stem the tide of a demonic communist force which threatened to engulf the world.

President Eisenhower indicated the pattern for America's response to communism in his first inaugural address, a pattern that had already been set by the Truman administration. Eisenhower portrayed the world as dividing itself into two opposing forces: "Freedom is pitted against slavery; lightness against the dark," and he called upon free people to unite against their common foe. "To produce this unity, to meet the challenge of our time, destiny has laid upon our country the responsibility of the free world's leadership." Eisenhower's secretary of state, John Foster Dulles, shared the president's vision of America's leadership in a divided world and acted to shape a foreign policy that sought to live up to that vision.

As a devout Presbyterian layman Dulles had directed a church commission in the 1940s that studied the "Bases of a Just and Durable Peace." As secretary of state he argued that the possibility of a stable world peace resided in the firm

---

2. For a summary of Eisenhower's religion (public and private) and its relation to his political views see Merlin Gustafson, "The Religion of a President," *Christian Century*, Apr. 30, 1969, pp. 610–13. Cf. William Lee Miller, *Piety Along the Potomac* (Boston: Houghton Mifflin Company, 1964).

leadership of the American nation, a nation called to its noble mission by God and specially equipped for that mission by the religious and moral principles which it possessed at the core of its political being.[3] Holding that conviction, Dulles worked for the strengthening of the North Atlantic Treaty Organization, piloted the formation of the Southeast Asia Treaty Organization, and generally sought to unify the Western alliance against the communist menace. Although the United States under Dulles's secretaryship did not attain either the secure world peace or the firm Western unity that he had envisaged (the Suez crisis and the weakness of SEATO were strong proofs to the contrary), he never ceased defending an American foreign policy dedicated to the energetic deterrence of an aggressive communism.

Secretary Dulles delineated the major features of his theory of foreign relations and grounded them in his view of American destiny in a speech of February 26, 1956. In that address, "Freedom's New Task," he described a recent shift in the Soviet "plan of conquest" from the tactics of "intolerance and violence" to the tactics of economic assistance. He designated the response that the United States must make and felt that the response would be readily forthcoming since our nation "was conceived with a sense of mission" and had been assigned by providence the task of extending freedom throughout the world.

Dulles's philosophy of foreign relations was called "brinkmanship" by his critics. Dulles himself invited the criticism when he said in 1956, "The ability to get to the verge without getting into the war is the necessary art. If you cannot master it, you inevitably get into war. If you try to run away from it, if you are scared to go to the brink, you are lost."[4] Brinkmanship as a method of dealing with crises in international affairs did not die with Secretary Dulles, and his conviction that America was providentially chosen to lead the free world in stopping the spread of communism certainly lived on after the man. Yet the arrival of the 1960s marked a transition to a somewhat less belligerent American attitude toward Russian communism and to an emphasis on negotiation. The change was reflected in the inaugural address of President John F. Kennedy. "Let us never negotiate out of fear," Kennedy said, "But let us never fear to negotiate." President Kennedy spurned catchwords like "godless communism" and "America's moral crusade" that had riddled the rhetoric of the 1950s and had pictured the world as divided into realms of light and darkness. He continued to speak of the need to check the spread of communism, particularly through economic aid to underdeveloped countries, but he insisted that the primary purpose of foreign aid programs should be not the winning of allies but the raising of living standards and the consolidation of democracies.

3. See Henry P. Van Dusen, ed., *The Spiritual Legacy of John Foster Dulles* (Philadelphia: Westminster Press, 1960), pp. 5–85.
4. *Life*, Jan. 16, 1956, p. 78.

America found itself on the verge of nuclear war during the Cuban missile crisis. After Khrushchev agreed, at Kennedy's firm insistence, to dismantle the rocket sites in Cuba, the Cold War between the Soviet Union and the United States thawed somewhat. Relations were further improved with the signing of the Nuclear Test-Ban Treaty by the United States, Great Britain, and the Soviet Union in August 1963. American fears of communism were now directed increasingly toward Red China, and talk of the American mission abroad focused more and more on Asia.

During the late 1960s and early 1970s the hottest item in the debate over the nature and extent of America's mission abroad became this country's costly involvement in the Vietnam War. In the SEATO agreements made during the 1950s, America pledged its protection of Southeast Asia against outside aggression. American leaders immediately found themselves dealing with an area plagued by bitter religious controversies, corrupt dictatorships insensitive to the needs of the people, and a style of political and social life unresponsive to the principles of Western democracy. Pleading obligation to aid South Vietnam in its struggle against the Viet Cong, the United States during the Kennedy years steadily increased its manpower and war material. As North Vietnam openly supported the Viet Cong with troops and supplies, the Johnson administration escalated the war with frequent bombings of the North and eventually stationed over 500,000 American servicemen in Vietnam. Spokesmen for the Johnson administration defended the American presence in Vietnam with the claim that the United States should meet its "long-standing commitments" to protect the right of independent nations to self-determination and "freedom from aggression." America's participation in the war was interpreted as an unfortunate but necessary means of preventing Asia from falling, area by area, under the control of communism.

The theme of American destiny, together with its religious underpinnings and its influence on American foreign policy in Southeast Asia, was forcefully brought to the attention of the American people by Senator J. William Fulbright, chairman of the Senate Foreign Relations Committee and foremost critic of U.S. policy in Vietnam. In the introduction to his *The Arrogance of Power* he summarized his criticisms of America's sense of omnipotence. Fulbright was convinced that the American presumption which confuses power with virtue and identifies fortunate national circumstances with the special blessings of God has led this nation into tragedies like the Vietnam War. Although Senator Fulbright attacked one traditional view of American destiny — the one that holds that America is obligated actively to convert the entire world to an American way of doing things — he did not deny that the nation has a service to perform in the world, namely the "service of her own example."

The issues respecting world mission raised by Fulbright did not disappear after U.S. troops were withdrawn from Vietnam by President Richard Nixon in 1973, and American national leaders continued to appeal to the theme of national destiny in their interpretations of America's international role. In his widely covered "evil empire" speech to the Annual Convention of the National Association of Evangelicals in 1983, President Ronald Reagan portrayed the Soviet Union as an immoral, materialistic, irreligious, aggressive force in the world that America, as a religious nation that keeps "alight the torch of freedom," must stand ready to resist, if necessary by force of arms.[5] In numerous other speeches President Reagan, as the country's "Great Communicator," invoked the civil religion theme of "supreme sacrifice"—death for the sake of the nation—as the very soul of America and an assurance of the destiny of preserving democratic freedom at home and abroad.[6] And President George Bush construed U.S. participation in the Gulf War, or "Desert Storm," in 1991 as simultaneously the stopping of Saddam Hussein's occupation of Kuwait and Iraq's eventual invasion of other parts of the Middle East, the defense of America's vital interests abroad (especially U.S. petroleum interests), and the pursuit of the destiny of a divinely blessed American nation that must do "what is right" on behalf of "all mankind."[7]

After the Vietnam War, however, the rhetoric of an aggressively pursued national destiny abroad seemed to connect less and less with the American experience. The failure of that long, costly war to deliver on several presidential administrations' promises to preserve democratic interests in the world rendered the rhetoric suspect. (As a consequence President Bush had to assure the American people that Desert Storm, unlike Vietnam, would be swift and its tools of war massive and effective.) Furthermore, the threat of the Cold War enemy, "godless communism," dissolved. The establishment of cordial relations with mainland China under President Nixon and the granting of full diplomatic recognition of China under President Carter stripped away fears of an Asian enemy. The creation of close relations between President Reagan and Soviet premier Gorbachev in 1988 and the collapse of communist governments in Eastern Europe in 1989 further dispelled anxieties about American interests being threatened by a powerful, sinister outside force. To be sure, the alleged "religious fanaticism" of a militant Islam in Iran and other countries raised the specter of a new enemy of American destiny, but it was an enemy no longer cast in terms of a world order balanced by the forces of superpowers. In fact, as journalist Daniel Schorr has observed, the late-twentieth-century

5. Ronald Reagan, *Speaking My Mind: Selected Speeches* (New York: Simon and Schuster, 1989), pp. 169–180.

6. See David Chidester, "Saving the Children by Killing Them: Redemptive Sacrifice in the Ideologies of Jim Jones and Ronald Reagan," *Religion and American Culture: A Journal of Interpretation*, Summer 1991, pp. 177–97.

7. Micah L. Sifry and Christopher Cerf, eds., *The Gulf War Reader: History, Documents, Opinions* (New York: Times Books of Random House, 1991), pp. 197–99, 228–29, 311–14, 449–51.

global situation is probably best described as a "new world disorder," or a world
disordered by local conflicts uncontrolled by the United States or any other
superpower. In 1993, for example, "when long-festering conflicts showed signs
of finally yielding to peaceful resolution [in South Africa, Northern Ireland,
and the Middle East], it was usually because of the internal dynamics of each
situation than because of outside intervention." By contrast, "during the Cold
War all conflicts, and efforts to resolve them, were measured on an index of
how they fitted into East-West confrontation."[8] The new disordered situation
would mute considerably any bold, self-confident claims about American destiny under God in the world at large.

The Black American

If the war in Vietnam became a crucial turning point in views of American
destiny abroad, the black American's struggle for equality and justice became a
turning point in the nation's sense of domestic destiny. The African American
struggles during the Civil Rights movement and afterward called attention to
the diseases of prejudice, poverty, inequity, and racism that had long afflicted
blacks and other minorities in the land. As a result some sharp questions regarding American destiny at home were posed. Should the downtrodden of
our society seek to become a redeeming remnant within the American Israel,
or are they called to separate themselves as a people from a thoroughly degenerate and hypocritical New Israel? Is their task one of rectifying America's
destiny under God, or one of discovering their own myths and their own independent destiny?

All of the motifs germane to the belief in the election of a people by God
are vital parts of black Americans' past. Themes like Deliverance from Bondage, Wilderness Wandering, Promised Land, and the Coming Kingdom of
God were firmly embedded in their experiences by slave songs and spirituals
and by the biblical preaching of the black church. Even after it ceased to be a
slave religion, black Christianity could be otherworldly in outlook and could
be endorsed by the white oppressors as a pie-in-the-sky religion for former
slaves and their heirs. Yet black Christianity did not always play such a role.
Despite white Christianity's persistent efforts to keep blacks in a subservient,
compliant status by providing an opiate religion, black religious zeal often
joined forces with a black passion for justice. The Old Testament, which furnished so much of the power of black Christian preaching, was too explicitly
this-worldly in its hope for the future, too prophetically critical of social injustice, too militantly aggressive in its words to the chosen people to be totally

8. Daniel Schorr, "The New World Disorder," *1994 Britannica Book of the Year*, p. 7.

glossed over as a pie-in-the-sky treatise. The slave preacher Nat Turner seems to have been at least partially motivated toward his famous rebellion by an Old Testament instinct for warfare against the enemies of the Lord, and his followers looked to him as a prophet chosen to lead them to the Promised Land of freedom.[9] As early as 1829 David Walker and Robert A. Young, both free Negro abolitionists, prophesied that there would arise among their people a Messiah who would lead in the liberation of the slaves.[10] Vincent Harding has observed that African American intellectual history is replete with hopes for a Black Messiah (conceived either individually or collectively) who will rise up to deliver black Americans from their bondage.[11] And James Cone has studied the manner in which black spirituals, sometimes interpreted as merely expressing hopes for salvation on the other side of the grave, in fact often give voice to longings for liberation from oppression in this life.[12]

Whatever strictly otherworldly accretions that may have adhered to the black view of destiny in the past have now been scrubbed off. In the Civil Rights movement black interpretations of themes like Chosen People, Messiah, and Promised Land took on an activistic thrust aimed directly at America's social maladies. As the following readings make clear, however, a debate has raged over the tactics and ideology proper to the realization of the black American's task and over the connection of that task with America as a whole.

Dr. Martin Luther King, Jr., was catapulted into national attention by the Montgomery, Alabama, bus boycott in 1955–56. As president of the Southern Christian Leadership Conference, he quickly became a moving force behind black Americans' bid for justice and an articulate interpreter of their mission in American society. Before his murder in the spring of 1968, King had come under severe criticism from black power militants as well as white segregationists, but he remained for large numbers of followers a Moses calling his people out of the bondage of segregation and discrimination. The vision that energized King's nonviolent campaign was much broader than the attainment of immediate goals like the integration of public transportation, restaurants, and schools or the winning of voting rights for black Americans. It was a vision often expressed in the rolling cadence of his speeches: a vision of America united by the bonds of justice and brotherhood. "I have a dream," King said in his speech during the March on Washington in August 1963. "It is a dream

9. See Leslie H. Fishel and Benjamin Quarles, eds., *The Negro American* (Glenview, Ill.: Foresman & Company, 1967), p. 120.

10. John Hope Franklin, *From Slavery to Freedom*, 3rd ed. (New York: Alfred A. Knopf, 1967), pp. 243, 250.

11. Vincent Harding, "The Religion of Black Power," in *The Religious Situation: 1968*, ed. Donald R. Cutler (Boston: Beacon Press, 1968), p. 13.

12. James H. Cone, *The Spirituals and the Blues: An Interpretation* (New York: Seabury Press, 1972), pp. 34–85.

deeply rooted in the American dream. I have a dream that one day this nation will rise up and live out the true meaning of its creed: 'We hold these truths to be self-evident, that all men are created equal.' "

King's view of the pressing urgency of the civil rights movement and its part in the realization of the American dream was the subject of his "Letter from Birmingham Jail." Written in response to the charge by several white Southern clergymen that civil rights agitation in Birmingham was "unwise and untimely," the letter was a stinging indictment of the disgruntled white moderate and an able description of the aims and techniques of "nonviolent direct action." The letter also portrayed American blacks as a remnant of the New Israel called to redeem America for its destiny of freedom and equality.

In the 1960s a new mood spread through the black revolutionary movement, a mood critical of the tactics, aims, and vision of King. Convinced that the techniques of nonviolent resistance were both humiliating and ineffectual, vocal groups of American blacks called for direct confrontation with an adamant white power structure—a confrontation that need not rule out returning violence for violence. Persuaded that integration was simply another means of submerging a distinct and healthy black identity in a sea of white middle-class mediocrity, they urged their people to turn to forms of separation and independence—separation in education, in politics, in dress and speech, in music, in living arrangements, in business. Believing that they had been asked by King to achieve the impossible task of loving whites while still harboring self-hatred, they issued a plea for self-love and the celebration of blackness. Feeling more affinity with the poor and oppressed people of the world than with an affluent white mainstream of American society, they sought connections with other nonwhite people and searched out the African roots of their heritage. Convinced that American destiny had been pursued at their expense but not on their behalf, they insisted that their own separate identity as a black people must be comprehended and actualized before they could—if ever—embrace the larger American destiny.

The black separatist viewpoint and its repudiation of King's vision of destiny were nowhere more apparent than in the doctrines of the Nation of Islam or the Black Muslim religion. Founded in Detroit in 1931 by Wali Fard, the Black Muslim movement came under the leadership of Elijah Muhammad in 1934, at first made slow progress, then spread rapidly after World War II as it struck a responsive chord in an emerging black consciousness in the United States. Particularly in the teeming black ghettos of the cities and among blacks in prison, expressions of Muslim belief have found attentive ears. The customary Black Muslim doctrines (periodically modified by more moderate leaders) that black people are a morally and culturally superior race, that they are the chosen people of Allah, that whites are a race of devils who have corrupted "the so-called Negro" with their Christian religion and civilization—all these doctrines found suitable soil for growth in the black frustrations created by an oppressive white society. And in the vision of Elijah Muhammad black Americans face a destiny quite separate from that of white America. Black people are to unify and purify themselves and prepare for the final conflict between good and evil, the conflict between the black community and the white community. White America's certain future is total ruin; out of the ashes Allah will erect a separate nation for his own Chosen Black People.[13]

Malcolm X (pre-Muslim name Malcolm Little) became the most visible and articulate spokesman for black nationalism and black separatism during his brief career as an African American leader. Converted to the Nation of Islam while serving a prison term for burglary, Malcolm X became an evangelist and organizer for Elijah Muhammad and, with a finely honed ability to speak the language of the streets, an effective challenger of Martin Luther King's softer, more moderate, Christian interpretation of the black American's role in the national destiny. In Malcolm's judgment, integration obscured the need for black pride, independence, and self-help; strategies of nonviolence regardless of circumstance required of blacks an attitude that did not apply to a violent white America; and demands for *civil rights* from the hand of government eclipsed the larger need to insist on basic *human rights* inherent within human existence itself. Many of these themes were uppermost in a speech that Malcolm X delivered to mostly black audiences in several cities in the U.S. in 1964, "The Ballot or the Bullet." Challenging King's notion that African Americans could participate in an American dream, Malcolm saw only an American nightmare for black people. Preferring the ballot exercised by blacks on behalf of blacks—and refusing to counsel the use of violence—he nevertheless believed that the bullet of violence was inevitable and justifiable if the ballot failed. And considering himself an African rather than an American, he believed his people to be the victims, not the beneficiaries, of the entire American system.

By the time Malcolm X delivered his "Ballot or Bullet" speech he had left the Nation of Islam. Courting the criticism of Black Muslim leaders for his reference to the assassination of President Kennedy as a "case of chickens coming home to roost" and prompting jealousy among those leaders by his increasing popularity, Malcolm was suspended from the Nation by Elijah Muhammad. In response he set about to form his own religious movement. (Three Black Muslims were convicted of his assassination by gunfire in the Audubon Ballroom in Harlem on February 21, 1965.) The "Ballot or Bullet" speech reflected Malcolm's independence from Elijah Muhammad's thinking. Although he still identified himself as a Muslim, Malcolm tied his remarks to

13. Elijah Muhammad, *Message to the Blackman in America* (Chicago: Muhammad Mosque of Islam No. 2, 1965), pp. 229–30, 269–75.

a unified black experience rather than to his Muslim convictions. He situated his pleas within a large contemporary international setting, and in welcoming the cooperation of all peoples moved away from radical black separatism. He also took an activist approach to dealing with problems of race rather than waiting for Allah to bring about a solution in a final conflagration. The central problem for Malcolm was still the white man, however, and unlike Martin Luther King, Jr., in "I Have a Dream" or "Letter from Birmingham Jail," Malcolm exhibited no confidence that solutions to the problems of race could be found in the documents, myths, or experiences of God's New Israel.

In the 1970s and the years following, the Nation of Islam revealed signs of further fragmentation. One branch of the religion under the leadership of Elijah Muhammad's son Wallace aligned itself with international Sunni Islam and advocated full participation of African Americans in American capitalism. Another branch under the leadership of Louis Farrakhan called for black independence and self-help as the appropriate ways of dealing with an irredeemably bigoted white power structure. Farrakhan's militant public pronouncements sometimes drew accusations from blacks and whites alike that he was anti-Semitic as well as antiwhite. Finally, however, it was Martin Luther King and Malcolm X who managed to capture enduring, distinctive readings of American destiny. King dreamed an American dream that embraced all citizens regardless of the color of their skin. He appropriated the myths and symbols of the American civil religion and of black Christianity and took hope from the democratic structures and processes that he believed to be deeply embedded in the American system. Malcolm X was possessed by a recurrent American nightmare filled with the horrors of racism. He castigated the pretensions of white American religious beliefs and practices and took no hope from a hypocritical, basically violent American system.

In another sense, however, these two fallen black heroes exemplify complementary dimensions of a continuing tradition. As African American theologian James Cone has said, "Martin and Malcolm illuminate the two roads to freedom that meet in the African-Americans' search for identity in the land of their birth."[14] The roads converge in part because Martin and Malcolm moved closer to the other's position toward the end of their lives. King's American dream was shattered between 1965 and 1968 by the violence and discrimination in American cities, by whites' demands for law and order as solutions to all problems, and by the war in Vietnam. His criticisms of an intractable American racism began to sound much like those of Malcolm. Malcolm X, on the other hand, dropped his "white devil" language following his Hajj or pilgrim-

14. James H. Cone, *Martin & Malcolm & America: A Dream or a Nightmare* (Maryknoll, N.Y.: Orbis Books, 1991), p. x.

age to Mecca in 1964, during which he was attracted to traditional Muslim as opposed to Black Muslim beliefs and was positively impressed by the fact that devout Muslims were of many different colors. His inclusive language and pleas for voting rights began to sound much like the speeches of King.

Beyond such personal changes, the positions of the two leaders coalesce in one effort for racial justice, one enduring dream for black Americans marked both by visionary hopes and by frightful nightmares. In Cone's words, "We need both of them and we need them *together*. Malcolm keeps Martin from being turned into a harmless American hero. Martin keeps Malcolm from being an ostracized black hero."[15] And together they embody an ardent hope for and a serious challenge to an American destiny under God—or under Allah.

National Morals

During the last twenty-five years or so, the sense of national purpose has been increasingly shaped by controversies over the moral order of America. The controversies have centered on a wide range of very public and very private issues: abortion, homosexuality, environmental pollution, family values, the drug trade, violent crime in the cities, the rights of minorities, prayer in the public schools, wealth and poverty, military spending, and a host of others. It has seemed to some social analysts that late-twentieth-century Americans became engaged in a series of "culture wars," with battle lines being drawn right down the middle of the country between cultural conservatives and cultural progressives.[16] Whether really engaged in a cultural war or not, Americans have entered into—and through the media have been surrounded by—debates about the moral destiny of the nation. The debates have often woven together religious and political values.

Sociologist Robert Wuthnow has suggested that the polar division over moral issues has resulted in two civil religions, each with its own set of beliefs and mythologies. On the political and social right, religious conservatives have looked back to the founding religious ideas and myths of the nation in order to define America as "Christian" or "Judeo-Christian" in its origins. They have also insisted that the nation has become immoral by departing from those origins. On the political and social left, religious liberals have tended to neglect American founding events, personalities, and myths in favor of con-

---

15. Ibid., p. 316.
16. See James Davison Hunter, *Culture Wars: The Struggle to Define America* (New York: Basic Books, 1991).

cern for common human problems, basic human rights, and ideas inclusive of the nations of the world.[17]

Christian conservatives, especially Protestant fundamentalists, evangelicals, and pentecostals, have come to stand for a right-wing version of the American civil religion and its rendition of the national destiny. Although those three religious groups differ in their theologies and religious practices, together they have expressed concerns about the moral decline of America and have reclaimed what they take to be the religious foundations of the country. Although they have not constituted a monolithic voting block in the United States,[18] they have become vocal supporters of political and social causes that accord with their religious views of the purpose and status of the nation. Thus they have been courted by conservative politicians, especially by conservatives in the Republican Party. The political and social activism of religious conservatives marks a new development for the twentieth century. In the early part of the century, religious conservatives retreated into a social and cultural enclave, disavowed overt political action, and abandoned any hopes for imbuing the nation with religious purpose. A turning point occurred in 1973, with the legalization of abortion on demand by the Supreme Court in the *Roe v. Wade* decision. Evangelicals and other conservatives began to assert their opinions on the moral issues of the day, frame those opinions in terms of the meaning of America, and join moral concerns with political activism.[19] The critique previously leveled by activist religious liberals against their conservative counterparts—that conservative Christianity was irrelevant to the pressing moral and social problems of the day—could be made no longer.

This important shift to the political is illustrated in the career of the founder of the Moral Majority, Jerry Falwell. A fundamentalist Baptist preacher who built up a huge congregation in Lynchburg, Virginia, and launched a popular radio and television ministry through his *Old-Time Gospel Hour*, Falwell had deliberately avoided political action on the grounds of the separation of church and state. The *Roe v. Wade* decision convinced him, however, that he must do more than preach against abortion and other behaviors in contem-

17. Robert Wuthnow, *The Restructuring of American Religion: Society and Faith since World War II* (Princeton, N.J.: Princeton University Press, 1988), pp. 241–67.

18. On the political diversity of religious conservatives see Lyman A. Kellstedt and Mark A. Noll, "Religion, Voting for President, and Party Identification, 1948–1984," in *Religion and American Politics: From the Colonial Period to the 1980s*, ed. Mark A. Noll (New York: Oxford University Press, 1990), pp. 370–76, and George Marsden, "Afterword: Religion, Politics, and the Search for an American Consensus," ibid., pp. 387–89. For evidence of diversity within one branch of the Religious Right see Harvey Cox's description of Pat Robertson's Regent University, "The Warring Visions of the Religious Right," *Atlantic Monthly*, Nov. 1995, pp. 59–69.

19. For a brief overview of the political transitions in Protestant evangelicalism from the late nineteenth century to the present see Mark A. Noll, *The Scandal of the Evangelical Mind* (Grand Rapids, Mich.: Eerdmans Publishing Co., 1994), pp. 149–75.

porary America that he considered immoral, so he organized people around such issues as abortion, pornography, and homosexuality in order to influence the voting public. Separation of church and state, he came to believe, did not mean the alienation of religion from politics but rather the denial of an established institutional church. And America, he came to think, was founded on the principles of "Holy Writ" to become a Christian nation, but the nation had landed itself in its current, sad moral state of affairs because it had departed from those principles.[20]

Pat Robertson's social and political conservatism was rooted in pentecostal evangelicalism rather than in fundamentalism, but he justified political action on many of the same grounds as Falwell. Robertson's bid for the presidential nomination in 1988, his influential Christian Broadcasting Network (CBN), and the talk-show format of his television show The 700 Club created a more sophisticated aura than Falwell's activities, but Robertson was on the same side of divisive moral issues as Falwell. In his book *The New World Order*, Robertson listed a string of social ills that he believed had prevented America from becoming the Christian agent of world peace to which God called it: "There will never be world peace until God's house and God's people are given their rightful place of leadership at the top of the world. How can there be peace when drunkards, drug dealers, communists, atheists, New Age worshipers of Satan, secular humanists, oppressive dictators, greedy moneychangers, revolutionary assassins, adulterers, and homosexuals are on top?"[21]

Ralph Reed, handpicked by Robertson in 1989 to direct the Christian Coalition organization, was a youthful, skillful, and articulate political organizer dedicated to moving the nation into a position for overcoming the moral woes listed by Robertson. In attempting to build a broad political coalition of moral conservatives, Reed sought connections between Christians and other Americans in his "pro-life" and "pro-family" critique of homosexual practices, teenage pregnancies, and widespread divorce, but the basis of all his claims was the conviction that Christians must serve as the "conscience of the nation" on moral issues.[22] And though he repudiated the notion that America should be a "Christian nation" that excludes other religious perspectives from the public sphere, Reed clearly believed that the moral destiny of the country has been most decisively shaped by a Christian national history. That belief is apparent in the following selection from Reed, "Separation of Church and State." While proposing that the American Civil Religion, a pillar of our social order, is an inclusive religious faith to be set against American secularism, the historic

20. Jerry Falwell, *If I Should Die before I Wake* (Nashville, Tenn.: Thomas Nelson Publishers, 1986), pp. 31–47; idem., *Listen, America!* (New York: Bantom Books, 1980), pp. 19–46.

21. Pat Robertson, *The New World Order* (Dallas, Tex.: Word Publishing Co., 1991), p. 227.

22. Ralph Reed, *Active Faith: How Christians Are Changing the Soul of American Politics* (New York: Free Press, 1996), pp. 27–28.

illustrations and language of Reed's Civil Religion are decidedly Christian. If Reed abandoned the idea of an exclusive Christian America, he by no means surrendered the idea that a religious America definitively formed by Christian beliefs and history was the only hope for calling the nation back to its high moral purposes.

As the Religious Right marks a return to the alleged religious origins of America for the sake of criticism of the current moral shape of the nation, so the position known as "ecofeminism" illustrates the liberal left appropriation of global ideas and common human problems for the sake of identifying moral problems of the day. Ecofeminism joins together two movements, feminism and ecology, that surged in popularity following the socially turbulent decade of the 1960s, and in its religious manifestations the movement has specified a set of moral issues crucial to the destiny of the nation and the world.

The origins of the feminist movement in the United States can be traced to the struggles for women's suffrage and other women's rights in the nineteenth and early twentieth centuries. Yet the movement took on a different tone and adopted different beliefs and strategies beginning in the 1960s. For example, the view so popular among women in the late nineteenth century that the male and female "natures" are meant to complement each other was largely scuttled by modern feminists. It appeared to the new breed of feminists that the theory of the complementarity of natures still implied the dependency of females on males and could be used by males to keep females in predetermined social roles.[23] In late-twentieth-century America feminism came to represent a wide spectrum of positions: from demands for equal employment opportunities for women and men, to criticisms of the misogyny of the capitalist system itself; from calls for the solidarity of all women against the injustices of a patriarchal society, to arguments for the establishment of separate female identities according to racial, ethnic, or class backgrounds; from pleas for the elimination of all sexism, to the shunning of all bonding with males considered oppressive by nature. Religious feminism also developed a range of viewpoints: from the discovery of women leaders and sexual equality in the history of traditional religions, to the dismissal of those religions as hopelessly patriarchal; from the celebration of the feminine features of the Jewish and Christian God, to the adoption of ancient goddesses as more appropriate to female experiences; from efforts to win equality for women in the contemporary churches, to the creation of new religious communities thought to be more sensitive to the needs and rights of women. Pervading most of the religious viewpoints, however, was the conviction that sexism is a serious basic moral problem with implications for the destiny of the globe.

---

23. See, for example, Rosemary Radford Ruether, *Disputed Questions: On Being a Christian* (Nashville, Tenn.: Abingdon Press, 1982), pp. 130–31.

A similar conviction has permeated the human ecology movement. According to the standard definitions, ecology is "the subdiscipline of biology that deals with interactions between organisms and their environment on the population, community and ecosystem levels of organization," whereas human ecology "focuses specifically on the relationships of human populations to the ecosystems of which they are a part."[24] Following the publication in 1962 of Rachel Carson's *Silent Spring*, which dramatically raised Americans' consciousness about the human pollution of the natural world, human ecology became a concern of many people outside as well as inside the boundaries of the biological sciences. Over time the human ecology or "green" movement would appear in a number of different organizations and adopt several political strategies, but it was unified in decrying the reckless, dangerous poisoning of nature by human actions and policies. Many religious interpretations arose to undergird pleas for a symbiotic relation between the human and the nonhuman realms of nature. Christian and Jewish theologians pointed to the responsibilities of human stewardship of the earth inherent within their religious teachings. Native Americans and others interested in indigenous religions celebrated the worshipful, nonexploitative relations with nature exhibited by many Native American peoples. Religious proponents of planetary and universal evolution called attention to both the positive and the deleterious effects that humans can bring to God's order of things.[25] These and other religious perspectives on human ecology insisted that the pollution of the earth's land, water, and atmosphere was a serious moral problem with basic human, international, and global ramifications.

Ecofeminism has brought together human ecology and feminism on the ground that both nonhuman nature and women have been dominated by males, most especially in modern European and American cultures. Furthermore, ecofeminists believe that those cultures have tended to relegate the realm of the feminine to the realm of nature. In the words of ecofeminist Ynestra King, "All human beings are natural beings. That may seem like an obvious fact, yet we live in a culture that is founded on the repudiation and domination of nature. This has a special significance for women because, in patriarchal thought, women are believed to be closer to nature than men. This gives women a particular stake in ending the domination of nature—in healing the alienation between human and nonhuman nature."[26] In her religious

24. Paul R. Ehrlich, Anne H. Ehrlich, and John P. Holdren, *Human Ecology: Problems and Solutions* (San Francisco: W. H. Freeman and Company, 1973), p. 6.

25. For a wide range of religious interpretations of ecology see Mary Evelyn Tucker and John A. Grim, eds., *Worldviews and Ecology* (Lewisburg, Pa.: Bucknell University Press, 1993).

26. Ynestra King, "The Ecology of Feminism and the Feminism of Ecology," in *Healing the Wounds: The Promise of Ecofeminism*, ed. Judith Plant (Philadelphia: New Society Publishers, 1989), p. 18.

interpretation of ecofeminism, American theologian Rosemary Ruether both criticizes the patterns of domination in human cultures and proposes the healing of the divisions between the human and the nonhuman.

In her book *Gaia and God*, Ruether argues that ecofeminism offers the possibility of a new consciousness of humans' nondominating relation to nature, a consciousness that goes beyond mere "technological fixes." God, the ultimate symbol in biblical and Christian religion, points to the need for human ethical responsibility for the earth and to the sacramental presence of the divine in nature. Gaia, the name for the Greek earth goddess and symbol of the planet as a living system,[27] calls up the image of communion among all parts of the planetary system and in particular the mutual interdependency of men, women, and nature. In her conclusion to the book (the following selection), Ruether proposes that the new religious consciousness born of the union of Gaia and God results in concrete courses of action and moral principles devoted to overcoming all instances of domination and dedicated to promoting the healing of the ecosystem. Ruether believes that human destiny and global destiny—purposes larger than those tied to national destiny alone—require the new ecological consciousness.

Even if Robert Wuthnow is correct that the moral issues of late-twentieth-century America led to two civil religions—one for the right and one for the left—each with its own distinctive set of symbols and myths, this does not necessarily describe the future. The possible emergence of a common enemy, previously such a powerful unifier of many Americans in times of national crisis, cannot be ruled out as a future factor that could overcome the mythic divisions between left and right. On the other hand, increasing social, cultural, and religious pluralism could very well fragment even further the American sense of destiny under God. In any event, the myth of divine destiny has shown considerable staying power throughout the history of the United States. Part of the myth's resilience is due to the ability of Americans to adjust their religious sense of the nation's destiny to changed circumstances and altered expectations. It is reasonable to conclude that the same resilience will be evident in the future.

SUGGESTED READING

America's World Role

Donaldson, Gary A. *America at War since 1945: Politics and Diplomacy in Korea, Vietnam, and the Gulf War*. Westport, Conn.: Praeger, 1996.

27. See J. E. Lovelock, *Gaia: A New Look at Life on Earth* (Oxford, England: Oxford University Press, 1979).

Marty, Martin E. *Under God, Indivisible: 1941–1960*. Vol. 3 of *Modern American Religion*. Chicago: University of Chicago Press, 1996.

Ramsey, Paul. *The Just War: Force and Political Responsibility*. Lanham, N.Y.: University Press of America, 1983.

Tucker, Robert W., and David C. Hendrickson. *The Imperial Temptation: The New World Order and America's Purpose*. New York: Council on Foreign Relations Press, 1992.

The Black American

Branch, Taylor. *Parting the Waters: America in the King Years, 1954–63*. New York: Simon & Schuster, 1988.

Lincoln, C. Eric. *The Black Muslims in America*. 3rd. ed. Grand Rapids, Mich.: Eerdmans Publishing Co., 1994.

Lincoln, C. Eric, and Lawrence H. Mamiya. *The Black Church in the African American Experience*. Durham, N.C.: Duke University Press, 1990.

Malcolm X (with Alex Haley). *The Autobiography of Malcolm X*. New York: Grove Press, 1964.

Raboteau, Albert J. *Slave Religion: The "Invisible Institution" in the Antebellum South*. New York: Oxford University Press, 1978.

National Morals

Bellah, Robert N., et al. *The Good Society*. New York: Knopf, 1991.

Diamond, Irene, and Gloria Feman Orenstein, eds. *Reweaving the World: The Emergence of Ecofeminism*. San Francisco: Sierra Club Books, 1990.

Keller, Rosemary Skinner. "Women and Religion." In *Encyclopedia of the American Religious Experience*, vol. 3, ed. Charles H. Lippy and Peter W. Williams. New York: Charles Scribner's Sons, 1988, pp. 1547–62.

Utter, Glenn H., and John W. Storey. *The Religious Right: A Reference Handbook*. Santa Barbara, Calif.: ABC-CLIO, 1995.

Wills, Garry. *Under God: Religion and American Politics*. New York: Simon & Schuster, 1990.

America's World Role

JOHN FOSTER DULLES

⊱⊰

Freedom's New Task

As we meet here at Independence Square, our thoughts inevitably turn to the world scene where freedom is at stake.

It is a moment of unusual significance. The Soviet rulers are reforming their lines. The Soviet 20th Congress, which adjourned last night, was busy revising the Soviet Communist creed. We cannot yet fully appraise what has happened. And, in any event, it takes time for doctrinal changes to get fully reflected in the mind and conduct of the party members.

But two things at least we know. One is that there is already a notable shift in Soviet foreign policy. And the other is that those Soviet policies which they change are being changed not because they succeeded, but because they have been thwarted by the free world.

Until recently, the foreign policy of Soviet communism was based on fanatical intolerance of all other systems and upon the organization of violence to overthrow all other systems. Marx, Lenin, and Stalin all taught that it was necessary to hate all who differed from the Soviet Communist creed; and they also taught that only by violence could international communism achieve its destined goals.

But the free nations, when confronted by this policy, grew more strong, more resolute and more united. Consequently the Soviet pattern of hatred and violence produced ever diminishing returns.

In Europe, the defensive strength of NATO, was rounded out by the addition of the Federal Republic of Germany.

In the western Pacific, freedom was consolidated by adding to our ANZUS, Philippine and Japanese treaties, the new mutual defense treaties with Korea and with the Republic of China. And the Congress, you will recall, authorized the President to use the Armed Forces of the United States in the Formosa area, if necessary, for its defense.

An address delivered to the Philadelphia Bulletin Forum, Philadelphia, Pennsylvania, February 26, 1956. From *Vital Speeches of the Day*, March 15, 1956, pp. 329–31.

In southeast Asia, the western powers joined with Asian powers in a treaty for collective security, and they transformed the Indochina struggle against colonialism to a struggle by truly independent nations—Vietnam, Laos, and Cambodia—to maintain their freedom.

In the Middle East, the northern tier concept, without challenging the concept of Arab unity, has drawn together for collective defense four nations which, for 2,500 miles, lie just south of Russia's frontiers.

Back of these formulations of free world resolve lay the vast mobile power of the United States which constituted a formidable deterrent to open armed aggression.

So the Soviets had either to give up their expansionist aims or turn to other means to advance them.

Lenin and Stalin had taught that, under these circumstances, there should be no giving up, but rather a shift to new methods.

So, last year, the Soviet rulers concluded that the time had come to change basically their approach to the non-Communist world.

II

In May of 1955, the Soviet rulers signed the Austrian State Treaty; they made their pilgrimage of repentance to Tito; they offered to establish diplomatic relations with Germany and to make a belated peace with Japan. In Asia, the Chinese Communists, at the Bandung Conference, gave at least lip service to methods other than outright violence.

The Soviet rulers trumpeted all this throughout the world as proof that Soviet Communist policy was no longer predatory.

We hoped that this was so. But we were highly skeptical. We well knew that under Leninism any tactic is admissible and that the change had come about, not through change of heart, but because old methods had failed.

On the other hand, we knew that the new Soviet tactics of increased tolerance and less dependence upon violence required a basic change in Soviet communist doctrine. This can, in the long run, have major internal consequences and set up within Russia powerful liberating trends.

But the fanatical teaching of a generation cannot be erased all at once. Also the change had not gone so far that there could not almost overnight be a sudden reversal to the old practice of intolerance and violence. Also we could only safely assume that the new tactics were designed as a new means of conquest. So we did not relax our vigilance or allow our military posture to slump.

But, on the other hand, we do not assume fatalistically that there can be no evolution within Russia or that Russia's rulers will always be predatory. Some day—I would not attempt to guess when—Russia will be governed by men who put the welfare of the Russian people above world conquest. It is our basic policy to seek to advance the coming of that day.

So last spring, when Soviet conduct began to change, we determined to do all that we safely could to make that change a first installment toward an eventual Russian state that would be a normal, not abnormal, member of the society of nations.

One major step we took was to join with Britain and France to invite the Russian rulers to a conference of heads of government. At that summit Conference at Geneva President Eisenhower did more than any other man could have done to open up to the Soviet rulers the vista of a new era of friendly relations between our countries.

We cannot yet measure what has been the full effect of that Conference. The gains will be measurable only in the future. For the time being the Soviet rulers, finding that the road of intolerance and violence was blocked, have subordinated those elements of their old creed in the hope that, in a new garb, they could still pursue conquest. Now they pursue their foreign-policy goals with less manifestation of intolerance and less emphasis on violence. Their foreign policy now puts large emphasis upon seeking political cooperation with left-wing Socialists, whom formerly they detested. Finally there is heavy emphasis on trade and economic assistance. It is this economic aspect of the Soviet "new look" that I would consider today.

III

This Soviet economic campaign is a varied one. It includes the barter of surplus arms into areas where tensions were already high. There are highly publicized purchases of agricultural commodities from a few countries where mounting surpluses have exposed the vulnerabilities of economies lacking in diversity. Incidentally the Soviet bloc, with typical cynicism, has re-exported some of these commodities to markets that the original sellers normally would supply. And the Soviet bloc has made loans to a selected number of countries.

This policy has been directed especially toward certain peoples in the Near East and South Asia. There the Soviet rulers believe that they can also exploit historic grievances for their own ends.

But the new Soviet policy roams far and wide. Even African and South American countries are receiving Soviet economic propositions.

What is the import of this new economic campaign of the Soviet bloc countries?

The first thing to note is that Soviet capital exports divert resources from the Soviet people who still lack many of the ordinary decencies of life. On this we have the testimony of Mr. Khrushchev in his recent speech to the Twentieth Communist Party Congress. There he stated:

"It must be said that we do not yet have an adequate quantity of consumer goods, that there is a shortage of housing, and that many of the important problems connected with raising the people's living standards have not yet been solved." Still quoting Mr. Khrushchev:

"Production of many important foodstuffs and manufactured goods still lags behind growing demands. Some towns and communities are still insufficiently supplied with such items as milk, butter, and fruit. There are even cases where supplies of potatoes and other vegetables are irregular. There are also difficulties in supplying the population with certain high-grade manufactured goods."

The Soviet Union, of course, has the capacity to do much to lift up the living standards of the Russian people, which Mr. Khrushchev described, and to give them opportunities for greater happiness. There was indeed a moment when it seemed that this might become the Soviet policy. Mr. Malenkov, as the Prime Minister who first succeeded Stalin, advocated more consumer goods and better quality goods for the Soviet people. But Mr. Malenkov was quickly removed from leadership, and his successors resumed the policy of forcing the Russian people to work primarily to build up the power machine of the state. The output of consumer goods—food, clothing, and housing—was firmly relegated to a secondary place.

Under these conditions, can we accept at face value the Soviet professions that its foreign economic activities are primarily designed to help others?

Actually in this campaign the Soviet Union is seeking to advance its interests.

It is important, therefore, to examine how the Soviet Union sees its interests.

IV

Throughout its 38 years of existence, the Soviet pattern has been unvarying. Whenever the opportunity has arisen the Soviet Union has swallowed up its neighbors, or made satellites of them, or subordinated them in other ways.

The future may well produce a different Russia. But today changes in creed and conduct are looked upon as ways to make it easier to achieve old goals of conquest. If there is less apparent intolerance and less reliance on violence, there is perhaps more reliance than ever on division, enticement, and duplicity.

On December 29, 1955, speaking to the Supreme Soviet, Mr. Khrushchev stated the fundamental precept: "If certain people think that our confidence in the victory of socialism, the teaching of Marxist-Leninism, is a violation of the Geneva spirit, they obviously have an incorrect notion of the Geneva spirit. They ought to remember once and for all that we never renounced and we will never renounce our ideas, our struggle for the victory of communism."

In his lengthy speech to the Twentieth Party Congress, Mr. Khrushchev promised "fundamental social transformations"—this means a Communist Party dictatorship—to any nation unwary enough to allow its political life to be undermined by the Communist apparatus.

We must assume that the intent behind the Soviet economic campaign is to subvert and communize the nations that are its targets.

V

The United States is engaged in programs of economic assistance to the less developed countries. Our programs have been in progress for a number of years and have totaled billions of dollars.

By these programs, we too hope to advance our legitimate national interests. We have never pretended otherwise.

But again the crucial question is: What are those interests and how are they intended to be served?

Our interests will be fully served if other nations maintain their independence and strengthen their free institutions. We have no further aims than these. We want a world environment of freedom. We have shown this time after time by electing to give freedom where we could have had conquest. Our historic policy, reflecting the will and the views of our own free people, is wholly compatible with the interests of the less-developed countries as their leaders themselves have defined them.

VI

The political leaders in the economically less-developed countries are entirely capable of judging the purposes and principles of other nations. They are, for the most part, men of political experience. In many cases they have had an active part in winning for their countries political independence. They have no desire to preside over the loss of that independence.

The wisdom and patriotism of the political leaders of the newly independent nations are among freedom's greatest assets. These men are not blind to Soviet purposes and past actions.

But we must also recognize that the Soviet Communist experiment has won for itself a considerable popular prestige in the less-developed countries. In these countries "industrialization" is a word of magic. It is a slogan that the people have come to believe will solve all domestic economic and political problems. The peoples of these countries do not like to be dependent upon the industrialized West for manufactured goods. For the most part, they now have political independence, but they do not yet have what they consider to be adequate economic independence.

The neighboring Asian peoples have seen the Soviet Union within a generation develop itself into a major industrial power. These observers are but dimly aware of the fact that the Soviet rate of progress was possible only because natural conditions favored, and that even so its cost in human servitude has been tragically high. They are like those of us who admire the pyramids, the palaces, the temples, and the coliseums which despotic rulers once produced out of slave labor. We are only dimly conscious of the cost in terms of human misery.

So it is with the peoples of less-developed lands who are informed in extravagant terms of the industrial monuments which have been built by the Soviet masters of 220 million subject peoples.

And when Soviet propaganda says to less-developed peoples, "See what we have done for ourselves; with our help, you can do the same," there is a strong temptation to accept that so-called help.

The political leaders of these countries, however wise they may be and however patriotic they may be, will find it difficult to resist the public pressures which Soviet propaganda arouses, unless there is some alternative.

The industrial nations of the West, with matured and vigorous economies and much well-being, can and must provide such an alternative.

VII

Western efforts to advance the economic well-being of the less-developed countries are nothing new. We need not be panicked by the new Soviet economic policy.

With or without the so-called competition of the Soviet Union, we propose to go forward with sound policies to aid the economic progress of less developed countries.

Normally, under our system, private capital could and should do the job. And, indeed, much private capital today flows into many less-developed countries. But it flows only where the political and economic risks are deemed tolerable. In much of the world, these risks are such that private capital is not ready to take them. If capital is to be found, a substantial part must be provided on a public basis which spreads the risk so that it is not appreciable in terms of any single individual.

This is one of the purposes of our mutual security program which now, in one form or another, is in its eighth year. The economic part of that program amounts this year (ending June 30) to about $1,700,000,000. Much of this is used to help our allies, particularly in the Far East and in Asia, to support adequate military establishments of their own. Of the total, approximately $600 million will assist, by loan or grant in capital developments in other lands.

This year we are asking Congress to appropriate for next year's economic program $100 million more than is available for this year. The capacity to spend wisely depends on many factors, and we should not appropriate, in a panic, merely because of Soviet economic activities. There is, however, need for somewhat greater flexibility, and for greater continuity, as regards support for long-range projects.

Some of the development projects which are most significant will take several years to complete. It is difficult for the countries concerned to arrange for financing these projects unless United States support can be relied upon not just for one year at a time, but for several years. Also, with United States support, it is easier for them to procure funds from other sources, such as the World Bank.

We believe, therefore, that the United States Government should have authority to commit some such amount as $100 million a year for several years for long-range projects which will develop to an important degree the economic strength of less-developed countries. Without that limited, long-range authority we take a risk which is quite unjustified having regard to the relatively small cost of avoiding it.

VIII

If our Nation and the other free nations play their proper part, we can face the future not with complacency—that would be disastrous—but with confidence.

I do not wish to minimize the threat of the Soviet "new look," of which the economic campaign is a part. Economic assistance knows no territorial limits. And we must count on the Soviets and their local Communist parties to press their policies with vigor.

But we should reflect that Communist successes in the world so far have come when Red armies were at hand. No people has willingly accepted the Soviet type of Communist dictatorship.

Communist open aggression has now been checked by the cohesion, resolution, vigilance, and strength of the free nations. Let us never forget that this is what deflected the Soviet rulers from primary reliance upon violence to which they were dedicated by creed and which they are skilled to practice.

They came up against the granite of a declared and strong resolve. If that granite should turn to putty, then violence and threat of war could again become the order of the day.

Meanwhile, we have new problems. These will require new efforts; without relaxation of the old cohesion, resolution, vigilance, and strength. But the new efforts will be of a kind that is in accord with our tradition. This Nation was conceived with a sense of mission and dedicated to the extension of freedom throughout the world. President Lincoln, speaking at this very Independence Hall, said of our Declaration of Independence, that there was "something in that Declaration giving liberty, not alone to the people of this country, but hope for the world for all future time. It was that which gave promise that in due time the weights should be lifted from the shoulders of all men and that all men should have an equal chance."

That has been the spirit which has animated our people since they came together as a nation. We have, it is true, acquired much for ourselves. But also we have had in large measure the greatest of all satisfactions—that is the situation which comes from creating and from sharing.

We have created at home and we have also created abroad. We have shared here at home and we have shared abroad. Today the greatest opportunity for creation and for sharing lies in those areas which, possessed of great economic and human potentials, have not yet realized the opportunities which are theirs.

We have unprecedented resources with which to create and with which to share. Our 160 million people, working in freedom and with ample leisure, produce over three times as much as do the 220 million of the Soviet Union working in servitude. Our industrial techniques are beyond compare. Our desire to create and to share with others is not a political plot; it is an expression of the spirit which has long animated our Nation. It is not a product of Government; it is a product of the faith of our people.

Let me conclude with words which Benjamin Franklin wrote from Paris on May 1, 1777:

> "It is a common observation here that our cause is the cause of all mankind, and that we are fighting for their liberty in defending our own. It is a glorious task assigned us by Providence; which has, I trust, given us spirit and virtue equal to it, and will at last crown it with success."

J. WILLIAM FULBRIGHT

The Arrogance of Power

America is the most fortunate of nations—fortunate in her rich territory, fortunate in having had a century of relative peace in which to develop that territory, fortunate in her diverse and talented population, fortunate in the institutions devised by the founding fathers and in the wisdom of those who have adapted those institutions to a changing world.

For the most part America has made good use of her blessings, especially in her internal life but also in her foreign relations. Having done so much and succeeded so well, America is now at that historical point at which a great nation is in danger of losing its perspective on what exactly is within the realm of its power and what is beyond it. Other great nations, reaching this critical juncture, have aspired to too much, and by overextension of effort have declined and then fallen.

The causes of the malady are not entirely clear but its recurrence is one of the uniformities of history: power tends to confuse itself with virtue and a great nation is peculiarly susceptible to the idea that its power is a sign of God's favor, conferring upon it a special responsibility for other nations—to make them richer and happier and wiser, to remake them, that is, in its own shining image. Power confuses itself with virtue and tends also to take itself for omnipotence. Once imbued with the idea of a mission, a great nation easily assumes that it has the means as well as the duty to do God's work. The Lord, after all, surely would not choose you as His agent and then deny you the sword with which to work His will. German soldiers in the First World War wore belt buckles imprinted with the words "*Gott mit uns*." It was approximately under this kind of infatuation—an exaggerated sense of power and an imaginary sense of mission—that the Athenians attacked Syracuse, and Napoleon and then Hitler invaded Russia. In plain words, they overextended their commitments and they came to grief.

I do not think for a moment that America, with her deeply rooted democratic traditions, is likely to embark upon a campaign to dominate the world in the manner of a Hitler or Napoleon. What I do fear is that she may be drifting into commitments which, though generous and benevolent in intent, are so far-reaching as to exceed even America's great capacities. At the same time, it is my hope—and I emphasize it because it underlies all of the criticisms and proposals to be made in these pages—that America will escape those fatal temptations of power which have ruined other great nations and will instead confine herself to doing only that good in the world which she *can* do, both by direct effort and by the force of her own example.

The stakes are high indeed: they include not only America's continued greatness but nothing less than the survival of the human race in an era when, for the first time in human history, a living generation has the power of veto over the survival of the next.

The Power Drive of Nations

When the abstractions and subtleties of political science have been exhausted, there remain the most basic unanswered questions about war and peace and why nations contest the issues they contest and why they even care about them. As Aldous Huxley has written:

> There may be arguments about the best way of raising wheat in a cold climate or of re-afforesting a denuded mountain. But such arguments never lead to organized slaughter. Organized slaughter is the result of arguments about such questions as the following: Which is the best nation? The best religion? The best political theory? The best form of government? Why are other people so stupid and wicked? Why can't they see how good and intelligent we are? Why do they resist our beneficent efforts to bring them under our control and make them like ourselves?[1]

Many of the wars fought by man—I am tempted to say most—have been fought over such abstractions. The more I puzzle over the great wars of history, the more I am inclined to the view that the causes attributed to them— territory, markets, resources, the defense or perpetuation of great principles— were not the root causes at all but rather explanations or excuses for certain unfathomable drives of human nature. For lack of a clear and precise understanding of exactly what these motives are, I refer to them as the "arrogance of power"—as a psychological need that nations seem to have in order to prove that they are bigger, better, or stronger than other nations. Implicit in

---

1. Aldous Huxley, "The Politics of Ecology" (Santa Barbara: Center for the Study of Democratic Institutions, 1963), p. 6.

this drive is the assumption, even on the part of normally peaceful nations, that force is the ultimate proof of superiority—that when a nation shows that it has the strongest army, it is also proving that it has better people, better institutions, better principles, and, in general, a better civilization.

Evidence for my proposition is found in the remarkable discrepancy between the apparent and hidden causes of some modern wars and the discrepancy between their causes and ultimate consequences.

The precipitating cause of the Franco-Prussian War of 1870, for example, was a dispute over the succession to the Spanish throne, and the ostensible "underlying" cause was French resistance to the unification of Germany. The war was followed by the completion of German unification—which probably could have been achieved without war—but it was also followed by the loss of Alsace-Lorraine, the humiliation of France, and the emergence of Germany as the greatest power in Europe, which could not have been achieved without war. The peace treaty, incidentally, said nothing about the Spanish throne, which everyone apparently had forgotten. One wonders to what extent the Germans were motivated simply by the desire to cut those haughty Frenchmen down to size and have a good excuse to build another monument in Berlin.

The United States went to war in 1898 for the stated purpose of liberating Cuba from Spanish tyranny, but after winning the war—a war which Spain had been willing to pay a high price to avoid—the United States brought the liberated Cubans under an American protectorate and incidentally annexed the Philippines, because, according to President McKinley, the Lord told him it was America's duty "to educate the Filipinos, and uplift and civilize and Christianize them, and by God's grace do the very best we could by them, as our fellowmen for whom Christ also died."[2]

Isn't it interesting that the voice was the voice of the Lord but the words were those of Theodore Roosevelt, Henry Cabot Lodge, and Admiral Mahan, those "imperialists of 1898" who wanted America to have an empire just because a big, powerful country like the United States *ought* to have an empire? The spirit of the times was expressed by Albert Beveridge, soon thereafter to be elected to the United States Senate, who proclaimed Americans to be "a conquering race": "We must obey our blood and occupy new markets and if necessary new lands," he said, because "In the Almighty's infinite plan . . . debased civilizations and decaying races" must disappear "before the higher civilization of the nobler and more virile types of man."[3]

In 1914 all Europe went to war, ostensibly because the heir to the Austrian throne had been assassinated at Sarajevo, but really because that murder be-

---

2. Quoted in Samuel Flagg Bemis, *A Diplomatic History of the United States* (New York: Holt, Rinehart & Winston, Inc., 1955), p. 472.

3. Quoted in Barbara Tuchman, *The Proud Tower* (New York: The Macmillan Company, 1966), p. 153.

came the symbolic focus of the incredibly delicate sensibilities of the great nations of Europe. The events of the summer of 1914 were a melodrama of abnormal psychology: Austria had to humiliate Serbia in order not to be humiliated herself, but Austria' effort at recovering self-esteem was profoundly humiliating to Russia; Russia was allied to France, who had been feeling generally humiliated since 1871, and Austria in turn was allied to Germany, whose pride required that she support Austria no matter how insanely Austria behaved and who may in any case have felt that it would be fun to give the German Army another swing down the Champs-Élysées. For these ennobling reasons the world was plunged into a war which took tens of millions of lives, precipitated the Russian Revolution, and set in motion the events that led to another world war, a war which took tens of millions more lives and precipitated the worldwide revolutions of our time, revolutions whose consequences are beyond the foresight of any of us now alive.

The causes and consequences of war may have more to do with pathology than with politics, more to do with irrational pressures of pride and pain than with rational calculations of advantage and profit. There is a Washington story, perhaps apocryphal, that the military intellectuals in the Pentagon conducted an experiment in which they fed data derived from the events of the summer of 1914 into a computer and that, after weighing and digesting the evidence, the machine assured its users that there was no danger of war. What this "proves," if anything, is that computers are more rational than men; it also suggests that if there is a root cause of human conflict and of the power drive of nations, it lies not in economic aspirations, historical forces, or the workings of the balance of power, but in the ordinary hopes and fears of the human mind.

It has been said that buried in every woman's secret soul is a drum majorette; it might also be said that in all of our souls there is a bit of the missionary. We all like telling people what to do, which is perfectly all right except that most people do not like being told what to do. I have given my wife some splendid suggestions on household management but she has been so consistently ungrateful for my advice that I have stopped offering it. The phenomenon is explained by the Canadian psychiatrist and former Director-General of the World Health Organization, Brock Chisholm, who writes:

> . . . Man's method of dealing with difficulties in the past has always been to tell everyone else how they should behave. We've all been doing that for centuries.
>
> It should be clear by now that this no longer does any good. Everybody has by now been told by everybody else how he should behave. . . . The criticism is not effective; it never has been, and it never is going to be. . . .[4]

4. Brock Chisholm, *Prescription for Survival* (New York: Columbia University Press, 1957), p. 54.

Ineffective though it has been, the giving—and enforcement—of all this unsolicited advice has at least until recently been compatible with the survival of the human race. Man is now, however, for the first time, in a situation in which the survival of his species is in jeopardy. Other forms of life have been endangered and many destroyed by changes in their natural environment; man is menaced by a change of environment which he himself has wrought by the invention of nuclear weapons and ballistic missiles. Our power to kill has become universal, creating a radically new situation which, if we are to survive, requires us to adopt some radically new attitudes about the giving and enforcement of advice and in general about human and international relations.

The enormity of the danger of extinction of our species is dulled by the frequency with which it is stated, as if a familiar threat of catastrophe were no threat at all. We seem to feel somehow that because the hydrogen bomb has not killed us yet, it is never going to kill us. This is a dangerous assumption because it encourages the retention of traditional attitudes about world politics when our responsibility, in Dr. Chisholm's words, is nothing less than "to re-examine all of the attitudes of our ancestors and to select from those attitudes things which we, on our own authority in these present circumstances, with our knowledge, recognize as still valid in this new kind of world. . . ."[5]

The attitude above all others which I feel sure is no longer valid is the arrogance of power, the tendency of great nations to equate power with virtue and major responsibilities with a universal mission. The dilemmas involved are pre-eminently American dilemmas, not because America has weaknesses that others do not have but because America is powerful as no nation has ever been before, and the discrepancy between her power and the power of others appears to be increasing. One may hope that America, with her vast resources and democratic traditions, with her diverse and creative populations, will find the wisdom to match her power; but one can hardly be confident because the wisdom required is greater wisdom than any great nation has ever shown before. It must be rooted, as Dr. Chisholm says, in the re-examination of "all of the attitudes of our ancestors."

It is a tall order. Perhaps one can begin to fill it by an attempt to assess the attitudes of Americans toward other peoples and some of the effects of America's power on small countries whom she has tried to help.

Innocents Abroad

There are signs of the arrogance of power in the way Americans act when they go to foreign countries. Foreigners frequently comment on the contrast

5. Ibid., p. 9.

between the behavior of Americans at home and abroad: in our own country, they say, we are hospitable and considerate, but as soon as we get outside our own borders something seems to get into us and wherever we are we become noisy and demanding and we strut around as if we owned the place. The British used to say during the war that the trouble with the Yanks was that they were "overpaid, oversexed, and over here." During a recent vacation in Mexico, I noticed in a small-town airport two groups of students on holiday, one group Japanese, the other American. The Japanese were neatly dressed and were talking and laughing in a manner that neither annoyed anybody nor particularly called attention to themselves. The Americans, on the other hand, were disporting themselves in a conspicuous and offensive manner, stamping around the waiting room in sloppy clothes, drinking beer, and shouting to each other as if no one else were there.

This kind of scene, unfortunately, has become familiar in many parts of the world. I do not wish to exaggerate its significance, but I have the feeling that just as there was once something special about being a Roman or a Spaniard or an Englishman, there is now something about the consciousness of being an American abroad, something about the consciousness of belonging to the biggest, richest country in the world, that encourages people who are perfectly well behaved at home to become boorish when they are in somebody else's country and to treat the local citizens as if they were not really there.

One reason Americans abroad may act as though they "own the place" is that in many places they very nearly do: American companies may dominate large segments of a country's economy; American products are advertised on billboards and displayed in shop windows; American hotels and snack bars are available to protect American tourists from foreign influence; American soldiers may be stationed in the country, and even if they are not, the population are probably well aware that their very survival depends on the wisdom with which America uses her immense military power.

I think that when any American goes abroad, he carries an unconscious knowledge of all this power with him and it affects his behavior, just as it once affected the behavior of Greeks and Romans, of Spaniards, Germans, and Englishmen, in the brief high noons of their respective ascendancies. It was the arrogance of their power that led nineteenth-century Englishmen to suppose that if they shouted at a foreigner loud enough in English he was bound to understand, or that now leads Americans to behave like Mark Twain's "innocents abroad," who reported on their travels in Europe that

> The people of those foreign countries are very, very ignorant. They looked curiously at the costumes we had brought from the wilds of America. They observed that we talked loudly at table sometimes. . . . In Paris they just simply opened their eyes and stared when we spoke to

them in French! We never did succeed in making these idiots understand their own language.[6]

The Fatal Impact

Reflecting on his voyages to Polynesia in the late eighteenth century, Captain Cook later wrote that "It would have been better for these people never to have known us." In a book on European explorations of the South Pacific, Alan Moorehead relates how the Tahitians and the Australian aborigines were corrupted by the white man's diseases, alcohol, firearms, laws, and concepts of morality, by what Moorehead calls "the long downslide into Western civilization." The first missionaries to Tahiti, says Moorehead, were "determined to recreate the island in the image of lower-middle-class Protestant England. . . . They kept hammering away at the Tahitian way of life until it crumbled before them, and within two decades they had achieved precisely what they set out to do."[7] It is said that the first missionaries to Hawaii went for the purpose of explaining to the Polynesians that it was sinful to work on Sunday, only to discover that in those bountiful islands nobody worked on any day.

Even when acting with the best of intentions, Americans, like other Western peoples who have carried their civilizations abroad, have had something of the same "fatal impact" on smaller nations that European explorers had on the Tahitians and the native Australians. We have not harmed people because we wished to; on the contrary, more often than not we have wanted to help people and, in some very important respects, we have helped them. Americans have brought medicine and education, manufactures and modern techniques to many places in the world; but they have also brought themselves and the condescending attitudes of a people whose very success breeds disdain for other cultures. Bringing power without understanding, Americans as well as Europeans have had a devastating effect in less advanced areas of the world; without knowing they were doing it, they have shattered traditional societies, disrupted fragile economies and undermined peoples' self-confidence by the invidious example of their own power and efficiency. They have done this in many instances simply by being big and strong, by giving good advice, by intruding on people who have not wanted them but could not resist them.

The missionary instinct seems to run deep in human nature, and the bigger and stronger and richer we are, the more we feel suited to the missionary task, the more indeed we consider it our duty. Dr. Chisholm relates the story of an

---

6. Mark Twain, *The Innocents Abroad* (New York: The Thistle Press, 1962), p. 494.

7. Alan Moorehead, *The Fatal Impact* (New York: Harper & Row, Publishers, 1966), pp. 61, 80–81.

eminent cleric who had been proselyting the Eskimos and said: "You know, for years we couldn't do anything with those Eskimos at all; they didn't have any sin. We had to teach them sin for years before we could do anything with them."[8] I am reminded of the three Boy Scouts who reported to their scoutmaster that as their good deed for the day they had helped an old lady to cross the street.

"That's fine," said the scoutmaster, "but why did it take three of you?"

"Well," they explained, "she didn't want to go."

The good deed above all others that Americans feel qualified to perform is the teaching of democracy. Let us consider the results of some American good deeds in various parts of the world.

Over the years since President Monroe proclaimed his doctrine, Latin Americans have had the advantages of United States tutelage in fiscal responsibility, in collective security, and in the techniques of democracy. If they have fallen short in any of these fields, the thought presents itself that the fault may lie as much with the teacher as with the pupils.

When President Theodore Roosevelt announced his "corollary" to the Monroe Doctrine in 1905, he solemnly declared that he regarded the future interventions thus sanctified as a "burden" and a "responsibility" and an obligation to "international equity." Not once, so far as I know, has the United States regarded itself as intervening in a Latin American country for selfish or unworthy motives—a view not necessarily shared, however, by the beneficiaries. Whatever reassurance the purity of our motives may give must be shaken a little by the thought that probably no country in human history has ever intervened in another except for motives it regarded as excellent.

For all our noble intentions, the countries which have had most of the tutelage in democracy by United States Marines have not been particularly democratic. These include Haiti, which is under a brutal and superstitious dictatorship; the Dominican Republic, which languished under the brutal Trujillo dictatorship for thirty years and whose second elected government since the overthrow of Trujillo is threatened, like the first, by the power of a military oligarchy; and of course Cuba, which, as no one needs to be reminded, has replaced its traditional right-wing dictatorships with a communist dictatorship.

Maybe, in the light of this extraordinary record of accomplishment, it is time for us to reconsider our teaching methods. Maybe we are not really cut out for the job of spreading the gospel of democracy. Maybe it would profit us to concentrate on our own democracy instead of trying to inflict our particular version of it on all those ungrateful Latin Americans who stubbornly oppose their North American benefactors instead of the "real" enemies whom we have so graciously chosen for them. And maybe—just maybe—if we left

8. Chisholm, *Prescription*, pp. 55–56.

our neighbors to make their own judgments and their own mistakes, and confined our assistance to matters of economics and technology instead of philosophy, maybe then they would begin to find the democracy and the dignity that have largely eluded them, and we in turn might begin to find the love and gratitude that we seem to crave.

Korea is another example. We went to war in 1950 to defend South Korea against the Russian-inspired aggression of North Korea. I think that American intervention was justified and necessary; we were defending a country that clearly wanted to be defended, whose army was willing to fight and fought well, and whose government, though dictatorial, was patriotic and commanded the support of the people. Throughout the war, however, the United States emphasized as one of its war aims the survival of the Republic of Korea as a "free society," something which it was not then and is not now. We lost 33,529 American lives in that war and have since spent $5.61 billion on direct military and economic aid and a great deal more on indirect aid to South Korea. The country, nonetheless, remained until recently in a condition of virtual economic stagnation and political instability. Only now is economic progress being made, but the truly surprising fact is that having fought a war for three years to defend the freedom of South Korea, most Americans quickly lost interest in the state of the ward for whom they had sacrificed so much. It is doubtful that more than a handful of Americans now know or care whether South Korea is a "free society."

We are engaged in a war to "defend freedom" in South Vietnam. Unlike the Republic of Korea, South Vietnam has an army which fights without notable success and a weak, dictatorial government which does not command the loyalty of the South Vietnamese people. The official war aims of the United States government, as I understand them, are to defeat what is regarded as North Vietnamese aggression, to demonstrate the futility of what the communists call "wars of national liberation," and to create conditions under which the South Vietnamese people will be able freely to determine their own future.

I have not the slightest doubt of the sincerity of the President and the Vice-President and the Secretaries of State and Defense in propounding these aims. What I do doubt, and doubt very much, is the ability of the United States to achieve these aims by the means being used. I do not question the power of our weapons and the efficiency of our logistics; I cannot say these things delight me as they seem to delight some of our officials, but they are certainly impressive. What I do question is the ability of the United States or any other Western nation to go into a small, alien, undeveloped Asian nation and create stability where there is chaos, the will to fight where there is defeatism, democracy where there is no tradition of it, and honest government where corruption is almost a way of life.

In the spring of 1966 demonstrators in Saigon burned American jeeps, tried to assault American soldiers, and marched through the streets shouting "Down with American imperialists," while a Buddhist leader made a speech equating the United States with the communists as a threat to South Vietnamese independence. Most Americans are understandably shocked and angered to encounter expressions of hostility from people who would long since have been under the rule of the Viet Cong but for the sacrifice of American lives and money. Why, we may ask, are they so shockingly ungrateful? Surely they must know that their very right to parade and protest and demonstrate depends on the Americans who are defending them.

The answer, I think, is that "fatal impact" of the rich and strong on the poor and weak. Dependent on it though the Vietnamese are, American strength is a reproach to their weakness, American wealth a mockery of their poverty, American success a reminder of their failures. What they resent is the disruptive effect of our strong culture upon their fragile one, an effect which we can no more avoid having than a man can help being bigger than a child. What they fear, I think rightly, is that traditional Vietnamese society cannot survive the American economic and cultural impact.

The evidence of that "fatal impact" is seen in the daily life of Saigon. A *New York Times* correspondent reported—and his information matches that of other observers on the scene—that many Vietnamese find it necessary to put their wives or daughters to work as bar girls or to peddle them to American soldiers as mistresses; that it is not unusual to hear a report that a Vietnamese soldier has committed suicide out of shame because his wife has been working as a bar girl; that Vietnamese have trouble getting taxicabs because drivers will not stop for them, preferring to pick up American soldiers who will pay outrageous fares without complaint; that as a result of the American influx bar girls, prostitutes, pimps, bar owners, and taxi drivers have risen to the higher levels of the economic pyramid; that middle-class Vietnamese families have difficulty renting homes because Americans have driven the rents beyond their reach, and some Vietnamese families have actually been evicted from houses and apartments by landlords who prefer to rent to the affluent Americans; that Vietnamese civil servants, junior army officers, and enlisted men are unable to support their families because of the inflation generated by American spending and the purchasing power of the G.I.'s. One Vietnamese explained to the *New York Times* reporter that "Any time legions of prosperous white men descend on a rudimentary Asian society, you are bound to have trouble." Another said: "We Vietnamese are somewhat xenophobe. We don't like foreigners, any kind of foreigners, so that you shouldn't be surprised that we don't like you."[9]

Sincere though it is, the American effort to build the foundations of freedom in South Vietnam is thus having an effect quite different from the one

9. Neil Sheehan, "Anti-Americanism Grows in Vietnam," *New York Times*, Apr. 24, 1966, p. 3.

intended. "All this struggling and striving to make the world better is a great mistake," said George Bernard Shaw, "not because it isn't a good thing to improve the world if you know how to do it, but because striving and struggling is the worst way you could set about doing anything."[10]

One wonders how much the American commitment to Vietnamese freedom is also a commitment to American pride—the two seem to have become part of the same package. When we talk about the freedom of South Vietnam, we may be thinking about how disagreeable it would be to accept a solution short of victory; we may be thinking about how our pride would be injured if we settled for less than we set out to achieve; we may be thinking about our reputation as a great power, fearing that a compromise settlement would shame us before the world, marking us as a second-rate people with flagging courage and determination.

Such fears are as nonsensical as their opposite, the presumption of a universal mission. They are simply unworthy of the richest, most powerful, most productive, and best educated people in the world. One can understand an uncompromising attitude on the part of such countries as China or France: both have been struck low in this century and a certain amount of arrogance may be helpful to them in recovering their pride. It is much less comprehensible on the part of the United States—a nation whose modern history has been an almost uninterrupted chronicle of success, a nation which by now should be so sure of its own power as to be capable of magnanimity, a nation which by now should be able to act on the proposition that, as George Kennan said, "there is more respect to be won in the opinion of the world by a resolute and courageous liquidation of unsound positions than in the most stubborn pursuit of extravagant or unpromising objectives."[11]

The cause of our difficulties in Southeast Asia is not a deficiency of power but an excess of the wrong kind of power, which results in a feeling of impotence when it fails to achieve its desired ends. We are still acting like Boy Scouts dragging reluctant old ladies across streets they do not want to cross. We are trying to remake Vietnamese society, a task which certainly cannot be accomplished by force and which probably cannot be accomplished by any means available to outsiders. The objective may be desirable, but it is not feasible. As Shaw said: "Religion is a great force—the only real motive force in the world; but what you fellows don't understand is that you must get a man through his own religion and not through yours."[12]

With the best intentions in the world the United States has involved itself

10. George Bernard Shaw, *Cashel Byron's Profession* (1886), chap. 5.

11. George F. Kennan, "Supplemental Foreign Assistance Fiscal Year 1966—Vietnam," *Hearings Before the Committee on Foreign Relations*, U.S. Senate, 89th Cong., 2nd sess. on S. 2793, Part I (Washington, D.C.: Government Printing Office, 1966), p. 335.

12. George Bernard Shaw, *Getting Married* (1911).

deeply in the affairs of developing nations in Asia and Latin America, practicing what has been called a kind of "welfare imperialism." Our honest purpose is the advancement of development and democracy, to which end it has been thought necessary to destroy ancient and unproductive modes of life. In this latter function we have been successful, perhaps more successful than we know. Bringing skills and knowledge, money and resources in amounts hitherto unknown in traditional societies, the Americans have overcome indigenous groups and interests and become the dominant force in a number of countries. Far from being bumbling, wasteful, and incompetent, as critics have charged, American government officials, technicians, and economists have been strikingly successful in breaking down the barriers to change in ancient but fragile cultures.

Here, however, our success ends. Traditional rulers, institutions, and ways of life have crumbled under the fatal impact of American wealth and power but they have not been replaced by new institutions and new ways of life, nor has their breakdown ushered in an era of democracy and development. It has rather ushered in an era of disorder and demoralization because in the course of destroying old ways of doing things, we have also destroyed the self-confidence and self-reliance without which no society can build indigenous institutions. Inspiring as we have such great awe of our efficiency and wealth, we have reduced some of the intended beneficiaries of our generosity to a condition of dependency and self-denigration. We have done this for the most part inadvertently: with every good intention we have intruded on fragile societies, and our intrusion, though successful in uprooting traditional ways of life, has been strikingly unsuccessful in implanting the democracy and advancing the development which are the honest aims of our "welfare imperialism."

American Empire or American Example?

Despite its dangerous and unproductive consequences, the idea of being responsible for the whole world seems to be flattering to Americans and I am afraid it is turning our heads, just as the sense of universal responsibility turned the heads of ancient Romans and nineteenth-century British.

In 1965 Henry Fairlie, a British political writer for *The Spectator* and *The Daily Telegraph*, wrote what he called "A Cheer for American Imperialism."[13] An empire, he said, "has no justification except its own existence." It must never contract; it "wastes treasure and life"; its commitments "are without rhyme or reason." Nonetheless, according to Fairlie, the "American empire" is uniquely benevolent, devoted as it is to individual liberty and the rule of

---

13. *The New York Times Magazine*, July 11, 1965.

law, and having performed such services as getting the author released from a Yugoslav jail simply by his threatening to involve the American Consul, a service which he describes as "sublime."

What romantic nonsense this is. And what dangerous nonsense in the age of nuclear weapons. The idea of an "American empire" might be dismissed as the arrant imagining of a British Gunga Din except that it surely strikes a responsive chord in at least a corner of the usually sensible and humane American mind. It calls to mind the slogans of the past about "manifest destiny" and "making the world safe for democracy," and the demand for "unconditional surrender" in World War II. It calls to mind President McKinley taking counsel with the Supreme Being about his duty to the benighted Filipinos.

The "Blessings-of-Civilization Trust," as Mark Twain called it, may have been a "Daisy" in its day, uplifting for the soul and good for business besides, but its day is past. It is past because the great majority of the human race is demanding dignity and independence, not the honor of a supine role in an American empire. It is past because whatever claim America may make for the universal domain of her ideas and values is balanced by the communist counter-claim, armed like our own with nuclear weapons. And, most of all, it is past because it never should have begun, because we are not God's chosen saviour of mankind, but only one of mankind's more successful and fortunate branches, endowed by our Creator with about the same capacity for good and evil, no more or less, than the rest of humanity.

An excessive preoccupation with foreign relations over a long period of time is more than a manifestation of arrogance; it is a drain on the power that gave rise to it, because it diverts a nation from the sources of its strength, which are in its domestic life. A nation immersed in foreign affairs is expending its capital, human as well as material; sooner or later that capital must be renewed by some diversion of creative energies from foreign to domestic pursuits. I would doubt that any nation has achieved a durable greatness by conducting a "strong" foreign policy, but many have been ruined by expending their energies in foreign adventures while allowing their domestic bases to deteriorate. The United States emerged as a world power in the twentieth century, not because of what it had done in foreign relations but because it had spent the nineteenth century developing the North American continent; by contrast, the Austrian and Turkish empires collapsed in the twentieth century in large part because they had so long neglected their internal development and organization.

If America has a service to perform in the world—and I believe she has—it is in large part the service of her own example. In our excessive involvement in the affairs of other countries we are not only living off our assets and denying our own people the proper enjoyment of their resources, we are also denying the world the example of a free society enjoying its freedom to the fullest. This is regrettable indeed for a nation that aspires to teach democracy to other nations, because, as Edmund Burke said, "Example is the school of mankind, and they will learn at no other."[14,15]

The missionary instinct in foreign affairs may, in a cautious way, reflect a deficiency rather than an excess of national self-confidence. In America's case the evidence of a lack of self-confidence is our apparent need for constant proof and reassurance, our nagging desire for popularity, our bitterness and confusion when foreigners fail to appreciate our generosity and good intentions. Lacking an appreciation of the dimensions of our own power, we fail to understand our enormous and disruptive impact on the world; we fail to understand that no matter how good our intentions — and they are, in most cases, decent enough — other nations are alarmed by the very existence of such great power, which, whatever its benevolence, cannot help but remind them of their own helplessness before it.

Those who lack self-assurance are also likely to lack magnanimity, because the one is the condition of the other. Only a nation at peace with itself, with its transgressions as well as its achievements, is capable of a generous understanding of others. Only when we Americans can acknowledge our own past aggressive behavior — in such instances, for example, as the Indian wars and the wars against Mexico and Spain — will we acquire some perspective on the aggressive behavior of others; only when we can understand the human implications of the chasm between American affluence and the poverty of most of the rest of mankind will we be able to understand why the American "way of life" which is so dear to us has few lessons and limited appeal to the poverty-stricken majority of the human race.

It is a curiosity of human nature that lack of self-assurance seems to breed an exaggerated sense of power and mission. When a nation is very powerful but lacking in self-confidence, it is likely to behave in a manner dangerous to itself and to others. Feeling the need to prove what is obvious to everyone else, it begins to confuse great power with unlimited power and great responsibility with total responsibility: it can admit of no error; it must win every argument, no matter how trivial. For lack of an appreciation of how truly powerful it is, the nation begins to lose wisdom and perspective and, with them, the strength and understanding that it takes to be magnanimous to smaller and weaker nations.

14. Edmund Burke, "On a Regicide Peace" (1796).

15. The services America can perform in the world — other than that of her own example — are discussed in Chapter 11. [In that chapter, Fulbright proposes a foreign aid program to replace bilateral foreign aid and its philanthropic orientation. Economic aid would be "conducted as a community enterprise, that is, through such international channels as the United Nations, the International Development Association of the World Bank, and the regional development banks." — Editor]

Gradually but unmistakably America is showing signs of that arrogance of power which has afflicted, weakened, and in some cases destroyed great nations in the past. In so doing we are not living up to our capacity and promise as a civilized example for the world. The measure of our falling short is the measure of the patriot's duty of dissent.

The Black American

MARTIN LUTHER KING, JR.

Letter from Birmingham Jail

April 16, 1963

My Dear Fellow Clergymen:

While confined here in the Birmingham city jail, I came across your recent statement calling my present activities "unwise and untimely." Seldom do I pause to answer criticism of my work and ideas. If I sought to answer all the criticisms that cross my desk, my secretaries would have little time for anything other than such correspondence in the course of the day, and I would have no time for constructive work. But since I feel that you are men of genuine good will and that your criticisms are sincerely set forth, I want to try to answer your statement in what I hope will be patient and reasonable terms.

I think I should indicate why I am here in Birmingham, since you have been influenced by the view which argues against "outsiders coming in." I have the honor of serving as president of the Southern Christian Leadership Conference, an organization operating in every southern state, with headquarters in Atlanta, Georgia. We have some eighty-five affiliated organizations across the South, and one of them is the Alabama Christian Movement for Human Rights. Frequently we share staff, educational and financial resources with our affiliates. Several months ago the affiliate here in Birmingham asked us to be on call to engage in a nonviolent direct-action program if such were deemed

AUTHOR'S NOTE: This response to a published statement by eight fellow clergymen from Alabama (Bishop C. C. J. Carpenter, Bishop Joseph A. Durick, Rabbi Hilton L. Grafman, Bishop Paul Hardin, Bishop Holan B. Harmon, the Reverend George M. Murray, the Reverend Edward V. Ramage and the Reverend Earl Stallings) was composed under somewhat constricting circumstances. Begun on the margins of the newspaper in which the statement appeared while I was in jail, the letter was continued on scraps of writing paper supplied by a friendly Negro trusty, and concluded on a pad my attorneys were eventually permitted to leave me. Although the text remains in substance unaltered, I have indulged in the author's prerogative of polishing it for publication.

necessary. We readily consented, and when the hour came we lived up to our promise. So I, along with several members of my staff, am here because I have organizational ties here.

But more basically, I am in Birmingham because injustice is here. Just as the prophets of the eighth century B.C. left their villages and carried their "thus saith the Lord" far beyond the boundaries of their home towns, and just as the Apostle Paul left his village of Tarsus and carried the gospel of Jesus Christ to the far corners of the Greco-Roman world, so am I compelled to carry the gospel of freedom beyond my own home town. Like Paul, I must constantly respond to the Macedonian call for aid.

Moreover, I am cognizant of the interrelatedness of all communities and states. I cannot sit idly by in Atlanta and not be concerned about what happens in Birmingham. Injustice anywhere is a threat to justice everywhere. We are caught in an inescapable network of mutuality, tied in a single garment of destiny. Whatever affects one directly, affects all indirectly. Never again can we afford to live with the narrow, provincial "outside agitator" idea. Anyone who lives inside the United States can never be considered an outsider anywhere within its bounds.

You deplore the demonstrations taking place in Birmingham. But your statement, I am sorry to say, fails to express a similar concern for the conditions that brought about the demonstrations. I am sure that none of you would want to rest content with the superficial kind of social analysis that deals merely with effects and does not grapple with underlying causes. It is unfortunate that demonstrations are taking place in Birmingham, but it is even more unfortunate that the city's white power structure left the Negro community with no alternative.

In any nonviolent campaign there are four basic steps: collection of the facts to determine whether injustices exist; negotiation; self-purification; and direct action. We have gone through all these steps in Birmingham. There can be no gainsaying the fact that racial injustice engulfs this community. Birmingham is probably the most thoroughly segregated city in the United States. Its ugly record of brutality is widely known. Negroes have experienced grossly unjust treatment in the courts. There have been more unsolved bombings of Negro homes and churches in Birmingham than in any other city in the nation. These are the hard, brutal facts of the case. On the basis of these conditions, Negro leaders sought to negotiate with the city fathers. But the latter consistently refused to engage in good-faith negotiation.

Then, last September, came the opportunity to talk with leaders of Birmingham's economic community. In the course of the negotiations, certain promises were made by the merchants—for example, to remove the stores' humiliating racial signs. On the basis of these promises, the Reverend Fred Shuttlesworth and the leaders of the Alabama Christian Movement for Human

Rights agreed to a moratorium on all demonstrations. As the weeks and months went by, we realized that we were the victims of a broken promise. A few signs, briefly removed, returned; the others remained.

As in so many past experiences, our hopes had been blasted, and the shadow of deep disappointment settled upon us. We had no alternative except to prepare for direct action, whereby we would present our very bodies as a means of laying our case before the conscience of the local and the national community. Mindful of the difficulties involved, we decided to undertake a process of self-purification. We began a series of workshops on nonviolence, and we repeatedly asked ourselves: "Are you able to accept blows without retaliating?" "Are you able to endure the ordeal of jail?" We decided to schedule our direct-action program for the Easter season, realizing that except for Christmas, this is the main shopping period of the year. Knowing that a strong economic-withdrawal program would be the by-product of direct action, we felt that this would be the best time to bring pressure to bear on the merchants for the needed change.

Then it occurred to us that Birmingham's mayoralty election was coming up in March, and we speedily decided to postpone action until after election day. When we discovered that the Commissioner of Public Safety, Eugene "Bull" Connor, had piled up enough votes to be in the run-off, we decided again to postpone action until the day after the run-off so that the demonstrations could not be used to cloud the issues. Like many others, we waited to see Mr. Connor defeated, and to this end we endured postponement after postponement. Having aided in this community need, we felt that our direct-action program could be delayed no longer.

You may well ask: "Why direct action? Why sit-ins, marches and so forth? Isn't negotiation a better path?" You are quite right in calling for negotiation. Indeed, this is the very purpose of direct action. Nonviolent direct action seeks to create such a crisis and foster such a tension that a community which has constantly refused to negotiate is forced to confront the issue. It seeks so to dramatize the issue that it can no longer be ignored. My citing the creation of tension as part of the work of the nonviolent-resister may sound rather shocking. But I must confess that I am not afraid of the word "tension." I have earnestly opposed violent tension, but there is a type of constructive, nonviolent tension which is necessary for growth. Just as Socrates felt that it was necessary to create tension in the mind so that individuals could rise from the bondage of myths and half-truths to the unfettered realm of creative analysis and objective appraisal, so must we see the need for nonviolent gadflies to create the kind of tension in society that will help men rise from the dark depths of prejudice and racism to the majestic heights of understanding and brotherhood.

The purpose of our direct-action program is to create a situation so crisis-packed that it will inevitably open the door to negotiation. I therefore concur with you in your call for negotiation. Too long has our beloved Southland been bogged down in a tragic effort to live in monologue rather than dialogue.

One of the basic points in your statement is that the action that I and my associates have taken in Birmingham is untimely. Some have asked: "Why didn't you give the new city administration time to act?" The only answer that I can give to this query is that the new Birmingham administration must be prodded about as much as the outgoing one, before it will act. We are sadly mistaken if we feel that the election of Albert Boutwell as mayor will bring the millennium to Birmingham. While Mr. Boutwell is a much more gentle person than Mr. Connor, they are both segregationists, dedicated to maintenance of the status quo. I have hope that Mr. Boutwell will be reasonable enough to see the futility of massive resistance to desegregation. But he will not see this without pressure from devotees of civil rights. My friends, I must say to you that we have not made a single gain in civil rights without determined legal and nonviolent pressure. Lamentably, it is an historical fact that privileged groups seldom give up their privileges voluntarily. Individuals may see the moral light and voluntarily give up their unjust posture; but, as Reinhold Niebuhr has reminded us, groups tend to be more immoral than individuals.

We know through painful experience that freedom is never voluntarily given by the oppressor; it must be demanded by the oppressed. Frankly, I have yet to engage in a direct-action campaign that was "well-timed" in the view of those who have not suffered unduly from the disease of segregation. For years now I have heard the word "Wait!" It rings in the ear of every Negro with piercing familiarity. This "Wait" has almost always meant "Never." We must come to see, with one of our distinguished jurists, that "justice too long delayed is justice denied."

We have waited for more than 340 years for our constitutional and God-given rights. The nations of Asia and Africa are moving with jetlike speed toward gaining political independence, but we still creep at horse-and-buggy pace toward gaining a cup of coffee at a lunch counter. Perhaps it is easy for those who have never felt the stinging darts of segregation to say, "Wait." But when you have seen vicious mobs lynch your mothers and fathers at will and drown your sisters and brothers at whim; when you have seen hate-filled policemen curse, kick and even kill your black brothers and sisters; when you see the vast majority of your twenty million Negro brothers smothering in an airtight cage of poverty in the midst of an affluent society; when you suddenly find your tongue twisted and your speech stammering as you seek to explain to your six-year-old daughter why she can't go to the public amusement park that has just been advertised on television, and see tears welling up in her eyes when she is told that Funtown is closed to colored children, and see ominous clouds of inferiority beginning to form in her little mental sky, and see her beginning to distort her personality by developing an unconscious bitterness toward white people; when you have to concoct an answer for a five-year-old son who is asking: "Daddy, why do white people treat colored people so mean?"; when you take a cross-country drive and find it necessary to sleep night after night in the uncomfortable corners of your automobile because no motel will accept you; when you are humiliated day in and day out by nagging signs reading "white" and "colored"; when your first name becomes "nigger," your middle name becomes "boy" (however old you are) and your last name becomes "John," and your wife and mother are never given the respected title "Mrs."; when you are harried by day and haunted by night by the fact that you are a Negro, living constantly at tiptoe stance, never quite knowing what to expect next, and are plagued with inner fears and outer resentments; when you are forever fighting a degenerating sense of "nobodiness"—then you will understand why we find it difficult to wait. There comes a time when the cup of endurance runs over, and men are no longer willing to be plunged into the abyss of despair. I hope, sirs, you can understand our legitimate and unavoidable impatience.

You express a great deal of anxiety over our willingness to break laws. This is certainly a legitimate concern. Since we so diligently urge people to obey the Supreme Court's decision of 1954 outlawing segregation in the public schools, at first glance it may seem rather paradoxical for us consciously to break laws. One may well ask: "How can you advocate breaking some laws and obeying others?" The answer lies in the fact that there are two types of laws: just and unjust. I would be the first to advocate obeying just laws. One has not only a legal but a moral responsibility to obey just laws. Conversely, one has a moral responsibility to disobey unjust laws. I would agree with St. Augustine that "an unjust law is no law at all."

Now, what is the difference between the two? How does one determine whether a law is just or unjust? A just law is a man-made code that squares with the moral law or the law of God. An unjust law is a code that is out of harmony with the moral law. To put it in the terms of St. Thomas Aquinas: An unjust law is a human law that is not rooted in eternal law and natural law. Any law that uplifts human personality is just. Any law that degrades human personality is unjust. All segregation statutes are unjust because segregation distorts the soul and damages the personality. It gives the segregator a false sense of superiority and the segregated a false sense of inferiority. Segregation, to use the terminology of the Jewish philosopher Martin Buber, substitutes an "I-it" relationship for an "I-thou" relationship and ends up relegating persons to the status of things. Hence segregation is not only politically, economically and sociologically unsound, it is morally wrong and sinful. Paul Tillich has said that sin is separation. Is not segregation an existential expression of man's tragic separation, his awful estrangement, his terrible sinfulness? Thus it is that I can urge men to obey the 1954 decision of the Supreme Court, for it is morally right; and I can urge them to disobey segregation ordinances, for they are morally wrong.

Let us consider a more concrete example of just and unjust laws. An unjust law is a code that a numerical or power majority group compels a minority group to obey but does not make binding on itself. This is *difference* made legal. By the same token, a just law is a code that a majority compels a minority to follow and that it is willing to follow itself. This is *sameness* made legal.

· · ·

I hope you are able to see the distinction I am trying to point out. In no sense do I advocate evading or defying the law, as would the rabid segregationist. That would lead to anarchy. One who breaks an unjust law must do so openly, lovingly, and with a willingness to accept the penalty. I submit that an individual who breaks a law that conscience tells him is unjust, and who willingly accepts the penalty of imprisonment in order to arouse the conscience of the community over its injustice, is in reality expressing the highest respect for law.

· · ·

I must make two honest confessions to you, my Christian and Jewish brothers. First, I must confess that over the past few years I have been gravely disappointed with the white moderate. I have almost reached the regrettable conclusion that the Negro's great stumbling block in his stride toward freedom is not the White Citizen's Counciler or the Ku Klux Klanner, but the white moderate, who is more devoted to "order" than to justice; who prefers a negative peace which is the absence of tension to a positive peace which is the presence of justice; who constantly says: "I agree with you in the goal you seek, but I cannot agree with your methods of direct action"; who paternalistically believes he can set the timetable for another man's freedom; who lives by a mythical concept of time and who constantly advises the Negro to wait for a "more convenient season." Shallow understanding from people of good will is more frustrating than absolute misunderstanding from people of ill will. Lukewarm acceptance is much more bewildering than outright rejection.

· · ·

In your statement you assert that our actions, even though peaceful, must be condemned because they precipitate violence. But is this a logical assertion? Isn't this like condemning a robbed man because his possession of money precipitated the evil act of robbery? Isn't this like condemning Socrates because his unswerving commitment to truth and his philosophical inquiries precipitated the act by the misguided populace in which they made him drink hemlock? Isn't this like condemning Jesus because his unique God-consciousness and never-ceasing devotion to God's will precipitated the evil act of crucifixion? We must come to see that, as the federal courts have consistently affirmed, it is wrong to urge an individual to cease his efforts to gain his basic constitutional rights because the quest may precipitate violence. Society must protect the robbed and punish the robber.

I had also hoped that the white moderate would reject the myth concerning time in relation to the struggle for freedom. I have just received a letter from a white brother in Texas. He writes: "All Christians know that the colored people will receive equal rights eventually, but it is possible that you are in too great a religious hurry. It has taken Christianity almost two thousand years to accomplish what it has. The teachings of Christ take time to come to earth." Such an attitude stems from a tragic misconception that there is something in the very flow of time that will inevitably cure all ills. Actually, time itself is neutral; it can be used either destructively or constructively. More and more I feel that the people of ill will have used time much more effectively than have the people of good will. We will have to repent in this generation not merely for the hateful words and actions of the bad people but for the appalling silence of the good people. Human progress never rolls in on wheels of inevitability; it comes through the tireless efforts of men willing to be coworkers with God, and without this hard work, time itself becomes an ally of the forces of social stagnation. We must use time creatively, in the knowledge that the time is always ripe to do right. Now is the time to make real the promise of democracy and transform our pending national elegy into a creative psalm of brotherhood. Now is the time to lift our national policy from the quicksand of racial injustice to the solid rock of human dignity.

You speak of our activity in Birmingham as extreme. At first I was rather disappointed that fellow clergymen would see my nonviolent efforts as those of an extremist. I began thinking about the fact that I stand in the middle of two opposing forces in the Negro community. One is a force of complacency, made up in part of Negroes who, as a result of long years of oppression, are so drained of self-respect and a sense of "somebodiness" that they have adjusted to segregation; and in part of a few middle-class Negroes who, because of a degree of academic and economic security and because in some ways they profit by segregation, have become insensitive to the problems of the masses. The other force is one of bitterness and hatred, and it comes perilously close to advocating violence. It is expressed in the various black nationalist groups that are springing up across the nation, the largest and best-known being Elijah Muhammad's Muslim movement. Nourished by the Negro's frustration over the continued existence of racial discrimination, this movement is made up of people who have lost faith in America, who have absolutely repudiated Christianity, and who have concluded that the white man is an incorrigible "devil."

I have tried to stand between these two forces, saying that we need emulate neither the "do-nothingism" of the complacent nor the hatred and despair of the black nationalist. For there is the more excellent way of love and nonviolent protest. I am grateful to God that, through the influence of the Negro church, the way of nonviolence became an integral part of our struggle.

If this philosophy had not emerged, by now many streets of the South would, I am convinced, be flowing with blood. And I am further convinced that if our white brothers dismiss as "rabble-rousers" and "outside agitators" those of us who employ nonviolent direct action, and if they refuse to support our nonviolent efforts, millions of Negroes will, out of frustration and despair, seek solace and security in black-nationalist ideologies—a development that would inevitably lead to a frightening racial nightmare.

Oppressed people cannot remain oppressed forever. The yearning for freedom eventually manifests itself, and that is what has happened to the American Negro. Something within has reminded him of his birthright of freedom, and something without has reminded him that it can be gained. Consciously or unconsciously, he has been caught up by the *Zeitgeist*, and with his black brothers of Africa and his brown and yellow brothers of Asia, South America and the Caribbean, the United States Negro is moving with a sense of great urgency toward the promised land of racial justice. If one recognizes this vital urge that has engulfed the Negro community, one should readily understand why public demonstrations are taking place. The Negro has many pent-up resentments and latent frustrations, and he must release them. So let him march; let him make prayer pilgrimages to the city hall; let him go on freedom rides—and try to understand why he must do so. If his repressed emotions are not released in nonviolent ways, they will seek expression through violence; this is not a threat but a fact of history. So I have not said to my people: "Get rid of your discontent." Rather, I have tried to say that this normal and health discontent can be challenged into the creative outlet of nonviolent direct action. And now this approach is being termed extremist.

But though I was initially disappointed at being categorized as an extremist, as I continued to think about the matter I gradually gained a measure of satisfaction from the label. Was not Jesus an extremist for love: "Love your enemies, bless them that curse you, do good to them that hate you, and pray for them which despitefully use you, and persecute you." Was not Amos an extremist for justice: "Let justice roll down like waters and righteousness like an ever-flowing stream." Was not Martin Luther an extremist: "Here I stand; I cannot do otherwise, so help me God." And John Bunyan: "I will stay in jail to the end of my days before I make a butchery of my conscience." And Abraham Lincoln: "This nation cannot survive half slave and half free." And Thomas Jefferson: "We hold these truths to be self-evident, that all men are created equal. . . ." So the question is not whether we will be extremists, but what kind of extremists we will be. Will we be extremists for hate or for love? Will we be extremists for the preservation of injustice or for the extension of justice? In that dramatic scene on Calvary's hill three men were crucified. We must never forget that all three were crucified for the same crime—the crime of extremism. Two were extremists for immorality, and thus fell below their environment. The other, Jesus Christ, was an extremist for love, truth and goodness, and thereby rose above his environment. Perhaps the South, the nation and the world are in dire need of creative extremists.

I had hoped that the white moderate would see this need. Perhaps I was too optimistic; perhaps I expected too much. I suppose I should have realized that few members of the oppressor race can understand the deep groans and passionate yearnings of the oppressed race, and still fewer have the vision to see that injustice must be rooted out by strong, persistent and determined action. I am thankful, however, that some of our white brothers in the South have grasped the meaning of this social revolution and committed themselves to it. They are still too few in quantity, but they are big in quality. Some—such as Ralph McGill, Lillian Smith, Harry Golden, James McBride Dabbs, Ann Braden and Sarah Patton Boyle—have written about our struggle in eloquent and prophetic terms. Others have marched with us down nameless streets of the South. They have languished in filthy, roach-infested jails, suffering the abuse and brutality of policemen who view them as "dirty nigger-lovers." Unlike so many of their moderate brothers and sisters, they have recognized the urgency of the moment and sensed the need for powerful "action" antidotes to combat the disease of segregation.

Let me make note of my other major disappointment. I have been so greatly disappointed with the white church and its leadership. Of course, there are some notable exceptions. I am not unmindful of the fact that each of you has taken some significant stands on this issue. I commend you, Reverend Stallings, for your Christian stand on this past Sunday, in welcoming Negroes to your worship service on a nonsegregated basis. I commend the Catholic leaders of this state for integrating Spring Hill College several years ago.

But despite these notable exceptions, I must honestly reiterate that I have been disappointed with the church. I do not say this as one of those negative critics who can always find something wrong with the church. I say this as a minister of the gospel, who loves the church; who was nurtured in its bosom; who has been sustained by its spiritual blessings and who will remain true to it as long as the cord of life shall lengthen.

When I was suddenly catapulted into the leadership of the bus protest in Montgomery, Alabama, a few years ago, I felt we would be supported by the white church. I felt that the white ministers, priests and rabbis of the South would be among our strongest allies. Instead, some have been outright opponents, refusing to understand the freedom movement and misrepresenting its leaders; all too many others have been more cautious than courageous and have remained silent behind the anaesthetizing security of stained-glass windows.

In spite of my shattered dreams, I came to Birmingham with the hope that the white religious leadership of this community would see the justice of our cause and, with deep moral concern, would serve as the channel through which our just grievances could reach the power structure. I had hoped that each of you would understand. But again I have been disappointed.

I have heard numerous southern religious leaders admonish their worshipers to comply with a desegregation decision because it is the law, but I have longed to hear white ministers declare: "Follow this decree because integration is morally right and because the Negro is your brother." In the midst of blatant injustices inflicted upon the Negro, I have watched white churchmen stand on the sideline and mouth pious irrelevancies and sanctimonious trivialities. In the midst of a mighty struggle to rid our nation of racial and economic injustice, I have heard many ministers say: "Those are social issues, with which the gospel has no real concern." And I have watched many churches commit themselves to a completely otherworldly religion which makes a strange, un-Biblical distinction between body and soul, between the sacred and the secular.

I have traveled the length and breadth of Alabama, Mississippi and all the other southern states. On sweltering summer days and crisp autumn mornings I have looked at the South's beautiful churches with their lofty spires pointing heavenward. I have beheld the impressive outlines of her massive religious-education buildings. Over and over I have found myself asking: "What kind of people worship here? Who is their God? Where were their voices when the lips of Governor Barnett dripped with words of interposition and nullification? Where were they when Governor Wallace gave a clarion call for defiance and hatred? Where were their voices of support when bruised and weary Negro men and women decided to rise from the dark dungeons of complacency to the bright hills of creative protest?"

Yes, these questions are still in my mind. In deep disappointment I have wept over the laxity of the church. But be assured that my tears have been tears of love. There can be no deep disappointment where there is not deep love. Yes, I love the church. How could I do otherwise? I am in the rather unique position of being the son, the grandson and the great-grandson of preachers. Yes, I see the church as the body of Christ. But, oh! How we have blemished and scarred that body through social neglect and through fear of being nonconformists.

There was a time when the church was very powerful—in the time when the early Christians rejoiced at being deemed worthy to suffer for what they believed. In those days the church was not merely a thermometer that recorded the ideas and principles of popular opinion; it was a thermostat that transformed the mores of society. Whenever the early Christians entered a town, the people in power became disturbed and immediately sought to convict the Christians for being "disturbers of the peace" and "outside agitators." But the Christians pressed on, in the conviction that they were "a colony of heaven," called to obey God rather than man. Small in number, they were big in commitment. They were too God-intoxicated to be "astronomically intimidated." By their effort and example they brought an end to such ancient evils as infanticide and gladiatorial contests.

Things are different now. So often the contemporary church is a weak, ineffectual voice with an uncertain sound. So often it is an arch-defender of the status quo. Far from being disturbed by the presence of the church, the power structure of the average community is consoled by the church's silent—and often even vocal—sanction of things as they are.

But the judgment of God is upon the church as never before. If today's church does not recapture the sacrificial spirit of the early church, it will lose its authenticity, forfeit the loyalty of millions, and be dismissed as an irrelevant social club with no meaning for the twentieth century. Every day I meet young people whose disappointment with the church has turned into outright disgust.

Perhaps I have once again been too optimistic. Is organized religion too inextricably bound to the status quo to save our nation and the world? Perhaps I must turn my faith to the inner spiritual church, the church within the church, as the true *ekklesia* and the hope of the world. But again I am thankful to God that some noble souls from the ranks of organized religion have broken loose from the paralyzing chains of conformity and joined us as active partners in the struggle for freedom. They have left their secure congregations and walked the streets of Albany, Georgia, with us. They have gone down the highways of the South on tortuous rides for freedom. Yes, they have gone to jail with us. Some have been dismissed from their churches, have lost the support of their bishops and fellow ministers. But they have acted in the faith that right defeated is stronger than evil triumphant. Their witness has been the spiritual salt that has preserved the true meaning of the gospel in these troubled times. They have carved a tunnel of hope through the dark mountain of disappointment.

I hope the church as a whole will meet the challenge of this decisive hour. But even if the church does not come to the aid of justice, I have no despair about the future. I have no fear about the outcome of our struggle in Birmingham, even if our motives are at present misunderstood. We will reach the goal of freedom in Birmingham and all over the nation, because the goal of America is freedom. Abused and scorned though we may be, our destiny is tied up with America's destiny. Before the pilgrims landed at Plymouth, we were here. Before the pen of Jefferson etched the majestic words of the Declaration of Independence across the pages of history, we were here. For more than two centuries our forebears labored in this country without wages; they made cotton king; they built the homes of their masters while suffering gross injustice and shameful humiliation—and yet out of a bottomless vitality they continued to thrive and develop. If the inexpressible cruelties of slavery could

not stop us, the opposition we now face will surely fail. We will win our freedom because the sacred heritage of our nation and the eternal will of God are
embodied in our echoing demands.

Before closing I feel impelled to mention one other point in your statement
that has troubled me profoundly. You warmly commended the Birmingham
police force for keeping "order" and "preventing violence." I doubt that you
would have so warmly commended the policemen if you were to observe their
ugly and inhumane treatment of Negroes here in the city jail; if you were to
watch them push and curse old Negro women and young Negro girls; if you
were to see them slap and kick old Negro men and young boys; if you were
to observe them, as they did on two occasions, refuse to give us food because
we wanted to sing our grace together. I cannot join you in your praise of the
Birmingham police department.

It is true that the police have exercised a degree of discipline in handling
the demonstrators. In this sense they have conducted themselves rather "nonviolently" in public. But for what purpose? To preserve the evil system of
segregation. . . .

I wish you had commended the Negro sit-inners and demonstrators of
Birmingham for their sublime courage, their willingness to suffer and their
amazing discipline in the midst of great provocation. One day the South will
recognize its real heroes. They will be the James Merediths, with the noble
sense of purpose that enables them to face jeering and hostile mobs, and with
the agonizing loneliness that characterizes the life of the pioneer. They will be
old, oppressed, battered Negro women, symbolized in a seventy-two-year-old
woman in Montgomery, Alabama, who rose up with a sense of dignity and
with her people decided not to ride segregated buses, and who responded with
ungrammatical profundity to one who inquired about her weariness: "My
feets is tired, but my soul is at rest." They will be the young high school and
college students, the young ministers of the gospel and a host of their elders,
courageously and nonviolently sitting in at lunch counters and willingly going
to jail for conscience' sake. One day the South will know that when these
disinherited children of God sat down at lunch counters, they were in reality
standing up for what is best in the American dream and for the most sacred
values in our Judaeo-Christian heritage, thereby bringing our nation back to
those great wells of democracy which were dug deep by the founding fathers
in their formulation of the Constitution and the Declaration of Independence.

Never before have I written so long a letter. I'm afraid it is much too long
to take your precious time. I can assure you that it would have been much
shorter if I had been writing from a comfortable desk, but what else can one
do when he is alone in a narrow jail cell, other than write long letters, think
long thoughts and pray long prayers?

If I have said anything in this letter that overstates the truth and indicates an unreasonable impatience, I beg you to forgive me. If I have said anything that understates the truth and indicates my having a patience that allows me to settle for anything less than brotherhood, I beg God to forgive me.

I hope this letter finds you strong in the faith. I also hope that circumstances will soon make it possible for me to meet each of you, not as an integrationist or a civil-rights leader but as a fellow clergyman and a Christian brother. Let us all hope that the dark clouds of racial prejudice will soon pass away and the deep fog of misunderstanding will be lifted from our fear-drenched communities, and in some not too distant tomorrow the radiant stars of love and brotherhood will shine over our great nation with all their scintillating beauty.

Yours for the cause of Peace and Brotherhood,
Martin Luther King, Jr.

MALCOLM X

The Ballot or the Bullet

Moderator, Brother Lomax, brothers and sisters, friends and enemies: I just can't believe everyone in here is a friend and I don't want to leave anybody out. The question tonight, as I understand it, is "The Negro Revolt, and Where Do We Go From Here?" or "What Next?" In my little humble way of understanding it, it points toward either the ballot or the bullet.

Before we try and explain what is meant by the ballot or the bullet, I would like to clarify something concerning myself. I'm still a Muslim, my religion is still Islam. That's my personal belief. Just as Adam Clayton Powell is a Christian minister who heads the Abyssinian Baptist Church in New York, but at the same time takes part in the political struggles to try and bring about rights to the black people in this country; and Dr. Martin Luther King is a Christian minister down in Atlanta, Georgia, who heads another organization fighting for the civil rights of black people in this country; and Rev. Galamison, I guess you've heard of him, is another Christian minister in New York who has been deeply involved in the school boycotts to eliminate segregated education; well, I myself am a minister, not a Christian minister, but a Muslim minister; and I believe in action on all fronts by whatever means necessary.

Although I'm still a Muslim, I'm not here tonight to discuss my religion. I'm not here to try and change your religion. I'm not here to argue or discuss anything that we differ about, because it's time for us to submerge our differences and realize that it is best for us to first see that we have the same problem, a common problem—a problem that will make you catch hell whether you're a Baptist, or a Methodist, or a Muslim, or a nationalist. Whether you're educated or illiterate, whether you live on the boulevard or in the alley, you're going to catch hell just like I am. We're all in the same boat and we all are going to catch the same hell from the same man. He just happens to be a white man. All of us have suffered here, in this country, political oppression at

From *Malcolm X Speaks: Selected Speeches and Statements*, ed. George Breitman (New York: Pathfinder Press, 1965, 1989), pp. 23–44. Copyright 1965, 1989 by Betty Shabazz and Pathfinder Press. Reprinted by permission.

the hands of the white man, economic exploitation at the hands of the white man, and social degradation at the hands of the white man.

Now in speaking like this, it doesn't mean that we're anti-white, but it does mean we're anti-exploitation, we're anti-degradation, we're anti-oppression. And if the white man doesn't want us to be anti-him, let him stop oppressing and exploiting and degrading us. Whether we are Christians or Muslims or nationalists or agnostics or atheists, we must first learn to forget our differences. If we have differences, let us differ in the closet; when we come out in front, let us not have anything to argue about until we get finished arguing with the man. If the late President Kennedy could get together with Khrushchev and exchange some wheat, we certainly have more in common with each other than Kennedy and Khrushchev had with each other.

If we don't do something real soon, I think you'll have to agree that we're going to be forced either to use the ballot or the bullet. It's one or the other in 1964. It isn't that time is running out—time has run out! 1964 threatens to be the most explosive year America has ever witnessed. The most explosive year. Why? It's also a political year. It's the year when all of the white politicians will be back in the so-called Negro community jiving you and me for some votes. The year when all of the white political crooks will be right back in your and my community with their false promises, building up our hopes for a letdown, with their trickery and their treachery, with their false promises which they don't intend to keep. As they nourish these dissatisfactions, it can only lead to one thing, an explosion; and now we have the type of black man on the scene in America today—I'm sorry, Brother Lomax—who just doesn't intend to turn the other cheek any longer.

Don't let anybody tell you anything about the odds are against you. If they draft you, they send you to Korea and make you face 800 million Chinese. If you can be brave over there, you can be brave right here. These odds aren't as great as those odds. And if you fight here, you will at least know what you're fighting for.

I'm not a politician, not even a student of politics; in fact, I'm not a student of much of anything. I'm not a Democrat, I'm not a Republican, and I don't even consider myself an American. If you and I were Americans, there'd be no problem. Those Hunkies that just got off the boat, they're already Americans; Polacks are already Americans; the Italian refugees are already Americans. Everything that came out of Europe, every blue-eyed thing, is already an American. And as long as you and I have been over here, we aren't Americans yet.

Well, I am one who doesn't believe in deluding myself. I'm not going to sit at your table and watch you eat, with nothing on my plate, and call myself a diner. Sitting at the table doesn't make you a diner, unless you eat some of what's on that plate. Being here in America doesn't make you an American.

Being born here in America doesn't make you an American. Why, if birth made you American, you wouldn't need any legislation, you wouldn't need any amendments to the Constitution, you wouldn't be faced with civil-rights filibustering in Washington, D.C., right now. They don't have to pass civil-rights legislation to make a Polack an American.

No, I'm not an American. I'm one of the 22 million black people who are the victims of Americanism. One of the 22 million black people who are the victims of democracy, nothing but disguised hypocrisy. So, I'm not standing here speaking to you as an American, or a patriot, or a flag-saluter, or a flag-waver—no, not I. I'm speaking as a victim of this American system. And I see America through the eyes of the victim. I don't see any American dream; I see an American nightmare.

These 22 million victims are waking up. Their eyes are coming open. They're beginning to see what they used to only look at. They're becoming politically mature. They are realizing that there are new political trends from coast to coast. As they see these new political trends, it's possible for them to see that every time there's an election the races are so close that they have to have a recount. They had to recount in Massachusetts to see who was going to be governor, it was so close. It was the same way in Rhode Island, in Minnesota, and in many other parts of the country. And the same with Kennedy and Nixon when they ran for president. It was so close they had to count all over again. Well, what does this mean? It means that when white people are evenly divided, and black people have a bloc of votes of their own, it is left up to them to determine who's going to sit in the White House and who's going to be in the dog house.

It was the black man's vote that put the present administration in Washington, D.C. Your vote, your dumb vote, your ignorant vote, your wasted vote put in an administration in Washington, D.C., that has seen fit to pass every kind of legislation imaginable, saving you until last, then filibustering on top of that. And your and my leaders have the audacity to run around clapping their hands and talk about how much progress we're making. And what a good president we have. If he wasn't good in Texas, he sure can't be good in Washington, D.C. Because Texas is a lynch state. It is in the same breath as Mississippi, no different; only they lynch you in Texas with a Texas accent and lynch you in Mississippi with a Mississippi accent. And these Negro leaders have the audacity to go and have some coffee in the White House with a Texan, a Southern cracker—that's all he is—and then come out and tell you and me that he's going to be better for us because, since he's from the South, he knows how to deal with the Southerners. What kind of logic is that? Let Eastland be president, he's from the South too. He should be better able to deal with them than Johnson.

In this present administration they have in the House of Representatives 257 Democrats to only 177 Republicans. They control two-thirds of the House vote. Why can't they pass something that will help you and me? In the Senate, there are 67 senators who are of the Democratic Party. Only 33 of them are Republicans. Why, the Democrats have got the government sewed up, and you're the one who sewed it up for them. And what have they given you for it? Four years in office, and just now getting around to some civil-rights legislation. Just now, after everything else is gone, out of the way, they're going to sit down now and play with you all summer long—the same old giant con game that they call filibuster. All those are in cahoots together. Don't you ever think they're not in cahoots together, for the man that is heading the civil-rights filibuster is a man from Georgia named Richard Russell. When Johnson became president, the first man he asked for when he got back to Washington, D.C., was "Dickey"—that's how tight they are. That's his boy, that's his pal, that's his buddy. But they're playing that old con game. One of them makes believe he's for you, and he's got it fixed where the other one is so tight against you, he never has to keep his promise.

So it's time in 1964 to wake up. And when you see them coming up with that kind of conspiracy, let them know your eyes are open. And let them know you got something else that's wide open too. It's got to be the ballot or the bullet. The ballot or the bullet. If you're afraid to use an expression like that, you should get on out of the country, you should get back in the cotton patch, you should get back in the alley. They get all the Negro vote, and after they get it, the Negro gets nothing in return. All they did when they got to Washington was give a few big Negroes big jobs. Those big Negroes didn't need big jobs, they already had jobs. That's camouflage, that's trickery, that's treachery, window-dressing. I'm not trying to knock out the Democrats for the Republicans, we'll get to them in a minute. But it is true—you put the Democrats first and the Democrats put you last.

Look at it the way it is. What alibis do they use, since they control Congress and the Senate? What alibi do they use when you and I ask, "Well, when are you going to keep your promise?" They blame the Dixiecrats. What is a Dixiecrat? A Democrat. A Dixiecrat is nothing but a Democrat in disguise. The titular head of the Democrats is also the head of the Dixiecrats, because the Dixiecrats are a part of the Democratic Party. The Democrats have never kicked the Dixiecrats out of the party. The Dixiecrats bolted themselves once, but the Democrats didn't put them out. Imagine, these lowdown Southern segregationists put the Northern Democrats down. But the Northern Democrats have never put the Dixiecrats down. No, look at that thing the way it is. They have got a con game going on, a political con game, and you and I are in the middle. It's time for you and me to wake up and start looking at it like it is, and trying to understand it like it is; and then we can deal with it like it is.

The Dixiecrats in Washington, D.C., control the key committees that run the government. The only reason the Dixiecrats control these committees is because they have seniority. The only reason they have seniority is because

they come from states where Negroes can't vote. This is not even a government that's based on democracy. It is not a government that is made up of
representatives of the people. Half of the people in the South can't even vote.
Eastland is not even supposed to be in Washington. Half of the senators and
congressmen who occupy these key positions in Washington, D.C., are there
illegally, are there unconstitutionally.

I was in Washington, D.C., a week ago Thursday, when they were debating
whether or not they should let the bill come onto the floor. And in the back
of the room where the Senate meets, there's a huge map of the United States,
and on that map it shows the location of Negroes throughout the country.
And it shows that the Southern section of the country, the states that are most
heavily concentrated with Negroes, are the ones that have senators and congressmen standing up filibustering and doing all other kinds of trickery to keep
the Negro from being able to vote. This is pitiful. But it's not pitiful for us any
longer; it's actually pitiful for the white man, because soon now, as the Negro
awakens a little more and sees the vise that he's in, sees the bag that he's in,
sees the real game that he's in, then the Negro's going to develop a new tactic.

These senators and congressmen actually violate the constitutional amendments that guarantee the people of that particular state or county the right
to vote. And the Constitution itself has within it the machinery to expel any
representative from a state where the voting rights of the people are violated.
You don't even need new legislation. Any person in Congress right now, who
is there from a state or a district where the voting rights of the people are
violated, that particular person should be expelled from Congress. And when
you expel him, you've removed one of the obstacles in the path of any real
meaningful legislation in this country. In fact, when you expel them, you
don't need new legislation, because they will be replaced by black representatives from counties and districts where the black man is in the majority, not
in the minority.

If the black man in these Southern states had his full voting rights, the key
Dixiecrats in Washington, D.C., which means the key Democrats in Washington, D.C., would lose their seats. The Democratic Party itself would lose its
power. It would cease to be powerful as a party. When you see the amount of
power that would be lost by the Democratic Party if it were to lose the Dixiecrat wing, or branch, or element, you can see where it's against the interests
of the Democrats to give voting rights to Negroes in states where the Democrats have been in complete power and authority ever since the Civil War.
You just can't belong to that party without analyzing it.

I say again, I'm not anti-Democrat, I'm not anti-Republican, I'm not anti-
anything. I'm just questioning their sincerity, and some of the strategy that
they've been using on our people by promising them promises that they don't
intend to keep. When you keep the Democrats in power, you're keeping the

Dixiecrats in power. I doubt that my good Brother Lomax will deny that. A vote for a Democrat is a vote for a Dixiecrat. That's why, in 1964, it's time now for you and me to become more politically mature and realize what the ballot is for; what we're supposed to get when we cast a ballot; and that if we don't cast a ballot, it's going to end up in a situation where we're going to have to cast a bullet. It's either a ballot or a bullet.

In the North, they do it a different way. They have a system that's known as gerrymandering, whatever that means. It means when Negroes become too heavily concentrated in a certain area, and begin to gain too much political power, the white man comes along and changes the district lines. You may say, "Why do you keep saying white man?" Because it's the white man who does it. I haven't ever seen any Negro changing any lines. They don't let him get near the line. It's the white man who does this. And usually, it's the white man who grins at you the most, and pats you on the back, and is supposed to be your friend. He may be friendly, but he's not your friend.

So, what I'm trying to impress upon you, in essence, is this: You and I in America are faced not with a segregationist conspiracy, we're faced with a government conspiracy. Everyone who's filibustering is a senator—that's the government. Everyone who's finagling in Washington, D.C., is a congress-man—that's the government. You don't have anybody putting blocks in your path but people who are a part of the government. The same government that you go abroad to fight for and die for is the government that is in a conspiracy to deprive you of your voting rights, deprive you of your economic opportu-nities, deprive you of decent housing, deprive you of decent education. You don't need to go to the employer alone, it is the government itself, the gov-ernment of America, that is responsible for the oppression and exploitation and degradation of black people in this country. And you should drop it in their lap. This government has failed the Negro. This so-called democracy has failed the Negro. And all these white liberals have definitely failed the Negro.

So, where do we go from here? First, we need some friends. We need some new allies. The entire civil-rights struggle needs a new interpretation, a broader interpretation. We need to look at this civil-rights thing from another angle—from the inside as well as from the outside. To those of us whose phi-losophy is black nationalism, the only way you can get involved in the civil-rights struggle is give it a new interpretation. That old interpretation excluded us. It kept us out. So, we're giving a new interpretation to the civil-rights struggle, an interpretation that will enable us to come into it, take part in it. And these handkerchief-heads who have been dillydallying and pussyfooting and compromising—we don't intend to let them pussyfoot and dillydally and compromise any longer.

How can you thank a man for giving you what's already yours? How then can you thank him for giving you only part of what's already yours? You haven't even made progress, if what's being given to you, you should have had already. That's not progress. And I love my Brother Lomax, the way he pointed out we're right back where we were in 1954. We're not even as far up as we were in 1954. We're behind where we were in 1954. There's more segregation now than there was in 1954. There's more racial animosity, more racial hatred, more racial violence today in 1964, than there was in 1954. Where is the progress?

And now you're facing a situation where the young Negro's coming up. They don't want to hear that "turn-the-other-cheek" stuff, no. In Jacksonville, those were teenagers, they were throwing Molotov cocktails. Negroes have never done that before. But it shows you there's a new deal coming in. There's new thinking coming in. There's new strategy coming in. It'll be Molotov cocktails this month, hand grenades next month, and something else next month. It'll be ballots, or it'll be bullets. It'll be liberty, or it will be death. The only difference about this kind of death—it'll be reciprocal. You know what is meant by "reciprocal"? That's one of Brother Lomax's words, I stole it from him. I don't usually deal with those big words because I don't usually deal with big people. I deal with small people. I find you can get a whole lot of small people and whip hell out of a whole lot of big people. They haven't got anything to lose, and they've got everything to gain. And they'll let you know in a minute: "It takes two to tango; when I go, you go."

The black nationalists, those whose philosophy is black nationalism, in bringing about this new interpretation of the entire meaning of civil rights, look upon it as meaning, as Brother Lomax has pointed out, equality of opportunity. Well, we're justified in seeking civil rights, if it means equality of opportunity, because all we're doing there is trying to collect for our investment. Our mothers and fathers invested sweat and blood. Three hundred and ten years we worked in this country without a dime in return—I mean without a *dime* in return. You let the white man walk around here talking about how rich this country is, but you never stop to think how it got rich so quick. It got rich because you made it rich.

You take the people who are in this audience right now. They're poor, we're all poor as individuals. Our weekly salary individually amounts to hardly anything. But if you take the salary of everyone in here collectively it'll fill up a whole lot of baskets. It's a lot of wealth. If you can collect the wages of just these people right here for a year, you'll be rich—richer than rich. When you look at it like that, think how rich Uncle Sam had to become, not with this handful, but millions of black people. Your and my mother and father, who didn't work an eight-hour shift, but worked from "can't see" in the morning until "can't see" at night, and worked for nothing, making the white man rich, making Uncle Sam rich.

This is our investment. This is our contribution—our blood. Not only did we give of our free labor, we gave of our blood. Every time he had a call to arms, we were the first ones in uniform. We died on every battlefield the white man had. We have made a greater sacrifice than anybody who's standing up in America today. We have made a greater contribution and have collected less. Civil rights, for those of us whose philosophy is black nationalism, means: "Give it to us now. Don't wait for next year. Give it to us yesterday, and that's not fast enough."

I might stop right here to point out one thing. Whenever you're going after something that belongs to you, anyone who's depriving you of the right to have it is a criminal. Understand that. Whenever you are going after something that is yours, you are within your legal rights to lay claim to it. And anyone who puts forth any effort to deprive you of that which is yours, is breaking the law, is a criminal. And this was pointed out by the Supreme Court decision. It outlawed segregation. Which means segregation is against the law. Which means a segregationist is breaking the law. A segregationist is a criminal. You can't label him as anything other than that. And when you demonstrate against segregation, the law is on your side. The Supreme Court is on your side.

Now, who is it that opposes you in carrying out the law? The police department itself. With police dogs and clubs. Whenever you demonstrate against segregation, whether it is segregated education, segregated housing, or anything else, the law is on your side, and anyone who stands in the way is not the law any longer. They are breaking the law, they are not representatives of the law. Any time you demonstrate against segregation and a man has the audacity to put a police dog on you, kill that dog, kill him, I'm telling you, kill that dog. I say it, if they put me in jail tomorrow, kill-that-dog. Then you'll put a stop to it. Now, if these white people in here don't want to see that kind of action, get down and tell the mayor to tell the police department to pull the dogs in. That's all you have to do. If you don't do it, someone else will.

If you don't take this kind of stand, your little children will grow up and look at you and think "shame." If you don't take an uncompromising stand—I don't mean go out and get violent; but at the same time you should never be nonviolent unless you run into some nonviolence. I'm nonviolent with those who are nonviolent with me. But when you drop that violence on me, then you've made me go insane, and I'm not responsible for what I do. And that's the way every Negro should get. Any time you know you're within the law, within your legal rights, within your moral rights, in accord with justice, then die for what you believe in. But don't die alone. Let your dying be reciprocal. This is what is meant by equality. What's good for the goose is good for the gander.

When we begin to get in this area, we need new friends, we need new allies. We need to expand the civil-rights struggle to a higher level—to the level of human rights. Whenever you are in a civil-rights struggle, whether you know it or not, you are confining yourself to the jurisdiction of Uncle

Sam. No one from the outside world can speak out in your behalf as long as your struggle is a civil-rights struggle. Civil rights comes within the domestic affairs of this country. All of our African brothers and our Asian brothers and our Latin-American brothers cannot open their mouths and interfere in the domestic affairs of the United States. And as long as it's civil rights, this comes under the jurisdiction of Uncle Sam.

But the United Nations has what's known as the charter of human rights, it has a committee that deals in human rights. You may wonder why all of the atrocities that have been committed in Africa and in Hungary and in Asia and in Latin America are brought before the UN, and the Negro problem is never brought before the UN. This is part of the conspiracy. This old, tricky, blue-eyed liberal who is supposed to be your and my friend, supposed to be in our corner, supposed to be subsidizing our struggle, and supposed to be acting in the capacity of an adviser, never tells you anything about human rights. They keep you wrapped up in civil rights. And you spend so much time barking up the civil-rights tree, you don't even know there's a human-rights tree on the same floor.

When you expand the civil-rights struggle to the level of human rights, you can then take the case of the black man in this country before the nations in the UN. You can take it before the General Assembly. You can take Uncle Sam before a world court. But the only level you can do it on is the level of human rights. Civil rights keeps you under his restrictions, under his jurisdiction. Civil rights keeps you in his pocket. Civil rights means you're asking Uncle Sam to treat you right. Human rights are something you were born with. Human rights are your God-given rights. Human rights are the rights that are recognized by all nations of this earth. And any time any one violates your human rights, you can take them to the world court. Uncle Sam's hands are dripping with blood, dripping with the blood of the black man in this country. He's the earth's number-one hypocrite. He has the audacity—yes, he has—imagine him posing as the leader of the free world. The free world!—and you over here singing "We Shall Overcome." Expand the civil-rights struggle to the level of human rights, take it into the United Nations, where our African brothers can throw their weight on our side, where our Asian brothers can throw their weight on our side, where our Latin-American brothers can throw their weight on our side, and where 800 million Chinamen are sitting there waiting to throw their weight on our side.

Let the world know how bloody his hands are. Let the world know the hypocrisy that's practiced over here. Let it be the ballot or the bullet. Let him know that it must be the ballot or the bullet.

When you take your case to Washington, D.C., you're taking it to the criminal who's responsible; it's like running from the wolf to the fox. They're all in cahoots together. They all work political chicanery and make you look like a chump before the eyes of the world. Here you are walking around in America, getting ready to be drafted and sent abroad, like a tin soldier, and when you get over there, people ask you what are you fighting for, and you have to stick your tongue in your cheek. No, take Uncle Sam to court, take him before the world.

By ballot I only mean freedom. Don't you know—I disagree with Lomax on this issue—that the ballot is more important than the dollar? Can I prove it? Yes. Look in the UN. There are poor nations in the UN; yet those poor nations can get together with their voting power and keep the rich nations from making a move. They have one nation—one vote, everyone has an equal vote. And when those brothers from Asia, and Africa and the darker parts of this earth get together, their voting power is sufficient to hold Sam in check. Or Russia in check. Or some other section of the earth in check. So, the ballot is most important.

Right now, in this country, if you and I, 22 million African-Americans—that's what we are—Africans who are in America. You're nothing but Africans. Nothing but Africans. In fact, you'd get farther calling yourself African instead of Negro. Africans don't catch hell. You're the only one catching hell. They don't have to pass civil-rights bills for Africans. An African can go anywhere he wants right now. All you've got to do is tie your head up. That's right, go anywhere you want. Just stop being a Negro. Change your name to Hoogagagooba. That'll show you how silly the white man is. You're dealing with a silly man. A friend of mine who's very dark put a turban on his head and went into a restaurant in Atlanta before they called themselves desegregated. He went into a white restaurant, he sat down, they served him, and he said, "What would happen if a Negro came in here?" And there he's sitting, black as night, but because he had his head wrapped up the waitress looked back at him and says, "Why, there wouldn't no nigger dare come in here."

So, you're dealing with a man whose bias and prejudice are making him lose his mind, his intelligence, every day. He's frightened. He looks around and sees what's taking place on this earth, and he sees that the pendulum of time is swinging in your direction. The dark people are waking up. They're losing their fear of the white man. No place where he's fighting right now is he winning. Everywhere he's fighting, he's fighting someone your and my complexion. And they're beating him. He can't win any more. He's won his last battle. He failed to win the Korean War. He couldn't win it. He had to sign a truce. That's a loss. Any time Uncle Sam, with all his machinery for warfare, is held to a draw by some rice-eaters, he's lost the battle. He had to sign a truce. America's not supposed to sign a truce. She's supposed to be bad. But she's not bad any more. She's bad as long as she can use her hydrogen bomb, but she can't use hers for fear Russia might use hers. Russia can't use hers, for fear that Sam might use his. So, both of them are weapon-less. They can't use the weapon because each's weapon nullifies the other's. So the only place where action can

take place is on the ground. And the white man can't win another war fighting on the ground. Those days are over. The black man knows it, the brown
man knows it, the red man knows it, and the yellow man knows it. So they
engage him in guerrilla warfare. That's not his style. You've got to have heart
to be a guerrilla warrior, and he hasn't got any heart. I'm telling you now.

I just want to give you a little briefing on guerrilla warfare because, before
you know it, before you know it—It takes heart to be a guerrilla warrior because you're on your own. In conventional warfare you have tanks and a whole
lot of other people with you to back you up, planes over your head and all
that kind of stuff. But a guerrilla is on his own. All you have is a rifle, some
sneakers and a bowl of rice, and that's all you need—and a lot of heart. The
Japanese on some of those islands in the Pacific, when the American soldiers
landed, one Japanese sometimes could hold the whole army off. He'd just wait
until the sun went down, and when the sun went down they were all equal.
He would take his little blade and slip from bush to bush, and from American
to American. The white soldiers couldn't cope with that. Whenever you see
a white soldier that fought in the Pacific, he has the shakes, he has a nervous
condition, because they scared him to death.

The same thing happened to the French up in French Indochina. People
who just a few years previously were rice farmers got together and ran the
heavily-mechanized French army out of Indochina. You don't need it—modern warfare today won't work. This is the day of the guerrilla. They did the
same thing in Algeria. Algerians, who were nothing but Bedouins, took a rifle
and sneaked off to the hills, and de Gaulle and all of his highfalutin' war machinery couldn't defeat those guerrillas. Nowhere on this earth does the white
man win in a guerrilla warfare. It's not his speed. Just as guerrilla warfare is
prevailing in Asia and in parts of Africa and in parts of Latin America, you've
got to be mighty naive, or you've got to play the black man cheap, if you
don't think some day he's going to wake up and find that it's got to be the
ballot or the bullet.

I would like to say, in closing, a few things concerning the Muslim Mosque,
Inc., which we established recently in New York City. It's true we're Muslims
and our religion is Islam, but we don't mix our religion with our politics and
our economics and our social and civil activities—not any more. We keep our
religion in our mosque. After our religious services are over, then as Muslims we become involved in political action, economic action and social and
civic action. We become involved with anybody, anywhere, any time and in
any manner that's designed to eliminate the evils, the political, economic and
social evils that are afflicting the people of our community.

The political philosophy of black nationalism means that the black man
should control the politics and the politicians in his own community; no
more. The black man in the black community has to be re-educated into the

science of politics so he will know what politics is supposed to bring him in return. Don't be throwing out any ballots. A ballot is like a bullet. You don't throw your ballots until you see a target, and if that target is not within your reach, keep your ballot in your pocket. The political philosophy of black nationalism is being taught in the Christian church. It's being taught in the NAACP. It's being taught in CORE meetings. It's being taught in SNCC [Student Nonviolent Coordinating Committee] meetings. It's being taught in Muslim meetings. It's being taught where nothing but atheists and agnostics come together. It's being taught everywhere. Black people are fed up with the dillydallying, pussyfooting, compromising approach that we've been using toward getting our freedom. We want freedom *now*, but we're not going to get it saying "We Shall Overcome." We've got to fight until we overcome.

The economic philosophy of black nationalism is pure and simple. It only means that we should control the economy of our community. Why should white people be running all the stores in our community? Why should white people be running the banks of our community? Why should the economy of our community be in the hands of the white man? Why? If a black man can't move his store into a white community, you tell me why a white man should move his store into a black community. The philosophy of black national-ism involves a re-education program in the black community in regards to economics. Our people have to be made to see that any time you take your dollar out of your community and spend it in a community where you don't live, the community where you live will get poorer and poorer, and the com-munity where you spend your money will get richer and richer. Then you wonder why where you live is always a ghetto or a slum area. And where you and I are concerned, not only do we lose it when we spend it out of the com-munity, but the white man has got all our stores in the community tied up; so that though we spend it in the community, at sundown the man who runs the store takes it over across town somewhere. He's got us in a vise.

So the economic philosophy of black nationalism means in every church, in every civic organization, in every fraternal order, it's time now for our people to become conscious of the importance of controlling the economy of our community. If we own the stores, if we operate the businesses, if we try and establish some industry in our own community, then we're developing to the position where we are creating employment for our own kind. Once you gain control of the economy of your own community, then you don't have to picket and boycott and beg some cracker downtown for a job in his business.

The social philosophy of black nationalism only means that we have to get together and remove the evils, the vices, alcoholism, drug addiction, and other evils that are destroying the moral fiber of our community. We ourselves have to lift the level of our community, the standard of our community to a higher level, make our own society beautiful so that we will be satisfied in our own social circles and won't be running around here trying to knock our way into a social circle where we're not wanted.

So I say, in spreading a gospel such as black nationalism, it is not designed to make the black man re-evaluate the white man—you know him already—but to make the black man re-evaluate himself. Don't change the white man's mind—you can't change his mind, and that whole thing about appealing to the moral conscience of America—America's conscience is bankrupt. She lost all conscience a long time ago. Uncle Sam has no conscience. They don't know what morals are. They don't try and eliminate an evil because it's evil, or because it's illegal, or because it's immoral; they eliminate it only when it threatens their existence. So you're wasting your time appealing to the moral conscience of a bankrupt man like Uncle Sam. If he had a conscience, he'd straighten this thing out with no more pressure being put upon him. So it is not necessary to change the white man's mind. We have to change our own mind. You can't change his mind about us. We've got to change our own minds about each other. We have to see each other with new eyes. We have to see each other as brothers and sisters. We have to come together with warmth so we can develop unity and harmony that's necessary to get this problem solved our selves. How can we do this? How can we avoid jealousy? How can we avoid the suspicion and the divisions that exist in the community? I'll tell you how.

I have watched how Billy Graham comes into a city, spreading what he calls the gospel of Christ, which is only white nationalism. That's what he is. Billy Graham is a white nationalist; I'm a black nationalist. But since it's the natural tendency for leaders to be jealous and look upon a powerful figure like Graham with suspicion and envy, how is it possible for him to come into a city and get all the cooperation of the church leaders? Don't think because they're church leaders that they don't have weaknesses that make them envious and jealous—no, everybody's got it. It's not an accident that when they want to choose a cardinal [as Pope] over there in Rome, they get in a closet so you can't hear them cussing and fighting and carrying on.

Billy Graham comes in preaching the gospel of Christ, he evangelizes the gospel, he stirs everybody up, but he never tries to start a church. If he came in trying to start a church, all the churches would be against him. So, he just comes in talking about Christ and tells everybody who gets Christ to go to any church where Christ is; and in this way the church cooperates with him. So we're going to take a page from his book.

Our gospel is black nationalism. We're not trying to threaten the existence of any organization, but we're spreading the gospel of black nationalism. Anywhere there's a church that is also preaching and practicing the gospel of black nationalism, join that church. If the NAACP is preaching and practicing the gospel of black nationalism, join the NAACP. If CORE is spreading and practicing the gospel of black nationalism, join CORE. Join any organization that has a gospel that's for the uplift of the black man. And when you get into it and see them pussyfooting or compromising, pull out of it because that's not black nationalism. We'll find another one.

And in this manner, the organizations will increase in number and in quantity and in quality, and by August, it is then our intention to have a black nationalist convention which will consist of delegates from all over the country who are interested in the political, economic and social philosophy of black nationalism. After these delegates convene, we will hold a seminar, we will hold discussions, we will listen to everyone. We want to hear new ideas and new solutions and new answers. And at that time, if we see fit then to form a black nationalist party, we'll form a black nationalist party. If it's necessary to form a black nationalist army, we'll form a black nationalist army. It'll be the ballot or the bullet. It'll be liberty or it'll be death.

It's time for you and me to stop sitting in this country, letting some cracker senators, Northern crackers and Southern crackers, sit there in Washington, D.C., and come to a conclusion in their mind that you and I are supposed to have civil rights. There's no white man going to tell me anything about my rights. Brothers and sisters, always remember, if it doesn't take senators and congressmen and presidential proclamations to give freedom to the white man, it is not necessary for legislation or proclamation or Supreme Court decisions to give freedom to the black man. You let that white man know, if this is a country of freedom, let it be a country of freedom; and if it's not a country of freedom, change it.

We will work with anybody, anywhere, at any time, who is genuinely interested in tackling the problem head-on, nonviolently as long as the enemy is nonviolent, but violent when the enemy gets violent. We'll work with you on the voter-registration drive, we'll work with you on rent strikes, we'll work with you on school boycotts—I don't believe in any kind of integration; I'm not even worried about it because I know you're not going to get it anyway; you're not going to get it because you're afraid to die; you've got to be ready to die if you try and force yourself on the white man, because he'll get just as violent as those crackers in Mississippi, right here in Cleveland. But we will still work with you on the school boycotts because we're against a segregated school system. A segregated school system produces children who, when they graduate, graduate with crippled minds. But this does not mean that a school is segregated because it's all black. A segregated school means a school that is controlled by people who have no real interest in it whatsoever.

Let me explain what I mean. A segregated district or community is a community in which people live, but outsiders control the politics and the economy of that community. They never refer to the white section as a segregated community. It's the all-Negro section that's a segregated community. Why? The white man controls his own school, his own bank, his own economy, his own politics, his own everything, his own community—but he also controls yours. When you're under someone else's control, you're segregated. They'll always give you the lowest or the worst that there is to offer, but it doesn't mean you're segregated just because you have your own. You've got to *control* your own. Just like the white man has control of his, you need to control yours.

You know the best way to get rid of segregation? The white man is more afraid of separation than he is of integration. Segregation means that he puts you away from him, but not far enough for you to be out of his jurisdiction; separation means you're gone. And the white man will integrate faster than he'll let you separate. So we will work with you against the segregated school system because it's criminal, because it is absolutely destructive, in every way imaginable, to the minds of the children who have to be exposed to that type of crippling education.

Last but not least, I must say this concerning the great controversy over rifles and shotguns. The only thing that I've ever said is that in areas where the government has proven itself either unwilling or unable to defend the lives and the property of Negroes, it's time for Negroes to defend themselves. Article number two of the constitutional amendments provides you and me the right to own a rifle or a shotgun. It is constitutionally legal to own a shotgun or a rifle. This doesn't mean you're going to get a rifle and form battalions and go out looking for white folks, although you'd be within your rights—I mean, you'd be justified; but that would be illegal and we don't do anything illegal. If the white man doesn't want the black man buying rifles and shotguns, then let the government do its job. That's all. And don't let the white man come to you and ask you what you think about what Malcolm says— why, you old Uncle Tom. He would never ask you if he thought you were going to say, "Amen!" No, he is making a Tom out of you.

So, this doesn't mean forming rifle clubs and going out looking for people, but it is time, in 1964, if you are a man, to let that man know. If he's not going to do his job in running the government and providing you and me with the protection that our taxes are supposed to be for, since he spends all those billions for his defense budget, he certainly can't begrudge you and me spending $12 or $15 for a single-shot, or double-action. I hope you understand. Don't go out shooting people, but any time, brothers and sisters, and especially the men in this audience—some of you wearing Congressional Medals of Honor, with shoulders this wide, chests this big, muscles that big—any time you and I sit around and read where they bomb a church and murder in cold blood, not some grownups, but four little girls while they were praying to the same god the white man taught them to pray to, and you and I see the government go down and can't find who did it.

Why, this man—he can find Eichmann hiding down in Argentina somewhere. Let two or three American soldiers, who are minding somebody else's business way over in South Vietnam, get killed, and he'll send battleships, sticking his nose in their business. He wanted to send troops down to Cuba and make them have what he calls free elections—this old cracker who doesn't have free elections in his own country. No, if you never see me another time in your life, if I die in the morning, I'll die saying one thing: the ballot or the bullet, the ballot or the bullet.

If a Negro in 1964 has to sit around and wait for some cracker senator to filibuster when it comes to the rights of black people, why, you and I should hang our heads in shame. You talk about a march on Washington in 1963, you haven't seen anything. There's some more going down in '64. And this time they're not going like they went last year. They're not going singing "We Shall Overcome." They're not going with white friends. They're not going with placards already painted for them. They're not going with round-trip tickets. They're going with one-way tickets.

And if they don't want that non-nonviolent army going down there, tell them to bring the filibuster to a halt. The black nationalists aren't going to wait. Lyndon B. Johnson is the head of the Democratic Party. If he's for civil rights, let him go into the Senate next week and declare himself. Let him go in there right now and declare himself. Let him go in there and denounce the Southern branch of his party. Let him go in there right now and take a moral stand—right now, not later. Tell him, don't wait until election time. If he waits too long, brothers and sisters, he will be responsible for letting a condition develop in this country which will create a climate that will bring seeds up out of the ground with vegetation on the end of them looking like something these people never dreamed of. In 1964, it's the ballot or the bullet. Thank you.

National Morals

RALPH REED

৯৵

Separation of Church and State: "Christian Nation" and Other Heresies

In 1992 I traveled to Oregon to debate John Frohnmayer, the former head of the National Endowment for the Arts, at a college symposium on the First Amendment. Our debate was spirited but cordial. He argued that any restrictions on the funding of the arts amounted to censorship. I argued that if taxpayers foot the bill, they should be free to set reasonable, common-sense guidelines to prevent the funding of obscenity or attacks on religion.

During the question-and-answer period, one man stepped to the microphone. "If you are allowed to pass laws based on your religious beliefs, where do you draw the line?" he pointedly asked. "What about the separation of church and state?" It was a good question. But it also betrayed a common misunderstanding about the First Amendment. I explained that the Constitution prohibited the government from establishing an official state religion. But equally important, the "free exercise" clause of the First Amendment prevented the government from restricting the citizenry from worshiping God according to the dictates of their conscience or freely expressing religious ideas.

What good is religious liberty, I asked, if it can only be practiced behind stained-glass windows on Sunday? If one desires to pass a law to prohibit people of faith from engaging in political action based on their beliefs, one would need to take a knife to our history books and cut out the pages on the antislavery crusade, the temperance movement, the women's movement, the civil rights struggle, and the anti–Vietnam War protests. All these social movements flowered in their day because religious people believed that the ideas of right and wrong they found in the Bible should be reflected in our laws. The only difference between these social movements and religious conservatives is the culture's view of what is politically correct.

Religious conservatives do not want a "Christian" nation, a "Jewish" nation, or a "Moslem" nation. They want a nation of strong families and basic goodness that respects the right of all individuals to express their faith and which does not prohibit faith to inform the laws that govern society. This is the kind of nation James Madison had in mind when he said, "We have staked the future . . . upon the capacity of each and all of us to govern ourselves, to control ourselves, to sustain ourselves according to the Ten Commandments of God."

Madison was right. Religious values are not a threat to democracy; they are essential to democracy. Indeed, the centrality of faith to the maintenance of democratic institutions was once considered axiomatic. For most of America's history, church pulpits flamed with sermons about social injustice; clergymen and women led social movements that embraced the highest ideals of faith-based reform; and the speeches, public statements, and proclamations of government officials brimmed with references to religion. No one suggested that these activities posed a threat to the separation of church and state. Americans resisted the establishment of a national religion but embraced faith as a vital ingredient in the body politic that was an essential counterbalance to government tyranny.

Only in recent times have religious conservatives, or religious people of any kind, been viewed as trying to transform this country into something that critics do not want to admit it has always been. The United States of America was founded on religious principles by religious people. Our society works best when we remember that fact and welcome into the public square those who act in its finest traditions.

Abraham Lincoln issued an order in 1862 requiring the observance of the sabbath in the Union army, noting that it corresponded "to the best sentiment of a Christian people."[1]

In the *Trinity* decision of 1892, the Supreme Court reviewed the Constitution, the Declaration of Independence, and other founding documents of America and concluded that they presupposed a Supreme Being and a religious citizenry. "Christianity," the Court stated, "general Christianity is and always has been a part of the common law. Not Christianity with an established church, but Christianity with liberty and conscience to all men."[2]

In 1931 Supreme Court Justice George Sutherland ruled that "the laws of the land . . . are not inconsistent with the will of God."[3] The North Atlantic summit in 1941 between Winston Churchill and Franklin Delano Roosevelt (who once described the United States as "the lasting concord between men

---

1. Don F. Fehrenbacher, ed., *Abraham Lincoln: Speeches and Writings, 1859–1865* (New York: Library of America, 1989), 382–83; Gary Wills, *Under God: Religion and American Politics* (New York: Simon and Schuster, 1990), 381.

2. *Church of the Holy Trinity v. U.S.*, 143 U.S. 457 (1892).

3. *U.S. v. MacIntosh*, 283 U.S. 605, 625 (1931).

and nations, founded on the principles of Christianity") featured Sunday services with a message from the Book of Joshua and the singing of hymns (selected by Winston Churchill) that climaxed with a windswept rendition of "Onward Christian Soldiers."[4] In 1947, in a letter to Pope Pius XII, President Harry Truman went further, asserting, "This is a Christian nation."

"We are a religious people whose system of government supposes a Supreme Being," concluded Justice William O. Douglas in *Zorach v. Clauson* in 1952. He added that there existed "no constitutional requirement which makes it necessary for government to be hostile to religion and to throw its weight against efforts to widen the effective scope of religious influence."[5]

"Our hard challenge and our sublime opportunity is to bear witness to the spirit of Christ in fashioning a truly Christian world," said Martin Luther King in 1963.[6]

These observations—many by liberal Democrats—reflected a consensus on civil religion that united Americans for the first three centuries of their history. They were not theological sermons but civil statements, some of them carrying the weight of law. They were not arguments for an established church but acknowledgements of a distinctly American piety that, until recently, permeated the entire culture, rendering the entanglement of government in religion superfluous and unnecessary.

This is the genius of America: we are a people of faith that stipulates, in order to protect the free exercise of our religion, that government stay out of the business of the church. In the 1830s, when the Second Great Awakening turned parts of western New York into a "burned over district" ablaze with the fires of revivalism, Alexis de Tocqueville observed that while religion was the first of America's civil institutions, the people nevertheless retained a healthy suspicion of government imposition of faith. "Religion in America," noted Tocqueville, "takes no direct part in the government of society, but it must be regarded the first of their political institutions; for if it does not impart a taste for freedom, it facilitates the use of it." He added that while "religion exercises but little influence upon the laws and upon the details of public opinion," it "directs the customs of the community, and by regulating domestic life, it regulates the state."[7]

Norman Sykes, in his classic *Church and State in England in the Eighteenth*

---

4. Eric Larrabee, *Commander in Chief: Franklin Delano Roosevelt, His Lieutenants, and Their War* (New York: Simon and Schuster, 1988), 239–40; Martin Gilbert, *Churchill: A Life* (New York: Holt, Henry and Company, 1992), 705; for a similar account of this incident and the preceding statements, see Larry Witham, "Christian Nation Now Fighting Words," *Washington Times*, November 23, 1992.

5. *Zorach v. Clauson*, 343 U.S. 306 (1952).

6. Martin Luther King, Jr., *Strength to Love* (Philadelphia: Fortress Press, 1963).

7. Alexis de Tocqueville, *Democracy in America*, ed. Phillips Bradley (1835; reprint, New York: Alfred A. Knopf, 1980), 304–5.

Century, argued that three "pillars" sustained the social order of Great Britain during the eighteenth century: the Protestant Succession, the Established Church, and tolerated Dissent.[8] Three equally important "pillars" have sustained the social order in the United States for over two centuries: the separation of powers, the Bill of Rights, and civil religion. The separation of powers has guarded against tyranny by preventing the power of the national government from residing in a single branch.

The Bill of Rights enumerates the rights of the citizenry against which government may not encroach. These rights were extended to all Americans by the Fourteenth Amendment to the Constitution, which granted former slaves equality before the law following the Civil War.

The third pillar, civil religion, has been the glue that held American society together, bridging ethnic and racial differences by expressing the common attributes of faith while assiduously avoiding the European practice of established churches. Civil religion, like the separation of powers and the Bill of Rights, provides an insurance policy against tyranny, something that was foremost in the minds of a people that had just fought a bloody war of independence from Great Britain. By inculcating a voluntary code of behavior that included respect for one's neighbor, honesty, frugality, piety, and self-sufficiency, it kept the government small and subdued.

None of this adds up to the conclusion that America is a "Christian nation" in the sense of a theocratic state or a unicultural society. That not only ignores the enormous contribution that Jews have made to America, but it is something of an anachronism. It makes just as much sense to say that Massachusetts is a Puritan colony or that Maryland is a Catholic state. Massachusetts may have been a Puritan commonwealth in the seventeenth or even the eighteenth centuries, but it hardly qualifies today. America is not solely a Christian nation, but a pluralistic society of Protestants, Catholics, Jews, Muslims, and other people of faith whose broader culture once honored religion, but which today increasingly reflects a hostility towards faith in the public sphere. What religious conservatives want is to accommodate the historic role of faith in American civic life. In short, they seek to restore the time-honored tradition of civil religion—not to establish Christianity by law or create an official church.

When former President Richard Nixon recently died, many analysts observed that probably only Nixon, stalwart Republican and staunch anticommunist, could have gone to China. Similarly, probably only a Democrat can bring our nation back to the tradition of civil religion.[9]

8. Norman Sykes, *Church and State in England in the Eighteenth Century* (Cambridge: Oxford University Press, 1934), 315.

9. Adam Clymer, "Tiff Over Governor's 'Christian' Remark Underscores Fault Line in G.O.P.," *New York Times*, November 22, 1992; Samuel Francis, "Pluralism Clouds Over Fordice," *Washington Times*, November 24, 1992.

There is some evidence that Bill Clinton would like to be that Democrat. While vacationing in Martha's Vineyard in the summer of 1993, Clinton read Yale Professor Stephen L. Carter's *The Culture of Disbelief* and found his theme of the marginalization of religion in American law and politics deeply compelling. Not long after returning to the White House, Clinton addressed an interfaith prayer breakfast of one hundred clergy in the State Dining Room and discussed the spiritual vacuum in America's soul. "Sometimes I think the environment in which we operate is entirely too secular," he confessed. "The fact that we have freedom of religion doesn't mean we need to try to have freedom from religion."[10] In a sun-drenched South Lawn ceremony celebrating the passage of the Religious Freedom Restoration Act on November 16, 1993, Clinton went further. The Democrats had recently made the centerpiece of the gubernatorial campaign in Virginia an assault on the Republican ticket for being too closely aligned with religious conservatives. The result was the largest landslide for a Republican candidate for governor in the twentieth century—and the near-election of home school attorney Mike Farris as lieutenant governor. "There is a great debate now abroad in the land which finds itself injected into several political races about the extent to which people of faith can seek to do God's will as political actors," Clinton noted. "I would like to come down on the side of encouraging everybody to act on what they believe is the right thing to do." He urged his audience to "respect one another's faith, fight to the death to preserve the right of every American to practice whatever convictions he or she has, but bring our values back to the table of American discourse to heal our troubled land."[11]

This presidential rhetoric is helpful not only because it reaffirms the importance of civil religion but also because it prevents religion from becoming a wholly-owned subsidiary of the Republican party. Clinton's remarks constituted a remarkable (if oblique) slap at his own party for failing to appreciate the role of religion in public life. President Clinton should be commended for speaking out on the essential role of people of faith in renewing our society and sustaining democracy.

However, this rhetoric will be found wanting unless it is matched with actions. Clinton's call for taxpayer funding of abortion, his appointments of persons such as Joycelyn Elders with harshly anti-Catholic views, his endorsement of special rights legislation based on sexual preference (issued, oddly, on Valentine's Day), and the recent reemergence of the character issue with the Whitewater scandal and allegations of sexual misconduct make it more diffi-

10. Statement by President Bill Clinton, August 30, 1993, White House Press Office; David Lauter, "Clinton Voices Concern U.S. May Be Too Secular," *Los Angeles Times*, August 31, 1993; Bill Nichols, "New Beginning for Clinton," *USA Today*, August 31, 1993.

11. Statement by Bill Clinton, November 16, 1993, White House Press Office; Peter Steinfels, "Clinton Signs Law Protecting Religious Practices," *New York Times*, November 17, 1993.

cult for him to appeal to religious values. As Terry Eastland of the Ethics and Public Policy Center notes, he "has named to his administration individuals like Surgeon General Joycelyn Elders who not only dismiss religious conservatives but cast aspersions upon them." Clinton should continue to use the bully pulpit of the presidency to urge a healthy respect for religious values, but he must also take action to insure that those values are reflected in both the policies and conduct of his presidency.[12]

This does not mean that only a president who agrees with every single element in the religious conservative agenda can reinstill public confidence in religion. Jimmy Carter, despite all his other shortcomings, did speak eloquently about his faith. Americans yearn for political leaders for whom faith is important in their daily lives.

Reviving Civil Religion

Whether Bill Clinton or another politician changes the terms of the debate about religion and politics, the decline in civil religion has accelerated as elected officials have grown wary of using religious language to frame public issues. Demographic changes during the twentieth century have had a devastating effect on religion as the common bond uniting all Americans. Urbanization has depersonalized society until many of us do not even know our neighbors' names. The anonymity and alienation of modern society stands in stark contrast to America during the nineteenth century, when everyone was accountable to parents, neighbors, church or synagogue, and the community. Today we live in fear of each other, with alarm systems on our homes, bars on our windows, alarms on our automobiles, and guns in the closet. We travel to and from work in hermetically-sealed automobiles, lost in thought or the blare of the radio, rarely exchanging glances with fellow motorists except to shake fists or shout expletives.

Even the church has become uprooted from a sense of community. My wife and I attended a large church in Atlanta, Georgia, with over 10,000 members. We often went to church twice a week, but outside of a young married couples' group, knew almost no one who sat next to us in the pews. Fifty years ago, they would have been our friends, our family, and our neighbors.

Human beings are social animals. They are not designed to function properly when disconnected from the love and concern of others. Sadly, the number of such individuals represents the fastest growing demographic group

12. Terry Eastland, "Religion, Politics, and the Clintons," *Commentary*, January 1994, 40–43. Some evangelical leaders have been enamored by Clinton's recent conversion to religion. Fred Barnes, "Rev. Bill: Clinton Courts Evangelical Leaders," *New Republic*, January 13, 1994.

in society. According to the U.S. Census Bureau, an astonishing 25 percent of all households consist of people living alone—one out of every four in the nation.[13] Among these roughly 22 million persons living alone, there are countless troubled people waiting to detonate. Estranged from dysfunctional families of origin, isolated from neighbors, unmarried, twisted by sexual or chemical addictions, and unaccountable to any faith community, some are the human consequences of an anonymous society.

Civil religion would help to soften the often brutal edges of our secular, modern society. It would not contemplate the establishment of an official church. But it would allow the healing influence of religion—all religions— to be freely expressed in the public square.

This was the original intent of our nation's founders when they framed the Constitution. Justice Joseph Story, who sat on the Supreme Court from 1811 until 1845 and taught law at Harvard University, stated unequivocally in his commentary on the Constitution: "The real object of the [First] Amendment was . . . to prevent any national ecclesiastical establishment which should give to a hierarchy the exclusive patronage of the national government." The objective was not, in Story's word, to "prostrate" Christianity by excluding it from the public square, but to prohibit the elevation of one sect or denomination above the others.[14]

Church and state jurisprudence has gradually shifted in recent decades to a point that the framers of the First Amendment would not recognize it. They saw the state as the threat; today the courts see the church as the threat. The founders viewed an established state religion as the embodiment of tyranny because it allowed the government to rule over citizens in matters of conscience. Today, we react harshly to religion itself, even when the government does not dictate its expression. The Supreme Court's opinion in *Employment Division v. Smith*, the so-called *peyote* case, in 1990 underscored our legal culture's hostility towards the free exercise of religion. In that case, the Court dropped the time-honored standard that government demonstrate a compelling reason for passing laws that had the effect (even when unintentional) of discriminating against religion. The ruling was later overturned by the passage of the Religious Freedom Restoration Act in 1993.[15]

This hostility contrasts sharply with the early republic, when religion was synonymous with patriotism, and Christianity became equated with republi-

13. Daniel Yankelovich, "How Changes in the Economy are Reshaping American Values," in *Values and Public Policy*, ed. Henry Aaron, et al. (Washington: Brookings Institute), 1994, 33–34.

14. John S. Baker, Jr., "The Establishment Clause as Intended: No Preference Among Sects and Pluralism in a Large Commercial Republic," in *The Bill of Rights: Original Meaning and Current Understanding*, ed. Eugene W. Hickok, Jr. (Charlottesville, Vir.: University Press of Virginia, 1991), 43.

15. *Employment Division v. Smith*, 110 S. Ct. 1595 (1990).

can virtue. In the famous 1811 blasphemy decision of *The People of New York v. Ruggles*, Federalist jurist Chancellor James Kent ruled that although the Constitution forbade an established church and New York had no specific statute banning blasphemy, for any citizen to denigrate Christianity was "to strike at the roots of moral obligation and weaken the security of social ties." Kent was not himself a committed Christian. But he agreed that religion was, in the words of Leverett Saltonstall of Massachusetts, "the great bond of civil society." This same conviction caused a New York judge in 1831 to disallow the testimony of a witness who declared himself an atheist. The judge ruled that faith in God "constituted the sanction of all testimony in a court of justice" and that no one could be "permitted to testify without such belief."[16]

No one is suggesting that we return to the days when the testimony of nonbelievers is excluded from courts of law. But if the pendulum then swayed too far in the direction of religion, can anyone deny that today it has swung too far in the opposite direction? When prosecutors are reprimanded because they quote from the Bible, when attorneys are told to remove ashes from their forehead on Ash Wednesday, and when a Rabbi's simple prayer is ruled unconstitutional, our zeal for separation of church and state has curdled into a sour distaste for religious expression. Today it is the religious person whose testimony or political activism may be called into question based solely on their belief in God.

16. Gordon S. Wood, *The Radicalism of the American Revolution* (New York: Alfred A. Knopf, 1992), 331, for Kent and Saltonstall quotations; de Tocqueville, *Democracy*, 306.

ROSEMARY RADFORD RUETHER

❧

Creating a Healed World:
Spirituality and Politics

In . . . two traditions, covenantal and sacramental, we hear two voices of divinity from nature. One speaks from the mountaintops in the thunderous masculine tones of "thou shalt" and "thou shalt not." It is the voice of power and law, but speaking (at its most authentic) on behalf of the weak, as a mandate to protect the powerless and to restrain the power of the mighty. There is another voice, one that speaks from the intimate heart of matter. It has long been silenced by the masculine voice, but today is finding again her own voice. This is the voice of Gaia. Her voice does not translate into laws or intellectual knowledge, but beckons us into communion.

Both of these voices, of God and of Gaia, are our own voices. We need to claim them as our own, not in the sense that there is "nothing" out there, but in the sense that what is "out there" can only be experienced by us through the lenses of human existence. We are not the source of life, but are latecomers to the planet. Our minds didn't fall from the skies, but are the flowering of organic body and its capacities to know itself. We can touch our fellow beings, and intuit the source of all life and thought that lies behind the whole. This contact, though humanly imaged, can be true. Its truth lies in the test of relationships; do our metaphors bear the fruits of compassion or of enmity?

We need both of these holy voices. We cannot depend on volunteerism alone to save rain forests and endangered species, set limits to the exploitation of animals and sanction abusers. We need organized systems and norms of ecological relations. Otherwise, not only will most people not comply, but will not be able to comply, because they have no way of fulfilling their daily needs except through the exigencies of the present system. But, without the second voice, our laws have no heart, no roots in compassion and fellow feeling. They fail to foster a motivating desire for biophilic living.

From *Gaia and God: An Ecofeminist Theology of Earth Healing* by Rosemary Radford Ruether (copyright 1992 by Rosemary Radford Ruether; reprinted by permission of HarperCollins Publishers, Inc.), pp. 254–74, 305–6.

To begin to define an ethic for ecological living, we need to revisit the questions of good and evil, sin and fallenness, discussed in Section Three of this book. That we have a "problem" is unquestionable, but how we define the nature of that problem will determine our solutions. Christians and their secular heirs inherit two definitions of the problem of evil. For the Hebraic tradition, the problem lies in the will to disobey. The commandments of God disclose the way of justice, but we choose injustice. Yet we remain free. We can choose the path of obedience and hence of abundant living. The solution does not lie outside history, but is to be worked out within the bounds of historical existence.

For the Greek tradition, the fault is metaphysical. We are a dualism of eternal mind and mortal body. The solution lies in withdrawing into the mind and controlling the body. Ultimately the solution lies beyond death, in the discarding of the body. Yet the power to do so lies with us. What we truly know, we can do. Christianity fused these two views and hence compounded the understanding of sin. Sin is both historical and metaphysical, both something for which we are totally guilty and yet which we are powerless to resolve by ourselves.

There is much in this combined sense of guilt and helplessness that has spoken and continues to speak to our experience, perhaps even more today, as the cumulative effects of human violence mount and we feel trapped in them. Yet it can lead to many perversions that reinforce the problem: passivity, contempt for what is possible to us here and now, the desire to flee to imagined perfections outside of embodied and historical existence, and finally the scapegoating of victims as the cause of the evils we seek to repudiate and to guard ourselves against.

We need a foundation for ethical theory that is not based on a dualistic negation of the "other," whether woman or animal or body, pagans, gentiles, or barbarians (or the countercultural reversals of these projections) as the bearers of our "shadow." This does not mean that there is no such thing as evil, or that ethical distinctions as such should be repudiated for an acceptance of all that is as good or, at least, necessary. The difference between starving a child or torturing a prisoner, and nurturing their lives, is real, and reflect decisions made by actual people.

But the reality of evil does not lie in some "thing" out there. It cannot be escaped, and indeed is exacerbated by efforts to avoid it by cutting ourselves off from that "thing." Rather, evil lies in "wrong relationship." All beings live in community, both with members of their own species and with others for which they depend for food, breath, materials for construction, and affective feedback. Yet there is a tendency in the life drive itself in each species to maximize its own existence and hence to proliferate in a cancerous way that destroys its own biotic support.

This is not just a human tendency. As Lynn Margulis has pointed out, even ancient bacteria tended toward this proliferating growth, in which the consuming of others finally threatens to destroy both the environment and the species.[1] The life force itself is not unequivocally good, but becomes "evil" when it is maximized at the expense of others. In this sense "good" lies in limits, a balancing of our own drive for life with the life drives of all the others in which we are in community, so that the whole remains in life-sustaining harmony. The wisdom of nature lies in the development of built-in limits through a diversity of beings in interrelation, so that none outruns its own "niche."

Humans, particularly since the development of agriculture, have been able to develop the food base to escape the built-in limits of other species, and even of their own species in the hunter-gatherer mode. They have been able to grow their own food base and thus maximize their own lives, using land, plants, and animals as objects of control and manipulation. In the process some humans (dominant males) also have learned to maximize their own lives, both for leisure and consumption, over against other humans. The human community itself was fissured into controlling "subjects" and exploited "objects."

It is more misleading than helpful to speak about this development of systems of domination as a "fall." It might be called a "loss of innocence" and the beginning of deceit. But we need to be clear that all was not idyllic before, nor did there enter into history at that time a totally new capacity for evil not present before. Rather, a possibility in nature, the maximizing of some against others, was appropriated in a new way, organized in such a way that self-correcting limits could be avoided by those who profited. The price of exploitation was borne by the exploited.

Only as the system of exploitation reaches its maximal stage does it begin to undermine the quality of life of those at the "top," and thus force them to recognize that the whole house of cards is about to topple. Their first instinct is to stave off this demise by accelerating the exploitation of those they dominate, while seeking to maintain their own comfortable life-style with the dwindling resources of the whole. The rich try to stay rich while the poor get poorer, and the destruction of the environment increases.

Eventually the whole system collapses. This has happened before, as in the disappearance of "lost civilizations," and in a more extensive way, in the "fall" of Rome. The difference today is that the system of exploitation is global, and the possibility of destruction correspondingly global. There are not the same spaces to retreat from the collapse. Thus we face a cancerous proliferation of

---

1. This analysis appeared in a talk by Lynn Margulis, "Gaia Minus Man," at the conference "Ecological Prospects: Theory and Practice," at Loyola Marymount University, Los Angeles, California, March 15, 1991. Margulis is one of the major theoreticians of the Gaia Hypothesis.

our species that could not only bring it to extinction, but pull much of the planetary life system down with it.

However, civilizations have not only created domination and cultures of deceit that justified domination. They have also created critical cultures designed to unmask deceit and spiritualities that awakened compassion for others, thus rebuilding culturally the balances of self-limitation and respect for the lives of others that make for good community. We inherit in our Christian tradition (as do others in their traditions) both cultures of domination and deceit and cultures of critique and compassion. We need to build on and develop the second culture to unmask and check the power of the first culture.

Envisioning a Good Society

Let us begin by envisioning something of the goal that we seek, not in the sense of a static "once-for-all" future perfection, but in the sense of healthy societies that can be sustained from season to season, which are no longer building up toxicities of destruction. This vision must start with a principle of equity: equity between men and women; between human groups living within regions; equity across human communities globally; equity between the human species and all other members to the biotic community of which we are a part; and finally equity between generations of living things, between the needs of those alive now and those who are to come.

Rebuilding human society for a sustainable earth will require far more than a plethora of technological "fixes" within the present paradigm of relations of domination. It will demand a fundamental restructuring of all these relations from systems of domination/exploitation to ones of biophilic mutuality. New technologies may well have their place, although there may also be a need to rediscover old techniques of agriculture, architecture, artisanry, and community-building as well. But technique cannot be divorced from its social and psychic contexts. A new technique or a recovery of an old one will not "take" without transformed political relations and cultural consciousness.

A healed earth is one in which all the patterns of destruction . . . have been deeply transformed, the patterns that are resulting in proliferating population, deepening poverty, famine, soil erosion, deforestation, the extinction of species, air and water pollution, energy crises, and militarism. Just as the patterns that are producing this vast reign of death are interrelated, so a new life-sustaining community of humans as part of the biosphere of Gaia are interrelated. This does not mean that there are not many incremental steps toward this new pattern, but these incremental steps have to be guided by a holistic vision.

Let us start by looking at some of these incremental shifts, envisioning, at each point, some of the interrelated transformations that would be involved. Let us start with the need to phase out petroleum and other fossil fuels as the primary energy sources of production, transportation, and home heating. The alternative energy sources are solar, wind, water, thermal, and biomass energies, as well as human and animal activity. There are many incremental steps along the way to this shift to renewable energy sources, to accommodate, not only the dwindling supplies of fossil fuels, but also the unacceptable price of polluting the atmosphere with their emissions.

Greatly increased efficiency of the machinery is one such step, getting much more work for the same amount of fuel. Another is control of the emissions. But finally one has to look at the organization of the system itself. In the case of transportation, the private automobile becomes an unacceptable mode of transportation. Phasing it out will require a whole new system of transportation that will combine much less polluting technologies of mass transit between centers, together with walking, biking, and small electric cars locally. But this also means reorganizing the locations of living, working, recreation, and marketing units, so that much less transportation is required to connect the segments of daily life.[2]

A new transportation system is an adjunct to rebuilding organic local communities no longer fragmented across distances that are only bridgeable by the private auto. Very quickly we move from the realm of technologies to the realm of political ordering of relations. Who profits from the present system of fuel-inefficient private autos, centralized workplaces separated from living places, and the class-ethnic segmentation of neighborhoods? To locate those who profit from this system is also to name those who will mobilize their political and economic power to prevent change.

Greatly improved insulation, including environmental designs such as homes built partly into the earth, together with solar and wind technologies for generating electricity, and biomass fuels, such as wood, can dramatically lessen the costs of heating and cooling houses, cooking, and lighting. Mass development of these sustainable home technologies demands political mobilization, locally and regionally. Subsidies must be put behind ecologically sound technologies, while subsidies are withdrawn from polluting and wasteful energy companies and builders, revealing the true costs of their methods.

The questions of local and regional control and decision making, over against the power of multinational corporations, is central to this political struggle. Oil is shipped to us from halfway around the world. Wood is locally produced. Solar energy for homes comes from panels on roofs possessed by the owners of the building. Electricity from windmills also could be owned

---

2. Marcia D. Lowe, "Rethinking Urban Transport," in *State of the World, 1991* (New York: Norton, 1991), 56–73.

by home units or organized in small local companies.[3] The age of mega-corporations is put in question, its inefficiency and true costs exposed. The state and its ownership also is revealed. The people seek to take control of the political systems for the commonweal of all, rather than the subsidization of the profits of the rich.

The question of raising and distributing food adequate to nourish the human population (and the animals they own), without depleting the fertility of the land from which it grows, also raises a host of interrelated issues. A shift toward sustainable food production and distribution calls for a phasing out of the long transportation chains that deliver great varieties of foods from all over the globe in all seasons to elites, while the majority of humans barely survive on a poor and limited diet. We need to return to seasonal patterns of food, produced and distributed in one or several contiguous bioregions.[4]

Another shift is toward eating lower on the food chain, greatly reducing meat-eating in favor of vegetable proteins. This not only releases a vast amount of grain, presently fed to animals destined for the dinner tables of the affluent, for human consumption, but also greatly reduces the ecological impact of cattle grazing and feedlots. Saving rain forests and preventing desertification of fragile grasslands is interdependent with great reduction of domesticated animal herds.

By withdrawing the subsidies from agribusiness methods of food production, its actual inefficiency is revealed. At the same time, the small farm using organic methods should be promoted. Then many traditional forms of agriculture can be recovered in more sophisticated forms. The organic farm reclaims the traditional integration of animals and crops. Animals provide a part of the farm work force, their excrement is returned as the natural fertilizer of soils, and they are fed with agricultural wastes and grasses. Organic pest control and integrated gardening, in which various types of plants renew soils for each other, are rediscovered and refined. These are elements of an agriculture that sustains the land for the generations to come.[5]

The concern to sustain the soil for the next generation also demands more rooted communities. Farmers sustain the land to be handed down to their children; corporations are uninterested in the next generation. They pillage the environment and then flee the scene. Creating rooted farming communi-

---

3. See Christopher Flavin and Nicholas Lenssen, "Designing a Sustainable Energy System," Lester Brown et al., editors, *State of the World, 1991* (New York: Norton), 21–38; also Amory B. Lovins, *Soft Energy Paths: Toward a Durable Peace* (Cambridge, MA: Ballinger Publishing Company, 1977).

4. Jeremy Rifkin, *Biosphere Politics: A New Consciousness for a New Century* (New York: Crown Publishers, 1991), 287–92; also Kirkpatrick Sale, *Dwellers in the Land: The Bioregional Vision* (San Francisco: Sierra Club Books, 1985).

5. Wes Jackson, *New Roots for Agriculture* (Lincoln: University of Nebraska Press, 1985).

ties also demands reversing the five-hundred-year trend of land confiscation. This trend has left most of the families of the world landless, while a few corporate landowners, the contemporary *latifundistas*, own, neglect, or deplete much of the agricultural land. Better agricultural methods that sustain the land go hand in hand with land reform that returns much of the land to local farmers in families and cooperative groups.[6]

Land reform also suggests an eventual reversal of the trends to urbanization, decentralizing the mega-urban centers and creating regional configurations in which business, educational, political, and cultural centers are integrated with their agricultural base. More hand labor and less mechanized labor would also mean more people working on and living directly from the land.

Return to the land means recovering something of the biorhythms of the body, the day, and the seasons from the world of clocks, computers, and artificial lighting that have almost entirely alienated us from these biorhythms.[7] This does not mean there is not a place for high-tech instruments of information processing and communication. But these need to become more accessible to all and organized in relation to the biotic base of life, rather than creating the delusion that this base of life has been replaced altogether.

Greatly reducing fossil fuels as the main source of energy, drastic reduction of grain-fed cattle in feedlots, shifting to organic pest control and fertilizers: these would greatly reduce major sources of air, soil and water pollution. But an ecologically sustainable society must also terminate as much as possible all forms of disposable waste. "Unnatural" toxic wastes, such as nuclear wastes and fluorocarbons, need to be phased out altogether, because these cannot be safely recycled. Human and animal body wastes need to be treated so they can be returned to rebuild soils. Agricultural and food wastes need to be part of composting systems, both on farms and in local communities. Packaging needs to be greatly reduced, and wastes from consumer goods of all kinds recycled. Finally all human artifacts should be made to be reused many times, rather than quickly discarded.[8] These shifts too will involve deep value changes, as well as political struggles with the forces that promote the "disposable society."

The real cost of throwing away twenty-five plastic wrappings and bags after each shopping, rather than reusing several sturdy cloth bags, needs to be made evident. One way of doing this would be to have the shopper pay for the actual costs of the plastic wrappings, costs that would be avoided by those

---

6. For example, the Spanish conquerers in the Americas created huge plantations, and this still shapes landholding patterns in these regions. Land reform remains the most central issue of social justice; see the pastoral letter by the Guatemalan bishops, *Clamor for Land*, published in *Reflections: The Guatemalan Church in Exile* (Managua, Nicaragua: May 1988).

7. Jeremy Rifkin, *Times Wars: The Primary Conflict in Human History* (New York: Simon and Schuster, 1989).

8. John E. Young, "Reducing Waste, Saving Materials," in *State of the World, 1991*, 39–55.

who brought their own bags, rather than hiding these costs in the costs of the food. The costs of the plastic wrapping must also include the costs of breaking them down and recycling them, as well as their initial production. Only when the true environmental costs are paid for by the producers and consumers, rather than passed on to the general public, will it be evident that the ecological society is the only truly "economical" society.

Although greatly reducing the environmental impact of human production, transportation, consumption, and waste is critical for a sustainable society, and must demand the greatest changes from the most affluent societies, a significant curbing and eventual reduction of human population itself is also necessary. If human population is allowed to double once again in forty years or less, and hits 8 billion to 10 billion in the first third of the twenty-first century, all the measures we have just discussed will go for naught. Humanity has no real alternative to population control. The question is, do we want population control to happen voluntarily, before conception, or violently by war, famine, and disease?

The promotion of effective birth control on a widespread basis sufficient to halt and reduce the world population explosion is only secondarily a matter of developing and distributing technologies, although this is not unimportant. It is, above all, a matter of how women and their bodies are socially and culturally appropriated. Many cultural, social, and economic forces impede the empowerment of women as moral agents of their own reproductive powers: poverty, demographic war, and the whole complex of attitudes that spring from patriarchy.[9]

Poor families, without adequate food or medicine for their children, but who also invest little in their children's future, will not cease to have many children as long as they fear that many of them will die, but also see that those who live can participate in the farming or scavenging that sustains the family unit. Communities under demographic threat from occupying peoples, such as the Palestinians in Israel, will not cease to have large families as long as this is the only way they have to assure the survival of their people.

Patriarchy has multiple impacts on reproductive patterns. Its valuing of the male over the female means that families cannot rest content with having produced two children, if both of these children are female. Often two males are desired to assure the patrilineage. Patriarchy also denies women control over their own sexuality and reproduction, and values women only to produce children, sharply curtailing other ways in which women can live satisfying lives and be held in esteem by their communities.

The empowerment of women as moral agents of their own sexuality and

---

9. Kathleen Newland, *Women and Population Growth: The Choice Beyond Childbearing*, Worldwatch Report no. 16 (Washington, D.C.: Worldwatch Institute, 1977).

reproduction is thus an integral part of any authentic population policy. The female child needs to be valued equally with the male. This is only possible if the adult female is also seen as an autonomous person who will be an active cultural and economic agent in her own right, and not just an adjunct to a male-centered society. Only when women can no longer be beaten by men, raped by men, and traded between men as commodities, can they cease to be treated or to see themselves as passive bodies to be acted upon by men.

Women need a sense of their own integrity and to have that integrity affirmed by males. They need to have a full range of life opportunities for their many creative roles, of which reproduction is only one. They need to have the knowledge and technology of birth control and the right to enforce these in sexual relations with men. They need to have a sense that their daughters, as much as their sons, will have these many options and will be given education for them. Finally they need to see themselves as responsible agents for a just and sustainable society in their communities.

Although the empowerment of women as moral, economic, and cultural agents in their own right is crucial for effective "family planning," it also lies at the base of all the value changes that will lead from cultures of domination to cultures of biophilic mutuality. The "liberation of women" cannot be seen simply as the incorporation of women into alienated male styles of life, although with far fewer benefits, for this simply adds women to the patterns of alienated life created by and for men. In fact, it is impossible to fully add women to this alienated life of males, since the male alienated life-style is only possible by the exploitation of women who remain tied to "nature."

Rather, what is necessary is a double transformation of both women and men in their relation to each other and to "nature." Women certainly need to gain some of the individuality that has been traditionally purchased by men at their expense. But this individuation should not be based on exploitative domination (of other women or subjugated men), but needs to remain in sustaining relation to primary communities of life. The ways of being a person for others and of being a person for oneself need to come together as reciprocal, rather than being split between female and male styles of life. It is the male rather than the female life-style that needs, however, the deeper transformation. Males need to overcome the illusion of autonomous individualism, with its extension into egocentric power over others, starting with the women with whom they relate. Men need to integrate themselves into life-sustaining relations with women as lovers, parents, and coworkers. They need to do regularly what they have hardly ever done, even in preagricultural societies: feed, clothe, wash, and hug children from infancy, cook food, and clean up wastes.

Only when men are fully integrated into the culture of daily sustenance of life can men and women together begin to reshape the larger systems of economic, social, and political life. They can begin to envision new cultural consciousness and organizational structures that would connect these larger systems to their roots in the earth and to sustaining the earth from day to day and from generation to generation.

Both the "liberation" of women into male styles of alienated pseudo-autonomy and the domestication of men into women's dependency are equally false compensations, if they function within the present pattern of distortion, and are not part of a larger transformation. The domestic-public split itself must yield to a new sense of a holistic culture that recognizes both men and women as individuated persons in mutual interdependency with each other and with the earth.[10]

From this familial base of relationships we turn to the largest system of dominating power: militarism. I have suggested that the isolated male ego that demands invulnerable and dominating power over others is shaped developmentally through negation of interdependency with women, in the context of woman-exploited childraising. But this type of masculine ego finds its most global manifestation in militarism, including the militarized economy and national security state.

. . . since 1950 the military state, with its appendages in professional armies and in rapacious business corporations, which produce military equipment as a major part of international trade, have taken over more and more of the wealth of the world. In a vast enclosure of the world commons, much of the land, sea, and even air space of the earth has been expropriated for the militarized corporate economy.[11] The poorest countries are forced into increasing debt and dependency within this system.

This military state operates out of a polarized, totalitarian worldview of absolute good against absolute evil. "Good" means our invulnerability and total power over other peoples and world resources. "Evil" is anything that challenges this invulnerability and control. The earth is reduced to "resources" to be used, and interdependency with nature or with other people is denied. In any situation of conflict, the other human community is demonized, justifying their annihilation, together with the entire infrastructure of their society. Ecological weapons are stock-in-trade of modern war, craterizing and poisoning cropland and forests. Although there is a pretense of hitting only "military targets," in fact everything is a military target. Modern war is total war.

When the former Soviet Union began to collapse in disarray, as a result of its efforts to keep up in the arms race, there was talk of a "new world order" in which conversion to a peacetime economy could happen around the world. But the national security state, with its military corporations and armies, refused to consider the reduction of their power. The United States oligarchies

10. Rifkin, *Biosphere Politics*, 319–26.
11. Rifkin, *Biosphere Politics*, 11–91.

particularly received the end of the Cold War, not as a chance to convert to an ecologically sustainable, peacetime economy, but as a victory for "our side," to be used to consolidate their global hegemony.

Immediately they began to search for new enemies to demonize, and thereby to justify new generations of weapons. They found one such enemy in Saddam Hussein, the leader of a middle-sized Arab country, who challenged their control over oil. And they proceeded to pulverize Iraq in a six-week air war in which they threw down upon it 50 percent more tonnage of bombs than were thrown on Vietnam over ten years.[12] They then declared with satisfaction that the "Vietnam Syndrome" is over; by which they meant that any disposition to question the righteousness of the military way of "solving" international disputes had been silenced.

Genuine demilitarization across the board, including the demilitarization of the United States and of Israel,[13] are the *sine qua non* of any genuine, ecologically sustainable, biospheric economy. It is not difficult to imagine the technological aspect of such conversion of the war industries to alternative production.[14] The cry that military production is necessary for economic prosperity can be refuted many times over, for such production employs far fewer people than any peacetime economy and employs them for purely destructive purposes.

The real resistance to conversion of the military industry lies, not in technology or genuine economic "sense," but in the power drives of the interlocking corporate elites of government, business, and professional military. It is their system of power that is the true "enemy of humanity" and of the earth. But the dismantling of this system of destructive power demands real "conversion," a *metanoia*, or change of heart and consciousness. This change of consciousness is one that recognizes that real "security" lies, not in dominating power and the impossible quest for total invulnerability, but rather in the acceptance of vulnerability, limits, and interdependency with others, with other humans and with the earth.

12. See March 20, 1991, United Nations Report on the damage done by United States bombing of Iraq: *International Socialist Review* (April 1991): 1–4.

13. Israel is usually ranked as the fourth largest military power, despite its small size, and has both nuclear and chemical weapons; see Jane Hunter, *Israel's Foreign Policy: South Africa and Central America* (Boston: South End Press, 1988).

14. See Michael Renner, "Converting to a Peaceful Economy," in *State of the World, 1990*, 154–72; also Kevin Cassidy, "Arms Control and the Home Front: Planning for the Conversion of Military Production Facilities to Civilian Manufacturing," in *Peace and Change* 14, no. 1 (January 1989): 46–64.

Building Communities of Celebration and Resistance

How do we carry on a struggle to heal the world and to build a new biospheric community in the face of this intransigent system of death? It is my belief that those who want to carry on this struggle in a sustained way must build strong base communities of celebration and resistance. By "base communities" I mean local face-to-face groups with which one lives, works, and prays. I do not mean that all these functions would necessarily come together for most people in one base community. Most people will find these different forms of support in a variety of groups and networks, although it is important that these many groups recognize their interconnections in one unified struggle.

There are three interrelated aspects of the work of such local communities. One is shaping the personal therapies, spiritualities, and corporate liturgies by which we nurture and symbolize a new biophilic consciousness. Second, there is the utilization of local institutions over which we have some control, our homes, schools, churches, farms, and locally controlled businesses, as pilot projects of ecological living. Third, there is the building of organizational networks that reach out, regionally, nationally, and internationally, in a struggle to change the power structures that keep the present death system in place.

We must start by recognizing that *metanoia*, or change of consciousness, begins with us. This does not happen all at once, but is an ongoing process. We all have been shaped to misname evil, to seek invulnerable power, or else to capitulate to such power demands in the hands of male authorities. We are tied to present systems of consumption and can hardly imagine alternatives to them that might give us greater peace and wholeness, even though the scramble to "keep up" in the present systems leaves us ever more insecure, anxious, and exhausted.

We need healing therapies and spiritualities of inner growth to let go of fears and open up to each other and to the world around us, to learn how to *be*, rather than to *strive*. The struggle to change the death system must be deeply rooted in joy in the goodness of life. Making healing and inner growth available to us all means unhooking them from professionalized "help," which comes with credentials and high price tags. Although there is a place for skilled people, most of what we need is fairly simple and "free."

We can survey ideas from a few good books, gather a group on a regular basis to discuss the ideas from "experts," and then begin to open up to each other and learn to become good "ears" for hearing each other's story. We also need to recover our body-psyche-spirit nexus, to learn to breathe again, to feel our life energy. Small groups can learn, perhaps with initial expert advice, and teach each other techniques of breathing, biofeedback, meditation, and massage.

We need to take the time to sit under trees, look at water, and at the sky, observe small biotic communities of plants and animals with close attention, get back in touch with the living earth. We can start to release the stifled intuitive and creative powers of our organism, to draw and to write poetry, and to know that we stand on holy ground.

In addition to personal therapies and spirituality, we need corporate liturgies as well, to symbolize and express our altered consciousness. Unfortunately most of our institutional forums of worship are tied to alienated, patriarchal consciousness. Much of their worship is literally "deadly," although some are open to partial transformation. Thus communities of new being and consciousness need to become their own liturgists. They need to learn to shape corporate liturgies to mourn together for violated lives, to midwife healing and new birth, and to taste a new creation already present.

Such communities can also learn to carry liturgy to the streets, in protest marches and demonstrations that cry out against the death system and visualize renewed life in ways that can catch the imagination of others who participate with them or watch them. We can call on all the arts—song and music, dance and mime, posters and banners, costumes and puppetry—to shape the public liturgies of biospheric politics. The Vermont-based Bread and Puppet Theatre is a model for such public liturgies of transformed consciousness.[15]

Another essential work of local communities is to begin to live now an ecologically healthful life. We can see our own homes and other institutions over which we have some control, such as schools or churches, as "pilot projects." We can form a local committee and study a basic manual of ecological living, such as Jeremy Rifkin's *Green Lifestyle Handbook: 1001 Ways You Can Heal the Earth*.[16] We can systematically check different aspects of our lives in this structure, our energy use in heating, cooling, and lighting, toxic cleaners, waste products, land use and transportation, and begin to implement some changes that bring our home or other institutions up to ecological "code."

Such efforts can only be pilot projects and will function as learning and consciousness-raising processes. As we try to implement some changes, it will become quickly evident that our church, school, and workplace, and even our home, are not autonomous. They are dependent parts of larger systems that operate, to a large extent, to tie them to present wasteful ways of functioning. As we try, for example, to implement recycling of household wastes, we run into city waste-disposal systems and resistance to new forms of trash collection that are integrated into recycling industries. We begin to recognize these

---

15. For more information write, The Bread and Puppet Theatre, Rural Delivery, Glover, VT 05839.

16. Jeremy Rifkin, *Green Lifestyle Handbook: 1001 Ways You Can Heal the Earth* (New York: Henry Holt and Company, 1990).

systems in their local and regional expressions, and even beyond, and to put names to those who control the decisions.

This leads us to the third role of local communities, to become political bases of organizing and action. Here again it is useful to start locally, where we can be concrete and where there is often some possibilities of real change. When our group has formulated some clear policy changes, for example, toward a recycling center coordinated with city waste collection, we can network with other groups in the city. We can form a larger organizational base, attend town council meetings, eventually run candidates for local office. We can find ways to pressure local business, both negatively through boycotts and positively through petitions and discussion.

Such local organizing efforts will also reveal the extent to which local government and business really have local control and the extent to which they too are dependent parts of national and international political and economic systems. This is a part of a learning process in which we put names to links in the chains of control, and imagine ways to put pressure for change on the weak links in those chains. Local "green committees" begin to link up with one another across the country.[17]

We ultimately have to think and also act globally, as well as locally. We need to become knowledgeable about parallel movements in Western and Eastern Europe, Asia, Africa, and Latin America, and also the distinct problems of different regions and their interconnection with our own lives. This global consciousness plays two roles. It makes us constantly aware that our local efforts are part of a global struggle, and we are all interdependent in that struggle. It also allows us, at times, to link up with movements internationally that have political forums through the United Nations and other international organizations.[18]

We need to amend the famous slogan of René Dubos: "Think globally and act locally."[19] We need to think both locally and globally and act both locally and globally. The struggle for local changes will lack depth unless it understands itself as an integral part of a global new consciousness. This needs to be more than an abstraction. We need to read about, and sometimes visit, groups who are organizing in other parts of the world and learn from what they are doing. We need to find ways to link up concretely in international forums where the defense of the global commons of forests, oceans, and atmosphere is being carried out against their corporate abusers.

17. In the United States, the Green political movement has taken the form of Green Committees of Correspondence, Clearinghouse, P.O. Box 30208, Kansas City, MO 64112.

18. For example, the World Conference on Environment and Development: see Lester R. Brown, *State of the World* (New York: Norton, 1990), 12–16.

19. Cited in Rifkin, *Green Lifestyle Handbook*, 286.

ROSEMARY RADFORD RUETHER

The time is short for major changes, if we are to save much of the biotic system of the earth that is in danger. The Worldwatch Institute estimates that we have about forty years for major global shifts to be carried out voluntarily (until 2030).[20] After that time major disasters of famine and collapse of life systems, under the pressures of exploitative use, will take place, and there could well be very dangerous militarist and totalitarian responses from threatened elites, as indeed is already happening.

In speaking about the urgency of the situation before audiences, I am often asked if I am "optimistic" about the possibilities for change. The assumption behind this question seems to be that we have two ideational stances toward these crises: optimism or pessimism. But I am inclined to think that both these stances get us off the hook. If we are "optimistic," it suggests that change is inevitable and will happen in the "natural" course of things, and so we need not make much effort ourselves. Someone else will take care of it. If we are "pessimistic," change is impossible, and therefore it is useless to try. In either case we have the luxury, as critical but comfortable elites in the United States, to question the present system without being responsible for it.

What we need is neither optimism nor pessimism, in these terms, but committed love. This means that we remain committed to a vision and to concrete communities of life no matter what the "trends" may be. Whether we are immediately "winning" or "losing" cannot shake our rooted understandings of what biophilic life is and should be, although we need to adapt our strategies to the changing fortunes of the struggle. We also remain clear that life is not made whole "once and for all," in some static millennium of the future. It is made whole again and again, in the renewed day born from night and in the new spring that rises from each winter.

Being rooted in love for our real communities of life and for our common mother, Gaia, can teach us patient passion, a passion that is not burnt out in a season, but can be renewed season after season. Our revolution is not just for us, but for our children, for the generations of living beings to come. What we can do is to plant a seed, nurture a seed-bearing plant here and there, and hope for a harvest that goes beyond the limits of our powers and the span of our lives.

20. *State of the World, 1990*, 172–90.

Index